CW00743047

Acknowledgments

The AA would like to thank the following for their help and co-operation in compiling this guide:

The British Horseracing Board
42 Portman Square, London W1H 0EN
Telephone: 0171-396 0011

The Jockey Club, Newmarket

The Irish Horseracing Authority
Leopardstown Racecourse, Foxrock, Dublin 18, Ireland
Telephone: 0353 1 289 2888

The Managers/Clerk of Courses of all the featured racecourses in Britain and Ireland for taking the time to fill in our questionnaire

Sadie Evans, The Racing Post; Lucy McDiarmid, Lambourn Trainers Association; Chris Thornton, Middleham Trainers Association; Racing Welfare Charities; Giles Anderson, The Turf Directory

The Automobile Association also wishes to thank the following libraries for their assistance in the preparation of this book.

ALLSPORT UK Ltd, Title page Royal Ascot 1992 (Chris Cole) Back Cover: (Pascal Rondeau)

THOROUGHBRED PHOTOGRAPHY: Front Cover. (Trevor Jones)

SPORTING PICTURES (UK) Ltd, 3 Tic Tac Man, 4 York Race Course, 5 Bookmakers, Cheltenham, 6 Cheltenham Races, 7 Looking through binoculars

and Mel Fordham, photos on pages 10-11

Contents

About the Book

If you speak to anyone who has never been to the races, the chances are that they will tell you that they have always wanted to go. Their reasons for absence may well include the fact that they don't know what's on, or when, or how to get there – and where's the fun in it if you don't even know how to place a bet?

This guide has the answers for all those people, as well as providing a useful reference to lifelong devotees of horse racing. All the course information has been supplied by the racecourses themselves; the directory of where to stay and where to eat comes from the AA's database of inspected establishments.

As with all guides of this kind, there are one or two things that have to be explained in order to avoid any misunderstandings along the way. We hope that the majority of the information we have compiled is completely self-explanatory and easy to use, but please read these few points that we felt we had to make.

ON THE COURSE

Admission prices

With a number of exceptions, the prices we have quoted are correct at the time of going to press. The courses do, of course, reserve the right to make any changes they feel necessary.

As in all things, you get what you pay for and the more expensive enclosures will provide the best facilities and sometimes the best view.

Dress

Along with the best facilities and view, the most expensive enclosures will also expect the best-dressed racegoers. This is not to say that you need a Royal Ascot outfit (unless, of course, that is where you are going), but men will usually need a

collar and tie or a polo-neck; jeans and T-shirts are rarely allowed and some will not allow open-necked or short-sleeved shirts. Ascot is, in fact, a good example – their 'no jeans' rule in the Members and Tattersalls enclosures is rigorously enforced by bowler-hatted gatemen.

Drinks

Some courses do not allow racegoers to take alcohol into the course with them and many have rules preventing you from wandering around the enclosures with a drink in your hand. To avoid embarrassment, check on arrival just what the rules are and stick to them.

Fixtures

The calendars of events cover racing fixtures month by month. Actual dates are given both there and on the pages for each course, but these will vary slightly from year to year. The details were correct at the time of publication, but some Irish fixtures were still to be announced and others will be subject to unavoidable last minute changes as circumstances change.

We strongly recommend that you check beforehand to avoid disappointment – a contact address and telephone number has been given for each course, or contact the British Horseracing Board, 42 Portman Square, London W1H 0EN ☎ 0171 396 0011.

WHERE TO STAY AND WHERE TO EAT

All of the accommodation and restaurants listed in this guide have been drawn from the AA's database of inspected establishments and includes hotels, restaurants, guesthouses, farmhouses, pubs and campsites. The general rule in selecting them for inclusion in this guide has been that they are within about a ten-mile radius of the racecourse to which we have attached them. Where we were unable to include a satisfactory number of places to stay using this rule, we did venture a little further afield, but they are rarely more than twenty miles away. More comprehensive information on the establishments listed, together with details of all the above kinds of accommodation throughout Britain and Ireland, can be found in the following AA annual guides:

AA Hotel Guide	**£13.99**
AA Bed and Breakfast in Britain and Ireland	**£8.99**
AA Camping and Caravanning in Britain and Ireland	**£7.99**
AA Best Restaurants in Britain	**£13.99**
AA Best Pubs & Inns	**£9.99**

AA CLASSIFICATIONS

Various classifications of accommodation and restaurants have been used. Firstly the AA's famous star ratings, which are subject to a rigorous and complicated system of inspection points and quality ratings. However, a simplified explanation of what they mean follows – remember that stars are for facilities; percentages, red stars and rosettes are for quality.

HOTEL CLASSIFICATIONS

★ Hotels generally of a small scale with good, but often simple furnishings, facilities and food. This category sometimes includes private hotels where requirements for public access and full lunch service may be relaxed. Not all bedrooms will necessarily have en suite facilities. These hotels are often managed by the proprietor and there may well be a more personal atmosphere than in larger establishments.

★★ Small to medium sized hotels offering more in the way of facilities such as telephones and televisions in bedrooms. Like one star hotels, this category can also include private hotels. At least half the bedrooms will have full en suite facilities. These can be proprietor managed or group owned.

★★★ Medium sized hotels offering more spacious accommodation and a greater range of facilities and services. Generally these will include a full reception service as well as more formal restaurant and bar arrangements. You can expect all rooms to provide en suite facilities, most of which will include a bath. Though often individually owned, this category encompasses a greater number of company owned properties.

★★★★ Generally large hotels with spacious accommodation including availability of private suites. This category of hotel normally provides a full range of formal hotel services including room service, reception and porterage and may well offer more than one dining operation. En suite facilities in all rooms should include both bath and shower. High standards of comfort and food are expected at this level.

7

★★★★★ Large luxury hotels offering the highest international standards of accommodation, facilities, services and cuisine.

(RED) Where you see this beside the star rating, it means that the hotel has been awarded Red Stars for outstanding levels of hospitality, service, food and comfort. There are around 150 Red Star hotels in the whole of Britain and Ireland.

You will notice that some of the hotels listed do not have a star rating beside them. These are lodges, which cannot be compared to traditional hotels. They offer reasonably priced accommodation catering for overnight stops and offering good, functional bedrooms with private facilities. They are usually situated adjacent to a motorway or roadside restaurant and have no food facilities of their own.

PERCENTAGES

Percentage ratings have been given to each of the hotels to represent the difference in quality between hotels within a particular star rating, reflecting the inspectors' experiences at the time of inspection:

50% - 59% A sound hotel which meets all the minimum standards for AA star rating and which overall provides modest but acceptable levels of accommodation, facilities and service.

60% – 69% A particularly sound hotel which exceeds the minimum requirements for its star rating by offering higher standards in certain areas of its operation.

70% – 79% Overall a very good hotel which can be strongly recommended for providing a high level of service, food and accommodation often with excellent standards in certain areas of its operation.

NB Red star hotels do not have percentage ratings because the award of red stars deems it unnecessary.

ROSETTES

These denote the quality of the food served at AA-inspected hotels and restaurants:

❀ Enjoyable food, carefully prepared, that reflects a high level of culinary skill.

❀❀ A high standard of food that demonstrates a serious, dedicated approach to cooking

❀❀❀ Very fine food prepared with considerable flair, imagination and originality

❀❀❀❀ Excellent standards of cuisine, service and wine, consistently achieved

❀❀❀❀❀ Outstanding cuisine, service and wine that reaches the highest international standards

CAMPSITE PENNANT RATINGS

Pennant ratings provide an objective guide to the basic range of facilities and equipment available on a site.

▶ **Site licence**

site density not more than 30 per acre of land suitable for camping

at least 6 pitches allocated to touring units and at least 10% of site capacity for tourers if there are more than 60 pitches

separate flush toilets with 2 washbasins and 2 WCs (ladies), 2 washbasins, 1 WC and 1 urinal (men) for 30 pitches

tap water supply of good quality and quantity

waste water disposal facilities within reasonable walking distance of any touring pitch

adequate arrangements for collection, storage and disposal of refuse, clearly indicated

fire precautions that meet local authority regulations

well-drained ground and provision of some level ground suitable for tents and motor caravans

entrance and access roads of adequate width and surface

► **all one-pennant facilities, plus:**

at least 15% of pitches allocated to tourers

separate washrooms with hot and cold water direct to each basin

point for disposal of chemical toilet contents with adjacent flushing and rinsing facilities (unless not allowed by local authority)

externally lit sanitary facilities

warden available at certain times of the day

►► **all the aforementioned, plus:**

one shower or bath with hot and cold water for each sex per 35 pitches

deep sinks for washing clothes, plus at least one washing machine and tumble dryer

electric shaver points, mirrors and sockets for hairdryers in washrooms

all-night lighting of sanitary facilities or push-button time switches

daily shopping facilities for basic foods on site or within reasonable walking distance

adequate roads to perimeter and services

warden in attendance during day; contact number for night-time emergencies

public telephone available 24 hours

some hardstandings and electric hookups

►►► **all the aforementioned, plus:**

at least 25% of pitches allocated for tourers

2 washbasins per sex for 25 pitches, 1 shower per sex for 30 pitches

all night permanent lighting of toilet blocks

washing up facilities with hot and cold water

signed reception office

signposted late arrivals enclosure, appropriately sited

well signed and properly maintained first aid room with washbasin

properly equipped site shop offering good selection of food, household and domestic products and camping/caravanning spares

access routes to essential facilities lit after dark

childrens playground, fenced or in safe area; area for ball games away from pitches and tents

some site landscaping

10% hard standings for touring van wheel runs and 50% hook-ups

►►►► **These sites are now designated as Holiday Centres because of the range of leisure facilities they offer on site:**

a comprehensive range of services and equipment

at least 40% of pitches allocated to tourers

24-hour supervision by warden on site

automated laundry with at least two of the following permanently installed: washing machines, tumble dryers, irons and ironing boards

2 washbasins per sex for 20 pitches, 1 shower per sex for 30 pitches

heated washrooms if site open between October and Easter

range of facilities for indoor and outdoor recreation for adults

indoor recreational facilities for children separate from those provided for adults

cafe or restaurant

visitors' car park

You may notice that some sites do not have a pennant rating at all. These are known as 'Venture' sites and they cater for self-contained campers and caravanners who take everything with them, including a toilet, and are literally just looking for a pitch, a water supply and chemical disposal point.

CREDIT CARDS
1 Access/Eurocard/Mastercard
2 American Express
3 Barclaycard/Visa
4 Carte Blanche
5 Diners

TRAINERS' OPEN DAYS

Open days are becoming increasingly popular up and down the country as the public's demand for knowledge and accessibility grows. The three main training centres at Lambourn, Middleham and Newmarket have each set aside a special day when the majority of stables are open to the public who are able to stroll around at will and see their equine heroes at close quarters. It is a fun day for the family at low cost and benefits both equine and human charities.

LAMBOURN, BERKSHIRE

Lambourn, some five miles north of the M4 (J14), is known as The Valley of The Racehorse. Primarily it is a centre for jumping yards but plenty of good flat horses are here too, by the likes of Peter Walwyn who handled the 1975 Derby winner Grundy, Dick Hern, Barry Hills and Willie Muir.

But the village, with its tiny suburb Upper Lambourn, houses far more jumping stables. Frequently, in recent years, it has played host to the homecoming of a Gold Cup winner such as Mr Mulligan (1997), Master Oats (1995) and Garrison Savannah (1991) or a Grand National hero such as Royal Athlete (1995), Party Politics (1992) and Mr Frisk (1990).

Many trainers such as Jenny Pitman, Kim Bailey and Nicky Henderson are household names, but all 35 members of the Lambourn Trainers Association open their gates on the Open Day, which is usually on Good Friday, a non racing day when all the horses and staff are available.

The Open Day which begins at 8.30am and lasts until around 5pm, provides a wonderfully memorable day. Some 10,000 people make the annual pilgrimage to Lambourn which is now geared up to receive crowds four times the size of the local population. It was in 1989 that Peter Walwyn, a trainer for 37 years and champion trainer twice, had the idea of creating on Open Day after consultation with a marketing expert, who felt that Lambourn was slow to sell itself as a centre of excellence. Now the whole village is commercially sponsored and the Lambourn Trainers Association was set up to promote the village.

Since then the Open Day has *growed and growed* like Topsy. Each individual yard has prizes on offer - in some cases the training of a racehorse for a year. There are tradestands, sideshows, raffles and catering tents.

During the afternoon there are such events as falconry displays, bungee jumping demonstrations, a parade of old equine heroes, camel racing and a silent auction. The proceeds from the latter go towards a housing project in the village for retired staff.

But the most exciting part of the day, even for the non racing person, is to visit the horses in their boxes and to chat to the likes of Jenny Pitman about them. All trainers love their horses and they imbue them with characteristics way beyond nature. It is fascinating to hear these stories.

Many personalities from the world of racing take part in the camel races. You may bump into television personalities such as Richard Pitman and John Francome. You may even meet racing's answer to Rory Bremner, Richard Phillips, the only trainer who admits to being a comedian.

NEWMARKET, SUFFOLK

This is traditionally known as the Headquarters of racing, principally because King Charles II, known as Old Rowley, decided in around 1665 that the wide open, flat terrain of the area was suitable for racing his horses - usually in match races. The Rowley Mile is named after him.

It was another 100 years before three stallions - the Darley Arabian, the Byerley Turk and the Godolphin Arabian - were introduced to the breed to instil speed and a fineness of bone. These animals became the forerunner of the modern thoroughbred, 3,000 of whom are trained in the Newmarket area, making it the largest training centre in Britain.

Newmarket houses the National Racing Museum, as well as the National Stud, the

Horserace Forensic Laboratories, The British Racing School, the Tattersalls sales complex and the Jockey Club rooms. More than 68 trainers are based in the immediate area which boasts the finest gallops in the world.

Newmarket's Open Day is usually held towards the end of August and around 25 yards participate, among them those of Luca Cumani, Michael Bell, Ed Dunlop, Ben Hanbury and Mark Tompkins. Other yards such as John Gosden's have individual open days, usually well advertised in the racing press.

Traditionally the stables are open from 9.30am until 1.30pm. Prior to that you can go on to Warren Hill gallop and see 100 well-known racehorses working. Take your binoculars with you and if you see Henry Cecil stop and ask him about his horses as he is very welcoming and informative.

There is plenty of fun and excitement for the family in the afternoon where the action is based at the Rookery Centre, Market Square and Tattersalls. There is usually a riding demonstration by pupils from the British Racing School and a Celebrity Question Time. Plentiful craft and trade exhibitions adorn the Square which also hosts such features as Punch & Judy shows, Morris dancing and Fancy Dress parades.

MIDDLEHAM, YORKSHIRE

Yorkshire folk believe that their county is God's own back garden, so beautiful and picturesque are the dales and moors. Few towns can match the splendour of Middleham which dominates Wensleydale with views from the High Moor which would delight a modern day Constable or Turner. Under the leadership of the late Neville Crump, who won the Grand National no fewer than four times, Middleham has enjoyed a revival in the past decade. Much of the credit for this goes to Chris Thornton, the Master of Spigot Lodge stables, who has nurtured the gallops and reformed the Middleham Trainers Association.

Like Lambourn Middleham's Open Day is held on Good Friday when all 13 racing stables open their doors to the public from 9am to 12.30pm. Local charities such as the Stable Lads Welfare Trust are the beneficiaries. For the first time for nearly 25 years a Classic winner (Mister Baileys) was trained in Yorkshire - by Mark Johnston to win the 2,000 Guineas in 1992. Mark has well over 100 horses in his care, including a number owned by Sheik Mohammed.

A complimentary bus service will take the visitor round the different stables, some of which are housed in part of the historic castle, and also to the Low Moor for the exciting afternoon activities. These include watching some two-year-olds galloping up the All Weather gallop and watching jumpers schooling over hurdles and fences. There is a parade of equine stars which recently included Desert Orchid and Milton (the show jumper).

Other events have included Shire horse racing - which proved to be hilarious, making idiots of the most experienced professional jockeys! Television personalities Richard Whiteley, Derek Thompson, Frazer Hines and Liz Hobbs are usually on hand to provide amusing commentaries.

All in all, each Open Day provides a great day out for kids of all ages from five to 105.

COLIN MACKENZIE

FURTHER INFORMATION

Lambourn Open Day

Lambourn Trainers Assciation Tel: 01488 71347 Fax: 01488 72664
* £5 adults, £2.50 senior citizens, children under 12 - free.

Newmarket Open Day

Racing Welfare Charities Tel: 01638 560763   Fax: 01638 560831
* £5 adults, £2.50 senior citizens, children under 12 - free.

Middleham Open Day

Middleham Trainers Association Tel: 01969 622237 (Mr Johnston) or 01969 623321 (Mr Bethell)
* £5 adults, reductions for senior citizens, children under 12 - free.

*prices and times correct at time of going to press

Racing in Ireland

No one is quite sure when Ireland's love affair with the horse and horse racing began, but it has certainly become an integral part of the national heritage. Its epicentre is The Curragh (whose gaelic interpretation is 'horse place') in County Kildare, with records of racing going back to the reign of the Celtic kings. At present there are nearly 1300 horses in training on the plains of the Curragh and its racecourse hosts no less than five Classics.

There are 27 courses in Ireland which offer varying degrees of facilities and racing, but one thing that is guaranteed at all of them is a tremendous atmosphere - few know how to enjoy themselves like the Irish, and the warmth of their welcome to visitors is renowned. Meetings are informal and children are always welcome. Five of the major Irish courses are featured in the guide, beginning on page 211, with a complete list of the rest on page 225.

Further information is available from:

The Irish Horseracing Authority
Leopardstown Racecourse, Foxrock, Dublin 18
☎ 01-289 2888 or 835 1965;
fax: 01-289 8412 or 01- 835 1964
E-mail: info@irishracing.iha.ie

or

The Irish Tourist Board
150 New Bond Street, London W1Y 0AQ
☎ 0171-493 3201

FESTIVAL MEETINGS IN IRELAND
Festival meetings are a great attraction, many of them having related activities to carry the festivities on beyond the gates of the racecourse. The Tralee Festival in August offers two evening meetings and four afternoons of racing during the same week that the town is alive with processions, music, theatre and the famous Rose of Tralee contest. Listowel's six-day September festival is part of the Harvest Festival of Ireland - a week-long carnival of fun through the streets - and Galway's Autumn Festival coincides with the opening of the oyster season and its associated celebrations. Please note that the dates of major fixtures may vary slightly from year to year. Please telephone course to check.

Fairyhouse Easter Festival - *April 13-15*

Punchestown Spring Festival - *April 28-30*

Killarney Spring Festival - *May 10-12*

Curragh Derby Festival - *June 26-28*

Bellewstown Summer Festival - *30 June-3 July*

Killarney Festival - *July 13-16*

Galway Summer Festival - *July 27-August 1*

Tramore Festival - *August 14-16*

The Rose of Tralee Festival - *August 24-29*

Galway Autumn Festival - *September 7-9*

Listowel Festival - *September 21-26*

Christmas Festival at Leopardstown - *Dec 26-29*

Christmas Festival at Limerick - *December 26-29*

HOW TO GET THERE
By air: Flights are available from most major British airports to Belfast, Dublin, Cork, Shannon, Knock, Kerry and Carrickfinn (Co Donegal), with internal flights from Dublin to Kerry, Galway and Sligo. A wide range of promotional fares are generally available.

By sea: Car and passenger ferry services operate on the following routes:

Holyhead - Dun Laoghaire (Stena Sealink)

Holyhead - Dublin (Irish Ferries)

Holyhead - Dublin (Sea Cat)

Fishguard - Rosslare (Stena Sealink)

Pembroke - Rosslare (Irish Ferries)

Swansea - Cork (Swansea Cork Ferries)

Cairnryan - Larne (P & O European Ferries)

Stranraer - Larne (Stena Sealink)

Stranraer - Belfast (Sea Cat Scotland)

Douglas - Dublin (Isle of Man Steam Packet Company)

TELEPHONING IRELAND
The international dialling code from Britain to the Republic of Ireland is 00 353.
The initial 0 of the area code is not needed when dialling from outside the Republic.

Aintree

Aintree plays host to the most famous race in the world - the Martell Grand National. This amazing spectacle attracts the largest viewing figures of any sporting event in Great Britain, with a total worldwide audience in excess of three hundred million.

Its popularity is not hard to fathom, for there can be no stiffer challenge for horse and jockey, and a fairy-tale result seems to emerge every year. The number of fatalities is now thankfully on the decline following recent modifications to the fences, especially the notorious Becher's Brook.

The quality of racing is second only to the Cheltenham Festival and there is always a huge attendance, particularly on the day of the big race when tickets will need to be purchased in advance for certain sections of the course. After a gap of twenty years, the early '90s saw the reintroduction of an autumn fixture, held in November and tremendously popular despite any inclement weather.

FURTHER INFORMATION

Aintree Racecourse Co Ltd
Ormskirk Road, Aintree, Liverpool L9 5AS
☎ 0151-523 2600

LOCATION AND HOW TO GET THERE

The course is on the outskirts of Liverpool on the A59, one mile south of its junction with the M57 and M58.
Nearest Railway Station: Aintree, adjacent to the course. From London Euston trains run to Liverpool Lime Street, from where there are local trains to Aintree.

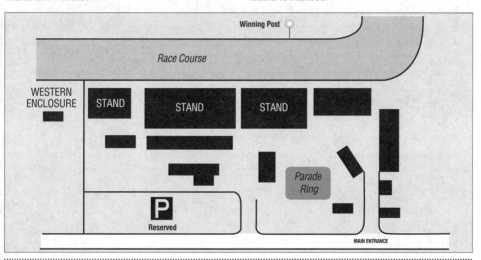

ADMISSION

All classes of day ticket give access to full betting facilities, including Tote.

Day Tickets:
From £7. Call for details – access to bars and restaurants

PADDOCK £11 Thursday & Friday, £18 Saturday – access to bars, restaurant and raised viewing area

STEEPLECHASE £7 Saturday – access to bars and refreshments

(Please note: These are 1997 prices and are subject to change in 1998)

COURSE FACILITIES

Banks:
there is a Foreign Exchange Unit on the course, open normal bank hours; there are cashpoint facilities.

For families:
Refreshment kiosk and toilets; Call for details.

CALENDAR OF EVENTS

April 2-4 – The Grand National Meeting; includes the Martell Cup Steeple Chase, Mumm Melling Steeple Chase, and the Martell Grand National

May 15 – Evening Meeting
November 21

WHERE TO STAY

HOTELS

★★★★ 57% Liverpool Moat House
Paradise Street,
☎ 0151-471 9988
fax: 0151-709 2706
251 bedrooms; double room £115-£120
Credit cards 1 2 3 5

★★★★ 57% Atlantic Tower Thistle
Chapel Street
☎ 0151-227 4444
fax: 0151-236 3973
226 bedrooms; double room £99-£106
Credit cards 1 2 3 5

Travel Inn (Liverpool North)
North Perimeter Road
☎ 0151-531 1497
fax: 0151-520 1842
43 bedrooms; double room £36.50
Credit cards 1 2 3 5

Campanile
Chaloner Street, Queens Dock
☎ 0151-709 8104
fax: 0151-709 8725
80 bedrooms; double room £38
Credit cards 1 2 3 5

Around Liverpool

★★★ 65% Blundellsands
The Serpentine, Blundellsands
☎ 0151-924 6515
fax: 0151-931 5364
37 bedrooms; double B&B £58.50-£90
Credit cards 1 2 3 5

★★★ 63% Royal
Marine Terrace, Waterloo
☎ 0151-928 2332
fax: 0151-949 0320
25 bedrooms; double B&B £48-£72
Credit cards 1 2 3 5

Travel Inn
Queensdrive, West Derby
☎ 0151-228 4724
fax: 0151-220 7610
40 bedrooms; double room £36.50
Credit cards 1 2 3 5

Travel Inn
Wilson Road, Tarbock
☎ 0151-480 9614
fax: 0151-480 9361
40 bedrooms; double room £36.50
Credit cards 1 2 3 5

★★ 72% Grove House
Grove Rd, Wallasey
☎ 0151-639 3947
fax: 0151-639 0028
14 bedrooms; double bedroom £49.50
Credit cards 1 2 3

BED AND BREAKFAST

QQQ Aachen Hotel
91 Mount Pleasant
☎ 0151-709 3477
fax: 0151-709 1126
Close to city centre; long established,
popular hotel with friendly and efficient
service.
17 bedrooms; double B&B £36-£44
Credit cards 1 2 3 5

Q Lyndhurst Guest House
101 King Street, Southport
☎ 01704 537520
Small guest house with modest, compact
bedrooms, close to town centre
7 bedrooms

QQQ Oakwood Private Hotel
7 Portland Street, Southport
☎ 01704 531858
Two combined semi-detached houses with
some spacious bedrooms, all non-smoking
7 bedrooms

QQ Rosedale Hotel
11 Talbot Street, Southport
☎ 01704-530 604
Large centrally situated house with good
compact accommodation
10 bedrooms; double B&B £40-£50
Credit cards 1 3

QQQ Blenheim
37 Arigburth Drive, Sefton Park
☎ 0151-727 7380
Early Victorian house 3 miles from city
centre
17 bedrooms

QQQ Ambassador Private Hotel
13 Bath Street, Southport
☎ 01704-543 998, fax:01704-536 269
A centrally situated private hotel with well-
equipped bedrooms.
8 bedrooms
Credit cards 1 2 3

QQQ White Lodge
12 Talbot Street, Southport
☎ 01704-536320
Comfortable, traditional hotel with modern
facilities
8 bedrooms; double B&B £40-£50

WHERE TO STAY

BED AND BREAKFAST

Around Liverpool

QQQ Treetops
506 Old Chester Road, Birkenhead
☎ (0151) 645 0740
8 bedrooms; double B&B £30–£40

CAMPSITES

►►► Abbey Farm Caravan Park
Dark Ln, Ormskirk
☎ 01695 572686; fax:01695 572686
North of Liverpool.
Pitch price £5–£8.50 per night

WHERE TO EAT

RESTAURANTS

❀ Beadles
15 Rosemount, Oxton,
Birkenhead
☎ 0151-653 9010
Good, well cooked food in a busy,
intimate restaurant.
Dinner only: 7-9
Credit cards 1 3

❀ Capitol
24 Argyle Street, Hamilton Square,
Birkenhead
☎ 0151-647 9212
A local Chinese with various dining areas
Lunch:11.30-2, £6 and à la carte
Dinner:6-11.30, £15 and à la carte
Credit cards 1 2 3

PUBS

Everyman Bistro
9 Hope Street, Liverpool
☎ (0151) 7089545; fax: (0151) 7090398
Free House
Beneath Everyman Theatre, popular city
meeting place for all ages and
backgrounds. Counter service offers
salads, snacks, pizza, quiches, and daily-
changing specials.
Open: 10am–12midnight
Principal Beers: Cains, Boddingtons

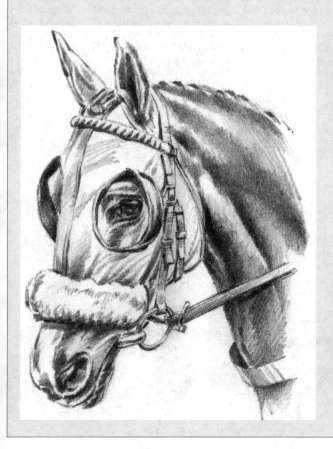

Ascot

Set in the heart of beautiful Berkshire countryside, Ascot deserves to be recognised as the jewel in the crown of British racecourses, an appropriate metaphor, since it forms part of the Royal Estates.

Facilities are among the best in the country, though inevitably this is reflected in admission prices, especially on Saturdays. Weekdays may lack atmosphere but are often cheaper and much better value for money. A word of warning - the 'no jeans' rule in the Members and Tattersalls enclosures is rigorously enforced by bowler-hatted gatemen.

Top-class action can be guaranteed throughout the year on Ascot's wide, triangular, galloping track. The highlight is the Royal meeting in June which provides the best week's Flat racing of the season, and remains one of the major events in the social calendar. There is a vibrant fashion scene and plenty of pomp and circumstance, with members of the Royal Family parading down the course in open carriages before the first race. Other important Flat races are the King George VI and Queen Elizabeth Diamond Stakes at the end of July, and the Queen Elizabeth II Stakes, part of the Festival of British Racing in September.

FURTHER INFORMATION

Racecourse Office,
Ascot Racecourse, Ascot, Berkshire SL5 7JN
☎ (01344) 22211; Fax: (01344) 28299
Credit hot-line booking ☎ (01344) 876456

LOCATION AND HOW TO GET THERE

The course is in Ascot town. From the south and east leave the M3 at junction 3 and take the A332 Bracknell Road; from the A30, take the A329 towards Bracknell; from the M4 eastbound, leave at junction 6 and take the A332 Windsor bypass; from the M4 westbound, leave at junction 10 and take the A329 towards Bracknell. The course is well signposted.

Nearest Railway Station: Ascot; the station is less than a mile from the course, approximately seven minutes' walk.

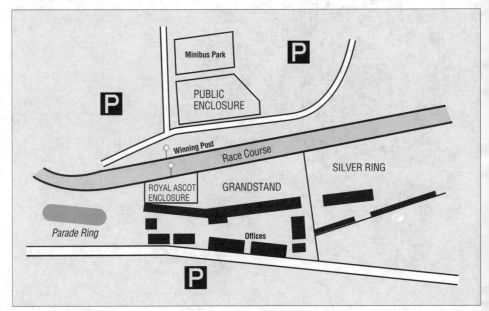

ADMISSION

All classes of day ticket give access to full betting facilities, including Tote.

Day Tickets:
Accompanied children under 16 are admitted free to all enclosures, except into the Royal Enclosure. Grandstand tickets must be booked in advance for all four days of the Royal Meeting.

MEMBERS/CLUB from £23, under 25s half price with proof of age – access to bars, restaurant, shops, champagne bars, excellent viewing, facilities for disabled racegoers

TATTERSALLS £8-£15 (£26 and £34 for Royal Meeting) – access to bars and restaurant.

SILVER RINGS £5 (£7-£10 for Royal Meeting) – access to bars and snack bars.

Transfers: from the Grandstand to the Members Stand available on all racedays except for the Royal Meeting and Diamond Day.

COURSE FACILITIES

Banks:
there is a Barclays Bank on the course, open during course opening hours, but no cashpoint facilities.

For families:
children's play area; free supervised creche for under 8s.

CALENDAR OF EVENTS

January 17 – National Hunt
January 23 – National Hunt
February 11
April 1 – National Hunt
April 8 – Long Distance Hurdle
April 28-29 – Tuesday: National Hunt; The Ascot Spring Evening Meeting. Wednesday: flat; Insulpak Victoria Cup Day
May 9
June 16-20 – Royal Meeting, includes St James's Palace Stakes, Coronation Stakes, Gold Cup and King's Stand Stakes; flat
June 20 – flat; London Clubs Fern Hill Rated Stakes

July 24-25 – flat; includes Princess Margaret Stakes
August 8 – flat
September 26-27 – flat; Tote Festival Handicap &. Tote Sunday Special Handicap
October 9-10 – flat; includes Bonusprint October Stakes & Princess Royal Stakes
October 31 – National Hunt
November 20-21 – National Hunt; Coopers & Lybrand Day &The First National Bank Gold Cup Steeplechase
December 19 – National Hunt; Betterware Day

WHERE TO STAY

HOTELS

★★★★ ❀ **68% Berystede**
Bagshot Rd, Sunninghill
☎ (01344) 23311, fax: (01344) 872301
91 bedrooms
Credit cards 1 2 3 5

★★★★ ❀ **69% Royal Berkshire**
London Rd, Sunninghill
☎ (01344) 23322, fax: (01344) 27100
63 bedrooms
Credit Cards 1 2 3 5

★★ **72% Highclere**
19 Kings Rd, Sunninghill
☎ (01344) 25220, fax: (01344) 872528
11 bedrooms; double B&B £70-£85
Credit Cards 1 2 3

Around Ascot

★★★★ (Red Star) ♨ ❀❀❀
Pennyhill Park
London Rd, Bagshot
☎ (01276) 471774, fax: (01276) 473217
89 bedrooms
Credit Cards 1 2 3 5

★★ **66% Brockenhurst**
Brockenhurst Road, Ascot
☎ (01344) 21912, fax: (01344) 873252
11 bedrooms; double B&B £79-£100
Credit cards 1 2 3 5

★★★★ ❀❀ **76% Coppid Beech**
John Nike Way, Bracknell
☎ (01344) 303333, fax: (01344) 301200
205 bedrooms; double B&B £160
Credit Cards 1 2 3 5

Hilton National
Bagshot Rd, Bracknell
☎ (01344) 424801, fax: (01344) 487454
167 bedrooms; double bedroom £135-£148
Credit Cards 1 2 3 5

★★★★ ❀ **70% Runnymede**
Windsor Rd, Egham
☎ (01784) 436171, fax: (01784) 436340
171 bedrooms; double bedroom £157-£175
Credit Cards 1 2 3 5

WHERE TO STAY

★★★★❀❀❀ 78% Fredrick's
Shoppenhangers Rd, Maidenhead
☎ (01628) 635934, fax: (01628) 771054
37 bedrooms; double B&B £188–£198
Credit Cards 1 2 3 5

★★★ 66% Thames Riviera
At the Bridge, Maidenhead
☎ (01628) 74057, fax: (01628) 776586
52 bedrooms; double £95
Credit Cards 1 2 3 5

★★★★★ (RED) ♨ ❀❀❀ Cliveden
Taplow, signposted from all directions
☎ (01628) 668561, fax: (01628) 661837
39 bedrooms
Credit cards 1 2 3 5

★★★★ ❀❀ 76% Oakley Court
Windsor Rd, Water Oakley, Windsor
☎ (01753) 609988, fax: (01628) 37011
114 bedrooms; double room £190–£205
(room only)
Credit cards 1 2 3 5

★★❀ 74% Aurora Garden
14 Bolton Av, Windsor
☎ (01753) 868686, fax: (01753) 831394
15 bedrooms
Credit cards 1 2 3 5

BED AND BREAKFAST

QQQQQ Beehive Manor
Cox Green Lane, Maidenhead
☎ (01628) 20980
A lovingly preserved house dating in part
from the 16th century with a special
atmosphere.
3 bedrooms; double bedroom £57

QQ Colnbrook Lodge
Bath Rd, Colnbrook
☎ (01753) 685958; fax:(01753) 685164
Comfortable and well equipped detached
house on the edge of the village of
Colnbrook
8 bedrooms; double B&B £39–£55
Credit cards 1 3

QQ Clarence Hotel
9 Clarence Rd, Windsor
☎ (01753) 864436, fax: (01753) 857060
Centrally placed old hotel offering attractive
and well coordinated rooms.
21 bedroom; double B&B £44–£52
Credit cards 1 2 3 5

QQQ Longford Guest House
550 Bath Rd, Longford
☎ (01753) 682969, fax: (01753) 794189
5 bedrooms; double B&B from £39
Credit cards 1 3

QQ Warbeck House
46 Queens Rd, Weybridge
☎ (01932) 848764, fax: (01932) 847290
Attractive Edwardian house close to town
centre. 10 bedrooms

QQQ Bridgettine Convent
Fulmer Common Rd, Iver Heath
☎ (01753) 662073, fax: (01753) 662172
Very pretty Tudor-style timbered house in
well-kept gardens, run by nuns.
13 bedrooms; double B&B £36–£40

QQ Antonio Guest House
41 Switchback Road North, Maidenhead
☎ (01628) 70537
3 bedrooms; double B&B £40–£50

Q Shepiston Lodge
31 Shepiston Lane, Hayes
☎ 0181-573 0266, fax: 0181-569 2536
Small guest house close to Heathrow
Airport.
13 bedrooms; double B&B £41.50

QQQQ Melrose House
53 Frances Rd, Windsor
☎ (01753) 865328, fax:(01753) 865328
Elegant Victorian house offering bright,
clean and very well equipped bedrooms.
9 bedrooms; double B&B £50
Credit cards 1 3

QQQ Glen Court
St Johns Hill Rd, Woking
☎ (01483) 764154, fax: (01483) 755737
Attractive Edwardian house set in 1.5 acres
of woodland.
12 bedrooms
Credit cards 1 2 3

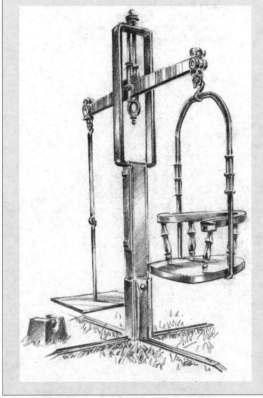

CAMPSITES

►►►⚑ California Chalet & Touring Park
Nine Mile Ride, Finchampstead. Signposted
☎ (01734) 733928
Southwest of Ascot off B3016; pitch price
£8.75 per night.

►►► Camping & Caravanning Club Site
Bridge Road, Chertsey
☎ (01932) 562405; fax:(01203) 694886
pitch prices £9.10-£12.10 a night

WHERE TO EAT

RESTAURANTS

❀❀❀❀ Waterside Inn
River Cottage, Ferry Rd, Bray
☎ (01628) 20691; fax:(01628) 784710
Excellent French cuisine prepared by
Michel Roux in picturesque riverside
setting.
Lunch: 12-2 from £30 and à la carte
Dinner: 7-10 from £66.50 and à la carte

❀❀❀ Pennyhill Park
London Rd, Bagshot
☎ (01276) 471774
An elegant hotel restaurant with fine
cooking
Lunch: £17.95 and à la carte
Dinner: £32 and à la carte

❀❀❀ Michels
13 High St, Ripley
☎ (01483) 224777; fax:(01483) 222940
Delicately prepared dishes with well-
balanced flavours showing evidence of fine
skill.
Lunch: 12-1.30 from £21
Dinner: 7-9 from £23 and à la carte

❀❀ New Mill
New Mill Rd, Eversley
☎ (01734) 732277 fax: (01734) 328780
Sound cooking in a lovely old mill on the
river.
Lunch: 12-2 from £10
Dinner: 7-10 from £19.50 and à la carte

❀ Jade Fountain
38 High St, Sunninghill
☎ (01344) 27070
Smart and friendly Chinese restaurant
offering high standard Chinese cuisine.
Lunch: 12-2 from £21.50 and à la carte
Dinner: 6-10.30, £22.50 and à la carte

❀ Royal Berkshire
London Rd, Sunninghill
☎ (01344) 23322; fax:(01344) 27100
Serious cuisine with an occasional touch of
ostentation.
Lunch: £24.75
Dinner: £34.50 and à la carte

❀❀ Cookham Tandoori
High St, Cookham
☎ (01628) 522584; fax:(01628) 533051
Mainly East Bengali cooking with
contemporary influences.
Lunch: 12-2.30 à la carte from £15
Dinner: 6-11 à la carte from £15

❀❀ Coppid Beech
John Nike Way, Bracknell
☎ (01344) 303333; fax:(01344) 301200
Traditional and modern style dishes served
in the main restaurant.
Lunch: à la carte from £29.50
Dinner: from £20.95 and à la carte

❀❀ Oakley Court
Windsor Rd, Water Oakley, Windsor
☎ (01753) 609988; fax:(01628) 37011
A range of skilfully produced traditional and
modern dishes served in two restaurants.
Lunch: 12.30-2, £24
Dinner: 7.30-10, £34 and à la carte

PUBS

Royal Foresters Hotel
London Road, Ascot
☎ (01344) 884747; fax:(01344) 884115
Open: 11am-11pm
Free House
Principal Beer: Morlands

Rose and Crown
Woodside, Winkfield
☎ (01344) 882051; fax:(01344) 885346
Open: 11am-11pm (Sun 12noon-7pm)
Brewery: Morlands
Principal Beers: Broadside, Bombadier,
Original

Ayr

This is without question the premier course in Scotland and it affords the only real opportunity for racegoers north of the border to see high-class horses in action.

The Stakis Scottish Grand National in April always attracts a select field (Red Rum was a past winner) and the three-day Great Western Meeting in September is immensely popular and has formed the backdrop to many happy holidays over the years. The major betting race of the week is the Ladbroke Ayr Gold Cup, an ultra-competitive sprint handicap in which a low draw was traditionally a huge advantage, although drainage work on the turf appears to have rectified that problem.

An extremely friendly track, renowned for its warm welcome and hospitality, it is also an ideal place to watch the horses being prepared for their races as the saddling boxes are situated right next to the parade ring. A recent addition is the Princess Royal Club Stand, completed in 1995.

FURTHER INFORMATION

The Western Meeting Club
Racecourse Office, 2 Whitletts Road, Ayr KA8 0JE
☎ (01292) 264179; Fax: (01292) 610140

LOCATION AND HOW TO GET THERE

The course is in Whitletts Road, Ayr. Leave the A77 at the Whitletts Roundabout and follow signs for Ayr.

Nearest railway Station: Ayr, one mile from the course; there are connecting bus services to the course for major events only.

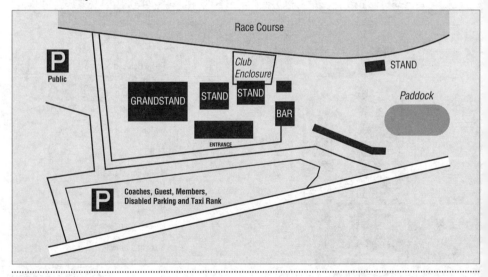

ADMISSION

All classes of day ticket give access to full betting facilities, including Tote.

Day Tickets:
CLUBSTAND £12-£20 – access to bar, restaurant, private rooms

GRANDSTAND £7-£12, reduction for senior citizens (£4) – access to bars, restaurant, private rooms
20% discount for parties of 10 or more, booked in advance. (Grandstand only)

COURSE FACILITIES

Banks:
there are no banks or cashpoint facilities on the course.

For families:
crèche; events are sometimes arranged for children.

CALENDAR OF EVENTS

January 2 – National Hunt
January 31 – National Hunt
February 14 – National Hunt
March 13-14 – National Hunt
April 17-18 – National Hunt; includes Samsung Electronics Scottish Champion Hurdle and Stakis Casinos Scottish National on Saturday
May 28-29
June 19-20 – flat
July 13

July 18 – flat; evening meeting
July 20 – flat
August 11 – flat
September 17-19 – flat; Western Meeting,includes Ladbrokes (Ayr) Gold Cup
October 12-13 – flat
November 14-15 – National Hunt
December 7
December 26 – National Hunt

WHERE TO STAY

HOTELS

★★★★ **65%** ❀❀
Fairfield House Hotel
12 Fairfield Road
☎ (01292) 267461; fax:(01292) 261456
33 bedrooms; double B&B £108-£180
Credit cards 1 2 3 5

★★★ **63% Savoy Park**
16 Racecourse Rd
☎ (01292) 266112, fax: (01292) 611488
15 bedrooms; double B&B £70-£95
Credit cards 1 2 3

★★★ **59% Quality Friendly Hotel**
Burns Statue Sq, Ayr
☎ (01292) 263268, fax: (01292) 262293
70 bedrooms; double room £71-£81
Credit cards 1 2 3 5

★★ **68% Aftongrange**
37 Carrick Rd
☎ (01292) 265679
8 bedrooms; double B&B £40-£50

★★ **67% Carrick Lodge**
46 Carrick Rd
☎ (01292) 262846, fax: (01292) 611101
8 bedrooms; double B&B £55
Credit cards 1 2 3

★★ **63% Elms Court**
21 Miller Rd
☎ (01292) 264191, fax: (01292) 610254
20 bedrooms; double B&B £60-£95
Credit cards 1 2 3

Travel Inn
Kilmarnock Road, Monkton
☎ (01292) 678262; fax:(01292) 678248
40 bedrooms; double room £36.50
Credit cards 1 2 3 5

Around Ayr

★★★★ **54% Hospitality Inn**
46 Annick Rd, Irvine
☎ (01294) 274272, fax: (01294) 277287
127 bedrooms; double room £105-£125
Credit cards 1 2 3 5

★★ **65% Carlton Toby Hotel**
187 Ayr Road, Prestwick
☎ (01292) 476811, fax: (01292) 474845
34 bedrooms: double B&B £54-£65
Credit cards 1 2 3

★★ **62% St Nicholas**
41 Ayr Rd, Prestwick
☎ (01292) 479568, fax: (01292) 475793
17 bedrooms
Credit cards 1 2 3 5

★★★★❀ **65% Marine Highland**
Troon
☎ (01292) 314444, fax: (01292) 316922
72 bedrooms; double B&B £130-£144
Credit cards 1 2 3 5

★★★❀❀ ⚘ **83% Lochgreen House**
Monktonhill Road, Southwood, Troon
☎ (01292) 313343 fax: (01292) 318661
14 bedrooms; double B&B from £140
Credit cards 1 2 3

★★★❀❀ **75% Highgrove House**
Old Loans Rd, Troon
☎ (01292) 312511, fax: (01292) 318228
9 bedrooms; double B&B £85
Credit cards 1 2 3

★★★ ❀**71% Piersland House Hotel**
Craigend Road, Troon
☎ (01292) 314747; fax:(01292) 315613
28 bedrooms; double B&B £110-£140
Credit cards 1 2 3 5

BED AND BREAKFAST

QQQQ **Glenmore**
35 Bellevue Cresent
☎ (01292) 269830; fax:(01292) 269830
5 bedrooms

QQQQ **Brenalder Lodge**
39 Dunure, Doonfoot
☎ (01292) 443939
Attractive bedrooms
3 bedrooms; double B&B £50-£70

QQQ **Craggallan**
8 Queens Terrace
☎ (01292) 264998
Attractive, nicely furnished bedrooms.
5 bedrooms; double B&B £36-£44

QQQ **Dargill**
7 Queens Terrace
☎ (01292) 261955
4 bedrooms

QQQ **Langley Bank**
39 Carrick Rd
☎ (01292) 264246, fax: (01292) 282628
Substantial period house
6 bedrooms; double B&B £32-£50
Credit cards 1 2 3

QQ **Windsor Hotel**
6 Alloway Place
☎ (01292) 264689
Full of character with 10 bright attractive bedrooms; double B&B from £44
Credit Cards 1 3

WHERE TO STAY

QQQQ Fairways Hotel
19 Links Rd, Prestwick
☎ (01292) 470396; fax:(01292) 470396
5 bedrooms; double B&B £48

QQQQ Golf View Hotel
17 Links Rd, Prestwick
☎ (01292) 671234, fax: (01292) 671244
Overlooking golf course, friendly owners
and high standard of bed and breakfast.
6 bedrooms
Credit Cards 1 3

QQQ Kincraig Private Hotel
39 Ayr Rd, Prestwick
☎ (01292) 479480
Spacious and well furnished bedrooms plus
comfortable lounge and attractive dining
room.
6 bedrooms

CAMPSITES

►►►► Sundrum Castle Holiday Park
Coylton
☎ (01292) 570057; fax:(01292) 570065
Ten minutes drive from the centre of Ayr off
the A70; pitch price from £9.50 per night.

►►► Camping & Caravanning Club Site
Culzean Castle, Maybole
☎ (01655) 760627 & (01203) 694995
South of Ayr off the A719; pitch price from
£8.70 per night.

►►► Middlemuir Park
Tarbolton
☎ (01292) 541647
Set in rolling farmland off the B743 Ayr-
Mauchline road

►► Cunningham Head Estate Caravan Park
Cunningham Head, Irvine
☎ (01294) 850238
A level farm site; pitch price from £6.50 per
night.

WHERE TO EAT

RESTAURANTS

✿✿ Fouters Bistro
2A Academy St, Ayr
☎ (01292) 261391; fax:(01292) 619323
Consistent quality and enthusiasm for new
ideas characterises the cuisine offered here
in this cosy basement restaurant.
Lunch: 12-2; from £4.95 and à la carte
Dinner: 7-10.30; from £19.50 and à la carte

✿✿ Lochgreen House
Monktonhill Rd, Southwood, Troon
☎ (01292) 313343, fax:(01292) 318661
A comfortable hotel where the cooking is
taken seriously.
Lunch: £17.95
Dinner: £28.50

✿ Marine Highland
Troon
☎ (01292) 314444, fax: (01292) 316922
A hotel restaurant offering fixed price and
carte menus that are rich in seafood.
Lunch: £14.95 and à la carte
Dinner: £19.95

✿✿ Fairfield House Hotel
12 Fairfield Road, Ayr
☎ (01292) 267461
fax: (01292) 261456
Lunch: 12-3.30 from £14.50
Dinner: 7-11.30 from £24

✿ Piersland House
Craigend Rd, Troon
☎ (01292) 314747
fax: (01292) 315613
Lunch: 12-2.30, £11.95
Dinner: 7-9.30, £19.95

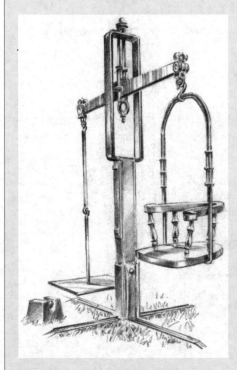

Bangor on Dee

This charming rural track is set in a bowl beside the River Dee and the surrounding banks afford excellent viewing, not only from the paddock area but also from the course car parks.

Due to its outstanding natural location, the management have never felt the need to build a grandstand, so be prepared for plenty of fresh air and a really enjoyable day out in the country. The best fixture is in late April, featuring a valuable three-mile handicap chase.

FURTHER INFORMATION

Bangor-on-Dee Races Ltd, The Racecourse, Bangor-on-Dee, Wrexham, LL13 0DA
☎ (01978) 780323; Fax: (01978) 780985

LOCATION AND HOW TO GET THERE

The course is 5 miles south of Wrexham off the A525 Wrexham-Whitchurch road. From the M53 take the A483 to bypass Wrexham; take the B5426 to Bangor, continue through Bangor village, then the B5069 Overton road for about a mile.

Nearest railway Station: Wrexham; there is an infrequent connecting bus service with the course.

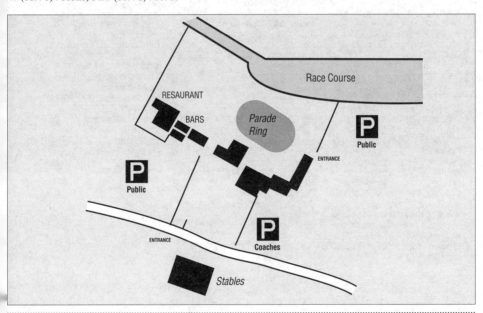

ADMISSION

All classes of day ticket give access to full betting facilities, including Tote.

Day Tickets:
Children under 16 are admitted free to all enclosures.

PADDOCK £9 – access to bars, buffet bar, cafeteria, facilities for disabled racegoers, facilities for private parties

COURSE £4 – access to bar, fast food

Annual membership: £85 includes reciprocal arrangements for 12 days racing at other courses, reserved car park, access to Members bar in the paddock.

COURSE FACILITIES

Banks:
there are no banks or cashpoint facilities on the course.

For families:
picnic area with refreshment kiosk and toilets.

CALENDAR OF EVENTS

February 13	August 15
March 11	September 12
March 28	October 10
April 18	October 26
May 1 - evening meeting	November 27
May 16	December 16
July 31	

WHERE TO STAY

HOTELS

Around Bangor-on-Dee

★★★ ⊛ 66% Broxton Hall Country House Hotel
Whitchurch Rd, Broxton
☎ (01829) 782321, fax: (01829) 782330
10 bedrooms; double B&B £70
Credit Cards 1 2 3 5

★★★ ⊛⊛ ⚘ 69% Bryn Howel
Llangollen
☎ (01978) 860331, fax: (01978) 860119
36 bedrooms; double B&B from £99
Credit cards 1 2 3

★★★ 62% The Royal
Bridge St, Llangollen
☎ (01978) 860202, fax: (01978) 861824
33 bedrooms; double B&B £70-£82
Credit cards 1 2 3 5

★★ ⊛ 67% Cross Lanes Hotel & Restaurant
Cross Lanes, Bangor Rd, Marchwiel
☎ (01978) 780555, fax: (01978) 780568
16 bedrooms; double B&B from £68
Credit cards 1 2 3 5

★★ 61% Redbrook Hunting Lodge
Wrexham Rd, Redbrook Maelor, Whitchuch
☎ (01948) 780204, fax: (01948) 780533
13 bedrooms; double B&B £49.50-£59.50
Credit cards 1 2 3

Travel Inn
Chester Rd, Greshford, Wrexham
☎ (01978) 853214; fax:(01978) 856838
38 bedrooms; double B&B £36.50

Travelodge
Mile End Service Area,
(junction A5/A483), Oswestry
☎ (01691) 658178; fax:(01691) 658178
40 bedrooms

★★★ ⊛ ⚘ 74% Llyndir Hall
Rossett
☎ (01244) 571648, fax: (01244) 571258
38 bedrooms
Credit cards 1 2 3 5

★★★ ⚘ 66% Llwyn Onn Hall
Cefn Rd, Wrexham
☎ (01978) 261225, fax: (01978) 363233
13 bedrooms; double B&B £79
Credit cards 1 2 3 5

★★★ 60% Wynnstay Arms
Yorke St, Wrexham
☎ (01978) 291010, fax: (01978) 362138
76 bedrooms; double room £34.50-£52.50
(room only)
Credit cards 1 2 3 5

Travelodge
Wrexham Bypass, Rhostyllen
☎ (01978) 365705; fax:(01978) 365705
32 bedrooms; double room from £34.50
(room only)
Credit cards 1 2 3 5

★★★ 67% The Wild Pheasant Hotel & Restaurant
Berwyn Road, Llangollen
☎ (01978) 860629, fax: (01978) 861837
34 bedrooms
Credit cards 1 2 3

BED AND BREAKFAST

QQQ Brackenwood
67 Wynnstay Lane, Marford
☎ (01978) 852866, fax: (01978) 852065
Family-run guest house set in beautiful gardens.
7 bedrooms; double B&B £30-£33

QQQ Hillcrest
Hill St, Llangollen
☎ (01978) 860208
Personally run private hotel located within a few minutes walk of the A5 and town centre.
7 bedrooms

QQQQ Golborne Manor
Platts Lane, Hatton Heath, Chester
☎ (01829) 770310; fax:(01244) 318084
Beautifully preserved and tastefully modernised Victorian country house.
3 bedrooms; double B&B £45-£60

QQQQQ Redland Private Hotel
64 Hough Green, Chester
☎ (01244) 671024, fax: (01244) 681309
A striking Victorian house with very individual bedrooms.
13 bedrooms; double B&B £60-£75

QQQQQ Laurel Farm
Chorlton Lane, Malpas
☎ (01948) 860291; fax: (01948) 860291
3 bedrooms; double B&B £50-£55

WHERE TO STAY

CAMPSITES

▶▶▶ Camping & Caravanning Club Site
The Racecourse, Signposted
☎ (01978) 781009 & (01203) 694995
pitch price from £8.10-£10.30 per night

▶▶▶ Plassey Touring Caravan & Leisure Park
Eyton
☎ (01978) 780277
fax: (01978) 780019
Situated off the B5426; pitch price from £10

▶▶▶ Ty-Ucha Farm
Maesmawr Rd, Llangollen
☎ (01978) 860677
Close to A5, 1 mile east of Llangollen; pitch price from £6

▶▶▶▶ Fernwood Caravan Park
Lyneal (near Ellesmere)
☎ (01948) 710221
Four miles southeast of Ellesmere off B5063

▶▶▶ Chester Southerly Caravan Pk
Balderton Lane, Marlston-Cum-Lache, Chester
☎ (01829) 270791
pitch price from £6.20-£8.80 per night

WHERE TO EAT

RESTAURANTS

🏵🏵 Bryn Howel
Llangollen
☎ (01978) 860331; fax:(01978) 860119
Daily-changing menus geared to market availability and quality produce
Lunch: 12-2; à la carte from £13
Dinner: 7-9; à la carte from £20

🏵 Llyndir Hall Hotel
Rossett
☎ (01244) 571648; fax:(01244) 571258
Interestiing cooking in an imposing country house hotel
Lunch: £12.50-£15.50 and à la carte
Dinner: £18.50 and à la carte

🏵 Broxton Hall County House
Whitchurch Rd, Broxton
☎ (01829) 782321 fax:(01829) 782330
Imaginative meals served in a popular hotel restaurant
Lunch: from £14.50
Dinner: £23.90

Bath

Situated just three miles outside the famous Roman and Georgian city, with its architectural splendours, lies this lovely course on a beautiful hill-top setting which offers panoramic views of the surrounding countryside.

A slight drawback is that it is fairly exposed to the elements, so be sure to wrap up well as a chill wind can blow even on the sunniest days, although a new stand may make all the difference. The track itself is very tight and a stiff uphill finish brings stamina into play. In sprint races, a low draw is absolutely vital as the course is constantly turning and lengths can be saved by hugging the rails.

There are over a dozen Flat meetings from April to October, with June and July probably the best time to go. The races are well supported by West Country folk and a good afternoon's entertainment is assured. As at most racecourses, private boxes or marquees can be hired for special occasions, but it is essential to book in advance.

FURTHER INFORMATION

The Bath Racecourse Co Ltd
Hopkins Farm, Lower Tysoe, Warwick.
CV35 0BN
☎ (01295) 688030; Fax: (01295) 688030

LOCATION AND HOW TO GET THERE

The course is two miles north of the city. Leave the M4 at junction 18 and take the A46 south for six miles; the course is signposted on racedays. **Nearest Railway Station:** Bath Spa; there is a special bus service to the course on race days.

ADMISSION

All classes of day ticket give access to full betting facilities, including Tote.

Day Tickets:
CLUB £13 – access to bar, luncheon room, boxes and private rooms

TATTERSALLS £8 – access to bar and snack bar

SILVER RING £4 – access to bar
COURSE £2 – access to bar

Parking: main parking free, central car park £5, including admission for one person

COURSE FACILITIES

Banks:
there are no banks or cashpoint facilities on the course.
For families:
picnic area with refreshment kiosk and toilets
Disabled:
New lift and toilet.

CALENDAR OF EVENTS

April 28	July 16
May 10	July 21
May 18	August 4
May 29 – evening meeting	August 11
June 13	September 7
June 27	September 28
July 6	October 27

WHERE TO STAY

HOTELS

★★★★★⊛⊛ 66% Bath Spa
Sydney Rd
☎ (01225) 444424
fax: (01225) 444006
98 bedrooms
Credit cards 1 2 3 5

★★ 70% The Old Mill Hotel
Tollbridge Road, Batheaston
☎ (01225) 858476; fax:(01225) 852600
26 rooms; double B&B £55
Credit cards 1 2 3

★★★★⊛⊛ 65% Combe Grove Manor Hotel & Country Club
Brassknocker Hill, Monkton Combe
☎ (01225) 834644, fax: (01225) 834961
40 bedrooms; double B&B from £99 –£285
Credit cards 1 2 3 5

★★★(Red)⊛⊛ The Priory
Weston Rd
☎ (01225) 331922
fax: (01225) 448276
29 bedrooms
Credit cards 1 2 3 5

★★★(Red)⊛⊛ Queensberry
Russel St
☎ (01225) 447928
fax: (01225) 446065
22 bedrooms; double B&B £90–£175
Credit cards 1 3

Hilton National
Walcot St, Bath
☎ (01225) 463411, fax (01225) 463411
150 bedrooms

★★ 70% The Bath Tasburg
Warminster Road
☎ (01225) 425096; fax:(01225) 463842
12 bedrooms; double B&B £65–£78
Credit cards 1 2 3 5

★★★ 65% Francis
Queen Square
☎ (01225) 424257
fax: (01225) 319715
94 bedrooms
Credit cards 1 2 3 5

★★★ 64% Compass Abbey
North Pde
☎ (01225) 461603
fax: (01225) 447758
60 bedrooms; double B&B £95–£105
Credit card 1 2 3 5

★★★ 64% Pratts
South Pde
☎ (01225) 460441
fax: (01225) 448807
46 bedrooms; double B&B £90
Credit cards 1 2 3 5

★★ 69% Duke's
Great Pulteney St
☎ (01225) 463512
fax: (01225) 483733
23 bedrooms; double B&B £65–£95
Credit Cards 1 2 3 5

★★ 71% Haringtons
8/10 Queen St
☎ (01225) 461728; fax(01225) 444804
13 bedrooms; double B&B £60–£85
Credit cards 1 2 3 5

Around Bath

★★★⊛⊛ 🏆 76% Woolley Grange
Woolley Green, Bradford on Avon
☎ (01225) 864705, fax: (01225) 864059
22 bedrooms; double B&B £99–£200
Credit cards 1 3

★★★★(Red) ⊛⊛⊛ Manor House
Castle Combe
☎ (01249) 782206
fax: (01249) 782159
45 bedrooms; double room £115–£350
(room only)
Credit cards 1 2 3 5

★★⊛ 64% Chelwood House
Chelwood
☎ (01761) 490730, fax (01761) 490730
12 bedrooms; double B&B £65–£88
Credit cards 1 2 3 5

★★★ 71% Centurion
Charlton Lane, Midsomer Norton
☎ (01761) 417711, fax (01761) 418357
44 bedrooms; double B&B £65–£70
Credit cards 1 2 3 5

★★⊛ 69% Country Ways
Marsh Lane,
Farrington Gurney
☎ (01761) 452449, fax: (01761) 452706
6 bedrooms; double B&B £65–£80
Credit cards 1 3

★★⊛ 69% White Hart Inn
Ford
☎ (01249) 782213, fax: (01249) 783075
11 bedrooms; double B&B £65
Credit cards 1 2 3 5

★★★ (Red)⊛⊛⊛⊛ 🏆 Homewood Park
Hinton Charterhouse
☎ (01225) 723731, fax: (01225) 723820
19 bedrooms; double B&B £105–£195
Credit cards 1 2 3 5

★★★ ⊛ 🏆 74% Cliffe Hotel
Crowe Hill, Limpley Stoke
☎ (01225) 723226; fax:(01225) 723871
11 bedrooms; double B&B £80–£105
Credit cards 1 2 3

★★★⊛ 66% Beechfield House
Beanacre, Melksham
☎ (01225) 703700, fax: (01225) 790118
21 bedrooms; double B&B £85–£110
Credit cards 1 2 3 5

WHERE TO STAY

BED AND BREAKFAST

Q Arney
99 Wells Rd
☎ (01225) 310020
Small Victorian terraced house offering
modest, value-for-money bed and breakfast
accommodation.
3 bedrooms; double B&B £37-£45

QQQ Ashley Villa Hotel
26 Newbridge Rd
☎ (01225) 421683; fax:(01225) 313604
Friendly small hotel with good range of
modern facilities
14 bedrooms; double B&B £59-£79
Credit Cards 1 3

QQQQ Bloomfield House
146 Bloomfield Rd
☎ (01225) 420105; fax:(01225) 481958
Stylishly decorated Georgian house with
period furniture on southern outskirts of
Bath.
8 bedrooms; double B&B £55-£95
Credit cards 1 3

QQQQ Brocks
32 Brock St
☎ (01225) 338374; fax:(01225) 334245
Bright and comfortable bedrooms, all
individually decorated with modern
facilities.
6 bedrooms; double B&B £58-£68
Credit cards 1 3

QQQQ Brompton House
St John's Rd
☎ (01225) 420972; fax:(01225) 420505
Renovated Victorian house providing
modern standards of comfort in city-centre
location.
18 bedrooms; double B&B £58-£78
Credit cards 1 2 3

QQQ Carfax Hotel
Great Pulteney St
☎ (01225) 462089, fax: (01225) 443257
Upgraded bedrooms, bright comfortable
public rooms on famous Bath street.
38 bedrooms; double B&B £51-£78
Credit cards 1 2 3

QQQQQ Cheriton House
9 Upper Oldfield Park
☎ (01225) 429862, fax: (01225) 428403
Well equipped bedrooms and bathrooms
with some fine views over the city.
9 bedrooms; double B&B £58-£72
Credit cards 1 2 3 5

QQQQ Cranleigh
159 Newbridge Hill
☎ (01225) 310197; fax:(01225) 423143
Spotlessly clean, airy and individually
styled rooms in a friendly, family-run
establishment.
5 bedrooms; double B&B £60-£78
Credit cards 1 3

QQQQ Devonshire House
143 Wellsway
☎ (01225) 312495; fax:(01225) 335534
On the outskirts of the city with comfortable,
individually styled bedrooms.
3 bedrooms; double B&B £48-£55
Credit cards 1 3

QQQQQ Dorian House
1 Upper Oldfield Park
☎ (01225) 426336, fax: (01225) 444699
In an elevated position off the A367, with
fine views over city and well equipped
bedrooms.
8 bedrooms; double B&B £66-£75
Credit cards 1 2 3 5

QQQ Eagle House
Church St, Bathford
☎ (01225) 859946; fax:(01225) 859946
Modern well equipped bedrooms in very
attractive listed Georgian house.
8 bedrooms; double B&B £44-£72
Credit cards 1 3

QQQ Edgar Hotel
64 Gt Pulteney St
☎ (01225) 420619; fax:(01225) 466916
Comfortable bed and breakfast
accommodation close to city centre.
16 bedrooms: double B&B £40-£65
Credit cards 1 3

QQQ Gainsborough Hotel
Weston Ln
☎ (01225) 311380; fax:(01225) 447411
16 bedrooms
Credit cards 1 2 3

QQQQ Highways House
143 Wells Rd
☎ (01225) 421238, fax: (01225) 481169
Comfortable and hospitable hotel.
7 bedrooms; double B&B £52-£64
Credit cards 1 3

QQQQQ Holly Lodge
8 Upper Oldfield Park
☎ (01225) 424042, fax: (01225) 481138
Exceptionally comfortable, beautifully
decorated bedrooms in hospitable
establishment.
7 bedrooms; double B&B £75-£89
Credit cards 1 2 3 5

QQQQQ Kennard Hotel
11 Henrietta St
☎ (01225) 310472, fax: (01225) 460054
Situated close to city centre, period house
offering bright, attractive bedrooms.
13 bedrooms; double B&B £65-£85
Credit cards 1 2 3 5

QQQQ Laura Place Hotel
3 Laura Place, Great Pulteney St
☎ (01225) 463815, fax: (01225) 310222
Very convenient location, tastefully
decorated with some very large and well
equipped bedrooms.
8 bedrooms; double B&B £60-£88
Credit cards 1 2 3

QQQQQ Leighton House
139 Wells Rd
☎ (01225) 314769; fax:(01225) 443079
Fine Victorian residence in elevated
position, with high quality bedrooms.
8 bedrooms; double B&B £62-£75
Credit cards 1 3

QQQQQ Meadowland
36 Bloomfield Park
☎ (01225) 311079
Bright and clean hotel in secluded grounds
on outskirts of city centre; charming
bedrooms.
3 bedrooms
Credit cards 1 3

QQQQQ Monkshill
Shaft Rd, Monkton Combe
☎ (01225) 833028; fax:(01225) 833028
On outskirts of city with superb views,
offering cosy, stylish bedrooms.
3 bedrooms
Credit cards 1 2 3 5

QQQQ Oakleigh House
19 Upper Oldfield Park
☎ (01225) 315698; fax:(01225) 448223
4 bedrooms
Credit cards 1 2 3

WHERE TO STAY

QQQQ Oldfields
102 Wells Rd
☎ (01225) 317984, fax: (01225) 444471
Hospitable, friendly atmosphere with richly
furnished and equipped bedrooms.
14 bedrooms; double B&B £50-£70
Credit cards 1 3

QQQQQ Old School House
Church St, Bathford
☎ (01225) 859593; fax:(01225) 859590
Cosy, individually styled, well equipped
bedrooms and very welcoming, hospitable
hosts.
4 bedrooms
Credit cards 1 3

QQQQ Paradise House Hotel
Holloway
☎ (01225) 317723, fax: (01225) 482005
Beautiful Georgian house with excellent
view of city and particularly comfortable
bedrooms.
8 bedrooms; double B&B £65-£80
Credit cards 1 2 3

QQQQ Somerset House Hotel & Restaurant
35 Bathwick Hill
☎ (01225) 466451; fax:(01225) 317188
Brightly decorated bedrooms in individual
styles in this listed property.
10 bedrooms; double B&B £79-£102
Credit cards 1 2 3

CAMPSITES

►►► Piccadilly Caravan Site
Folly Ln, Chippenham
☎ (01249) 730260
East of Bath, 4 miles south of Chippenham;
pitch price from £7 per night.

►►►► Bath Marina & Caravan Park
Brassmill Lane, Newbridge
☎ (01225) 428778; fax:(01225) 424301
On the edge of Bath;
pitch prices £10-£10.50 per night.

►►►► Newton Mill Caravan and Camping Park
Newton St. Loe
☎ (01225) 333909; fax:(01225) 461556
Tranquil terraced site;
pitch prices £9.50-£12.95 per night.

WHERE TO EAT

RESTAURANTS

❀❀❀ Royal Crescent
16 Royal Crescent
☎ (01225) 823333; fax:(01225) 339401
Sumptuously furnished restaurant serving
superb foot.
Lunch: 12.30-2; £14.50 and à la carte
Dinner: 7-9.30; £33 and à la carte

❀❀ Woods
9-13 Alfred St
☎ (01225) 314812; fax:(01225) 443146
Excellently balanced flavours and generous
portions are offered in this popular local
venue.
Lunch: 12-3 ; from £6 and à la carte
Dinner: 6-11; from £10 and à la carte

❀❀ Clos du Roy
1 Seven Dials, Sawclose
☎ (01225) 444450; fax:(01225) 404044
Smart modern restaurant offering light
lunches and a lengthier evening carte.
Lunch: 12-2.30; £8.95 and à la carte
Dinner 6-10.30; £19.50 and à la carte

❀ Rajpoot Tandoori
Rajpoot House, 4 Argyle St
☎ (01225) 466833, fax; (01225) 442462
Stylish Indian restaurant serving classical
Tandoori, Mughlai and Bengali dishes.
Lunch: 12-2.30; from £6.95 and à la carte
Dinner 6-11; £18.95 and à la carte

❀❀ No 5 Bistro
5 Argyle St
☎ (01225) 444499; fax:(01225) 318668
Informal bistro serving light lunchtime
meals and snacks and more serious
evening meals.
Lunch: 12-2.30
Dinner 6.30-10.30

❀❀ The Hole in the Wall
16 George St
☎ (01225) 425242; fax:(01225) 425242
Smart, comfortable city centre restaurant
serving Italian food
Lunch: 12-2; £11.50 and à la carte
Dinner 6-10.30; £22.50 and à la carte

PUBS

The Cross Keys
Midford Road, Combe Down
☎ (01225) 832002
On the upper outskirts of Bath, this old
coaching inn's garden has a well-stocked
aviary. Home-made pies are a speciality.
Open: 11am-2.30pm, 6pm-11pm
(Sat: 11am-3pm, 7pm-11pm, Sun: 12am-
3pm, 7pm-10.30pm) No dinner Sunday
Principle Beers: Founders, Ushers, Courage

The Old Green Tree
12 Green Street
 (01225) 448259
This pub can be traced back to 1752 and
was completely oak-panelled in 1923. Run
on old-fashioned lines with good beer,
wine, food and company.
Open: 11am-11pm (Sun 7pm-10.30)
Principle Beers: from local micro-
breweries.

Beverley

There is a fine history behind this attractive venue - its track was initially laid out towards the end of the 17th century - and the site still possesses plenty of old-fashioned charm.

The stands have been the subject of recent modernisation without the course losing any of its individual character.

The right-handed track is a galloping, roughly oval circuit. There is a separate chute for five-furlong races (horses drawn high have a distinct advantage) and this provides a stiff test of stamina for sprinters as the home straight rises steadily throughout. Lots of close finishes occur as a result and many a winner has triumphed with a late flourish.

FURTHER INFORMATION

Beverley Race Company Ltd
The Grandstand, York Road, Beverley,
East Yorkshire HU17 8QZ
☎ (01482) 867488 / 882645
fax: (01482) 863892

LOCATION AND HOW TO GET THERE

The course is signposted from the M62.
Nearest Railway Station: Beverley

ADMISSION

All classes of day ticket give access to full betting facilities, including Tote.

Day Tickets:
Accompanied children under 16 admitted free.

CLUB £12, £8 junior (16-21 years) – access to bar, restaurant, boxes

TATTERSALLS £8 – access to bar and restaurant

SILVER RING £3 – access to bar and restaurant

NUMBER 3 RING £2

Annual Membership:
£90 single, £140 associate, £50 junior (under 25)

Parking: picnic parking £2 per car, plus £2 per person on course. Free parking elsewhere.

COURSE FACILITIES

Banks:
there are no banks or cashpoint facilities on the course.

For families:
picnic area with refreshment kiosk and toilet; children's play area

CALENDAR OF EVENTS

April 23 – flat
May 9-10 – flat
May 19 – flat
June 3 – flat; evening meeting
June 10 – flat
June 23
July 3-4 – flat; evening meeting on Friday
July 14 – flat

July 20 – flat; evening meeting
July 28 – flat
August 12-13 – flat
August 24 – flat
August 29
September 16 – flat
September 22 – flat

WHERE TO STAY

HOTELS

★★★ **66% Beverley Arms**
North Bar Within
☎ (01482) 869241, fax: (01482) 870907
57 bedrooms; double room from £75 (room only)
Credit cards 1 2 3 5

★★★ ❀ **65% Tickton Grange**
Tickton
☎ (01964) 543666, fax: (01964) 542556
18 bedrooms
Credit cards 1 2 3 5

★★ **67% Lairgate**
30-34 Lairgate
☎ (01482) 882141, fax: (01482) 861067
22 bedrooms; double B&B £55-£80
Credit cards 1 3

30

WHERE TO STAY

Around Beverley

★★ 68% Burton Lodge
Brandesburton
☎ (01964) 542847, fax: (01964) 542847
10 bedrooms; double B&B £46–£50
Credit cards 1 2 3

★★ 65% Fox and Coney Inn
Market Pl, South Cave
☎ (01430) 422275, fax: (01430) 421552
8 bedrooms; double room £39–£42.50
Credit cards 1 2 3

Campanile
Beverley Rd, Freetown Way, Hull
☎ (01482) 325530
fax: (01482) 587538
50 bedrooms; double room £36.50
Credit cards 1 2 3 5

★★★ ⚬ 65% Rowley Manor
Rowley Rd, Little Weighton
☎ (01482) 848248, fax: (01482) 849900
16 bedrooms; double B&B £70–£90
Credit cards 1 2 3 5

★★★ ⚬ 70% Willerby Manor
Well Ln, Willerby
☎ (01482) 652616
fax: (01482) 653901
51 bedrooms; double bedroom £75–£82
Credit cards 1 2 3

BED AND BREAKFAST

QQQ Earlsmere Hotel
76/78 Sunnybank, Spring Bank West, Hull
☎ (01482) 341977
fax: (01482) 473714
7 bedrooms
Credit cards 1 3 5

QQQ The Eastgate
7 Eastgate
☎ (01482) 868464, fax: (01482) 871899
Friendly town centre guesthouse with cosy bedrooms
18 bedrooms; double B&B £30–£44

QQ New Inn
44 South St, Leven
☎ (01964) 542223
4 bedrooms
Credit cards 1 2 3

CAMPSITES

►►► Silver Birches Tourist Park
Waterside Rd, Barton upon Humber
☎ (01652) 632509
South of Beverley, close to the Humber Bridge; pitch price from £5.50 per night.

►►► Dacre Lakeside Park
Brandesburton
☎ (01964) 543704
fax; (01964) 543851
Northeast of Beverley; pitch price from £6.50 per night.

►►► Burton Constable Caravan Park
Old Lodges, Sproatley
☎ (01964) 562508
Beautiful site close to boating and fishing lakes; pitch price from £6.25 per night.

WHERE TO EAT

RESTAURANTS

⚬ Cerutti's
10 Nelson St, Hull
☎ (01482) 328501, fax: (01482) 587597
Fresh fish, competently cooked, in a pleasant waterside setting.
Lunch: 12-2, £13.50 à la carte
Dinner: 7-9.30, £13.50 à la carte

⚬ Willerby Manor
Well Lane, Willerby
☎ (01482) 652616
fax: (01482) 653901
Interesting selection of classic French and British dishes with modern interpretations
Lunch: 12-2; £12 and à la carte
Dinner: 7-9.30; £14.50 and à la carte

⚬⚬ Manor House
Northlands, Walkington
☎ (01482) 881645
fax:(01482) 866501
Dinner: 7-11; £16.50 and à la carte

PUBS

White Horse
22 Hengate, Beverley
☎ (01482) 861973
Grade I listed building dating back to the 16th century with unspoilt interior. A Samuel Smiths pub serving tasty and substantial bar meals. Children are allowed in any of the rooms, except the one with the bar in. Open: 11am-11pm Monday to Saturday; 10.30am-12pm Sunday
Bar food: 12-2 but not Monday evenings

Dacre Arms
Main Street, Brandesburton
☎ (01964) 542392
Open: 11.30am-2.30pm, 6pm-11pm. (weekend: all day, Fri: 11.30am-2.30pm, 5.30pm-11pm)
Principal beer: John Smiths
Bar Meals: Lunch: 12-2, Dinner: 6-10.30

Half Moon
16 Main St, Skidby
☎ (01482) 843403
A John Smiths pub dating in parts back to the 17th century. Popular range of bar meals are plentiful and good value for money. Children are permitted in the pub and there is a garden with climbing nets, slides etc. Open 11am-11pm
Bar food: 12-9.30pm

The Bell
Market Place, Driffield
☎ (01377) 256661
fax:(01377) 253225
Open 10am-11pm
Bar meals; Lunch 12-1.30, Dinner 7-10
Principal beers: Stones, Hambleton Ales, Malton.

Brighton

The unique feature of this popular seaside course is its U-shaped track, one of the very few in Britain not to form a complete circuit. Consequently the start of long-distance contests (the furthest is 1.5 miles) is barely visible from the stands and much of the action will be missed without a good pair of binoculars (they can be hired).

The finish is also interesting, because jockeys have to be pretty smart at pulling up as the course comes to an abrupt halt. In many other ways, the track resembles Epsom, with its long downhill stretch round a sharp left-hand bend before the ground rises again slightly in the final furlong. Look out for course specialists who have shown past ability at handling the unusual contours.

With the Channel clearly visible in the background, except on the rare occasions when the sea mists roll in and obliterate everything, this is a very attractive setting. Nineteen fixtures are scheduled. Finding a seat in the stands is no problem, and for an exciting head-on view, try the open roof-top opposite the winning post.

FURTHER INFORMATION

The Racecourse office
Lingfield Park 1991 Ltd
Lingfield, Surrey, RH7 6PQ
☎ (01342) 834800; Fax:(01342) 832833

LOCATION AND HOW TO GET THERE

The course is on the hill above Brighton Marina. It is well signposted from both the A23 London Brighton road and the A27.

Nearest Railway Station: Brighton; there is courtesy bus service to the course on racedays.

ADMISSION

All classes of day ticket give access to full betting facilities, including Tote.

Day Tickets:
Accompanied children under 16 are admitted free to all enclosures, except Club.

CLUB £12 – access to restaurant, boxes, private rooms

TATTERSALLS £8 – access to snack bar, boxes, private rooms

Picnic park £4 per car and £4 per occupant – access to bar and snack bar

Annual membership: £130

COURSE FACILITIES

Banks:
there are no banks or cashpoint facilities on the course.

For families:
picnic area with refreshment kiosk and toilet family room

CALENDAR OF EVENTS

April 20	July 1	September 2
April 30	July 13-14	September 30
May 5	July 23	October 5
May 22	August 5	October 22
May 28	August 12	November 5
June 2	August 18	
June 15	August 24	

WHERE TO STAY

HOTELS

★★★ 71% Old Ship
Kings Rd
☎ (01273) 329001, fax: (01273) 820718
152 bedrooms; double B&B £52–£110
Credit cards 1 2 3 5

★★★ 65% Imperial
First Avenue
☎ (01273) 777320, fax: (01273) 777310
76 bedrooms; double B&B £60–£90
Credit cards 1 2 3 5

★★★ 58% Sackville
189 Kingsway
☎ (01273) 736292
fax: (01273) 205759
45 bedrooms
Credit cards 1 2 3 5

★★ 60% St Catherines Lodge
Seafront, Kingsway
☎ (01273) 778181, fax: (01273) 774949
50 bedrooms; double B&B £40–£65
Credit cards 1 2 3 5

★★★★ ❀ 68% Brighton Thistle
Kings Rd
☎ (01273) 206700, fax: (01273) 820692
204 bedrooms; double B&B £102–£170
Credit cards 1 2 3 5

★★★ 63% Brighton Oak
West St
☎ (01273) 220033, fax: (01273) 778000
138 bedrooms; double room £62–£105
Credit cards 1 2 3 5

★★★★★ 63% Grand
Kings Rd
☎ (01273) 321188, fax: (01273) 202694
200 bedrooms; double B&B £180–£270
Credit cards 1 2 3 5

BED AND BREAKFAST

QQQQ Adelaide Hotel
51 Regency Square
☎ (01273) 205286, fax: (01273) 220904
Freshly decorated and tastefully furnished
bedrooms; the proprietors are welcoming.
12 bedrooms; double B&B £62–£78
Credit cards 1 2 3 5

QQQ Allendale Hotel
3 New Steine
☎ (01273) 675436, fax: (01273) 602603
Charming proprietors and smart, modern
bedrooms, exceptionally well equipped.
12 bedrooms
Credit cards 1 2 3 5

QQQ Ambassador Hotel
22 New Steine
☎ (01273) 676869, fax: (01273) 689988
Family-run hotel offers of a range of neat,
well equipped bedrooms.
21 bedrooms; double B&B £42–£65
Credit cards 1 2 3 5

QQQQ Arlanda Hotel
20 New Steine
☎ (01273) 699300, fax: (01273) 600930
Regency-style house offers a mixed style of
accommodation.
12 bedrooms; double B&B £46–£80
Credit cards 1 2 3 5

QQQQ Ascott House Hotel
21 New Steine, Marine Pde
☎ (01273) 688085, fax: (01273) 623733
Small personally run hotel close to the
seafront, offering bright, freshly decorated
bedrooms
12 bedrooms; double B&B £40–£80
Credit cards 1 2 3 5

QQQ Cavalaire House
34 Upper Rock Gardens
☎ (01273) 696899, fax: (01273) 600504
Well maintained guest house with compact
but thoughtfully equipped bedrooms.
9 bedrooms; double B&B £40–£58
Credit cards 1 2 3

QQ Dudley House
10 Madeira Place
☎ (01273) 676794
Smart terraced house with immaculate
bedrooms.
6 bedrooms; double B&B £32–£50

QQQ Gullivers
10 New Steine
☎ (01273) 695415, fax: (01252) 372774
Attractive bedrooms feature in this Regency
residence close to the seafront.
9 bedrooms; double B&B £38–£54
Credit cards 1 2 3 5

QQQ Kempton House
33/34 Marine Parade
☎ (01273) 570248, fax: (01273) 570248
Small informal Regency hotel on sea front.
12 bedrooms; double B&B £44–£64
Credit cards 1 2 3

QQQQ New Steine Hotel
12a New Steine, Marine Pde
☎ (01273) 681546
Smart, comfortable accommodation.
11 bedrooms; double B&B £40–£49

QQQ Paskins Town House
18/19 Charlotte Street
☎ (01273) 601203
fax:(01273) 621973
Friendly, helpful owners in an attractively
decorated and well-designed guest house
19 bedrooms; double B&B £40–£80
Credit cards 1 2 3 5

QQQ Trouville Hotel
11 New Steine, Marine Pde
☎ (01273) 697384
Seafront, family-run guesthouse offering
freshly decorated bedrooms.
9 bedrooms; double B&B £38–£49
Credit cards 1 2 3

CAMPSITES

▶ Harwoods Farm
West End Lane, Henfield
☎ (01273) 492820.
Unspoilt 'Venture' site for tents and motor
caravans only, down narrow lane; pitch
price from £4.50

WHERE TO EAT

RESTAURANTS

❀ Brighton Thistle Hotel
Kings Rd
☎ (01273) 206700
fax:(01273) 820692
Formal hotel restaurant serving enjoyable
dishes with well-balanced flavours
Lunch: 12.30-2.30; £18.50
Dinner: 7-10; £26.50

❀❀ One Paston Place
1 Paston Place
☎ (01273) 606933
fax: (01273) 675686
Down to earth and flavoursome cooking in a
relaxed friendly atosphere.
Lunch: 12.30-2; from £16.50 and à la carte
Dinner: 7.30-10

❀❀ Whyte's
33 Western St, Brighton
☎ (01273) 776618
Cosy, small restaurant near the seafront,
serving sound, honest cooking in French
and English styles.
Dinner: 7-9.30; from £19.50

❀❀ Black Chapati
12 Circus Parade, New England Rd
☎ (01273) 699011
Unassuming little restaurant serving dishes
with influences from around Asia.
Dinner: 7-10.30; £9.50 and à la carte

❀❀ Quentin's
42 Western Rd, Hove
☎ (01273) 822734
Eclectic international dishes using modern
English, Mediterranean and Oriental recipes
Lunch: 12-2, £5.95
Dinner: from £17.95

❀ La Marinade
77 St George Road, Kemp Town
☎ (01273) 600992
fax: (01273) 600992
Lunch: 12-2, from £12.80
Dinner: 7-10; £18.50

❀ Terre a Terre
7 Pool Valley
☎ (01273) 729051
fax: (01273) 327561
Lunch: 12-5.30; £17 à la carte
Dinner: 5.30-10.30, £17 à la carte

PUBS

The Juggs
The Street, Kingston, nr Lewes
☎ (01273) 472523
Traditional Kentish-style building in
attractive garden with a good play area.
Fairly standard pub meals; draught beers
include Harveys and King & Barnes; wine
list features around 30 bottles. Children are
welcome anywhere in the pub and there is a
children's menu.
Open: 11am-3pm, 6-11pm
Bar food: 12-2pm, 6-9.30pm
Restaurant: times as bar food

Carlisle

This friendly Cumbrian racecourse is situated between the Lake District and the Borders and is therefore an ideal place to visit for people wishing to explore the colourful countryside of the surrounding areas.

Access is easy and a warm welcome is sure to be extended to any newcomers to the sport. Facilities are good, with a fair selection of bars and restaurants to choose from, and both the admission charges and catering prices are very reasonable.

There are 20 fixtures held here every year under both codes, with the highlight being the late June meeting which features the Carlisle Bell and the Cumberland Plate, the two most important contests in the calendar. The roughly pear-shaped, undulating track provides an extremely stiff test of stamina and the general consensus among racing professionals is that it is the most demanding course in the north. The final home stretch rises steeply uphill and only the most resolute of gallopers are able to overcome this severe climb in heavy ground.

FURTHER INFORMATION

Carlisle Racecourse Co Ltd
Grandstand Office, The Racecourse, Blackwell, Carlisle, Cumbria CA2 4TS
☎ (01228) 22973

LOCATION AND HOW TO GET THERE

Carlisle racecourse is two miles south of the city at Blackwell. From M6 junction 42, follow signs on Dalston Road.
Nearest Railway Station: Carlisle; the number 66 bus runs between the station and the racecourse on racedays.

ADMISSION

All classes of day ticket give access to full betting facilities, including Tote.

Day Tickets:
MEMBERS £12 – access to members' stand with seating, bars and restaurants.

GRANDSTAND & PADDOCK £6, pensioners £3, accompanied children under 16 free – access to private rooms, bars and cafeteria, and parade ring.

TRACKSIDE PARKING AND PICNIC AREA £3, £5 Saturdays and Bank Holidays

Annual membership:
£100 single, £145 double, junior membership (under 21) £50 – includes admission to ten other racecourses on certain days in the year.

COURSE FACILITIES

Banks:
There are no banks or cashpoint facilities on the course.

For families:
picnic area with toilet; children's play area and baby changing facilities on busy days only; lost children centre and crèche.

CALENDAR OF EVENTS

January 20 – jumping
February 10 – jumping
March 12 – jumping
April 11 – jumping
April 13 – jumping
April 24 – flat
May 8 – flat
June 11 – flat
June 24-25 – flat
July 4 – flat; evening meeting

July 17 – flat
August 3 – flat; evening meeting
August 26 – flat
September 19 – jumping
October 9 – jumping; Club Visitors Day
October 24 – jumping
November 9 – jumping
November 26 – jumping
December 30 – jumping

WHERE TO STAY

HOTELS

★★★ 67% Cumbria Park
32 Scotland Rd, Stanwix
☎ (01228) 22887, fax: (01228) 514796
48 bedrooms; double B&B £87.50-£120
Credit cards 1 2 3 5

★★★ 60% Central Plaza
Victoria Viaduct
☎ (01228) 20256, fax: (01228) 514657
84 bedrooms
Credit cards 1 2 3 5

Forte Posthouse Carlisle
Parkhouse Rd, Kingstown
☎ (01228) 31201, fax: (01228) 43178
93 bedrooms
Credit cards 1 2 3 5

★★★ 64% Swallow Hilltop
London Rd
☎ (01228) 29255
fax: (01228) 25238
92 bedrooms; double B&B £99
Credit cards 1 2 3 5

★★ 65% County
9 Botchergate
☎ (01228) 31316, fax: (01228) 515456
84 bedrooms; double room £39.95-£64.95
(room only)
Credit cards 1 2 3 5

★★ 60% Pinegrove
262 London Rd
☎ (01228) 24828, fax: (01228) 810941
32 bedrooms; double B&B from £40-£56
Credit cards 1 2 3 5

★★★ ❀ 74% Crown
Wetheral
☎ (01228) 561888, fax: (01228) 561637
51 bedrooms; double B&B £116-£136
Credit cards 1 2 3 5

★ 63% Vallum House Garden
Burgh Rd
☎ (01228) 21860
9 bedrooms; doubleB&B £45-£50
Credit cards 1 3

Around Carlisle

Travelodge
Gretna Green
☎ (01461) 337566
64 bedrooms; double room £34.95-£49.95
(room only)

**★★★❀ ♨ 73% Crosby Lodge
Country House Hotel**
High Crosby, Crosby-on-Eden
☎ (01228) 573618, fax: (01228) 573428
11 bedrooms; double B&B £98-£125
Credit card 1 2 3

BED AND BREAKFAST

QQQQ Angus Hotel
14 Scotland Rd
☎ (01228) 23546
fax: (01228) 31895
Pleasant well run guesthouse offering
simple, well maintained accommodation.
12 bedrooms; double B&B £36-£51.50
Credit cards 1 2 3

QQQ Crossroads House
Brisco
☎ (01228) 28994
Modern detached house set in open
countryside.
6 bedrooms; double B&B £36-£42

QQ East View
110 Warwick Rd
☎ (01228) 22112
Friendly, family owned and run guesthouse.
8 bedrooms

QQQ Kingstown Hotel
246 Kingstown Rd
☎ (01228) 515292, fax: (01228) 515292
8 bedrooms; double B&B £45
Credit cards 1 2 3

QQQ The Warren
368 Warwick Road
☎ (01228) 33663
fax: (01228) 33663
Once known as the Star Inn, now offering
prettily decorated bedrooms.
6 bedrooms; double B&B from £36

QQQQ Howard House
27 Howard Place
☎ (01228) 29159
5 bedrooms
Credit cards 1 3

QQQQQ Number Thirty One
Shaftesbury House, 31 Howard Place
☎ (1228) 597080
fax: (1228) 597080
3 bedrooms; double B&B £60-£80

Around Carlisle

Q Gelt Hall Farm
Castle Carrock
☎ (01228) 70260
A pleasant little farmhouse with natural
charm.
3 bedrooms

CAMPSITES

►►► Dandy Dinmont Caravan Site
Blackford
☎ (01228) 74611
North of Carlisle;
pitch price £5.75-£7.25 per night

**►►► Orton Grange Caravan &
Camping Park**
Orton Grange, Wigton Rd, Carlisle
☎ (01228) 710252
fax: (01228) 710252
Pitch price from £6.60 per night

►►► Dalston Hall Caravan Park
Dalston Hall Estate, Dalston
☎ (01228) 710165
Southwest of Carlisle adjacent to the A35;
pitch price from £6-£7.50 per night

WHERE TO STAY

►►► Camelot Caravan Park
Sandysike, Longtown
☎ (01228) 791248
On the A7 north of Carlisle;
pitch price from £6.70

►►► Irthing Vale Holiday Park
Old Church Lane, Brampton
☎ (016977) 3600
In a rural setting on the edge of the market
town;
pitch price from £9.50 per night

►►►► Clea Hall Holiday Park
Westward
☎ (016973) 42880
fax: (016973) 42880
3 miles south of A595;
pitch price £10-£12 per night

►►► Cairndale Caravan Park
Cumwhitton
☎ (01768) 896280
Lovely grass site in Eden Valley;
pitch price from £4.50 per night

WHERE TO EAT

RESTAURANTS

✸ Crosby Lodge Country House Hotel
High Crosby, Crosby-on-Eden
☎ (01228) 573618
fax: (01228) 573428
Extensive range of dishes served in a
delightful hotel setting
Lunch: 12-1.30; £16 and à la carte
Dinner: 7-9; £28 and à la carte

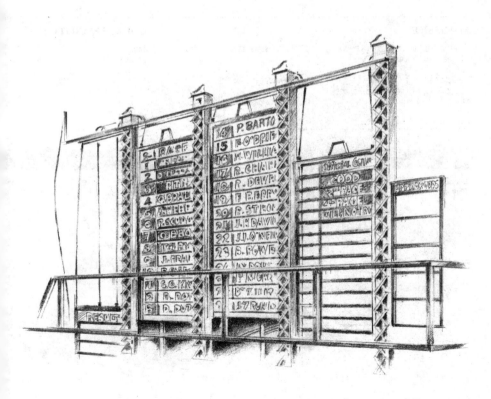

Cartmel

Amidst stunningly beautiful Lake District scenery, this delightful little course provides a truly idyllic site for jump racing. Even the journey to the course is a real pleasure, but allow lots of time because it is not a well-kept secret and crowds are always huge.

Part of the reason for this is that only two meetings are run here every year, with six days' racing spread over the Spring Bank Holiday in May and the August Bank Holiday.

Fun is the order of the day, with plenty of other attractions besides the horses (these are often moderate due to firm ground, although fields are big and the exceptionally long run-in of half a mile usually witnesses exciting finishes). Exhibitions of hound-trailing are sometimes held before racing, and a fun-fair is always in attendance with the Ferris Wheel providing a unique perspective of the action as the runners pass virtually underneath. A charming course with a terrific atmosphere; it is well worth planning a holiday in the area around one of the meetings.

FURTHER INFORMATION

Cartmel Steeplechases Ltd
Estate Office, Lowther, Penrith,
Cumbria CA10 2HG
☎ (01539) 536340 (Recorded Information Line)

LOCATION AND HOW TO GET THERE

The course is approximately 2 miles west of Grange over Sands. Leave the M6 at junction 36 and take the A590. Later turn left for Cartmel. **Nearest Railway Station:** Cark in Cartmel; there is a connecting bus service to the course on racedays.

ADMISSION

All classes of day ticket give access to full betting facilities, including Tote.

Day tickets:
PADDOCK £10, senior citizens £5 – access to bar, restaurant and grandstand

COURSE £4, senior citizens £2 – access to bar

Annual membership: £70

Parking: free in Course Enclosure, £5 in Paddock Enclosure

COURSE FACILITIES

Banks:
there are no banks or cashpoint facilities on the course.

CALENDAR OF EVENTS

May 23 – jumping
May 25 – jumping

May 27 – jumping
August 27 – evening meeting

August 29 – jumping
August 31 – jumping

WHERE TO STAY

HOTELS

★★ ⚜ 75% Anysome Manor
☎ (015395) 36653, fax: (015395) 36016
12 bedrooms; double B&B £90-£108
(including dinner)
Credit cards 1 2 3

Around Cartmel

★★★ 68% Grange
Station Square,
Grange-over-Sands
☎ (015395) 33666, fax: (015395) 35064
41 bedrooms; double B&B £88
Credit cards 1 2 3 5

★★★ 65% Netherwood
Lindale Rd,
Grange-over-Sands
☎ (015395) 32552, (015395) 34121
29 bedrooms; double B&B £90-£110
Credit cards 1 3

★★★ ⚜ 63% Graythwaite Manor
Fernhill Rd, Grange-over-Sands
☎ (015395) 32001 & 33755,
fax: (015395) 35549
21 bedrooms
Credit cards 1 2 3

★★ ⚜ 67% Hampsfell House
Hampsfell Rd, Grange-over-Sands
☎ (015395) 32567
9 bedrooms; double B&B £45-£54
Credit cards 1 3

★★★ 67% Whitewater
The Lakeland Village, Newby Bridge
☎ (015395) 31133, fax; (015395) 31881
35 bedrooms; double B&B £95-£120
Credit cards 1 2 3 5

★ (Red) ⚜ ⚜⚜ Old Vicarage Country House Hotel
Church Rd, Witherslack
☎ (015395) 52381, fax;(015395) 52373
14 bedrooms; double B&B £70-£95
Credit cards 1 2 3

★★★ 69% Swan
Newby Bridge
☎ (015395) 31681, fax; (015395) 31917
36 bedrooms; double B&B £96-£140
Credit cards 1 2 3

★ 73% Clare House
Park Rd, Grange-over-Sands
☎ (015395) 33026 & 34253
17 bedrooms; double B&B £86-£92
(includes dinner)

★★ 72% Grizedale Lodge
Grizedale
☎ (015395) 36532, fax: (015395) 36572
9 bedrooms; double B&B and dinner £97-£110
Credit cards 1 3

BED AND BREAKFAST

QQQQ Crosthwaite House
Crosthwaite
☎ (015395) 68264
Set in beautiful countryside; the house
is well furnished and cared for.
6 bedrooms; double B&B £40-£44
Credit cards 2

QQ Birchleigh Guest House
Kents Bank Rd, Grange-over-Sands
☎ (015395) 32592
Small, friendly guesthouse.
4 bedrooms
Credit cards 2

QQQQ Hill Crest
Brow Edge, Newby Bridge
☎ (015395) 31766
fax: (015395) 31986
A split level, lakeland stone bungalow with
two luxurious bedrooms
Double B&B £36-£40

QQQ Ashley Private Hotel
371 Marine Rd, Promenade East, Morecambe
☎ (01524) 412034; fax (01524) 421390
Family-run hotel with superb views.
13 bedrooms; double B&B £32.40-£36
Credit cards 1 2 3

QQQ Beach Mount Hotel
395 Marine Rd East, Morecambe
☎ (01524) 420753
Comfortable accommodation with excellent
views.
23 bedrooms; double B&B £41
Credit cards 1 2 3 5

QQ New Hazelmere Hotel
391 Promenade East, Morecambe
☎ (01524) 417876, fax; (01524) 414488
Large sea-front hotel with a nautical theme.
50 bedrooms
Credit cards 1 2 3

Q Browside Cottage
Ayside, Newby Bridge
☎ (015395) 31500
A cosy country cottage with 2 comfortable
bedrooms
Double B&B £30-£40

QQQ Lakes End
Newby Bridge
☎ (015395) 31260; fax:(015395) 43275
Friendly family-run guesthouse with well
furnished, comfortable accommodation.
8 bedrooms; double B&B £37-£39

QQQQQ The Bower
Yealand Conyers
☎ (01524) 734585
Comfortable rooms with pine and antique
furniture.
2 bedrooms; double B&B £46-£56

CAMPSITES

►►► Oak Head Caravan Park
Ayside
☎ (015395) 31475
Close to A590 north of Cartmel; pitch price
from £8.50 per night

►► Detron Gate Farm
Bolton-le-Sands
☎ (01524) 732842 & 733617 (evening)
Overlooking Morecambe Bay off A6; pitch
price £4.50-£7 per night

►►► Black Beck Caravan Park
Bouth
☎ (01229) 861274; fax:(01229) 861041
Northwest of Cartmel
pitch price £5.50-£11.50 per night

►►► Old Hall Caravan Park
Capernwray
☎ (01524) 733276 & 735996
fax (01524) 734488
Situated southeast of Cartmel; pitch price
from £8.50-£10 per night

►►► Lambhowe Caravan Park
Crosthwaite
☎ (015395) 68483
On A5074 between Lancaster and
Windermere; pitch price £9-£11 per night.

►►► Lakeland Leisure Park
Moor Ln, Flookburgh
☎ (015395) 58556
South of Cartmel

WHERE TO STAY

►►► Bigland Hall Caravan Park
Haverthwaite
☎ (015395) 31702
West of Cartmel; pitch price from £6 per night.

►►►► Fell End Caravan Park
Slackhead Rd, Hale, Milnthorpe
☎ (015395) 62122; fax:(015395) 63810
East of Cartmel; pitch price from £9.50 per night.

►►►►► Holgate's Caravan Park
Cove Rd, Silverdale
☎ (01524) 701508; fax:(01524) 701580
Southeast of Cartmel; pitch price from £14.25 per night.

WHERE TO EAT

RESTAURANTS

❀❀ Uplands
Haggs Lane, Cartmel
☎ (015395) 36248; fax:(015395) 36848
Imaginative, consistently good cooking at very reasonable prices in a relaxed country-house hotel.
Lunch:£15
Dinner:£27

❀❀ Bay Horse Inn
Ulverston
☎ (01229) 583972, fax: (01229) 580502
Sound, imaginative cooking at reasonable prices, superb views and a convivial atmosphere.
Lunch: 12-1.30; £15.75
Dinner: Last Dinner 8; £20 à la carte.

❀ Aynsome Manor
Grange over Sands, Cartmel
☎ (015395) 36653; fax:(015395) 36016
A panelled hotel dining room serving intersting, well-produced meats.
Lunch: (Sun only) £11.95
Dinner: from £16

❀❀ Old Vicarage Country House Hotel
Witherslack
☎ (015395) 52381, fax: (015395) 52373
A high standard of cooking is served in this cosy hotel restaurant.
Lunch: 12.30-2; £13.50
Dinner: 7.30-9; £27.50

Catterick Bridge

Catterick offers a good mixture of Flat and National Hunt racing and is one of a select band of courses that stages a meeting in every month of the year.

With over two dozen fixtures scheduled annually, there is every opportunity to catch local runners in action because the cards are always well supported by trainers from nearby Middleham, the major training centre in the north, whose size and popularity is increasing all the time thanks to the tremendous success that some of the handlers based there have been enjoying of late.

The course, like the area, makes no pretensions to grandeur, but there is a genuine country feel to the place which is most appealing. The undulating track is extremely sharp and the soil drains superbly so good ground can nearly always be guaranteed, even in very wet conditions. This means that races are run at an exceptionally fast pace, suiting the nippy type of horse who is able to lie handily or make all the running.

FURTHER INFORMATION

The Racecourse Office
Catterick Racecourse, Catterick Bridge, Richmond, North Yorkshire DL10 7PE
☎ (01748) 811478

LOCATION AND HOW TO GET THERE

The racecourse is situated on the outskirts of Catterick village, approximately five miles south of Scotch Corner. Leave the A1 at the exit for Catterick and proceed through the village. **Nearest Railway Stations:** Darlington or Northallerton; there are connecting bus services to the course.

ADMISSION

All enclosures have access to bookmakers and Tote points, but the Course Enclosure does not have access to the betting office or the Tote Credit Office.

Day Tickets:
MEMBERS £11 – access to parade ring, winners' enclosure, bar and bar meals, plus all facilities in Paddock (see below)

TATTERSALLS AND PADDOCK £7 – access to parade ring, winners' enclosure, bars, dining room, self-service restaurant, private rooms and facilities for disabled racegoers

COURSE £2.50 – access to bar and cafeteria; no access to winners enclosure

Annual membership:
£75 single, £135 joint

Parking: there is free parking outside the course; on-course parking £2 per day or £30 for the year; parking for disabled racegoers in centre of course.

COURSE FACILITIES

Banks:
there are no banks or cashpoint facilities on the course

For families:
baby changing facilities; lost children centre

CALENDAR OF EVENTS

January 1 – jumping	**April 22** – flat	**September 19** – flat
January 8 – jumping	**May 29-30** – flat	**October 3** – flat
January 24 – jumping	**June 5** – flat	**October 15-16** – flat
February 6 – jumping	**July 2** – flat	**November 3** – flat
February 14 – jumping	**July 15** – flat	**November 21** – jumping
March 3 – jumping	**July 22** – flat	**December 2** – jumping
March 11 – flat	**August 4** – flat	**December 16-17** – jumping
April 1 – flat	**August 14** – flat; evening meeting	**December 31** – jumping

WHERE TO STAY
HOTELS

★★ 61% Bridge House
☎ (01748) 818331, fax; (01748) 818331
16 bedrooms; double B&B £50–£65
Credit cards 1 2 3 5

Around Catterick Bridge

★★ 63% Motel Leeming
Great North Rd, Bedale
☎ (01677) 422122, fax: (01677) 424507
40 bedrooms; double room £29.95–£39.50
Credit cards 1 2 3 5

★★★ 69% Hallgarth Country House
Coatham Mundeville, Darlington
☎ (01325) 300400, fax: (01325) 310083
41 bedrooms; double room £60–£75
Credit Cards 1 2 3 5

★★★ 68% Headlam Hall
Headlam, Gainford, Darlington
☎ (01325) 730238, fax: (01325) 730790
28 bedrooms; double B&B £78–£98
Credit cards 1 2 3 5

★★ 60% White Rose
Leeming Bar
☎ (01677) 422707 & 424941,
fax: (01677) 425123
18 bedrooms; double B&B from £45
Credit cards 1 2 3 5

★ 68% Buck Inn
Thornton Watlass
☎ (01677) 422461
fax: (01677) 422447
7 bedrooms; double B&B £52
Credit cards 1 2 3 5

★★ 59% Frenchgate
59-61 Frenchgale, Richmond
☎ (01748) 822087, fax: (01748) 823596
13 bedrooms; double B&B £53–£60
Credit cards 1 2 3 5

★★ 69% King's Head
Market Pl, Richmond
☎ (01748) 850220, fax: (01748) 850635
30 bedrooms; double B&B £75–£99
Credit cards 1 2 3 5

★★★ 67% Quality Scotch Corner
Scotch Corner
☎ (01748) 850900
fax: (01748) 825417
90 bedrooms; double room £61–£92 (room only)
Credit cards 1 2 3 5

Travelodge
Skeeby, Scotch Corner
☎ (01748) 823768
fax: (01748) 823768
40 bedrooms; double room £34.95–£49.95 (room only)
Credit cards 1 2 3 5

Travelodge
A1/A66 Middleton Tyas, Scotch Corner
☎ (01325) 377177, fax: (01325) 377890
50 bedrooms; double room £34.95–£49.95
Credit cards 1 2 3 5

BED AND BREAKFAST

QQQQ The Countryman's
Hunton, Bedale
☎ (01677) 450554
fax: (01677) 450570
Well appointed bedrooms in charming old stone built inn.
7 bedrooms; double B&B £45–£60
Credit cards 1 3

QQQQ Elmfield House
Arrathorne, Bedale
☎ (01677) 450558 ;fax:(01677) 450557
Spacious, beautifully decorated and furnished bedrooms with good views, friendly hosts.
9 bedrooms; double B&B £42–£48
Credit cards 1 3

QQQQQ Clow Beck House
Monk End Farm, Croft on Tees, Darlington
☎ (01325) 721075; fax: (01325) 720419
Luxuriously furnished bedrooms
11 bedrooms; double B&B £50
Credit cards 1 2 3

QQQ Alverton
26 South Pde, Northallerton
☎ (01609) 776207
Comfortably furnished rooms, in attractive Victorian house.
5 bedrooms

QQQ Windsor
56 South Pde, Northallerton
☎ (01609) 774100
Thoughtfully furnished and equipped bedrooms.
6 bedrooms; double B&B £32–£40

QQ Pottergate Guest House
4 Pottergate, Richmond
☎ (01748) 823826
A Georgian terraced with six compact, well equipped bedrooms
double B&B £34–£36

QQQ Vintage
Scotch Corner, Richmond
☎ (01748) 824424
8 bedrooms
Credit cards 1 2 3 5

QQQQQ Whashton Springs Farm
Richmond
☎ (01748) 822884
Charming farmhouse offering a warm welcome and friendly hospitality.
8 bedrooms; double room £42

QQQ Mount Pleasant Farm
Whashton, Richmond
☎ (01748) 822784
Good modern bedrooms in a Victorian farm house
6 bedrooms

CAMPSITES

►►►► Brompton-on-Swale Caravan Park
Brompton-on-Swale, Richmond
☎ (01748) 824629
fax: (01748) 824629
1.5m SE of B6271; pitch price from £5–£10.40 per night.

►►► Swale View Caravan Site
Reeth Rd, Richmond
☎ (01748) 823106
Level grassy site on the banks of the R. Swale; pitch price from £4.90 per night.

►►► Scotch Corner Caravan Park
Scotch Corner
☎ (01748) 822530 & 826272
Off A6108 slightly north of Catterick; pitch price £7–£10 per night.

►►► Constable Burton Caravan Pk
Constable Burton
☎ (01677) 450428
Off A684 but screened behind old deer park walls; pitch price £8.20 per night.

WHERE TO EAT
RESTAURANTS

Black Bull Inn
Moulton
☎ (01325) 377289, fax: (01325) 377422
Four different settings in which to enjoy honest, competently prepared food.
Lunch: 12-2; Dinner: 7-10.15

Cheltenham

This is the undisputed Home of National Hunt Racing and a visit to the course is an absolute must for anyone remotely interested in the jumping game.

Overlooked by the beautiful Cotswold Hills, it really is the perfect site to watch the best chasers and hurdles in the world. Facilities match the setting, with improvements continually being made, such as the new saddling area and link tunnel to the Parade Ring. A recent innovation is the Cheltenham Hall of Fame, which tells the story of the Racecourse's history and the illustrious figures, both equine and human, that have graced its turf over the years.

The track is best known for the National Hunt Festival in March, the top three-day meeting of the season which features the Gold Cup and Champion Hurdle and attracts some 50,000 spectators from all over Europe. Advance booking is essential for Gold Cup Day and recommended for the other days of the National Hunt Festival. Other fixtures include the Murphy's Gold Cup meeting in November.

FURTHER INFORMATION

Cheltenham Racecourse
Prestbury Park, Cheltenham
Glos GL50 4SH
☎ (01242) 513014

LOCATION AND HOW TO GET THERE

The course is a mile north of Cheltenham on the A435. Leave the M5 at junction 10 southbound or 11 northbound.
Nearest Railway Station: Cheltenham Spa; there is a connecting bus service to the course on major racedays.

ADMISSION

All classes of day ticket give access to full betting facilities, including Tote.

Day Tickets:
Accompanied children under 16 are admitted free to all enclosures, except during the National Hunt Festival in March, when full rates will apply. On Feature and Premier days, Club and Tattersalls are one enclosure. There are substantial reductions for advance booking for the National Hunt Festival Meeting. It is essential to book in advance for Gold Cup Day (Thursday).

CLUB Feature days £12, junior £8; Premier days £14, junior £8; Classic Day £20, junior £12; National Hunt Festival prices from £40 on Tues & Wed; £45 on Thurs. Plus £20-£25 for a Guinness Grandstand seat – access to viewing seats, restaurant, bars, buffets and boxes; during the National Hunt Festival the Tented Village is in the Club enclosure; seats should be booked in advance

TATTERSALLS Feature Day £12, Premier Day £14, Classic Day £15; National Hunt Festival from £20 on Tues & Wed, £25 on Thurs plus £20-£25 for a Guinness Grandstand Seat – access to paddock, centre of course, viewing steps, restaurants, bars and boxes; during the National Hunt Festival extra seating, the

Guinness Village and entertainments are provided

COURAGE Feature and Premier days £5, Classic day £7; National Hunt Festival from £8 on Tues & Wed, from £10 on Thurs – excellent viewing directly opposite the main stands, access to bars, buffets and snack bars; temporary stands, marquees and entertainments provided during National Hunt Festival

Parking: during the National Hunt Festival there is a charge of £5; advance purchase of parking vouchers provides a space nearest the entrance. At other meetings, parking is free, but can be reserved for a fee.

Annual membership:
Full: £165 plus £100 enrolment – includes free admission and parking on all racedays, admission to viewing seats, bars and buffet on Level 3 of the Grandstand on all Feature and Premier days, reciprocal arrangements with other racecourses on certain days.

COURSE FACILITIES

Banks:
Bank of Ireland and Allied Irish Bank at National Hunt Festival Meeting only (17-19 March); open 11am-4pm. Midland cashpoint in Courage enclosure.

For families:
lost children centre.

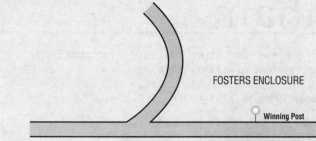

FOSTERS ENCLOSURE

Winning Post

TATTERSALLS

CLUB

TATTERSALLS

GRANDSTAND

TENTED VILLAGE (CLUB)

Parade Ring

CALENDAR OF EVENTS

January 1
January 31 – includes Cleeve Hurdle
March 17-19 – National Hunt Festival; includes Smurfitt Champion Hurdle Day on Tuesday, Queen Mother Champion Chase on Wednesday and Tote Cheltenham Gold Cup on Thursday
April 15-16

April 29 – evening meeting
October 27-28 – National Hunt
November 13-14 – includes Murphys Gold Cup on Saturday
November 24
December 11-12 – includes Tripleprint Gold Cup Chase

WHERE TO STAY

HOTELS

★★★★⊛ **67% Golden Valley Thistle**
Gloucester Rd
☎ (01242) 232691 fax: (01242) 221846
122 bedrooms; double bedroom £86-£118
Credit cards 1 2 3 5

★★★★ **61% The Queen's**
Promenade
☎ (01242) 514724
fax: (01242) 224145
74 bedrooms
Credit cards 1 2 3 5

★★★⊛⊛⊛⊯ (RED) **Greenway**
Shurdington
☎ (01242) 862352, fax: (01242) 862780
19 bedrooms; double B&B £135-£225
Credit cards 1 2 3 5

★★★ **66% Carlton**
Parabola Rd
☎ (01242) 514453, fax: (01242) 226487
75 bedrooms
Credit cards 1 2 3 5

★★★ **64% White House**
Gloucester Rd
☎ (01452) 713226
fax: (01452) 857590
49 bedrooms; double B&B £60-£90
Credit cards 1 2 3 5

★★★ **62% The Prestbury House Hotel & Restaurant**
The Burgage, Prestbury,
☎ (01242) 529533, fax: (01242) 227076
17 bedrooms; double B&B £70-£88
Credit cards 1 2 3 5

★★★ **57% Hotel de la Bere**
Southam
☎ (01242) 237771, fax: (01242) 236016
57 bedrooms
Credit cards 1 2 3 5

★★★ **66% Charlton Kings**
London Rd, Charlton Kings
☎ (01242) 231061, fax: (01242) 241900
14 bedrooms; double B&B £62-£94
Credit cards 1 2 3

WHERE TO STAY

★🏵 74% Regency House
50 Clarence Sq
☎ (01242) 582718, fax: (01242) 262697
8 bedrooms; double B&B £46-£58
Credit cards 1 2 3

★★ 67% George Hotel
St George's Rd
☎ (01242) 235751, fax: (01242) 224359
39 bedrooms; double B&B £56-£66
Credit cards 1 2 3 5

★★★ 67% Wyastone
Parabola Rd
☎ (01242) 245549,
fax: (01242) 522659
13 bedrooms; double B&B from £69
Credit cards 1 2 3

★★ 62% Allards
Shurdington
☎ (01242) 862498, fax: (01242) 863017
12 bedrooms; double B&B £45-£50
Credit cards 1 2 3

★★ 64% Cotswold Grange
Pittville Circus Rd
☎ (01242) 515119, fax: (01242) 241537
25 bedrooms; double B&B £65
Credit cards 1 2 3 5

Around Cheltenham

★★★ 65% Royal George
Birdlip
☎ (01452) 862506
fax: (01452) 862277
34 bedrooms; double B&B £75
Credit cards 1 2 3 5

★★★ 65% Rising Sun
Cleeve Hill
☎ (01242) 676281
fax: (01242) 673069
24 bedrooms; Double B&B £79.50
Credit cards 1 2 3 5

★★★🏵🏵 68% Corse Lawn House
Corse Lawn
☎ (01452) 780479 & 780771,
fax: (01452) 780840
19 bedrooms; double B&B £100-£135
Credit cards 1 2 3 5

★★★🏵 76% Hatton Court
Upton Hill, Upton St Leonards, Gloucester
☎ (01452) 617412
fax: (01452) 612945
45 bedrooms; double B&B £105-£145
Credit cards 1 2 3 5

Travel Inn
Tewkesbury Rd, Uckington
☎ (01242) 233847
fax: (01242) 244887
40 bedrooms; double room £36.50

Forte Posthouse Gloucester
Crest Way, Barnwood, Gloucester
☎ (01452) 613311
fax: (01452) 371036
123 bedrooms; double room £59
(room only)
Credit cards 1 2 3 5

★★★🏵 62% Hatherley Manor Down
Hatherley Ln, Gloucester
☎ (01452) 730217, fax: (01452) 731032
56 bedrooms; double B&B from £70
Credit cards 1 2 3 5

★★★ 68% Tewkesbury Park Hotel Country Club Resort
Lincoln Green Ln, Tewkesbury
☎ (01684) 295405
fax: (01684) 292386
78 bedrooms; double B&B £75
Credit cards 1 2 3 5

WHERE TO STAY
BED AND BREAKFAST

QQQ Battledown Hotel
125 Hales Rd
☎ (01242) 233881
Bright clean and comfortable bedrooms; friendly hosts.
8 bedrooms; double £45-£50

QQQQ Beechworth Lawn Hotel
133 Hales Rd
☎ (01242) 522583; fax: (01242) 522583
Congenial guesthouse; excellent value for money.
8 bedrooms; double B&B £45-£52

QQQQQ Cleeve Hill Hotel
Cleeve Hill
☎ (01242) 672052
Good hospitality and tasteful, quality surroundings provide excellent bed and breakfast accommodation.
10 bedrooms; double B&B £60-£78
Credit cards 1 2 3

QQQ Hannaford's
20 Evesham Rd
☎ (01242) 515181; fax:(01242) 257571
Off the A435 Evesham road. Spacious well equipped bedrooms.
8 bedrooms; double B&B £55-£65
Credit cards 1 2 3

QQQQ Hollington House Hotel
115 Hales Rd
☎ (01242) 256652, fax: (01242) 570280
Comfortable bedrooms; friendly relaxed atmosphere.
9 bedrooms; double B&B £40-£60
Credit cards 1 2 3

QQ North Hall Hotel
Pittville Circus Rd
☎ (01242) 520589, fax: (01242) 216953
Central position, well equipped comfortable bedrooms.
20 bedrooms; double B&B from £50.50-£60
Credit Cards 1 2 3

QQ Ivy Dene Guest House
145 Hewlett Rd
☎ (01242) 521726
Detached Victorian house offering modern well-equipped accommodation.
9 bedrooms; double B&B £40-£45

QQQ Wishmoor Guest House
147 Hales Rd
☎ (01242) 238504
fax: (01242) 226090
Comfortable guest house with bright, neat bedrooms.
11 bedrooms; double B&B £36-£45
Credit Cards 1 3

QQQQ Stretton Lodge
Western Rd
☎ (01242) 570771, fax; (01242) 528724
Rich interior architecture, nicely decorated bedrooms.
4 bedrooms; double B&B £50-£75
Credit cards 1 2 3

Around Cheltenham

QQQQ Colesbourne
Colesbourne
☎ (01242) 870376, fax: (01242) 870397
Former coaching inn steeped in history.
9 bedrooms
Credit cards 1 3

Q Claremont
135 Stroud Rd, Gloucester
☎ (01452) 529540 & 529270
Cosy guesthouse on the Stroud road.
6 bedrooms; double B&B £35-£38

QQ The Abbey Hotel
67 Church St, Tewkesbury
☎ (01684) 294247
fax: (01684) 297208
Family-run hotel situated in the main street.
16 bedrooms
Credit cards 1 2 3

QQQQ Beaumont House Hotel
56 Shurdington Road
☎ (01242) 245986, fax: (01242) 520044
A distinctive Victorian hotel with various styles of accommodation
16 bedrooms; Double B&B £48-£62
Credit cards 1 2 3

CAMPSITES

►►► Caravan Club Site
Cheltenham
☎ (01242) 523102
One and a half miles north of town on A435; pitch price £8-£9 per night.

►►► Longwillows Camping Site
Station Rd, Woodmancote, Cheltenham
☎ (01242) 674113
fax: (01242) 678731
Three and a half miles north of Cheltenham; pitch price from £5.50-£6 per night.

►►► Red Lion Caravan Park
Wainlode Hill, Norton, Gloucester
☎ (01452) 730251
West of Cheltenham; pitch price from £5 per night.

►►►► Leedon's Park
Childswickham Rd, Broadway
☎ (01386) 852423
Large site on edge of Vale of Evesham; pitch price per night £7-£9

WHERE TO EAT

RESTAURANTS

❀❀❀❀ Le Champignon Sauvage
24 Suffolk Rd
☎ (01242) 573449
fax: (01242) 573449
Predominantly classic French cooking in a
friendly relaxed style.
Lunch: 12-1.30; from £17.50
Dinner: 7-9.30; from £29.50

❀❀ Cleeveway House
Bishops Cleeve
☎ (01242) 672585
Small Cotswold manor house hotel with
reliable, straightforward cooking.
Lunch: 12-1.45; £22 à la carte.
Dinner: 7-9.45; £22 à la carte.

❀ Mayflower Chinese
32-34 Clarence St
☎ (01242) 522426 & 511580,
fax: (01242) 251667
Comfortable and popular Chinese
restaurant, serving mainly Cantonese
dishes.
Lunch: 12-1.45; £6.75 and à la carte
Dinner: 6-10.30; £25 and à la carte

❀❀ Wesley House
High St, Winchcombe
☎ (01242) 602366
fax: (01242) 602405
Half-timbered merchant's house with
popular three course lunch and good value
set dinner.
Lunch: 12-2
Dinner: 7-9.30; £26

❀ Kingshead House
Birdlip
☎ (01452) 862299
Twice-weekly changing fixed price menus in
an appealing country restaurant.
Lunch: 12.15-1.45; £17 à la carte
Dinner: 7.15-9.45; £25

❀❀❀ The Lygon Arms
High Street, Broadway
☎ (01386) 852255
fax: (01386) 858611
A superior mix of modern English and haute
cuisine.
Lunch: 12-2; £20.50
Dinner: 7-9.15; £32

❀❀ Restaurant on the Park
38 Evesham Rd
☎ (01242) 518898
fax: (01242) 511526
Charming little hotel with a talented new
chef.
Lunch: 12-2
Dinner: 7-9; £21.50

❀❀❀ Greenway Hotel
Shurdington
☎ (01242) 862352
One of Cheltenham's finest restaurants, in a
beautiful location.
Lunch: 12-2; £16
Dinner: 7-9.30; £27.50

PUBS

Kilkeney Inn
Andoversford, nr Cheltenham
☎ (01242) 820341
fax: (01242) 820133
Long, low Cotswold stone building with a
pretty garden. Imaginative dishes are served
in generous portions. Draught beers
includes John Smiths, Ruddles Best; there
is an extensive wine list and range of malt
whiskies.
Open: 11.30am-2.30pm, 6.30-11pm;
Food: 12-3pm, 7-10pm

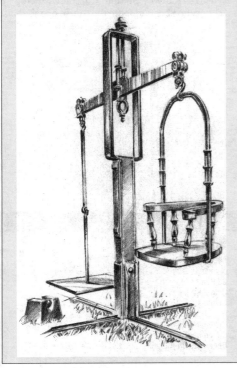

Chepstow

Chepstow stands alone as the sole course in Wales, a surprising statistic considering the tremendous enthusiasm that the Welsh have for their racing. As a result, meetings attract sizeable turnouts with plenty of knowledgeable locals in evidence.

Patrons are well served by a broad mixture of events under both codes, although the National Hunt cards tend to be of a much higher standard. This is particularly true around Christmas with the running of the Coral Welsh National, one of the major staying handicap chases of the season. Favourites have an outsanding record in this event as does top trainer Martin Pipe, who has monopolised the race virtually to the exclusion of all others in recent years.

Most Saturday jump meetings will stage at least one valuable contest, but traffic congestion can be notoriously bad on big days, with the Severn Bridge (vital for access, along with the second Severn crossing a few miles further south) and nearby roundabouts sometimes grinding to a complete standstill, so set off early. Soft ground is usually prevalent, putting stamina at a premium, as does the undulating track that dips out of sight at the start of the home straight. Flat racing is of a lower calibre, but evening meetings are popular and feature many of the top jockeys.

FURTHER INFORMATION

Chepstow Racecourse plc
The Racecourse, Chepstow, Gwent NP6 5YH
☎ (01291) 622260; Fax:(01291) 625550

LOCATION AND HOW TO GET THERE

The course is on the northern edge of the town, off the A466. Leave the M4 at junction 22 on the western side of the Severn Bridge and take the A48 northwards, later taking the A446 Monmouth road.
Nearest Railway Station: Chepstow; there is a connecting bus service to the course on racedays.

ADMISSION

All classes of day ticket give access to full betting facilities, including Tote

Day Tickets:
MEMBERS £14, £20 on Welsh National day – access to bars, restaurant, boxes, private rooms

TATTERSALLS £10 on Saturdays, £15 on Welsh National day – access to bars, snack bar, facilities for disabled racegoers including special viewing

PUBLIC & CENTRE COURSE £5 – available all Sundays and Bank Holidays; access to bar and snack bar

Annual membership: £138

COURSE FACILITIES

Banks:
there are no banks or cashpoint facilities on the course

For families:
picnic area with refreshments kiosk and toilets

CALENDAR OF EVENTS

February 21 – jumping	**July 10** – flat; evening meeting
March 4 – jumping	**July 24** – flat; evening meeting
March 14 – jumping	**August 13** – flat
March 24 – jumping	**August 31** – flat
April 13 – jumping	**September 10** – flat
April 21 – jumping	**October 3** – jumping
May 6 – jumping	**October 21** – jumping
May 13 – jumping	**November 7** – jumping
May 25 – flat	**November 25** – jumping
June 12 – flat; evening meeting	**December 5** – jumping
June 30 – flat	**December 28** – jumping; includes Coral Welsh National
July 4 – flat	

WHERE TO STAY

HOTELS

★★★★❀ 72% Marriot St Pierre Hotel & Country Club
St Pierre Park.
☎ (01291) 625261
fax: (01291) 629975
148 bedrooms; double bedroom £115-£165
Credit cards 1 2 3 5

★★ 67% Castle View
16 Bridge St
☎ (01291) 620349, fax: (01291) 627397
13 bedrooms; double room £52.95-£59.95
Credit cards 1 2 3 5

★★ 67% The George
Moor St
☎ (01291) 625363, fax: (01291) 627418
14 bedrooms
Credit cards 1 2 3 5

★★❀ 67% Beaufort
Beaufort Sq, St Mary St
☎ (01291) 622497, fax: (01291) 627389
18 bedrooms; double room £42.50-£49
Credit cards 1 2 3 5

★★★ 63% The Old Course
Newport Road
 (01291) 626261, fax: (01291)626263
31 bedrooms; Double room £42.50 (room only)
Credit cards 1 2 3 5

Around Chepstow

★★❀ ⚜ 74% Rangeworthy Court
Church Ln, Wotton Rd, Rangeworthy
☎ (01454) 228347 fax: (01454) 228945
Approximately 16 miles east of Chepstow, via the M4.
14 bedrooms; double B&B £58–£86
Credit cards 1 2 3 5

★★★❀ 74% Alveston House
Alveston
☎ (01454) 415050, fax: (01454) 415425
30 bedrooms; double B&B £81.50-£91.50
Credit cards 1 2 3 5

Forte Posthouse Alveston
Thornbury Rd, Alveston
☎ (01454) 412521
fax: (01454) 413920
74 bedrooms; double room £43-£59 (room only)
Credit cards 1 2 3 5

★★★ 67% Wyndham Arms
Clearwell
☎ (01594) 833666, fax: (01594) 836450
17 bedrooms; double B&B £61-£65
Credit cards 1 2 3 5

★★★★ ❀❀ 65% Cwrt Bleddyn Hotel & Country Club
LLangybi
☎ (01633) 450521, fax: (01633) 450220
33 bedrooms; double B&B £135-£195
Credit cards 1 2 3 5

★★★ (Red) ❀❀ ⚜ Thornbury Castle
Thornbury
☎ (01454) 281182, fax: (01454) 416188
18 bedrooms; double B&B £95-£225
Credit cards 1 2 3 5

★★❀ 70% Royal George
Tintern
☎ (01291) 689205, fax: (01291) 689448
19 bedrooms; double B&B £62-£85
Credit cards 1 2 3 5

★★❀ 67% Parva Farmhouse Hotel & Restaurant
Tintern
☎ (01291) 689411, fax; (01291) 689557
9 bedrooms; double B&B £60-£70
Credit cards 1 2 3

WHERE TO STAY

BED AND BREAKFAST

QQQQ Abbotts Way
Gloucester Rd, Almondsbury
☎ (01454) 613134
fax: (01454) 613134
6 bedrooms; double B&B from £40-£42
Credit cards 1 2 3 5

QQQQQ Tudor Farmhouse Hotel
Clearwell
☎ (01594) 833046, fax: (01594) 837093
Listed Tudor farmhouse full of charm and
character.
13 bedrooms
Credit cards 1 2 3

Q Brown's Hotel & Restaurant
Llandogo
☎ (01594) 530262
Set in beautful Wye Valley; good ensuite
facilities in bedrooms.
7 bedrooms

QQQ The Sloop
Llandogo
☎ (01594) 530291
fax: (01594) 530935
Modern well furnished bedrooms with good
views.
4 bedrooms; double B&B £39-£47
Credit cards 1 2 3

QQQ Viney Hill Country Guest House
Viney Hill, Lydney
☎ (01594) 516000
fax: (01594) 516018
Charming cottage-style guesthouse.
6 bedrooms; double B&B from £44
Credit cards 1 3

**QQQQ Brickhouse Country Guest
House**
Redwick
☎ (01633) 880230, fax: (01633) 882441
Delightful farmhouse with spotlessly clean
and spacious bedrooms.
7 bedrooms; double B&B £40

QQ Rowan Lodge
41 Gloucester Rd. North, Filton Park, Bristol
☎ (0117) 9312170
Well-equipped bedrooms in a large
detached house.
6 bedrooms
Credit cards 1 3

QQQ Valley House
Raglan Rd, Tintern
☎ (01291) 689652
fax: (01291) 689805
Off the A466; situated in tranquil
surroundings
with good standard rooms.
3 bedrooms
Credit cards 2

QQ Fountain
Trellech Grange, Tintern
☎ (01291) 689303
Seventeenth century inn two miles west of
the village.
5 bedrooms; double B&B £39
Credit cards 1 2 3

CAMPSITES

►►► Salthouse Farm Caravan Site
Severn Beach
☎ (01454) 632274 & 632699
Adjacent to Severn Estuary and beach, off
A403;
pitch price £7.80 per night

**►►► Christchurch Forest Park
Camping Ground**
Coleford
☎ (01594) 833376
Northeast of Chepstow; pitch price from
£5.20-£9.40 per night

**►►► Bridge Caravan and Camping
Site**
Bridge Farm, Dingestow
☎ (01600) 740241
Excellent site in quiet village; pitch price
£7-£8.50 per night

WHERE TO EAT

RESTAURANTS

❀❀ Thornbury Castle
Thornbury
☎ (01454) 281182
fax: (01454) 416188
Classic English and French cuisine in an
impressively grand setting.
Lunch; 12-2, £16.50 and a la carte
Dinner; 7-10, £34.50 and a la carte

❀ Royal George
Tintern
☎ (01291) 689205
fax: (01291) 689448
Reliable cooking with top-quality local
produce.
Lunch; 12-2, £11.95
Dinner; 7-9.30 £18

❀❀❀❀ Restaurant Lettonie
9 Druid Hill, Stoke Bishop, Bristol
☎ (0117) 9686456
Smart restaurant serving adventurous food
with intense flavours.
Lunch; 12-2
Dinner; 7-10

❀ Marriot St Pierre Hotel
St Pierre Park
☎ (01291) 625261
fax: (01291) 629975
A range of skilfully prepared and accurately
cooked dishes.
Lunch: 12-2.30; £15 and a la carte
Dinner: 7-10; £20 and a la carte

Chester

Chester has the oldest racecourse in the country - The Roodee - overlooked by the medieval walls of the city. The tight, circular track enables every spectator to get a close-up perspective of the action.

It also means that runners are almost always on the turn which will not suit long-striding animals. Instead, the smaller, handy type of horse is greatly favoured here with speed out of the gate also a necessary attribute in sprint races.

The highlight of the racing calendar is the Festival Meeting in May; huge crowds pack the grandstands in anticipation of seeing some potentially top-class horses. The County Stand provides excellent facilities and affords panoramic views. Indeed, about the only criticism that could be levelled at this delightful course is that there are not enough fixtures to satisfy demand.

FURTHER INFORMATION

Chester Racecourse Co Ltd
The Racecourse, Chester CH1 2LY
☎ (01244) 323170. Fax: (01244) 344971

LOCATION AND HOW TO GET THERE

The racecourse is within easy walking distance of the centre of Chester. By road, join the Inner Ring road and take the A548 Queensferry Road. The racecourse and car parks are on the left hand side, immediately beyond the city walls.

Nearest Railway Station: Chester General; there are frequent bus services to the city centre from where the course can be reached by walking down Watergate Street, across the Inner Ring Road and through the Watergate.

ADMISSION

All classes of day ticket give access to full betting facilities, including Tote.

Day Tickets:
COUNTY ENCLOSURE Adult £16, Junior (up to 17 years) £3, seats free; May Festival Meeting £22 per day or £60 for 3 days, Junior £4 per day, reserved seats £20 for 3 days – access to bars, restaurant, boxes, tented village during May Festival Meeting.

TATTERSALLS AND PADDOCK £10; May Festival Meeting £12 – access to new entrance building, bars, fast food

DEE STANDS £4 – access to open bars, fast food

COURSE £2

Parking: £2; £5 for 3 days reserved parking during May Festival Meeting.

Annual membership:
£160 including free parking

COURSE FACILITIES

Banks:
there are no banks or cashpoint facilities on racecourse.

For families:
Picnic area with refreshment kiosk and toilets, baby changing facilities, lost children centre.

CALENDAR OF EVENTS

May 5-7 – Festival Meeting including Chester Vase, Tote Chester Cup and Ormonde and Dee Stakes
June 3 – flat; evening meeting
June 24 – flat; evening meeting
July 10-11 – evening meeting on Friday

August 2 – flat
August 21-22 – flat
September 23 – flat

WHERE TO STAY

HOTELS

★★★★★🏵🏵🏵 75% The Chester Grosvenor
Eastgate St
☎ (01244) 324024
fax: (01244) 313246
85 bedrooms; double bedroom £140-£210
Credit cards 1 2 3 5

★★★★ 66% Chester Moat House
Trinity St
☎ (01244) 899988
fax: (01244) 316118
152 bedrooms; double B&B £112-£150
Credit Cards 1 2 3 5

★★★★🏵 65% Mollington Banastre
Parkgate Rd
☎ (01244) 851471
fax: (01244) 851165
63 bedrooms; double B&B £84-£105
Credit cards 1 2 3 5

★★★🏵🏵🏵 79% Crabwall Manor
Parkgate Rd, Mollington
☎ (01244) 851666
fax: (01244) 851400
48 bedrooms; double room £110-£150
Credit cards 1 2 3 5

★★★★ 64% Queen
City Rd
☎ (01244) 350100, fax: (01244) 318483
128 bedrooms; double B&B £110-£125
Credit cards 1 2 3 5

Forte Posthouse Chester
Wrexham Rd
☎ (01244) 680111, fax: (01244) 674100
105 bedrooms
Credit cards 1 2 3 5

★★★ 65% Blossoms
Saint John St
☎ (01244) 323186
fax: (01244) 346433
64 bedrooms; double room £85 (room only)
Credit cards 1 2 3 5

★★ 60% Eaton
29/31 City Rd
☎ (01244) 320840, fax: (01244) 320850
18 bedrooms; double B&B £42.50-£52.50
Credit cards 1 2 3 5

★★ 68% Green Bough
60 Hoole Rd
☎ (01244) 326241, fax: (01244) 326265
20 bedrooms; double B&B £52-£65
Credit cards 1 2 3 5

★★ 66% Brookside
Brook Ln
☎ (01244) 381943, fax: (01244) 379701
26 bedrooms; double B&B £48-£52
Credit cards 1 3

★ 63% Leahurst Court
74 Hoole Rd, Hoole
☎ (01244) 327542, fax: (01244) 344889
14 bedrooms; double B&B from £39-£46
Credit cards 1 3

Around Chester

Travel Inn
High St, Bromborough
☎ 0151-334 2917
fax: 0151-334 0443
31 bedrooms; double room £36.50
Credit cards 1 2 3 5

★★★🏵 66% Broxton Hall Country House
Whitchurch Rd, Broxton
☎ (01829) 782321, fax: (01829) 782330
10 bedrooms; double B&B £70
Credit cards 1 2 3 5

★★★ 66% Woodhey Hotel
Welsh Rd, Little Sutton, Ellesmore Port
☎ 0151-339 5121, fax: 0151-339 3214
53 bedrooms; double room £85-£95
Credit cards 1 2 3 5

Travel Inn
Childer Thornton, Ellesmore Port
☎ 0151-339 8101
fax: 0151- 347 1401
31 bedrooms; double room £36.50

★★ 65% Bryn Awel
Denbigh Rd, Mold
☎ (01352) 758622, fax: (01352) 758625
17 bedrooms; double B&B from £48-£50
Credit cards 1 2 3 5

★★★ 63% Holiday Inn Garden Court
Gateway Services, Westbound A55
☎ (01244) 550011, fax: (01244) 550763
55 bedrooms
Credit cards 1 2 3

BED AND BREAKFAST

Q Gables Guest House
5 Vicarage Rd, Hoole
☎ (01244) 323969
Small Victorian guest house with compact bedrooms.
6 bedrooms

QQ Eversley Hotel
9 Eversley Park
☎ (01244) 373744
Simple accommodation in personally-run hotel.
11 bedrooms
Credit cards 1 3

QQQ Gloster Lodge Hotel
44 Hoole Rd, Hoole
☎ (01244) 348410 & 320231
Modern, well-equipped bedrooms with en suite facilities.
8 bedrooms
Credit cards 1 2 3

QQQQ Green Gables
11 Eversley Park
☎ (01244) 372243, fax: (01244) 376352
Fully modernised small hotel on outskirts with smart bedrooms.
4 bedrooms; double B&B £36

WHERE TO STAY

QQQ Egerton Lodge
57 Hoole Rd, Hoole
☎ (01244) 320712
Spacious bedrooms with modern
furnishings.
4 bedrooms; double B&B £38

QQQ Bawn Park Hotel
10 Hoole Rd, Hoole
☎ (01244) 324971
fax: (01244) 310951
Converted Victorian semi 1 mile from city
centre.
7 bedrooms; double B&B £36-£46
Credit cards 1 2 3

QQQQ Golborne Manor
Hatton Heath
☎ (01829) 770310, fax: (01829) 318084
A tastefully modernised mid-Victorian
house with spacious guest bedrooms
3 bedrooms; double B&B £45-£60

QQQQ Grove House
Holme Street, Tarvin
☎ (01829) 740893, fax: (01829) 741769
Bright, spacious and very comfortable
accommodation
3 bedrooms; double B&B £46-£56

CAMPSITES

►►► Camping & Caravanning Club Site
Bangor-on-Dee
☎ (01978) 781009 (in season)
  & (01203) 694995
fax: (01203) 694886
On the A525 south of Chester; pitch price
£8.10-£10.30 per night.

►►► Plassey Touring Caravan & Leisure Park
Eyton.
☎ (01978) 780277
fax: (01978) 780019
South of Chester; pitch price £6.50-£8.50
per night.

►►► Chester Southerley
Balderton Lane, Marlston-cum-lache
☎ (01829) 270791 & 270697
Well tended rural site on south side of city
close to bypass; pitch price £6.20-£8.80 per
night.

WHERE TO EAT

RESTAURANTS

🕸🕸 Craxton Wood
Parkgate Rd, Puddington
☎ 0151-339 4717, fax: 0151-339 1740
Classical food and attentive service in a
hotel restaurant.
Lunch: 12.30-2; £19.85 and à la carte
Dinner: 7.30-10; £19.85 and à la carte

🕸 Mollington Banastre Hotel
Parkgate Road
☎ (01244) 851471
fax: (01244) 851165
Lunch: 12.30-2; £16 and à la carte
Dinner: 7-9.45; £20 and à la carte

🕸🕸🕸 The Arkle Restaurant at the Chester Grosvenor
Eastgate St
☎ (01244) 324024
fax: (01244) 313246
Artistically presented French and modern
British cuisine, strongly featuring seafood
and offal.
Lunch: 12-2.30, £22.50 and à la carte
Dinner: 7-9.30 £40 and à la carte

🕸🕸🕸 Crabwall Manor Hotel
Parkgate Road, Mollington
☎ (01244) 851666
fax: (01244) 851400
An elegant Manor house serving
imaginative modern dishes
Lunch: 12-2, £35 à la carte
Dinner: 7-9.30, £35 à la carte

PUBS

Ye Olde Kings Head
48-50 Lower Bridge Street, Chester
☎ (01244) 324855
Open: 11am-11pm; Sunday 12-3, 7-10.30
Bar food: 12-2pm
Restaurant: 12-2pm, 6-9.30pm; Sunday
12-9pm

The Copper Mine
Nantwich Rd, Broxton
☎ (01829) 782293
Bar food: 12-2.30, 7-9.30

Doncaster

This Yorkshire venue has undergone a major programme of improvements in recent years after being the subject of some justified criticism in the 80s for its boring atmosphere and lack of soul.

Nearly £10million has been sunk into its redevelopment and the construction of a spanking new grandstand has done much to change its image and restore its reputation as a Grade One racecourse. Facilities, including the family enclosure have been similarly refurbished .

The quality of racing on this flat, galloping track has never been in question. Doncaster boasts a fine tradition as home to the fifth and oldest Classic, the St Leger, the highlight of a vibrant four-day meeting in September. Its late March fixtures also hold an important place in the calendar as they herald the opening of the new Flat season, with the Lincoln, a lottery of a handicap, as the principal race. Several major two-year-old contests take place during the summer and it also plays host to the last important Flat meeting of the year in early November before jumping fans get a chance to see some action during the winter months.

FURTHER INFORMATION

International Racecourse Management Ltd Doncaster Racecourse, Grand Stand, Leger Way Doncaster DN2 6BB
Tel (01302) 320066/7; Fax:(01302) 323271

LOCATION AND HOW TO GET THERE

The course is on the southeastern outskirts of Doncaster, alongside the M18 (junctions 3 and 4). The M18 connects directly with the M1, A1(M), M180 and M62.
Nearest Railway Station: Doncaster.
Doncaster airport is adjacent to the course and there is a helicopter landing pad.

ADMISSION

All classes of day ticket give access to full betting facilities, including Tote.

Day Tickets:
MEMBERS £14-£16, St Leger Festival £22, or £65 for a 4-day ticket – access to bar, restaurant, boxes, private rooms

GRANDSTAND £8-£10, St Leger Festival £12.50, or £40 for a 4-day ticket – access to bar, restaurant, boxes, private rooms
ENCLOSURE £3-£5, St Leger Festival £5 – access to bar, restaurant, boxes, private rooms

Annual membership: £100 single, £180 dual, £50 junior, includes exclusive use of 'Flying Fox' room, reciprocal days at other courses for certain meetings

COURSE FACILITIES

Banks:
No Banks or Cashpoint facilities

For families:
baby-changing facilities, lost children centre, creche at Saturday meetings for children over 2 years, children's entertainment at summer meetings

CALENDAR OF EVENTS

January 30-31 – jumping
February 24 – jumping
March 6-7 – jumping
March 3 – jumping
March 26-28 – flat; includes Worthington Lincoln Handicap
May 4 – flat
May 23 – flat
June 6 – flat

June 27-28 – flat; evening meeting on Saturday
July 15-16 – flat; evening meeting on Wednesday
July 29-30 – flat; evening meeting on Wednesday
September 9-12 – flat; St Leger Festival
October 23-24 – flat; includes Racing Post Trophy
November 6-7 – flat; includes Tote Credit November Handicap
December 11-12 – jumping

WHERE TO STAY

HOTELS

★★★ 66% Doncaster Moat House
Warmsworth
☎ (01302) 799988, fax: (01302) 310197
100 bedrooms; double room £96-£110
Credit cards 1 2 3 5

★★★ 63% Danum Swallow
High St
☎ (01302) 342261
fax: (01302) 329034
66 bedrooms; double B&B £75-£95
Credit cards 1 2 3 5

★★ 69% Regent
Regent Square
☎ (01302) 364180, fax: (01302) 322331
50 bedrooms; double B&B £65-£75
Credit cards 1 2 3 4 5

Campanile
Doncaster Leisure Park Bawtry Rd
☎ (01302) 370770, fax: (01302) 370813
50 bedrooms; double room £29.95-£36.50
Credit cards 1 2 3 5

Around Doncaster

★★★ 69% Elton
Main St, Bramley, Rotherham
☎ (01709) 545681, fax; (01709) 549100
29 bedrooms; double B&B £50-£70
Credit cards 1 2 3 5

★★★ 65% Mount Pleasant
Great North Rd, Rossington
☎ (01302) 868696 & 868219,
fax: (01302) 865130
33 bedrooms; double B&B £79-£92
Credit cards 1 2 3 4 5

★★★ 65% Crown
High St, Bawtry
☎ (01302) 710341, fax: (01302) 711798
57 bedrooms; double bedroom £56-£66
Credit cards 1 2 3 5

Campanile
Hellaby Industrial Estate, Lowton Way, off
Denby Way, Rotherham
☎ (01709) 700255, fax: (01709) 545169
50 bedrooms; double room £29.95-£36.50
Credit cards 1 2 3 5

★★ 68% Belmont
Horsefair Green, Thorne
☎ (01405) 812320
fax: (01405) 740508
23 bedrooms; double B&B £64.95-£74.95
Credit cards 1 2 3 5

BED AND BREAKFAST

QQ Almel Hotel
20 Christchurch Rd,
☎ (01302) 365230, fax: (01302) 341434
Town centre guesthouse with light,
quite compact rooms.
30 bedrooms; double B&B £36-£40
Credit cards 1 2 3 5

QQQQ Canda Lodge
Hampolbalk Laner, Skellow
☎ (01302) 724028
6 bedrooms

QQQQ Stonecroft
Main St, Bramley, Rotherham
☎ (01709) 540922; fax:(01709) 540922
Delightful stone-built farmhouse with cosy
accommodation
8 bedrooms
Credit cards 1 3

CAMPSITES

►► Hatfield Marina Water Sports Centre
Hatfield
☎ (01302) 841572 & 737343
Situated northeast of Doncaster; pitch price
£3.30-£6.20 per night.

WHERE TO EAT

RESTAURANTS

❀❀ Greenhead House
84 Buncross Rd, Chapeltown
☎ (0114) 2469004
Enjoyable French-based cooking in cottage-
style restaurant.
Lunch: 12-2.30; £13.50 a la carte.
Dinner: 7-9; from £29.50

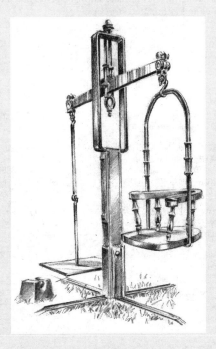

Epsom Downs

Epsom is, of course, famous as the home of the Derby, the most prestigious contest in the British racing calendar and an event which has been run over this course for some 200 years.

Derby Day traditionally falls in June, when huge crowds always pack the beautiful downs, lining the rails several deep right down to Tattenham Corner. There is a real carnival atmosphere with open-topped buses, fun-fairs, a tented village and plenty of gypsies gazing into their crystal balls. The course also plays host to the fillies' Classic, the Oaks (run on the Friday of the meeting), as well as the Coronation Cup, an important Group One event for older horses. Sadly though, spectators are few at the other meetings staged here, and this is a track which really only comes alive once a year.

The huge white building of the Queen's Stand opened in the early nineties, offers superb facilities and a spectacular view of the racing. Its design did not meet with universal approval (likened by some to an ocean liner), but it is certainly a substantial improvement on the previous antiquated structure.

FURTHER INFORMATION

United Racecourses (Holdings) Ltd
The Grandstand, Epsom Downs
Surrey KT18 5LQ
☎ (01372)726311 or 470047
Fax: (01372) 748253

LOCATION AND HOW TO GET THERE

The course is two miles south of Epsom on the B290. From M25 junction 8 take the A217; from junction 9 take the A24.
Nearest Railway Stations: Epsom, Epsom Downs or Tattenham Corner; there are connecting bus services to the course on racedays. There are fast and frequent trains from Waterloo or Victoria to Epsom. There is a 15-minute helicopter service from London Heliport and from Sandown Park Racecourse in Esher.

ADMISSION

All classes of day ticket give access to full betting facilities, including Tote.

Day Tickets:
QUEEN'S STAND £16 (more for Oaks & Derby Days)– access to bar, restaurant, boxes, private rooms; morning dress required on Derby Day

GRANDSTAND £10,(more for Oaks & Derby Days) – access to paddock, club enclosure, bar, restaurant, boxes, private rooms

LONSDALE & TATTENHAM £5 – access to bars; Lonsdale enclosure is opposite the Grandstand, for good head-on views of racing and final furlong rails position

CLUB ENCLOSURE £20 Oaks Day, £40 Derby Day – all seats can be booked in advance; access also to the Grandstand and Paddock

Transfers to the Queen's Stand are available on all days, space permitting, apart from Derby Day.

COURSE FACILITIES

Banks:
National Westminster bank on course during Derby Week only; open 10.30am-4.30pm on Derby Day, 11.30am-4.30pm other days; there are no cashpoint facilities on the course.

For families:
picnic area with refreshment kiosk and toilets.

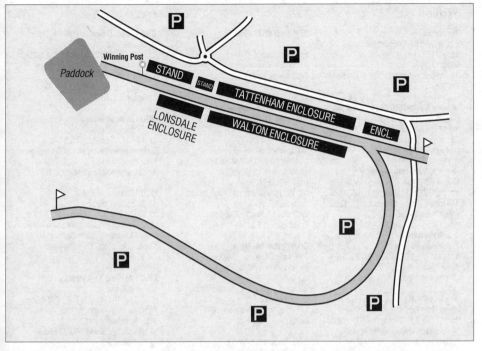

CALENDAR OF EVENTS

April 22 – flat
June 5-6 – Derby Week, including the Vodaphone Derby; the
    Vodaphone Coronation Cup and the Vodaphone Oaks
June 24 – evening meeting

July 29 – evening meeting
August 9 – flat
August 31
September 4-5

WHERE TO STAY

HOTELS

Epsom

★★ 64% Driftbridge Hotel
Reigate Road, Epsom
☎ (01737) 352163
fax: (01737) 370477
34 bedrooms; double B&B £58-£75
Credit cards 1 2 3

Around Epsom

★★★★ 66% The Burford Bridge
Burford Bridge, Box Hill, Dorking
☎ (01306) 884561, fax: (01306) 880386
48 bedrooms; double bedroom from £65
Credit cards 1 2 3 5

★★★ 60% The White Horse
High St, Dorking
☎ (01306) 881138, fax: (01306) 887241
68 bedrooms
Credit cards 1 2 3 5

Travelodge
Reigate Rd, Dorking
☎ (01306) 740361
fax: (01306) 740361, Central Reservations:
(01800) 850950
54 bedrooms; double room £34.95-£49.94
Credit cards 1 2 3 5

★★★★ ❀ ❀ 76% Cannizaro House
West Side, Wimbledon Common, London
SW19
☎ 0181-879 1464
fax: 0181-879 7338
46 bedrooms; double room from £155-
£220 (room only)
Credit cards 1 2 3 4 5

★★★★ ❀ ❀ 70% Nutfield Priory
Nutfield
☎ (01737) 822066, fax: (01737) 823321
60 bedrooms; double room £135-£300
Credit cards 1 2 3 5

WHERE TO STAY

Travel Inn
Leatherhead Rd, Chessington
☎ (01372)744060
fax: (01372) 720889
42 bedrooms; double bedroom £36.50
Credit cards 1 2 3 5

★★★★⊛⊛ 75% Coulsdon Manor
Coulsdon Court Rd, Coulsdon, Croydon
☎ 0181-668 0414, fax; 0181-668 3118
35 bedrooms; double room £80-£120
Credit cards 1 2 3 5

★★★★ 63% Holiday Inn
Gibson Rd, Sutton
☎ 0181-770 1311, fax; 0181-770 1539
116 rooms; double bedroom £125-£255
Credit cards 1 2 3 5

★★ 65% Haven
Portsmouth Rd, Esher
☎ 0181-398 0023, fax; 0181-398 9463
20 bedrooms; double B&B £79
Credit cards 1 2 3 5

★★★ 65% Reigate Manor Hotel
Reigate Hill, Reigate
☎ (01737) 240125, fax: (01737) 223883
50 bedrooms; double room £93-£100
Credit cards 1 2 3 5

★★★⊛ 63% Bridge House
Reigate Hill, Reigate
☎ (01737) 246801 & 244821
fax: (01737) 223756
39 bedrooms; double bedroom £65-£77
Credit cards 1 2 3 5

★★★★ ⊛ 65% Woodlands Park
Woodlands Ln, Stoke D'Abernon
☎ (01372) 843933, fax; (01372) 842704
59 bedrooms; double bedroom £115
Credit cards 1 2 3 5

BED AND BREAKFAST

Around Epsom

QQQ Kings Lodge
5 Kings Rd, London SW19
☎ 0181-545 0191, fax: 0181-545 0381
Bedrooms furnished to very high standard.
7 bedrooms; double B&B £59-£79
Credit cards 1 2 3 5

QQ Trochee Hotel
21 Malcolm Rd, London SW19
☎ 0181-946 1579 & 3924,
fax: 0181-785 4058
Old-fashioned but soundly maintained
guesthouse.
17 bedrooms; double B&B £48-£51
Credit cards 1 2 3

QQ Wimbledon Hotel
78 Worple Rd, London SW19
☎ 0181-946 9265 & 946 1581
fax: 0181-946 9265
Detached Victorian house offering a choice
to suit everyone.
14 bedrooms; double B&B £65-£75
Credit cards 1 2 3 5

QQQ Worcester House
38 Alwyne Rd, London SW19
☎ 0181-946 1300, fax: 0181-785 4058
Choice of brightly decorated bedrooms, all
equipped with modern amenities.
9 bedrooms; double B&B £57.50-£62.50
Credit cards 1 2 3 5

QQQQ Ashleigh House Hotel
39 Redstone Hill, Redhill
☎ (01737) 764763;
fax: (01737) 780308
Modestly furnished bedrooms; hospitable
owners; ideally located for town centre and
station.
8 bedrooms; double B&B £40-£52
Credit cards 1 3

QQQ The White House
Downs Hill Rd, Epsom
☎ (01372) 722472, fax: (01372) 744447
Late Victorian house with generally
spacious first floor bedrooms and more
modest ground floor rooms.
15 bedrooms; double B&B £49.50-£69.50
Credit cards 1 3

QQQ Epsom Downs Hotel
9 Longdown Rd
☎ (01372) 740643, fax; (01372) 723259
Friendly hotel offering small, modestly
furnished bedrooms
15 bedrooms; double B&B £49-£65
Credit cards 1 3 5

QQQ Lynwood House
50 London Rd, Redhill
☎ (01737) 766894 & 778253
Clean and comfortable rooms in a friendly
small guesthouse.
9 bedrooms; double B&B £38-£45

QQQQ Cranleigh Hotel
41 West St, Reigate
☎ (01737) 223417, fax: (01737) 223734
Ideally located for town centre, with many
orginal features; attractive bedrooms.
9 bedrooms; double B&B £69-£89
Credit cards 1 2 3 5

QQQQ Ashling Tara Hotel
50 Rosehill, Sutton
☎ 0181-641 6142, fax: 0181-644 7872
Particularly well-furnished bedrooms,most
with private bathrooms.
14 bedrooms; double B&B £50-£70
Credit cards 1 2 3

QQ Warwick
321 Ewell Rd Surbiton
☎ 0181-296 0516
fax:0181-296 0517
Small guest house convenient for A3
9 bedrooms; double B&B £40-£46
Credit cards 1 3

WHERE TO EAT

CAMPSITES

▶▶▶ Camping & Caravanning Club Site
Ockham Rd North, East Horsley
☎ (01483) 283273 & (01203) 694995
fax: (01203) 694886
pitch price £9.10-£12.10 per night

▶▶▶ Long Acres Farm Caravan & Camping
Newchapel Rd, Lingfield
☎ (01342) 833205 & 884307
Southeast of Epsom; pitch price from £7.50 per night.

RESTAURANTS

✿✿ Le Raj
211 Firtree Rd,
☎ (01737) 371371
fax: (01737) 211903
Excellent Indian cuisine in stylish air conditioned restaurant.
Lunch 12-2.30; £20 à la carte
Dinner: 6-10.30; £20 à la carte

Around Epsom

✿✿ Partners West Street
West Street 2,3 & 4 West St, Dorking
☎ (01306) 882826
fax: (01306) 885741
Stylish and unpretentious modern cooking with decor to match, at reasonable prices.
Lunch: 12-2.30; £30 à la carte
Dinner: 7-10.30; £30à la carte

✿✿ Le Petit Pierrot
4 The Parade, Claygate
☎ (01372) 465105, fax; (01372) 467642
Small, intimate restaurant serving interesting dishes in the Modern French style.
Lunch:£18.75
Dinner:£21.75

✿ The Good Earth
14-18 High St, Esher
☎ (01372) 462489
fax: (01372) 465588
Smart restaurant serving mainly Cantonese style dishes plus Mandarin, Szechuan and Pekinese choices.
Lunch: 12-3; £12 and à la carte
Dinner: 6-11.15; £28 à la carte

✿✿ C'est La Vie
17 High St, Ewell
☎ 0181-394 2933
fax: 0181-786 7123
High quality dishes making good use of fresh produce.
Lunch: 12-3; £8.75 and à la carte
Dinner: 7-11; £14.75 and à la carte

✿✿ Ayudhya
14 Kingston Hill, Kingston-upon-Thames
☎ 0181-549 5984
Popular restaurant on three floors with a wide choice of dishes.
Lunch: 12-2.30; £20 à la carte
Dinner: 7-11; £20 à la carte

PUBS

Cricketers
Downside Cobham
☎ (01932) 862105
fax: (01932) 868186
Pretty and cottage-like 16th-century pub with an atmosphere of civilised calm, overlooking common. Ruddles County and Best, and Webster's Yorkshire beers available. Spacious restaurant with table d'hote lunch and a la carte menu; blackboard menu offers cheaper alternatives.
Open 11am-2.30pm, 3-12pm
Bar food: 12-2pm, 6.30-10pm
Restaurant: 12.15-2.30, 7.15-11
Closed Sunday evening and all day Monday

Exeter

This is a majestic country venue in the heart of Devon that thoroughly merits a visit. Situated on the top of Haldon Hill, the breathtaking landscape can provide a welcome distraction if backing a winner is proving too difficult.

It is also not unknown for stags to jump out of the nearby woods and, on an infamous occasion, one even changed the result of a race by knocking over the leading horse which was 15 lengths clear at the time. As it was a foggy day, this incident was not visible from the stands and so everyone thought the jockey was suffering from concussion when he proffered his explanation for not completing the course. In fact, he had almost been sent to hospital by the time the other riders backed up his bizarre but true story.

Such a freak occurrence is unlikely to be repeated but racegoers can be sure of seeing some exciting jumping action on this big, galloping track. Viewing is pretty good, apart from a slight dip in the back straight where the horses momentarily pass out of sight, and the catering is first rate. The only disappointment is that, with the exception of the valuable William Hill Haldon Gold Cup Chase in early November, the course does not attract the calibre of runner it deserves due to the lack of prize money. Nevertheless, the early season evening meeting in August is a wonderful occasion when the sun is shining, and the New Year's Day fixture always attracts a good turnout.

FURTHER INFORMATION

Exeter Racecourse
Haldon Hill, Kennford, Nr Exeter, Devon
☎ (01392) 832599/811346. Fax:(01392) 833454

LOCATION AND HOW TO GET THERE

The course is five miles west of Exeter. From the end of the M5, continue on the A38 Plymouth road the course is two miles east of Chudleigh. **Nearest Railway Station:** Exeter St Davids; there is a connecting bus service to the course.

ADMISSION

All classes of day ticket give access to full betting facilities, including Tote.

Day Tickets:
Accompanied children under 16 are admitted free to all enclosures.

GRANDSTAND AND PADDOCK £10 – access to bar, restaurant, boxes, hospitality rooms

COURSE £5 – access to bar and snacks

Annual membership: £90. Parking on the rails £2, elsewhere free

COURSE FACILITIES

Banks:
there are no banks or cashpoint facilities on the course.

For families:
picnic area with toilets; lost children centre.

CALENDAR OF EVENTS

January 1 – jumping
January 9
March 10 – jumping
March 25
April 2 – jumping
April 14 – jumping

April 29 – jumping
May 5 – jumping
May 21 – jumping
September 28
October 7 – jumping
October 20 – jumping

November 3 – jumping; includes William Hill Haldon Gold Cup
November 20
December 4 – jumping
December 17 – jumping

WHERE TO STAY

HOTELS

★★★❀❀ 70% Edgemoor
Haytor Rd, Bovey Tracey
☎ (01626) 832466, fax: (01626) 834760
17 bedrooms; double B&B £75.95-£89.95
Credit cards 1 2 3 5

★★ 63% Riverside Inn
Fore St, Bovey Tracey
☎ (01626) 832293, fax: (01626) 833880
10 bedrooms; double B&B £39.50
Credit cards 1 3

★★ 65% Coombe Cross
Coombe Cross, Bovey Tracey
☎ (01626) 832476, fax: (01626) 835298
24 bedrooms; double B&B £68
Credit cards 1 2 3 5

★★★ 67% Langstone Cliff
Dawlish Warren, Dawlish
☎ (01626) 865155
fax: (01626) 867166
68 bedrooms; double room £82-£90
Credit cards 1 2 3 5

★★★★ 67% The Southgate
Southernhay East, Exeter
☎ (01392) 412812
fax: (01392) 413549
110 bedrooms; double room £69-£90
(room only)
Credit cards 1 2 3 5

★★★ 68% Royal Clarence
Cathedral Yard
☎ (01392) 319955
fax: (01392) 439423
57 bedrooms; double room £69-£99
Credit cards 1 2 3 5

★★★ 71% Rougemont Thistle
Queen St
☎ (01392) 254982
fax: (01392) 420928
90 bedrooms; double B&B from £95
Credit cards 1 2 3 5

Travel Inn
398 Topsham Rd, Countess Wear
Roundabout, Exeter Bypass
☎ (01392) 875441,
fax: (01392) 876174
44 bedrooms; double room £36.50
Credit cards 1 2 3 5

★★★❀❀ 69% St Olaves Court
Mary Arches St
☎ (01392) 217736, fax: (01392) 413054
15 bedrooms; double B&B £65-£95
Credit cards 1 2 3 5

★★★❀❀ 75% Buckerell Lodge
Topsham Rd
☎ (01392) 221111
fax: (01392) 491111
54 bedrooms; double room £64-£89 (room
only)
Credit cards 1 2 3 5

★★★ 60% Travelodge
Moor Ln, Sandygate
☎ (01392) 74044, fax: (01392) 410406
73 bedrooms; double room £34.95-£49.95
(room only)
Credit cards 1 2 3 5

★★★ 66% Gipsy Hill
Monkerton, Exeter
☎ (01392) 465252
fax: (01392) 464302
37 bedrooms; double B&B £70-£90
Credit cards 1 2 3

★★★ 70% Devon Hotel
Exeter Bypass, Exeter
☎ (01392) 259268
fax: (01392) 413142
41 bedrooms; double B&B £55-£75
Credit cards 1 2 3 5

★★ 66% Exeter Arms Toby
Rydon Ln, Middlemoor, Exeter
☎ (01392) 435353, fax: (01392) 420826
37 bedrooms; double B&B £58-£62.50
Credit cards 1 2 3

★★ 72% St Andrews
28 Alphington Rd, Exeter
☎ (01392) 276784, fax: (01392) 250249
16 bedrooms; double B&B £50-£56
Credit cards 1 2 3 5

★★ 57% Red House
2 Whipton Village Rd, Exeter
☎ (01392) 56104, fax: (01392) 435708
12 bedrooms
Credit cards 1 2 3 5

★★ 69% Fairwinds
Kennford
☎ (01392) 832911
fax: (01392) 832911
7 bedrooms; double B&B £49-£52
Credit cards 1 3

★★★ 71% Passage House
Hackney Ln, Kingsteignton
☎ (01626) 55515, fax: (01626) 63336
39 bedrooms; double B&B £75-£85
Credit cards 1 2 3 5

★★★❀❀ 68% Ebford House
Exmouth Road
☎ (01392) 877658, fax: (01392) 874424
16 bedrooms; double B&B £75-£87
Credit cards 1 2 3

WHERE TO STAY

★★ 74% The White Hart
The Square, Moretonhampstead
☎ (01647) 440406, fax: (01647) 440565
20 bedrooms; double B&B from £65-£73
Credit cards 1 2 3 5

★★ 64% Queens
Queen St, Newton Abbot
☎ (01626) 63133 & 54106, fax: (01626) 64922
22 bedrooms; double B&B £56-£66
Credit cards 1 2 3 5

★ 62% Hazelwood
33A Torquay Rd, Hazelwood
☎ (01626) 66130, fax: (01626) 65021
8 bedrooms; double B&B £40-£49
Credit cards 1 3

★★ 68% Ness House
Marine Dr, Shaldon, Teignmouth
☎ (01626) 873480, fax: (01626) 873486
12 bedrooms; double B&B £70-£85
Credit cards 1 2 3

★★ 65% Belvedere
Parnpark Rd, Teignmouth
☎ (01626) 774561
13 bedrooms; double B&B £40-£45
Credit cards 1 2 3

★ 67% Glenside
Ringmoor Rd, Shaldon, Teignmouth
☎ (01626) 872448
9 bedrooms; double B&B £37-£49

BED AND BREAKFAST

Q Braeside
21 New North Rd, Exeter
☎ (01392) 56875
Easy walk from city centre, offering simple furnished bedrooms.
7 bedrooms; double B&B £29-£31
Credit cards 1 3

QQQQ The Edwardian
30/32 Heavitree Rd, Exeter
☎ (01392) 276102 & 254699
fax: (01392) 276102 & 254699
Convenient location, with simply furnished bedrooms.
13 bedrooms; double B&B £44-£52
Credit cards 1 2 3

Q Dunmore
22 Blackall Rd, Exeter
☎ (01392) 431643
7 bedrooms; double B&B £28-£34
Credit cards 1 3

QQQ Hotel Gledhills
32 Alphington Rd, Exeter
☎ (01392) 2430469 & 271439
fax: (01392) 430469
En suite comfortable bedrooms in this hotel situated on the edge of the city.
12 bedrooms; double B&B £40-£44
Credit cards 1 3

QQQ Park View Hotel
8 Howell Rd, Exeter
☎ (01392) 271772, fax: (01392) 253047
Particularly well equipped bedrooms feature in this hotel close to the city centre.
15 bedrooms; double B&B £35-£45
Credit cards 1 2 3

QQ Sunnymede
24 New North Rd, Exeter
☎ (01392) 273844
fax: (01392) 424436
Georgian house providing bright, well equipped rooms.
9 bedrooms; double B&B £34-£38
Credit cards 1 3

Q Telstar Hotel
77 St Davids Hill, Exeter
☎ (01392) 272466
Clean comfortable bedrooms; close to the city centre.
18 bedrooms; double B&B £26-£40

QQ Trees Mini Hotel
2 Queen's Crescent, York Rd, Exeter
☎ (01392) 59531
Immaculate bedrooms, close to city centre and with friendly resident proprietors.
12 bedrooms
Credit cards 1 3

WHERE TO STAY

QQQQ Cleavelands St Mary
Lustleigh, Newton Abbot
☎ (01647) 277349
fax: (01647) 277349
3 bedrooms; double B&B £40-£50

QQQQ Fonthill
Torquay Rd, Shaldon, Teignmouth
☎ (01626) 872344
fax: (01626) 872344
The Graeme family warmly welcome non-smoking guests to their home.
3 bedrooms; double B&B £48-£52

QQQ Hill Rise Hotel
Winterbourne Rd, Teignmouth
☎ (01626) 773108
Edwardian house offering light, airy accommodation.
8 bedrooms; double B&B £28-£32

QQQQ Wytchwood
West Buckeridge
☎ (01626) 773482
6 bedrooms; double B&B £37-£50

QQQQQ Thomas Luny House
Teign St, Teignmouth
☎ (01626) 772976
Bedrooms furnished with great flair and thoughtful touches. A lovely house, restored to its 18th-century style.
4 bedrooms; double B&B £60-£70

QQ Rowhorne House
Whitestone
☎ (01392) 274675
Splendid rural views, spacious bedrooms.
3 bedrooms; double B&B £30
Credit cards 1 2 3 5

CAMPSITES

►►►► Cofton Country Holiday Park
Dawlish
☎ (01626) 890111
fax: (01626) 891572
South of Exeter on A379; pitch price £5-£9.50 per night.

►►►► Kennford International Caravan Park
Kennford
☎ (01392) 833046
fax: (01392) 833046
Just west of Exeter off the A38; pitch price from £9 per night.

►►► Springfield Holiday Park
Tedburn Rd, Tedburn St Mary
☎ (01647) 24242
fax: (01647) 24131
One and a half miles east of Tedburn; pitch price £5-£10 per night.

►►►► Peppermint Park
Warren Rd, Dawlish
☎ (01626) 863436 & 862211
Well managed site; pitch price from £5.50 per night.

►►►► Lady's Mile Touring & Caravan Park
Dawlish
☎ (01626) 863411
fax: (01626) 888689
Well laid out site, 1 mile north of Dawlish
Pitch price £5.50-£10.50

►►► Barley Meadow Caravan and Camping Park
Crockernwell
☎ (01647) 2281629
Off old A30, now bypassed and isolated; pitch price £5.75-£6.50 per night.

WHERE TO EAT

RESTAURANTS

✿✿ River House
The Strand, Lympstone
☎ (01395) 265147
Accomplished light, modern cooking, with
plenty of fish, in a pretty waterside location.
Lunch: 12-1.30; from £28.95 and à la carte
Dinner: 7-9.30; from £28.95 and à la carte

✿✿ St Olaves Court
Mary Arches St
☎ (01392) 217736
fax: (01392) 413054
Carefully prepared dishes listed on a
handwriten carte.
Lunch: £13.50 and à la carte
Dinner: £13.50 and à la carte

✿✿ Buckerell Lodge
Topsham Rd
☎ (01392) 221111
fax: (01392) 491111
Interesting dishes which achieve very high
standards.
Lunch: £14.50 and à la carte
Dinner: £14.50 and à la carte

PUBS

Nobody Inn
Doddiscombsleigh
☎ (01647) 252394
fax: (01647) 252978
A combination of 260 whiskies, a superior
wine list, Nobody Beer, Bass, a guest beer
and local farm cider; well cooked,
reasonably priced bar meals.
Open: 12-2.30pm, 6-11pm, (7-11pm in
winter)
Bar food: pub hours
Restaurant: Tuesday-Saturday 7.30-9.15pm
Accommodation: double room £48-£59

Turf
Turf Lock, Exminster
☎ (01392) 833128
fax: (01392) 832545
Informal pub in a beautiful setting on the
Exe estuary; ideal for families. Range of real
ales on draught and superb home-cooked
dishes; outdoor barbecue menu available in
summer. Morning coffee and afternoon tea
available.
Open: 11am-11pm, Closed November-
February
Bar food: pub hours
Accommodation: from £25 per person

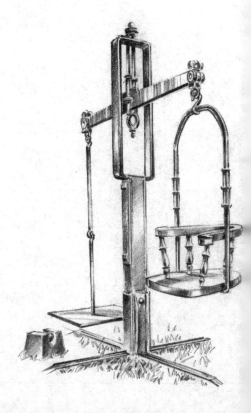

Fakenham

Hidden away in the peaceful surroundings of rural Norfolk lies this small, friendly course. Opportunities to visit are limited, however, as there are only half a dozen National Hunt meetings run here every year, the most popular fixtures being held in May when a large attendance is as certain as the warm reception you will receive.

There is always an appealing atmosphere at Fakenham that draws spectators from a wide circumference.

Facilities are relatively sparse and this is an ideal place to take a picnic - drive into the centre of the track (known as the course enclosure) and make a proper day of it with all the family. Entrance fees are comparatively cheap and should certainly not break the budget. The action is fast and furious round the sharp, left-handed circuit, with horses galloping flat out all the way. Long-striding animals are not suited to the tight turns, so look out for small, nippy types who will be able to scoot round the bends.

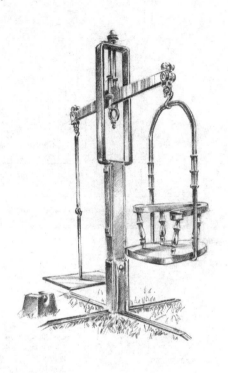

FURTHER INFORMATION

Fakenham Racecourse Ltd
The Racecourse , Fakenham, Norfolk NR21 7NY
☎ (01328) 862388; Fax:(01328) 855908

LOCATION AND HOW TO GET THERE

The course is a mile from the outskirts of Fakenham on the B146 Dereham road. It is signposted from all main junctions on the approach to Fakenham.
Nearest Railway Station: King's Lynn or Norwich; there are no connecting bus services to the racecourse.

ADMISSION

All classes of day ticket give access to full betting facilities, including Tote.

Day Tickets:
Accompanied children under 16 are admitted free to all enclosures.

MEMBERS £12-£14 – access to bar, restaurant, viewing stand for disabled racegoers. Car parking £7-£8

GRANDSTAND/PADDOCK £6-£10 – access to bar and restaurant

COURSE £5 – access to bar and snack bar.

Transfers: Paddock to Members £5; Course to Grandstand/Paddock £4

Annual membership: £44 single, £65 double.

COURSE FACILITIES

Banks:
There are no banks or cashpoint facilities on the course.

For families: picnic area with refreshment kiosk and toilets.

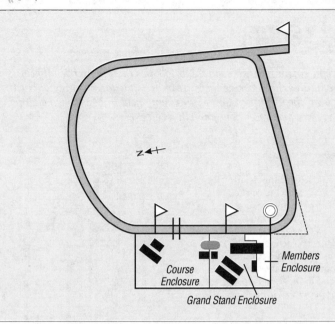

Course Enclosure

Grand Stand Enclosure

Members Enclosure

CALENDAR OF EVENTS

February 20 – jumping
March 20 – jumping
April 13 – jumping

May 17 – jumping
October 23 – jumping
December 7 – jumping

WHERE TO STAY

HOTELS

Around Fakenham

★★★ 71% Blakeney
The Quay, Blakeney
☎ (01263) 740797, fax: (01263) 740795
60 bedrooms; double B&B £110-£186
Credit cards 1 2 3 5

★★(Red) ❀❀❀ Morston Hall
Morston, Blakeney
☎ (01263) 741041
fax: (01263) 740419
6 bedrooms; double B&B £70-£90
including dinner.
Credit cards 1 2 3

★★ 62% Manor
Blakeney
☎ (01263) 740376, fax: (01263) 741116
37 bedrooms; double B&B £56-£84

★★ 60% Crown
The Buttlands, Wells-next-the-Sea
☎ (01328) 710209, fax; (01328) 711432
15 bedrooms; double B&B £60-£70
Credit cards 1 2 3 5

★ 70% Scarborough House
Clubbs Lane, Wells-Next-The-Sea
☎ (01328) 710309 & 711661
14 bedrooms; double B&B £48-£68
Credit cards 1 2 3 5

★★ 65% Crown
Market Place
☎ (01328) 851418, fax: (01328) 862433
11 bedrooms
Credit cards 1 2 3

BED AND BREAKFAST

QQQQ The Old Brick Kilns
Little Barney, Barney
☎ (01328) 878305
fax: (01328) 878948
Hospitality is assured at this immaculate
guesthouse, with period furniture in the
bedroom.
3 bedrooms; double B&B £40-£48
Credit cards 1 3

QQQ Flintstones
Wiveton, Holt
☎ (01263) 740337
In quiet village setting; modern bedrooms,
with bright, fresh decor.
5 bedrooms; double B&B £33-£37

WHERE TO STAY

QQQ Kings Head Hotel
Crossroads, North Elmham
☎ (01362) 668856
fax: (01362) 668856
Small country inn dating back to 16th-century. Enthusiastic management encourages a relaxed atmosphere.
2 bedrooms; double B&B £45
Credit cards 1 2 3

QQ Rookery Farm
Thurning, Melton Constable
☎ (01263) 860357
Seventeenth century, detached red-brick farmhouse; spacious and comfortable bedrooms.
2 bedrooms; double B&B £30-£32

QQQ Lawns Private Hotel
Station Rd, Holt
☎ (01263) 713390
Old red-brick building with attractive garden and comfortable accommodation.
11 bedrooms; double B&B £50-£70
Credit cards 1 2 3

CAMPSITES

►►► Camping & Caravanning Club Site
The Sandringham Estate, Double Lodges
☎ (01485) 542555 (in season)
& (01203) 694995
fax: (01203)m 694886
A well-landscaped prestige site; pitch price £9.10-£12.10 per night.

►►►► The Old Brick Kilns
Little Barney, Barney
☎ (01328) 878305
fax: (01328) 878948
East of Barney off A148; price from £8.25 per night

WHERE TO EAT

RESTAURANTS

☯☯ Moorings
6 Freeman St, Wells-next-the-Sea
☎ Fakenham (01328) 710949
Fresh, local ingredients cooked with free-ranging imagination – and served with charm.
Lunch: 12.30-2; £25 a la carte
Dinner: 7-8.30; £25 a la carte

☯☯ Hoste Arms
Burnham Market
☎ (01328) 738777
fax: (01328) 730103
Good value, freshly produced meals.
Dinner; £18.50 a la carte

☯☯☯ Morston Hall
Blakeney
☎ (01263) 741041
fax: (01263) 740419
Good British cooking of flare and imagination in a warmly hospitable hotel dining room
Lunch: (Sun only) £15
Dinner: 7.30 for 8; £26

PUBS

Boar Inn
Great Ryburgh
☎ (01328) 829212
Open: 11am-2.30pm, 6.30-11pm
Beers include: Adnams, Carlsberg, Kilkenny
Bar food: 12-2pm, 7-9.30pm
Restaurant: times as bar food

Folkestone

A dual purpose, bread-and-butter type course, whose main virtue is its easy access from all parts of the country, thanks to the M25 (traffic jams permitting) and M20. Situated on the southeast coast, not far from Dover, this Kent track is rightly famous for the excellence of its fish stalls with delicious fresh seafood and tasty fish and chips at very reasonable prices – one definite advantage of a seaside venue.

There is never any shortage of runners and, though they may not be of the highest quality, there is the occasional prestigious contest sprinkled among the mixed calendar of events. One of the biggest crowds of the year is always seen at the United Hunts meeting, an evening fixture in mid-May to which local point-to-point enthusiasts flock in droves. All the participants are amateurs, creating a very warm and friendly atmosphere, and displays of various other country pursuits help to provide an interesting evening's entertainment with the post race celebrations of winning connections often extending long into the night.

FURTHER INFORMATION

The Racecourse Office
Lingfield Park 1991 Ltd
Lingfield, Surrey, RH7 6PQ
☎ (01342) 834800

LOCATION AND HOW TO GET THERE

The course is six miles west of Folkestone at Westenhanger, near Stanford. Leave the M20 at junction 11 and take the A20 southwards towards Sellindge and Stanford, following AA signposting. **Nearest Railway Station:** Westenhanger; only 2 minutes from course.

ADMISSION

Day Tickets:
MEMBERS £9, children 12-16 free access to Westenhanger Club, Members' bar and Members' dining room

TATTERSALLS £9, accompanied children under 16 free – access to grandstand, bars, restaurant, boxes, Orchard Suite and Tote

COURSE £4, car £4, accompanied children under 16 free – access to bar, hot and cold snacks. There is no betting shop in the Course Enclosure.

Annual membership: £130

COURSE FACILITIES

Banks:
there are no banks or cashpoint facilities on the course.

For families:
picnic area with refreshment kiosk and toilets; children's play area at certain meetings; lost children in weighing room.

CALENDAR OF EVENTS

January 5 – jumping	**July 8** – flat
January 14 – jumping	**July 15** – flat
January 30 – jumping	**July 27** – flat
February 25 – jumping	**August 6** – flat
March 20 – jumping	**August 14** – flat
April 1 – flat	**August 28** – flat
April 7 – flat	**September 25** – flat
April 21 – flat	**October 20** – flat
May 13 – steeplechasing; evening meeting	**November 30** – flat
May 27 – flat	**December 15** – steeplechasing
June 3 – flat; evening meeting	
June 26 – flat	

WHERE TO STAY

HOTELS

★★★ 68% Clifton
The Leas, Folkestone
☎ (01303) 851231
fax; (01303) 851231
80 bedrooms; double B&B £65-£90
Credit cards 1 2 3 5

★★★ 62% Wards
39 Earls Av, Folkestone
☎ (01303) 245166, fax: (01303) 254480
10 bedrooms; double bedroom £67-£95
Credit cards 1 2 3 5

★★★★ (RED) 🏵🏵🏵 Eastwell Manor Park
Boughton Lees, Ashford
☎ (01233) 219905
fax: (01233) 635530
23 bedrooms; double bedroom £160-£180
Credit cards 1 2 3 5

★★★★ 63% Ashford International
Simone Weil Av, Ashford
☎ (01233) 219988
fax: (01233) 627708
200 bedrooms
Credit cards 1 2 3 5

Forte Posthouse
Canterbury Rd, Ashford
☎ (01233) 625790, fax: (01233) 643176
60 bedrooms; double bedroom £56
Credit cards 1 2 3 5

★★★ 64% Master Spearpoint
Canterbury Rd, Kennington, Ashford
☎ (01233) 636863
fax: (01233) 610119
35 bedrooms; double B&B £70-£75
Credit cards 1 2 3 5

★★★★ 🏵 75% The Hythe Imperial
Princes Pde, Hythe
☎ (01303) 267441
fax: (01303) 264610
100 bedrooms; double bedroom £100-£140
Credit cards 1 2 3 5

★★★ 🏵 70% Stade Court
West Pde, Hythe
☎ (01303) 268263
fax: (01303) 261803
42 bedrooms; double B&B from £82.50
Credit cards 1 2 3 5

Travel Inn
Folkestone Rd, Dover
☎ (01304) 213339
62 bedrooms; double bedroom £36.50

★★★ 63% County
Townwall St, Dover
☎ (01304) 509955, fax: (01304) 213230
79 bedrooms; double room £69-£73
Credit cards 1 2 3 5

BED AND BREAKFAST

QQQ Croft Hotel
Canterbury Rd, Kennington, Ashford
☎ (01233) 622140
fax: (01233) 622140
Well kept grounds and a choice of well
equipped bedrooms; friendly hosts.
28 bedrooms; double B&B £45-£55
Credit cards 1 2 3

QQ Chantry Hotel
Sycamore Gardens, Dymchurch
☎ (01303) 873137
Situated off the A259; most bedrooms retain
period character; friendly proprietors.
6 bedrooms; double B&B £39.50-£45
Credit cards 1 2 3

QQ Waterside
15 Hythe Rd, Dymchurch
☎ (01303) 872253
Attractive detached roadside building with
extensive rear views over Romney Marsh.
7 bedrooms; double B&B £30-£38

QQQ The White House
27 Napier Gardens, Hythe
☎ (01303) 266252
Close to the sea, with individually furnished
bedrooms and friendly service.
3 bedrooms; double B&B £36-£38

QQ Dell
233 Folkestone Rd, Dover
☎ (01304) 202422
Bright, simply furnished bedrooms,
immaculately maintained
5 bedrooms

QQQ Peverell House Hotel
28 Park Ave, Dover
☎ (01304) 202573 & 205088
Impressive detached Victorian house with
attractively furnished bedrooms.
6 bedrooms

CAMPSITES

►► Little Switzerland Camping & Caravan Site
Wear Bay Rd
☎ (01303) 252168
Small site on cliffs over Dover Straits; pitch
price £6.50-£8.50 per night.

►►►► Hawthorn Farm Caravan & Camping Site
Martin Mill
☎ (01304) 852658 & 852914
Pleasant rural site; pitch price £8.55-£10.80
per night.

►►► Little Satmar Holiday Park
Winehouse Ln, Capel Le Ferne, Folkestone
☎ (01303) 251188
Two miles west, off A20; pitch price from
£8.10 per night.

►► Camping and Caravanning Club Site
The Warren, Folkestone
☎ (01303) 255093 & (01203) 694995
pitch price £9.30-£10

►►►► Broad Hembury Farm
Steeds Ln, Kingsnorth
☎ (01233) 620859
fax: (01233) 620859
Four miles from Ashford off the B2070;
pitch price from £6-£12

WHERE TO EAT

RESTAURANTS

🏵🏵🏵 Walletts Court
West Cliffe, St Margaret's at Cliffe, Dover
☎ (01304) 852424
fax: (01304) 853430
Interesting dishes in candle-lit setting.
Lunch: 12-2; £25 à la carte
Dinner: 7-9; £25 à la carte

🏵 Hythe Imperial
Princes Parade, Hythe
☎ (01303) 267441
fax: (01303) 264610
Attractive restaurant in an impressive
seafront hotel.
Lunch: 12.30-2, £16 and à la carte
Dinner: 7-9.30, £22 and à la carte

Fontwell Park

This must be one of the very best courses in Britain for first-time racegoers to visit. Newcomers to the sport are welcomed with open arms and nothing is too much trouble for the courteous and ever helpful staff. Facilities are compact and the catering is of a high standard.

Unfortunately, it is not the easiest place to reach, but the route is well signposted and it is well worth the effort.

Racing is over the sticks and the chase course is one of only two in the country (the other is at Windsor) to be run on a figure-of-eight circuit. Consequently, runners are never far out of sight and for a really exciting close-up view of the action, walk over to the centre of the track where it is possible to see the horses jumping the first obstacle in the back straight before moving across to watch them negotiate the final fence. Meetings are well supported by the top trainers and all the necessary ingredients are present for an enjoyable day's racing.

FURTHER INFORMATION

Pratt & Company
11 Boltro Road, Haywards Heath, West Sussex
RH16 1BP

LOCATION AND HOW TO GET THERE

The course is mid-way between Arundel and Chichester at the junction of the A27 with the A29.

Nearest Railway Station: Barnham; there is a connecting bus service to the course on racedays.

ADMISSION

All classes of day ticket give access to full betting facilities, including Tote.

Day Tickets:
CLUB £13 – access to bars, restaurant and private boxes

TATTERSALLS AND PADDOCK £9 – access to bars, seafood bar, mobile catering, boxes and private rooms

SILVER RING £5 – access to bar, mobile catering, picnic area (£4 per car, plus £4 per occupant)

Annual membership: £100, plus £10 for car badge if required

Please note: These prices are for 1997 and will be subject to change in 1998.

COURSE FACILITIES

Banks:
there are no banks or cashpoint facilities on the course.

For families:
picnic area with refreshment kiosk and toilet children's play area on Bank Holidays and August Meeting only.

CALENDAR OF EVENTS

January 19 – jumping	May 4	October 28
February 9 – jumping	May 25	November 9
February 23 – jumping	August 31	December 2
March 24 – jumping	September 3	December 31
April 6	September 22	
April 23	October 6	

WHERE TO STAY

HOTELS

Travelodge
Fontwell
☎ (01243) 543973
32 bedrooms; double room £36.50 (room only)
Credit cards 1 2 3 5

Around Fontwell

★★★ (Red) ☸☸ Amberley Castle
Amberley
☎ (01798) 831992, fax: (01798) 831998
15 bedrooms; double B&B £130-£300
Credit cards 1 2 3 5

★★★ ☸ 68% Norfolk Arms
High St, Arundel
☎ (01903) 882101, fax: (01903) 884275
34 bedrooms; double B&B from £90
Credit cards 1 2 3 5

★★☸ 75% Burpham Country
Old Down, Burpham, Arundel
☎ (01903) 882160
fax: (01903) 884627
10 bedrooms; double B&B £76-£83
Credit cards 1 3

★★ 68% Black Mill House
Princess Av, Aldwick, Bognor Regis
☎ (01243) 821945 & 865596, fax: (01243) 821316
26 bedrooms
Credit cards 1 2 3 5

★★★ ☸ 73% The Millstream
Bosham Ln, Bosham
☎ (01243) 573234, fax: (01243) 573459
29 bedrooms; double B&B £91-£113
Credit cards 1 2 3 5

★★★ ☸☸ 79% Bailiffscourt
Climping
☎ (01903) 723511, fax: (01903) 723107
27 bedrooms; double B&B £125-£285
Credit cards 1 2 3 5

★★★ 64% Robin Hood
Main Rd, Shripney, Bognor Regis
☎ (01243) 822323, fax: (01243) 841430
24 bedrooms; double B&B from £55

★★ 69% Suffolk House
3 East Row, Chichester
☎ (01243) 778899 ;fax: (01243) 787282
9 bedrooms; double B&B £89-£118
Credit cards 1 2 3 5

★★★ ☸ 63% Ship
North St, Chichester
☎ (01243) 778000, fax: (01243) 788000
32 bedrooms; double B&B £72-£150
Credit cards 1 2 3 5

★★ 68% Bedford
Southgate, Chichester
☎ (01243) 785766, fax: (01243) 533175
20 bedrooms; double B&B £70-£80
Credit cards 1 2 3 5

★★★★ ☸☸ 71% Goodwood Park
Goodwood,
☎ (01243) 775537, fax: (01243) 520120
88 bedrooms
Credit cards 1 2 3 5

★★★ ☸☸☸ 77% Angel
North St, Midhurst
☎ (01730) 812421, fax: (01730) 815928
21 bedrooms; double B&B £90
Credit cards 1 2 3 5

★★★ ☸☸ 73% Spread Eagle
South St, Midhurst
☎ (01730) 816911, fax: (01730) 815668
41 bedrooms; double B&B £110
Credit cards 1 2 3 5

BED AND BREAKFAST

QQQ Arden
4 Queens Ln, Arundel
☎ (01903) 882544
Quietly situated off the main road; freshly decorated, neat, well equipped bedrooms.
8 bedrooms; double B&B £30-£40

QQQ Bridge House
18 Queen St, Arundel
☎ (01903) 882779 & 0500 323224 (free)
Bedrooms of various sizes; good views of the castle.
19 bedrooms; double B&B £36-£42
Credit cards 1 3

QQQQQ The Park House Hotel
Bepton
☎ (01730) 812880, fax: (01730) 815643
Dating back to 17th-century, with charm and tranquility throughout.
14 bedrooms; double B&B from £90
Credit cards 1 2 3

QQQQQ Kenwood
Off A259, Bosham
☎ (01243) 572727, fax: (01243) 572738
Individually furnished, spacious bedrooms, some with distant harbour views.
3 bedrooms; double B&B £40-£45

QQQ Trotton Farm
Rogate
☎ (01730) 813618
fax :(01730) 816093
Two modern bedrooms in a converted barn.
3 bedrooms; double B&B £35-£40

QQQQ Kenmore
Claigmar Rd, Rustington
☎ (01903) 784634
fax:(01903) 784634
Located in quiet residential area with well equipped rooms.
7 bedrooms; double B&B £45-£50
Credit cards 1 2 3

QQQQQ The White Horse
Sutton
☎ (01798) 869221, fax: (01798) 869291
Attractive surroundings, friendly staff fresh food, real ales and five splendid bedrooms.
5 bedrooms; double B&B £58-£68
Credit cards 1 2 3 5

WHERE TO STAY

CAMPSITES

►►► Southern Leisure Lakeside Village
Vinnetrow Rd, Chichester
☎ (01243) 787715
Fax: (01243) 533643
West of Fontwell

►►►►► Warner Farm Touring Park
Warner Ln, Selsey, Chichester
☎ (01243) 604121 & 604499
fax; (01243) 604499
Pitch price £6–£21 per night.

►►► Wicks Farm Caravan Park
Redlands Ln, West Wittering
☎ (01243) 513116
fax: (01243) 511296
Pleasant rural site; pitch price £8–£9.50 per night.

►► Caravan Club Site
Goodwood Racecourse, Goodwood
☎ (01243) 774486
Five miles north of Chichester; pitch price from £10.50 per night.

►► Camping & Caravanning Club Site
Great Bury, Graffham
☎ (01798) 867476 & (01203) 694995
From A285 towards Petworth, first left after Duncton; pitch price £9.30–£10 per night.

►►► White Rose Touring Park
Littlehampton
☎ (01903) 716176
Close to Arundel; pitch price from £6.75 per night.

WHERE TO EAT

RESTAURANTS

❀❀ George & Dragon
Burpham, Arundel
☎ (01903) 883131
fax: (01903) 883341
Honest, tasty cooking with good use of fresh local produce in warm friendly atmosphere.
Lunch (Sunday): 12.15-2; £15.95
Dinner: 7.15-9.45; £19.50

❀❀ Cliffords Cottage
Bracklesham Ln, Bracklesham
☎ (01243) 670250
Reasonably priced traditional French-style food in a charming 17th-century thatched cottage.
Lunch: Sunday only; £12.50
Dinner: 7-9.30; from £19 and à la carte

❀❀ Comme Ca
Broyle Rd, Chichester
☎ (01243) 788724
fax: (01243) 530052
Simple French dishes in a prettily Gallicised country inn.
Lunch: 12-2; £17.45 and à la carte
Dinner: 6-10.30; £21 à la carte

❀ Little London
38-39 Little London, Chichester
☎ (01243) 530735
fax: (01243) 533011
Lunch: 12-2.30; £12.50 and à la carte
Dinner: 6-10.30; £15.50 and à la carte

❀❀ White Horse Inn
Chilgrove
☎ (01243) 535219
fax: (01243) 535301
Popular, pretty country inn with skilful, unpretentious cooking and an exceptional wine list.
Lunch: 12-3; £19.50
Dinner: 6-12; £23.50

❀❀ Stane Street Hollow
Codmore Hill, Pulborough
☎ (01798) 872819
Traditional, carefully cooked Swiss and French dishes, in a relaxed country setting.
Lunch: 12.30-1.15; from £15.50
Dinner: 7-9.15; from £25 à la carte

❀❀❀ Manleys
Manleys Hill, Storrington
☎ (01903) 742331
fax: (01903) 740649
Rich, imaginative European cooking and friendly, professional service in elegant intimate atmosphere.
Lunch: 12.15-1.45; £19.60 and à la carte
Dinner: 7.15-9; £31.50 and à la carte

❀❀ Old Forge
6a Church St, Storrington
☎ (01903) 743402
fax: (01903) 742540
Modern English cooking using quality produce.
Lunch: 12.15-1.30; £15 and à la carte
Dinner: 7.15-9; £21.50 and à la carte

Goodwood

There is no course in the country that can match this marvellous setting on a summer's day. With the beautiful South Downs providing an idyllic backdrop, this magical venue offers a near perfect combination of top-class racing and outstanding facilities.

One of the most enjoyable week's racing to be found anywhere in the world is the five-day 'Glorious Goodwood' meeting run here in late July, a fixture which rivals Royal Ascot in importance. The cards are a great mixture of competitive handicaps and conditions events. The two-year-old maidens are nearly always won by potential Classic horses. The undoubted highlight of the week, however, is the Sussex Stakes, arguably Europe's most important mile race for older horses. A meeting and a course not to be missed.

FURTHER INFORMATION

Goodwood Racecourse Ltd
Goodwood, Chichester, West Sussex PO18 0PS
☎ (01243) 755022; (01242) 755025

LOCATION AND HOW TO GET THERE

Four miles north of Chichester, signposted from A27 2 miles south and from A285 2 miles north. **Nearest Railway Station:** Chichester; special bus service from the station to the course on racedays.

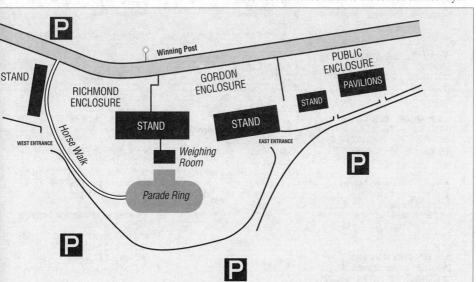

ADMISSION

ll classes of day ticket give access to full etting facilities, including Tote.

ay Tickets:
ICHMOND ENCLOSURE £16, (available to embers only during July meeting) – access Charlton Hunt Restaurant, bars and boxes.

JBLIC ENCLOSURE £5, July meeting £6 arty discount on advance bookings)– ccess to bars and fast food areas.

GORDON ENCLOSURE £10, July meeting £17 (party discount on advance bookings) – access to Gordon Restaurant (July meeting), fast food bar and private rooms.

Annual membership: £160 (£35 joining fee)

COURSE FACILITIES

Banks:
Richmond Enclosure Barclays Bank is open 1 hour before the first race until the start of the penultimate race. There are no cashpoint facilities on the course.

For families:
picnic area with toilets; children's play area; baby changing facilities; lost children centre in Operations HQ.

CALENDAR OF EVENTS

May 19-21
June 5 – evening meeting
June 11
June 12 – evening meeting
June 19 – evening meeting
June 26 – evening meeting

June 28
July 28-August 1 –Festival Meeting
August 28-29
September 11-12
September 23-24

WHERE TO STAY

HOTELS

Around Goodwood

Travelodge
Fontwell
☎ (01243) 543973
fax: (01243) 543973
32 bedrooms; double room £34.95-£49.95
(room only)
Credit cards 1 2 3 5

★★★(Red) ❀❀ Amberley Castle
Amberley
☎ (01798) 831992, fax: (01798) 831998
15 bedrooms; double B&B £130-£300
Credit cards 1 2 3 5

★★★ ❀ 68% Norfolk Arms
High St, Arundel
☎ (01903) 882101, fax: (01903) 884275
34 bedrooms; double B&B from £90
Credit cards 1 2 3 5

★★❀ 75% Burpham Country
Old Down, Burpham, Arundel
☎ (01903) 882160
fax: (01903) 884627
10 bedrooms; double B&B £76-£83
Credit cards 1 3

★★ 68% Black Mill House
Princess Av, Aldwick, Bognor Regis
☎ (01243) 821945 & 865596, fax: (01243) 821316
26 bedrooms
Credit cards 1 2 3 5

★★★ ❀ 73% The Millstream
Bosham Ln, Bosham
☎ (01243) 573234, fax: (01243) 573459
33 bedrooms; double B&B £109-£112
Credit cards 1 2 3 5

★★ 69% Suffolk House
3 East Row, Chichester
☎ (01243) 778899
fax: (01243) 787282
11 bedrooms; double B&B £89-£118
Credit cards 1 2 3 5

★★ 68% Bedford
Southgate, Chichester
☎ (01243) 785766, fax: (01243) 533175
20 bedrooms; double B&B £70-£80
Credit cards 1 2 3 5

★★ 70% Crouchers Bottom
Birdham Rd, Chichester
(01243) 784995
fax:(01243) 539797
9 bedrooms; double B&B £65-£85
Credit cards 1 2 3

★★★ 69% Brookfield
Havant Rd, Emsworth
☎ (01243) 373363 & 376383,
fax: (01243) 376342
40 bedrooms; double B&B from £79.50
Credit cards 1 2 3 5

★★★★ ❀❀ 71% Marriot Goodwood Park
Goodwood.
☎ (01243) 775537, fax: (01243) 533802
94 bedrooms
Credit cards 1 2 3 5

★★★ 62% The Bear
East St, Havant
☎ (01705) 486501
fax: (01705) 470551
42 bedrooms; double B&B £70
Credit cards 1 2 3 5

★★★ ❀❀❀ 77% Angel
North St, Midhurst
☎ (01730) 812421, fax: (01730) 815928
28 bedrooms; double B&B £90
Credit cards 1 2 3 5

★★★ ❀❀ 73% Spread Eagle
South St, Midhurst
☎ (01730) 816911, fax: (01730) 815668
41 bedrooms; double B&B £110
Credit cards 1 2 3 5

WHERE TO STAY

BED AND BREAKFAST

QQQ Arden
4 Queens Ln, Arundel
☎ (01903) 882544
Quietly situated off the main road; freshly decorated, neat, well equipped bedrooms.
8 bedrooms; double B&B £30-£40

QQQ Bridge House
18 Queen St, Arundel
☎ (01903) 882779 & 0500 323224 (free)
fax: (01903) 883600
Bedrooms of various sizes; good views of the castle.
19 bedrooms; double B&B £36-£42
Credit cards 1 3

QQQQQ The Park House Hotel
Bepton
☎ (01730) 812880, fax: (01730) 815643
Dating back to 17th-century, with charm and tranquility throughout.
14 bedrooms; double B&B from £90
Credit cards 1 2 3

QQQ Jingles Hotel
77 Horndean Rd, Emsworth
☎ (01243) 373755
fax: (01243) 373755
Bright well-kept bedrooms and garden with rural views.
13 bedrooms; double B&B £42-£54
Credit cards 1 3

QQQQQ Mizzards Farm
Rogate
☎ (01730) 821656
fax: (01730) 821655
Lovely 16th-century house in tranquil rural setting. High standard of bedrooms.
3 bedrooms; double B&B £50-£60

QQQQQ The White Horse
Sutton
☎ (01798) 869221, fax: (01798) 869291
Attractive surroundings, friendly staff fresh food, real ales and five splendid bedrooms.
5 bedrooms; double B&B £68
Credit cards 1 2 3 5

QQQ Trotton Farmhouse
Trotton, Rogate
☎ (01798) 813618
fax: (01798) 816093
Converted farmhouse with beams, antique pine and a friendly family atmosphere.
3 bedrooms; double B&B £40

QQQQQ Kenwood
Off A259, Bosham
☎ (01243) 572727, fax: (01243) 572738
Individually furnished and spacious bedrooms, some with distant harbour views.
3 bedrooms; double B&B £40-£45

QQQQ Crown Hotel
8 High St, Emsworth
☎ (01243) 372806, fax: (01243) 370082
9 bedrooms
Credit cards 1 2 3

CAMPSITES

►►► Southern Leisure Lakeside Village
Vinnetrow Rd, Chichester
☎ (01243) 787715
fax: (01243) 533643
South of Goodwood.

►► Caravan Club Site
Goodwood Racecourse, Goodwood
☎ (01243) 774486
Five miles north of Chichester; pitch price from £11.50 per night.

►►► Camping & Caravanning Club Site
Great Bury, Graffham
☎ (01798) 867476 & (01203) 694995
fax: (01203) 694886
From A285 towards Petworth, first left after Duncton; pitch price from £8.70 per night.

WHERE TO STAY

▶▶▶ **White Rose Touring Park**
Littlehampton
☎ (01903) 716176
fax: (01903) 732671
Close to Arundel; pitch price from £7 per night.

▶▶▶ **Wicks Farm Caravan Park**
Redlands Ln, West Wittering
☎ (01243) 513116
fax: (01243) 511296
Pleasant rural site; pitch price £8–£9.50 per night.

▶▶▶▶▶ **Warner Farm Touring Park**
Warner Ln, Selsey, Chichester
☎ (01243) 604121, fax; (01243) 604499
Pitch price £6–£21 per night.

WHERE TO EAT

RESTAURANTS

❀❀ **George & Dragon**
Burpham, Arundel
☎ (01903) 883131
fax: (01903) 883341
Honest, tasty cooking with good use of fresh local produce in warm friendly atmosphere.
Lunch (Sunday): 12.15-2; £15.95
Dinner: 7.15-9.45; £19.50

❀❀ **Cliffords Cottage**
Bracklesham Ln, Bracklesham
☎ (01243) 670250
Reasonably priced traditional French-style food in a charming 17th-century thatched cottage.
Lunch: Sunday only; £12.50
Dinner: 7-9.30; from £19 and à la carte

❀❀ **Comme Ca**
Broyle Rd, Chichester
☎ (01243) 788724
fax: (01243) 530052
Simple French dishes in a prettily Gallicised country inn.
Lunch: 12-2; £17.45 and à la carte
Dinner: 6-10.30; £21 à la carte

❀❀ **White Horse Inn**
Chilgrove
☎ (01243) 535219
fax: (01243) 535301
Popular, pretty country inn with skilful, unpretentious cooking and an exceptional wine list.
Lunch: 12-3; £19.50
Dinner: 6-12; £23.50

❀❀❀ **36 On The Quay**
47 South St, Emsworth
☎ (01243) 375592 & 372257
Innovative French cooking served with modern presentation in a quayside restaurant.
Lunch: 12-1.45; from £19.55 and à la carte
Dinner: 7-9.45; 7-10; £29.95 à la carte

❀❀ **Stane Street Hollow**
Codmore Hill, Pulborough
☎ (01798) 872819
Traditional, carefully cooked Swiss and French dishes, in a relaxed country setting.
Lunch: 12.30-1.15; from £15.50
Dinner: 7-9.15; from £25 à la carte

❀ **Little London**
38-39 Little London, Chichester
☎ (01243) 530735
fax: (01243) 533011
Lunch: 12-2.30; £12.50 and à la carte
Dinner: 6-10.30; £15.50 and à la carte

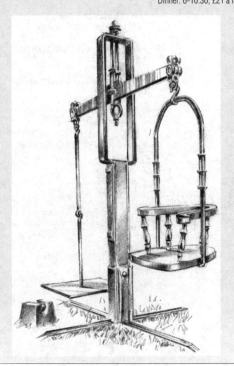

Hamilton Park

A small track, this is somewhat overshadowed by its near neighbour Ayr yet still manages to put on worthwhile meetings. Attendances have improved, especially at the summer evening meetings where there can be a very happy atmosphere.

The compact facilities contain plenty of bars, and families are well catered for.

Racing is restricted to the Flat with meetings being staged from April right through to September. The standard of competition has improved and top northern trainer Jack Berry usually dominates the two-year-old events. The most positive aspect of the track is that it is possible to see the start of long distance races close up, with the horses being loaded into the stalls right in front of the stands. This is because of the unusual configuration of the course which consists of a six furlong straight with a pear-shaped loop attached. Runners in contests of around a mile and a half therefore begin by racing away from the winning post before going round the loop and heading back towards the stands.

FURTHER INFORMATION

Hamilton Park Racecourse Co Ltd
Bothwell Rd, Hamilton, ML3 0DW
☎ (01698) 283806

LOCATION AND HOW TO GET THERE

The course is on Bothwell Road, Hamilton. Leave the M74 at junction 5 and follow signs to Hamilton. **Nearest Railway Station:** Hamilton West; there is no connecting bus service to the course.

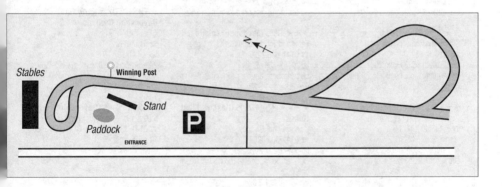

ADMISSION

All classes of day ticket give access to full betting facilities, including Tote.

Day Tickets:
CLUB £12 – access to bars, restaurant, private rooms

TATTERSALLS AND PADDOCK £7, senior citizens and students £4 – access to bars, cafeteria, fast food

Annual membership: £125 single, £200 per couple*
(* the term 'couple' applies only to a man and a woman)

(Please note that these are 1997 prices and are due for review in 1998.)

COURSE FACILITIES

Banks: there are no banks or cashpoint facilities on the course.

For families:
children's play area; lost children centre in the racecourse office.

CALENDAR OF EVENTS

March 30 – flat
April 4 – flat
May 3
May 7
May 15 – evening meeting
June 1
June 10 – evening meeting
June 17
June 24 – evening meeting

June 30
July 3 – evening meeting
July 10 – evening meeting
August 1 – evening meeting
August 12 – evening meeting
August 17
September 7
September 28

WHERE TO STAY

HOTELS

Roadchef Lodge
M74 Northbound,
☎ (01698) 891904, fax: (01698) 891682
36 bedrooms; double room £43.50 (room only)
Credit cards 1 2 3 5

Around Hamilton

★★★ 67% Bothwell Bridge
89 Main St, Bothwell
☎ (01698) 852246
fax: (01698) 854686
90 bedrooms; double B&B £50–£68
Credit cards 1 2 3 5

★★ 62% Silvertrees
Silverwells Crescent, Bothwell
☎ (01698) 852311
fax: (01698) 852311 ext 200
26 bedrooms; double B&B £75–£85
Credit cards 1 2 3 5

★★★ 63% Bruce Swallow
Cornwall St, East Kilbride
☎ (013552) 29771
fax: (013552) 42216
78 bedrooms; double B&B £99
Credit cards 1 2 3 5

★★★ 61% Stuart
2 Cornwall Way, East Kilbride
☎ (013552) 21161, fax: (013552) 64410
39 bedrooms; double B&B £80–£135
Credit cards 1 2 3 5

Travel Inn
Glasgow Rd, Newhouse, Motherwell
☎ (01698) 860277
fax: (01698) 861353
40 bedrooms; double bedroom £36.50

Travel Inn
Brunel Way, The Murray, East Kilbride
☎ (01355) 222809
fax: (01355) 230517
40 bedrooms; double bedroom £36.50

★★★ 65% Macdonald Thistle
Eastwood Toll, Giffnock
☎ 0141-638 2225
fax: 0141-638 6231
56 bedrooms; double bedroom £70–£99
Credit cards 1 2 3 5

★★★★ 🏵🏵 71% Glasgow Moat House
Congress Rd, Glasgow
☎ 0141-306 9988
fax: 0141-221 2022
284 bedrooms; double room £155 (room only)
Credit cards 1 2 3 5

★★★★ 66% Glasgow Marriott
Argyle St, Anderston, Glasgow
☎ 0141-226 5577
fax: 0141-221 7676
300 bedrooms; double B&B £58–£144
(room only)
Credit cards 1 2 3 5

Forte Posthouse
Bothwell St, Glasgow
☎ 0141-248 2656
fax: 0141-221 8986
251 bedrooms; double room £99 (room only)
Credit cards 1 2 3 5

★★★ (RED) 🏵🏵🏵 One Devonshire Gardens
1 Devonshire Gardens, Glasgow
☎ 0141-339 2001
fax: 0141-337 1663
27 bedrooms; double room £125–£200
(room only)
Credit cards 1 2 3 5

★★★ 76% 🏵 Devonshire
5 Devonshire Gardens, Glasgow
☎ 0141-339 7878, fax: 0141-339 3980
14 bedrooms
Credit cards 1 2 3 5

WHERE TO STAY

★★★★ 62% Copthorne Hotel
George Square, Glasgow
☎ 0141-332 6711
fax: 0141-332 4264
141 bedrooms; double room £65-£130
(room only)
Credit cards 1 2 3 5

★★★ 63% Tinto Firs Thistle
470 Kilmarnock Rd, Glasgow
☎ 0141-637 2353
fax: 0141-633 1340
28 bedrooms; double B&B £80-£100
Credit cards 1 2 3 5

★★★ 67% Swallow
517 Paisley Rd, Glasgow
☎ 0141-427 3146
fax: 0141-427 4059
117 bedrooms; double B&B £70-£110
Credit cards 1 2 3 5

★★★ 64% Quality Central
99 Gordon St, Glasgow
☎ 0141-221 9680
fax: 0141-226 3948
222 bedrooms; double room £76.50-£92
(room only)
Credit cards 1 2 3 5

★★★ 68% Popinjay
Lanark Rd, Rosebank
☎ (01555) 860441
fax: (01555) 860204
47 bedrooms; double B&B £ 60-£150
Credit cards 1 2 3 5

★★★ ✿ 66% Strathaven
Hamilton Rd, Strathaven
☎ (01357) 521778, fax: (01357) 520789
22 bedrooms; double B&B £60-£80
Credit cards 1 2 3 5

★★ 67% Redstones
8-10 Glasgow Rd, Uddingston
☎ (01698) 813774 & 814843,
fax: (01698) 815319
18 bedrooms; double B&B £50-£74
Credit cards 1 2 3 5

★★★ 61% Carrick
377 Argyle St, Glasgow
☎ 0141-248 2355
fax: 0141-221 1014
121 bedrooms; double bedroom £55-£65
Credit cards 1 2 3 5

★★★ 67% King's Park
Mill Street, Rutherglen, Glasgow
0141-647 5491
fax: 0141-613 3022
26 bedrooms; double B&B £50-£75
Credit cards 1 2 3 5

BED AND BREAKFAST

Around Hamilton

QQ Rosslee
107 Forrest St, Airdrie
☎ (01236) 765865
Run by enthusiastic owners and catering for
both tourist and commercial trade.
6 bedrooms; double B&B £40-£50

QQQ Deauvilles
62 St Andrews Dr, Pollockshields,
Glasgow
☎ 0141-427 1106
fax: 0141-427 1106
Small family-run hotel with thoughtfully
equipped bedrooms.
6 bedrooms
Credit cards 1 2 3

QQQ Hotel Enterprise
144 Renfrew St, Glasgow
☎ 0141-332 8095
fax: 0141-332 8095
In the heart of the city offering a good
standard of accommodation.
6 bedrooms
Credit cards 1 2 3

QQ Kelvin Private Hotel
15 Buckingham Terrace, Great Western
Road, Hillhead
☎ (0141) 3397143, fax: (0141) 339 5215
Good value bed and breakfast
accomodation.
21 bedrooms; double B&B £38-£54
Credit cards 1 2 3

QQQ Botanic Hotel
1 Alfred Ter, Great Western Rd, Glasgow
☎ 0141-339 6955; fax: 0141-339 6955
Spacious, commfortable bedrooms are a
feature of this well run hotel.
11 bedrooms
Credit cards 1 2 3

QQ Lomond Hotel
6 Buckingham Terrace, Great Western Road,
Hillhead
☎ (0141) 339 2339, fax: (0141) 339 5215
Friendly family-run hotel in a tree-lined
Victorian terrace.
17 bedrooms; double B&B £38-£54
Credit cards 1 2 3

WHERE TO STAY

Q Braidenhill Farm
Braidenhill, Glenmavis
☎ (01236) 872319
Unassuming working farm, modest
accommodation and cheery hospitality.
3 bedrooms; double B&B £33-£40
Credit cards 1 2 3

QQ Dykecroft
Kirkmuirhill
☎ (01555) 892226
A modern bungalow situated 1.5m west of
Kirkmuirhill. Compact cosy accommodation
in friendly environment.
3 bedrooms

QQ Springvale Hotel
18 Letham Rd, Strathaven
☎ (01357) 21131
Personal, friendly service, well equipped
bedrooms; cheerful dining room with nice
view.
14 bedrooms

CAMPSITES

►►► Strathclyde Country Park
366 Hamilton Rd, Motherwell
☎ (01698) 266155
Junction 5 of M74; pitch price from £7.75
per night.

WHERE TO EAT

RESTAURANTS

Around Hamilton

❀❀ Buttery
652 Argyle St, Glasgow
☎ 0141-221 8188
fax: 0141-204 4639
An atmospheric Victorian setting for plush
modern cooking.
Lunch: 12-2.30; £14.85 and à la carte
Dinner: 7-10.30; from £25 à la carte
Credit cards 1 2 3 5

❀❀ Rogano
11 Exchange Place, Glasgow
☎ 0141-248 4055
fax: 0141-248 2608
A stylish Thirties setting for skilful modern
cooking with an emphasis on fish.
Lunch: 12-2.30; from £16
Dinner: 6.30-10.30; from £16.50 à la carte
Credit cards 1 2 3 5

❀❀ Hilton Hotel
1 Williams Street
☎ 0141- 204 5555
fax: 0141- 204 5004
Scottish/British cooking in a striking
modern building
Lunch: 12-2, from £19.50
Dinner: 7-10.30, from £38 and à la carte

❀❀ La Parmigiana
447 Great Western Road
☎ 0141 334 0686
fax: 0141- 332 3533
Traditional Italian restaurant offering
classical specialities
Lunch: 12-2.30, £7.50
Dinner: 6-11, from £12 à la carte

❀ Papingo
104 Bath St
☎ 0141-332 6678
fax: 0141-332 6549
Lunch: 12-3
Dinner: 5-10.30; from £17.95

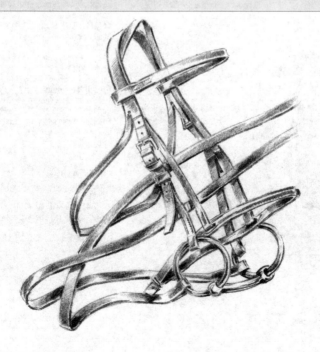

Haydock Park

Haydock Park is the top course in the northwest of England, offering an excellent standard of racing under both codes at the 28 or so meetings that are held here throughout the year. The facilities at this Grade One venue match the high quality of competition.

The catering is especially praiseworthy as there is a broad range of dining areas, serving everything from fast foods to à la carte cuisine. The viewing from the large stands is outstanding and the place always seems to be buzzing with excitement and eager anticipation - the crowds get really involved in the contests, giving their fancies lots of vociferous support.

The oval track is galloping in nature and the very stiff fences will catch out any shoddy jumpers. January and February see two important handicaps run over these imposing obstacles in the shape of the Peter Marsh Chase and Greenalls Grand National Trial, while the mixed May Bank Holiday card features the last valuable contest of the jumps season, the Crowther Homes Swinton Handicap Hurdle. Connoisseurs of the Flat, meanwhile, get the opportunity to sample some high-class racing during the summer. Particularly attractive is the three-day fixture at the start of July which culminates on the Saturday with the Letheby & Christopher Old Newton Cup and Lancashire Oaks. Best of all, though, is the Haydock Sprint Cup in early September, a contest which regularly attracts the cream of Europe's speed merchants.

FURTHER INFORMATION

The Haydock Park Racecourse Co Ltd
Newton-le-Willows, Lancashire WA12 0HQ
☎ (01942) 725963; Fax: (01942) 270879

Clubcall is a recorded message service giving information on
1. Going report and trainers information
2. Previews of next meeting
3. prices and facilities
☎ (01891) 800828

LOCATION AND HOW TO GET THERE

Between Manchester and Liverpool. Leave the M6 at junction 23 then take the A49; it is possible that, up to an hour before racing, the police may direct the majority of traffic from the M6 down the A580 to enter the racecourse at the eastern end. Because of the one way system in the car park, it may not be possible for cars to reach the Owners and Trainers, or A, B, C, or D Car Parks, and an alternative area is provided.

Nearest Railway Station: Wigan or Newton le Willows; from Wigan take bus number 320.

ADMISSION

All classes of day ticket give access to full betting facilities, including Tote.

Day Tickets:
Accompanied children under 16 and wheelchair users are admitted free; senior citizens are admitted into Tattersalls and Newton Enclosures at half price. There is also an NUS discount. On ladies evenings, ladies are admitted at half price.

COUNTY STAND £15 midweek, £17 weekends and bank holidays– access to boxes, private rooms, restaurant, several bars and dining areas.

TATTERSALLS £9, £10 weekends and bank holidays– access to several bars and snack kiosks

NEWTON £4, £5 weekends and bank holidays– access to bar and cafe

Annual membership: £190, Junior (under 21) £65, includes free and reserved parking and reciprocal arrangements at certain other courses on certain days. A supplement of £10 per day is charged for admission to the Park Suite.

COURSE FACILITIES

Banks:
There are no banks or cashpoint facilities on the course.

For families:
children's play area; lost children centre.

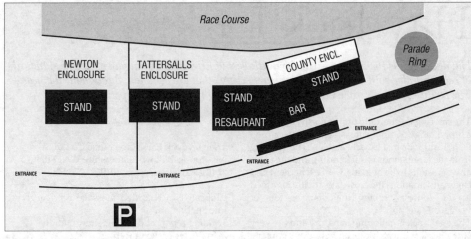

CALENDAR OF EVENTS

January 10 – jumping; Newton Steeple Chase
January 24 – jumping; includes Premier Long Distance Hurdle
February 27-28 – jumping; includes Greenalls Grand National Trial
   on Saturday
April 11 – flat
May 2 – jumping; includes Crowther Homes Swinton Hurdle
May 10 – flat
May 22-23 – flat; racing includes Silver Bowl and Leahurst Sandy
   Lane Stakes
June 4-6 – flat; includes The John O'Gaunt Stakes
July 2-4 – flat; includes July Trophy,Lancashire Oaks and Old
   Newton Cup
July 12
August 6-8 – flat; includes Petros Rose of Lancaster Stakes

September 4-5 – flat;includes Sprint Cup
September 25-26
October 14 – flat
November 5 – jumping; Open Morning
November 18 – jumping
November 28 – jumping
December 12 – jumping
December 29 – jumping

WHERE TO STAY

HOTELS

★★★★ 63% Haydock Thistle
Penny Lane, Haydock
☎ (01942) 272000
fax: (01942) 711092
139 bedrooms; double room from £70
(room only)
Credit cards 1 2 3 5

Forte Posthouse Haydock
Lodge Ln, Newton-Le-Willows, Haydock
☎ (01942) 717878, fax: (01942) 718419
136 bedrooms; double room £59-£69
(room only)
Credit cards 1 2 3 5

Travelodge
Piele Rd, Haydock
☎ (01942) 272055
fax: (01942) 272055
40 bedrooms; double room £36.50 (room
only)
Credit cards 1 2 3

★★★★ 68% Park Royal International
Stretton Rd, Stretton, Warrington
☎ (01925) 730706, fax: (01925) 730740
114 bedrooms; double bedroom £88-£116
Credit cards 1 2 3 5

Travelodge
Burtonwood Motorway Service (M62)
☎ (01925) 710376
40 bedrooms; double room £36.50 (room
only)
Credit cards 1 2 3

★★★★ 65% Daresbury Park
Chester Rd, Daresbury
☎ (01925) 267331, fax: (01925) 265615
140 bedrooms; double B&B £120-£130
Credit cards 1 2 3 5

WHERE TO STAY

★★★ 🏵 65% Lymm
Whitbarrow Rd, Lymm
☎ (01925) 752233, fax: (01925) 756035
62 bedrooms
Credit cards 1 2 3 5

★★ 62% Kirkfield
2-4 Church St, Newton-le-Willows
☎ (01925) 228196
fax: (01925) 291540
14 bedrooms
Credit cards 1 3

★★★ 🏵🏵 69% Holland Hall
6 Lafford Ln, Upholland
☎ (01695) 624426, fax: (01695) 622433
34 bedrooms; double B&B £47-£72
Credit cards 1 2 3 5

★★★ 66% Fir Grove
Knutsford Old Rd, Warrington
☎ (01925) 267471, fax: (01925) 601092
40 bedrooms; double B&B £48-£75
Credit cards 1 2 3 5

★★ 🏵 73% Rockfield
Alexandra Rd, Grappenhall
☎ (01925) 262898, fax: (01925) 263343
12 bedrooms; double B&B £45-£58
Credit cards 1 2 3 5

★ 69% Kenilworth
2 Victoria Rd, Grappenhall, Warrington
☎ (01925) 262323 & 268320
14 bedrooms
Credit cards 1 2 3

★★★ 65% Oak
Riverway, Wigan
☎ (01942) 826888, fax (01942) 825800
88 bedrooms; double bedroom £59
Credit cards 1 2 3 5

★★ 64% Bel-Air
236 Wigan Ln, Wigan
☎ (01942) 241410, fax; (01942) 243967
12 bedrooms
Credit cards 1 3

★★★★ 🏵🏵 67% Kilhey Court
Chorley Road, Standish
☎ (01257) 472100, fax: (01257) 422401
63 bedrooms; double room from £100
Credit cards 1 2 3 5

BED AND BREAKFAST

QQQ Broomfield Hotel
33-35 Wigan Rd, Deane, Bolton
☎ (01204) 61570, fax; (01204) 650932
15 bedrooms; double B&B £42
Credit cards 1 2 3

QQQ Astley House Hotel
3 Southport Rd, Chorley
☎ (01257) 272315
Attractive Laura Ashley style bedrooms
6 bedrooms; double B&B £44
Credit cards 1 2 3 5

QQ Aalton Court
23 Upper Dicconson St, Wigan
☎ (01942) 322220
fax: (01942) 322220
Compact but well equipped bedrooms;
conveniently situated Victorian terraced
house.
6 bedrooms

CAMPSITES

►►► Holly Bank Caravan Park
Warburton Bridge Rd, Rixton
☎ 0161-775 2842
Off A57 close to the Manchester Ship Canal;
pitch price from £10

WHERE TO EAT

RESTAURANTS

🏵🏵 High Moor
Highmoor Ln, Wrightington
☎ (01257) 252364
fax: (01257) 255120
Careful, unpretentious cooking and a cosy
period style setting for a formal but relaxing
evening out.
Lunch: 12-2
Dinner: 5.30-10

🏵🏵 Wrightington Hotel & Restaurant
Moss Ln, Wrightington
☎ (01257) 425803
fax: (01257) 425830
Lunch: 12.30-2; from £9.95
Dinner: 7-9.30; from £17.50

Hereford

A nice little National Hunt course which has always found wide favour among jumping enthusiasts. Part of the reason for its popularity is that the stands, parade ring and saddling boxes are all situated within a short distance of each other, eliminating the need to rush about madly in order to see all the action.

Rather, this is a place where everything can be done at a leisurely pace, allowing plenty of time to savour the friendly, easy-going atmosphere that makes this such an appealing venue.

The hilly track is unusual in that it is almost square-shaped, with the turn into the home straight being particularly sharp, a feature which tends to suit front-runners. Fields will, by and large, consist of moderate horses, but do not be put off by that as the programmes have been deliberately structured to create competitive racing, albeit of a lesser quality. There are some 15 fixtures scheduled here annually and a trip to the evening meeting in June will probably prove most rewarding.

FURTHER INFORMATION

Hereford Racecourse Company Ltd
Shepherd's Meadow, Eaton Bishop
Hereford HR2 9UA
☎ (01981) 250436/250192

LOCATION AND HOW TO GET THERE

The course is on the northern outskirts of the city, a quarter of a mile west of the A49 at its junction with the northern Roman Road Ring Road. **Nearest Railway Station:** Hereford; there is no connecting bus service to the course.

ADMISSION

Day Tickets:
There is free access to racing for those staying on the adjacent campsite – see under Where to Stay.

CLUB £12 – access to excellent viewing, bar, restaurant, cloakrooms, private boxes, toilets for the disabled.

TATTERSALLS £9 – access to excellent viewing, bar, snack restaurant, private boxes

COURSE £5 – access to grandstand, bar and Tote facilities. Racecourse betting is only available in the course enclosure on Bank Holidays.

COURSE FACILITIES

Banks:
there are no banks or cashpoint facilities on the course

For families:
picnic area with toilets; parking free; under 16s free

CALENDAR OF EVENTS

February 16	September 21
March 21	October 1
April 4	October 16
April 13	November 18
May 2	December 4
May 12	December 15
May 25	December 26
June 1 – evening meeting	

WHERE TO STAY

HOTELS

★★★ 62% The Green Dragon
Broad St,
☎ (01432) 272506
fax: (01432) 352139
87 bedrooms; double room from £70 (room only)
Credit cards 1 2 3 5

★★ 66% Merton Hotel & Governors Restaurant
28 Commercial Rd
☎ (01432) 265925, fax: (01432) 354983
19 bedrooms; double B&B £65-£70
Credit cards 1 2 3 5

★★ 63% Castle Pool
Castle St
☎ (01432) 356321
fax: (01432) 356321
26 bedrooms; double B&B £58-£72
Credit cards 1 2 3 5

★★★ 62% Belmont Lodge & Golf Course
Belmont
☎ (01432) 352666
fax: (01432) 358090
30 bedrooms; double B&B £62.50
Credit cards 1 2 3 5

Travel Inn
Holmer Rd, Holmer
☎ (01432) 274853
fax: (01432) 343003
40 bedrooms; double room £36.50
Credit cards 1 2 3 5

★★★ 63% Pilgrim
Ross Rd, Much Birch
☎ (01981) 540742
fax: (01981) 540620
20 bedrooms; double B&B £45-£90
Credit cards 1 2 3 5

BED AND BREAKFAST

QQQQ Hermitage Manor
Canon Pyon
☎ (01432) 760317
Impressive manor house with magnificent oak panelling and spacious accommodation. It is surrounded by 11 acres of grounds bordering woodland.
3 bedrooms; double B&B £40-£50

QQQ Hopbine Hotel
Roman Rd
☎ (01432) 268722
fax: (01432) 268722
Simple and modest, but well equipped accommodation to the north of the city centre.
20 bedrooms

QQQQ Sink Green Farm
Rotherwas
☎ (01432) 870223
16th-century ivy-clad farmhouse with lots of exposed timbers and excellent bedrooms, including one four-poster.
3 bedrooms; double B&B from £36-£42

QQQQ Grafton Villa Farm
Grafton
☎ (01432) 268689; fax: (01432) 268689
Early 18th-century farmhouse with fresh, bright bedrooms.
3 bedrooms; double B&B £39-£41

QQQQ Maund Court
Bodenham
☎ (01568) 797282
Attractive creeper-clad farmhouse with well-equipped bedrooms.
4 bedrooms

QQQQ Cwm Craig
Little Dewchurch
☎ (01432) 840250
Spacious bedrooms and several very comfortable seating areas.
3 bedrooms; double B&B £30-£36

QQQ Bowens Country House
Fownhope
☎ (01432) 860430; fax: (01432) 860430
Attractive accommodation with co-ordinating decor and furnishings.
12 bedrooms
Credit cards 1 3

QQQQ The Old Mill
Hoarwithy
☎ (01432) 840602
Cottage style guest rooms in a converted mill.
6 bedrooms

QQQ Butchers Arms
Woolhope
☎ (01432) 860281
Half-timbered 14th-century building with good facilities.
3 bedrooms

CAMPSITES

►► Hereford Racecourse Camp Site
Roman Rd
☎ (01432) 272364
fax: (01432) 352807
Quiet, well maintained sloping grass site on the perimeter of the racecourse. Free access to racing on racedays.

►►► Poston Mill Caravan & Camping Park
Peterchurch
☎ (01981) 550225 & (01584) 711280
fax: (01981) 550885
Pitch price from £6.50 per night

WHERE TO EAT

RESTAURANTS

❀❀ Hope End Hotel
Hope End, Ledbury
☎ (01531) 633613
fax: (01531) 636366
Fresh local produce in a short but well-balanced menu
Dinner: 7.30-8.30, £30

❀❀ Pengethley Manor
Pengethley Park, Ross-on-Wye
☎ (01989) 730211
fax: (01989) 730238
Lunch: 12-2; £16 and a la carte
Dinner: 7-9.30; £25 and a la carte

PUBS

Around Hereford

Ancient Camp
Ruckhall Common, nr Eaton Bishop
☎ (01981) 250449; fax (01981) 251581
Wood Parish Bitter and Hook Norton Bitter, a choice of malt whiskies and an above-average wine list; food on offer is of good quality and variety. Children welcome anywhere during the day, but in the evening only if eating; no children under eight accommodated overnight.
Open: Tuesday to Saturday 12-2.30pm, 6-11pm; Sunday 12-2.30pm, 7-10.30pm; Monday 6-11pm
Bar food: Tuesday to Saturday 12-3pm,

Hexham

Hexham is quite simply a delight. Its location in the heart of the unspoilt Northumberland countryside, just a short distance south of Hadrian's Wall, is one of the most attractive to be found anywhere in Britain.

It is a great place to leave behind the hustle and bustle of Newcastle's city life (some twenty miles to the east) and escape to a different world where peace and tranquillity reign in a charming, rural venue. This is also one of the highest sites where racing is held as the course is some 800 feet above sea level, the upshot being that it is totally open to the elements, so be sure to take plenty of extra layers of clothing to keep warm.

On account of its exposed setting, this National Hunt track has very sensibly taken the decision not to stage any meetings during the bleak winter months of January and February, preferring instead to concentrate most of its fixtures from March through to May with a few more in the autumn. The mile and a half circuit is considered to be exceptionally testing due to its steep undulations, and races finish on a separate spur which runs along right in front of the stands. For a great day out in the country where a cracking atmosphere is ensured, this is the place to come.

FURTHER INFORMATION

Hexham Steeplechase Co Ltd
The Riding, Hexham, Northumberland
NE46 4PF
☎ (01434) 606881, Fax:(01434) 605814

LOCATION AND HOW TO GET THERE

The course is 1½ miles south of Hexham. It is signposted from the Bridge End Roundabout on the A69, which connects with the M6 at Carlisle and with the A1 at Newcastle.
Nearest Railway Station: Hexham; there is a free connecting bus service to and from the course.

ADMISSION

All classes of day ticket give access to full betting facilities, including Tote.

Day Tickets:
There is a reduced rate for caravanners using the adjacent caravan site on racedays.

CLUB £9 – access to bars and exclusive viewing area

TATTERSALLS £6, pensioners £4 – access to bars and restaurant

COURSE FACILITIES

Banks:
There are no banks or cashpoint facilities on the course.

For families:
picnic area with refreshment kiosk and toilets, children's play area. Dogs on leads allowed.

CALENDAR OF EVENTS

March 19	June 13 – jumping; evening meeting
March 30	June 19 – jumping; evening meeting
April 20	October 2 – jumping
May 2 – jumping	October 10
May 9 – jumping	November 6 – jumping
May 23 – jumping	November 25 – jumping
May 26 – evening meeting; jumping	December 9 – jumping

WHERE TO STAY

HOTELS

★★★ ❀ 66% Beaumont
Beaumont St
☎ (01434) 602331; fax: (01434) 606184
23 bedrooms; double room from £76
Credit cards 1 2 3 5

★★ 62% Country
Priestpopple
☎ (01434) 602030
fax: (01434) 603202
9 bedrooms; double B&B £58
Credit cards 1 2 3

Around Hexham

★★ 68% Angel Inn
Main Street, Corbridge
☎ (01434) 632119
fax: (01434) 632119
5 bedrooms; double B&B from £64
Credit cards 1 2 3 5

★★ ❀ 69% Lord Crewe Arms
Blanchland
☎ (01434) 675251, fax: (01434) 675337
19 bedrooms; double B&B £110
Credit cards 1 2 3 5

★★★ ❀❀ 71% George
Chollerford
☎ (01434) 681611, fax: (01434) 681727
46 bedrooms; double B&B from £110
Credit cards 1 2 3 5

★★(Red) ❀❀ Lovelady Shield Country House
Alston
☎ (01434) 381203, fax: (01434) 381515
12 bedrooms; double B&B £65–£118
Credit cards 1 2 3 5

★★★ 65% Nent Hall Country House
Alston
☎ (01434) 381584, fax: (01434) 382668
19 bedrooms
Credit cards 1 2 3

★★ 67% Lowbyer Manor Country House
Alston
☎ (01434) 381230, fax: (01434) 382937
12 bedrooms; double B&B £70
Credit cards 1 2 3 5

★★ 68% Riverdale Hall
Bellingham
☎ (01434) 220254; fax: (01434) 220457
20 bedrooms; double B&B £69–£80
Credit cards 1 2 3 5

BED AND BREAKFAST

QQQ Rye Hill Farm
Hexham
☎ (01434) 673259
fax: (01434) 673608
Converted barn and cow shed; bright, modern and sensibly furnished, including lovely family room.
6 bedrooms; double B&B from £40

QQQ Priorfield
Hippingstones Ln
☎ (01434) 633179
A handsome Edwardian house in its own grounds with good facilities.
2 bedrooms; double B&B £36–£40

QQQ Rose & Crown
Main St, Slaley, Hexham
☎ (01434) 673263
fax: (01434) 673305
An attractive inn with three well-furnished guest rooms.
3 bedrooms; double B&B £40–£50

QQQQQ The Courtyard
Mount Pleasant, Sandhoe, Corbridge
☎ (01434) 606850
fax: (01434) 606632
A remarkable conversion of once derelict farm buildings, restored in country style.
3 bedrooms; double B&B £55–£75

QQQ Crindledykes
Housesteads, Bardon Mill
☎ (01434) 344316
Traditional old stone farmhouse with spotlessly clean, character accommodation.
2 bedrooms; double B&B £30–£34

QQQ Greenhead
Carterway Heads, Shotley Bridge, Consett
☎ (01207) 255676
A charming guest house with beams and exposed stone walls.
3 bedrooms; double B&B £32

CAMPSITES

►►► Caravan Club Site
Hexham Racecourse,
☎ (01434) 606847
Overlooking Hexham Moors

►►► Causey Hill Caravan Park
Benson's Fell Farm,
☎ (01434) 602834 & 604647
fax: (01434) 604647
Pitch price from £7.50 per night

► Ascroft Farm
Bardon Mill
☎ (01434) 344409
Adjacent to A69 between Haltwhistle and Hexham; pitch price from £2.50 per night.

►►► Allensford Caravan & Camping Park
Castleside
☎ (01207) 591043
Gently sloping parkland

WHERE TO EAT

RESTAURANTS

❀ Lord Crewe Arms
Nr Consett, Blanchland
☎ (01434) 675251
fax: (01434) 675 337
Interesting menus in a historic inn.
Lunch: 12.30-2; £13.50
Dinner: 7-9.15; £26 à la carte

❀❀ George Hotel
Chollerford, Hexham
☎ (01434) 681611
fax: (01434) 681727
Lunch: 12-2; £13.50 and à la carte
Dinner: 6.30-9.30; £24 and à la carte

Huntingdon

A pretty market town whose most famous son is Oliver Cromwell, although it has more recently come to prominence as the constituency of the former Prime Minister, John Major. He is an occasional visitor to the track and his daughter even rode in a charity race here, unfortunately falling off near the finish due to exhaustion.

The racecourse lies just outside Huntingdon itself by the small village of Brampton and is set in the flat fen lands that are so typical of this Cambridgeshire area. This has resulted in a level, sharp circuit which places a greater premium on speed than stamina, while a particularly nice feature is the siting of an open ditch in front of the grandstand, providing an added spectacle for spectators.

The fifteen or so jumps meetings regularly draw large crowds of enthusiastic racegoers with the two highest attendances normally being seen at the Boxing Day and Easter Monday fixtures. The standard of the runners on both these occasions is usually nothing to write home about, but the course has begun to go slightly more up-market in recent years and there is now a growing number of valuable contests, most prestigious of which is the Peterborough Chase, a Grade Two event in November that carries some £30,000 in prize money.

FURTHER INFORMATION

Huntingdon Racecourse
Brampton, Huntingdon, Cambs PE18 8NN
☎ (01480) 453373/454610

LOCATION AND HOW TO GET THERE

The course is at Brampton near Huntingdon. From the end of the M11 continue on the A604, turning off at Spitals Link (signposted). From the A1, take the A604 east for a mile.

Nearest Railway Station: Huntingdon; there are no connecting bus services to the course.

ADMISSION

All classes of day ticket give access to full betting facilities, including Tote.

Day Tickets:
MEMBERS £12 – access to bar dining room, restaurant, private rooms, boxes

TATTERSALLS £8 – access to bars, restaurants, dining rooms

COURSE CENTRE £4 – access to bar and restaurant

Annual membership: £85 single, £150 double; £50 junior (16-24)

COURSE FACILITIES

Banks:
there are no banks or cashpoint facilities on the course

For families:
picnic area with toilets

CALENDAR OF EVENTS

January 21	April 28 – evening meeting	November 21 – includes the Peterborough
January 29	May 13 – evening meeting	Chase
February 12	May 25	December 8
February 20	August 31	December 26
February 26	September 18	
March 7	September 27	
March 18	October 9	
April 13	November 10	

WHERE TO STAY

★★★ ✿ 73% The Old Bridge
Huntingdon
☎ (01480) 452681, fax: (01480) 411017
26 bedrooms; double B&B £89.50-£139.50
Credit cards 1 2 3 5

★★★ 62% The George
George St
☎ (01480) 432444, fax: (01480) 453130
24 bedrooms; double room £75 (room only)
Credit cards 1 2 3 5

★★ 64% Grange
115 High St, Brampton
☎ (01480) 459516
fax: (01480) 459391
9 bedrooms
Credit cards 1 3

Travelodge
A604 Huntingdon Rd, Fenstanton
☎ (01954) 230919
fax: (01954) 230919
40 bedrooms; double room £36.50 (room only)
Credit cards 1 2 3

★★★ 67% Olivers Lodge
Needingworth Rd, St Ives
☎ (01480) 463252, fax: (01480) 461150
16 bedrooms; double B&B £70-£85
Credit cards 1 2 3

★★★ 66% Slepe Hall
Ramsey Rd, St Ives
☎ (01480) 463122, fax: (01480) 300706
16 bedrooms; double B&B £70-£90
Credit cards 1 2 3 5

★★★ 66% Dolphin
London Rd, St Ives
☎ (01480) 466966, fax: (01480) 495597
47 bedrooms; double B&B £80-£90
Credit cards 1 2 3 5

★★ 59% Papworth
Ermine St South, Papworth Everard
☎ (01954) 718851, fax: (01954) 718069
20 bedrooms; double B&B from £40
Credit cards 1 2 3 5

Travelodge
Huntingdon Rd, Lolworth
☎ (01954) 781335
fax: (01954) 781335
20 bedrooms; double bedroom £36.50

★★ 64% Abbotsley Golf
Eynesbury Hardwicke, St Neots
☎ (01480) 474000, fax: (01480) 471018
15 bedrooms; double B&B from £65
Credit cards 1 3 5

BED AND BREAKFAST

QQ Cross Keys
Molesworth
☎ (01832) 710283; fax:(01832) 710098
Archetypal village inn; with friendly
proprietor; high standard of accommodation
and good bar meals.
10 bedrooms; double B&B £37-£42
Credit cards 1 3

QQQ The Manor House Hotel
Chapel St. Alconbury
☎ (01480) 890423, fax: (01480) 891663
Popular inn , once a 16th-century manor
house, with comfortable bedrooms.
4 bedrooms
Credit cards 1 3

QQQ Prince of Wales
Potton Rd, Hilton
☎ (01480) 830257, fax: (01480) 830257
Small, friendly public house with well-fitted
bedrooms.
4 bedrooms; double B&B £40-£50
Credit cards 1 2 3

QQQ Gransden Lodge Farm
Longstowe Rd, Little Gransden
☎ (01767) 677365, fax: (01767) 677647
Proudly kept farmhouse accommodation for
non-smokers.
3 bedrooms; double B&B £34-£40

CAMPSITES

►►► Park Lane Touring Park
Godmanchester, Huntingdon
☎ (01480) 453740; fax: (01480) 453740
Just off the B1043 between Godmanchester
and Huntingdon; pitch price from £8 per
night.

►►► Quiet Waters Caravan Park
Hemingford Abbots
☎ (01480) 463405
One mile from the A604; pitch price from £8
per night.

WHERE TO EAT

►► Houghton Mill Caravan & Camping Park
Mill St, Houghton
☎ (01480) 462413 & 492811
East of Huntingdon; pitch price £8.50 £9
per night.

►►► Camping & Caravanning Club Site
Rush Meadow, St Neots
☎ (01480) 474404 & (01203) 694995
South of Huntingdon; pitch price £9.10-
£12.10 per night.

RESTAURANTS

✿✿ Pheasant Inn
Keyston
☎ (01832) 710241
fax: (01832) 710340
Competent modern cooking with some
exotic flavours in a cosy, beamed pub
restaurant.
Lunch: 12-2; from £20 a la carte
Dinner: 6-10; from £20 a la carte

✿ Bennett's
The White Hart, Bythorn
☎ (01832) 710226
fax: (01832) 710226
Lunch: 12-3; £23.50 a la carte
Dinner: 7-11; £23.50 a la carte

PUBS

Old Ferry Boat Inn
Holywell, nr St Ives
☎ (01480) 463227
Low-built, whitewashed and thatched pub
claiming to be the oldest in Britain
(documents show that liquor was sold here
as long ago as AD560, though foundations
have been dated even earlier). Draught
beers include Bass, Nethergates and
Courage. Varied menu of interesting dishes.
Children's area and children's menu
available.
Open: 11am-3pm, 6-11pm; Sunday 12-
3pm, 7-10.30pm
Bar food: 12-2pm, 6.30-9.30pm
Accommodation: double B&B £55-£75

Kelso

The glorious Scottish Border country is home to Kelso, one of the most picturesque racecourses in Britain. Far removed from any major urban settlements, this small venue is full of character.

For instance, the old grandstand was originally constructed in 1822 and is still going strong today, albeit with most of the original amenities having been replaced over the intervening 170 years. Even so, an old-fashioned feel has deliberately been preserved with special touches like the lighting of log fires to provide extra warmth during the winter.

This is real jumping country and the love of National Hunt racing is deeply ingrained in the local psyche. The track is quite wide (there is enough room for a golf course to have been located in its centre) and the extremely long and demanding run-in of two furlongs has seen many a clear leader swallowed up by the chasing pack in the closing stages. This is definitely not a course where it is safe to start counting the winnings until the horses have passed the post.

FURTHER INFORMATION

Kelso Racecourse
18-20 Glendale Road, Wooler, Northumberland
NE71 6DW
☎ (01668) 281611

LOCATION AND HOW TO GET THERE

The racecourse is just north of the town on the A698. Take the A6089 from Edinburgh, or the A699 from the west.

Nearest Railway Station: Berwick-upon-Tweed; there are no connecting bus services to the racecourse.

ADMISSION

All classes of day ticket give access to full betting facilities, including Tote.

Day Tickets:
Accompanied children under 16 are admitted free.

MEMBERS £10-£12 – access to full facilities including restaurant, bars, snack bar, corporate rooms and facilities for disabled racegoers.

TATTERSALLS £7, senior citizens £4 – access to restaurant, bars and fast food.

Annual membership: £75 single, £140 double, £55 senior citizens – includes reciprocal arrangements with certain other courses on certain days.

COURSE FACILITIES

Banks:
there are no banks or cashpoint facilities on the course, but the Secretary will cash cheques.

For families:
baby changing facilities, lost children centre.

CALENDAR OF EVENTS

January 23
February 5
March 6
March 27
April 6
April 29 – evening meeting
May 20
October 4

October 17
October 31
November 11
November 30
December 21

WHERE TO STAY

HOTELS

★★★ ❀❀ 73% Sunlaws House
Heiton
☎ (01573) 450331, fax: (01573) 450611
22 bedrooms; double B&B £145
Credit cards 1 2 3 5

★★★ 67% Ednam House
Bridge St
☎ (01573) 224168, fax: (01573) 226319
32 bedrooms; double B&B £70-£102
Credit cards 1 3

★★★ 61% Cross Keys
36-37 The Square
☎ (01573) 223303, fax: (01573) 225792
24 bedrooms; double B&B £55-£65
Credit cards 1 2 3 5

★★★ 76% Dryburgh Abbey
St Boswells
☎ (01835) 822261, fax: (01835) 823945
26 bedrooms; double B&B £84-£165
Credit cards 1 3

★★ 69% Buccleuch Arms
The Green, St Boswells
☎ (01835) 822243, fax: (01835) 823965
18 bedrooms; double B&B £50-£85
Credit cards 1 3

★★ 68% Bon Accord
Market Sq. Melrose
☎ (01896) 822645, fax: (01896) 823474
10 bedrooms; double B&B from £70
Credit cards 1 2 3

★★★❀❀ 65% Burt's
The Sq, Melrose
☎ (01896) 822285, fax: (01896) 822870
21 bedrooms
Credit cards 1 2 3 5

★★ 65% George & Abbotsford
High St, Melrose
☎ (01896) 822308, fax: (01896) 822308
30 bedrooms; double B&B £55-£97
Credit cards 1 2 3 5

★★★❀ 72% Tillmouth Park
Cornhill-on-Tweed
☎ (01890) 882255, fax: (01890) 882540
14 bedrooms; double B&B £110
Credit cards 1 2 3 5

BED AND BREAKFAST

Around Kelso

QQQQQ The Spinney
Langlee, Jedburgh
☎ (01835) 863525
fax: (01835) 863525
Delightful house 2 miles south of Jedburgh;
inviting, individually decorated bedrooms.
3 bedrooms; double B&B £40-£42

QQQQ Froylehurst
Friars Jedburgh
☎ (01835) 862477
fax: (01835) 862477
Handsome Victorian house in quiet area;
attractive fabrics individually deocrated
bedrooms.
5 bedrooms; double B&B £32-£34

QQQ Kenmore Bank Hotel
Oxnam Rd, Jedburgh
☎ (01835) 862369
Off the A68, friendly family-run guesthouse.
Compact brightly decorated and furnished
bedrooms.
6 bedrooms; double B&B £37-£44
Credit cards 1 3

QQQQ Willow Court
The Friars, Jedburgh
☎ (01835) 863702
fax: (01835) 864601
Standing in 2 acres of gardens above the
town centre. Warm and welcoming
atmosphere.
4 bedrooms

QQ Ferniehirst Mill Lodge
Jedburgh
☎ (01835) 863279
Modern purpose-built lodge; compact neat
bedrooms.
9 bedrooms; double B&B £46
Credit cards 1 3

QQQQ Dunfermline House
Buccleuch St, Melrose
☎ (01896) 822148; fax((01896) 822148
Delightful Victorian house.
5 bedrooms; double B&B £44

CAMPSITES

►►► Camping & Caravanning Club Site
Elliot Park, Edinburgh Rd, Jedburgh
☎ (01835) 863393 & (01203) 694995
fax: (01203) 694886
North of Jedburgh off A68; pitch price from
£8.10 per night.

►►►► Springwood Caravan Park
Kelso
☎ (01573) 224596
fax: (01573) 224033
One mile west of town; pitch price from £8
per night

►►► Jedwater Caravan Park
Jedburgh
☎ (01835) 840219
fax: (01835) 840219
Quiet riverside site close to A68; pitch price
from £7.50 per night

WHERE TO EAT

RESTAURANTS

❀❀ Sunlaws House Hotel
Kelso
☎ (01573) 450331
Grand surroundings for accomplished
Scottish-French cooking.
Lunch: 12.30-2; from £12.50
Dinner: 7.30-9.30;from £27

❀ Wheatsheaf
Swinton
☎ (01890) 860257
fax: (01890) 860257
A country inn with a reputation for good
food.
Lunch: 12-2; £20 à la carte
Dinner: 6.30-9.30; £20 à la carte

Kempton Park

Located just 15 miles from central London, this first-rate venue has some of the finest facilities of any racecourse in the country. These will no doubt be drastically improved by an £8.5 million redevelopment of the Grandstand and Parade Ring which will hopefully be complete by Boxing Day 1997.

There is a wide selection of places to eat, varying from the main restaurant, which offers an excellent three-course meal, to the numerous snack bars serving light refreshments. And for those who want to toast their good fortune or drown their sorrows, there is a broad range of well-stocked bars from which to choose.

If the facilities are good, then the quality of the racing is even better. The majority of the fixtures are run on the Flat with the Easter Saturday meeting featuring a couple of significant Classic trials, while the September Stakes sometimes gives a few pointers towards the Arc result. Although they are fewer in number, it is with the jumps meetings that this delightful course really excels itself. One of the main highlights of the National Hunt season is the two-day Christmas Festival which starts on Boxing Day and includes the Pertemps King George VI Chase, a race which the now retired Desert Orchid virtually made his own in recent years. Not surprisingly, massive crowds flock to see this prestigious contest, causing horrible tail-backs on the roads, so allow twice the normal time for your journey.

FURTHER INFORMATION

The Club Secretary,
Kempton Park Racecourse, Sunbury-on-Thames, Middlesex TW16 5AQ
☎ (01932) 782292; Fax: (01932) 782044

LOCATION AND HOW TO GET THERE

Fifteen miles from central London via the A316 and A308. From outside London, leave the M3 at junction 1 and take the A308 towards Kingston-upon-Thames.
Nearest Railway Station: Kempton Park; there is an excellent service from Waterloo.

ADMISSION

All classes of day ticket give access to full betting facilities, including Tote.

Day Tickets:
Accompanied children under 16 are admitted free to all enclosures.

CLUBHOUSE – reserved exclusively for Annual Members and their guests. No children under 10.

MEMBERS – £10 feature days, £15 premium days, £25 Boxing day; junior (16 – 25 years) £8 feature days, £12 premium days, £16 Boxing Day – access to viewing terrace encircling parade ring and winners enclosure, bar, restaurant, snack bar, Tote

GRANDSTAND – £10 feature days, £10 premium days, £15 Boxing Day – access to viewing terrace, bar, restaurant, snack bar, Tote

SILVER RING – £5 feature days, £5 premium day, £7 Boxing Day – access to bar, restaurant, snack bar, Tote.

Parking: – main car park £2, Silver Ring and Centre free.

Annual membership: £155, junior £70 includes free Members Car Park label and reciprocal visits to certain other race meetings.

(Please note: The above prices refer to the 1997 season, as details of changes were not available at the time of going to press.)

COURSE FACILITIES

Banks:
there are no banks or cashpoint facilities on the course. Cheques may be cashed at racecourse office and Tote betting vouchers may be purchased with banker's card.

For families:
Picnic area with refreshment kiosk and toilets; children's play area; baby changing facilities; lost children centre; creche

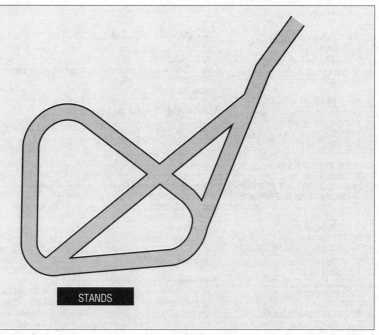

STANDS

CALENDAR OF EVENTS

January 16 – jumping
January 24
February 27-28 – jumping
April 11
April 13
May 4 – flat; includes Jubilee Handicap
May 17 – flat
May 23 – flat
May 30 – evening meeting
June 10 – evening meeting
July 1 – evening meeting

July 8 – evening meeting
August 5 – flat; evening meeting
August 19 – evening meeting
September 9 – flat; includes Sirenia Stakes
September 21 – flat
October 17 – jumping
November 4 – jumping
November 18 – jumping
December 26 & 28 – jumping; includes Pertemps King George VI
   Tripleprint Chase and Christmas Hurdle

WHERE TO STAY

HOTELS

Around Kempton Park

★★★★ **70% London Heathrow Hilton**
Terminal 4, Heathrow Airport
☎ 0181-759 7755; fax:0181-759 7579
395 bedrooms; double bedroom from £99
Credit cards 1 2 3 5

★★★ **64% Shepperton Moat House**
Felix Ln, Shepperton
☎ (01932) 241404, fax: (01932) 245231
156 bedrooms
Credit cards 1 2 3 5

★★★★ ⊛ **71% Oatlands Park**
146 Oatland Dr, Weybridge
☎ (01932) 847242, fax: (01932) 842252
128 bedrooms; double B&B £75-£145
Credit cards 1 2 3 5

★★★ ⊛ **71% Ship Thistle**
Monument Green, Weybridge
☎ (01932) 848364, fax: (01932) 857153
39 bedrooms; double bedroom £86-£125
Credit cards 1 2 3 5

WHERE TO STAY

★★ 65% Haven
Portsmouth Rd, Esher
☎ 0181-398 0023, fax: 0181-398 9463
20 bedrooms; double B&B £79
Credit cards 1 2 3 5

★★★ 63% Master Robert
Great West Rd, Hounslow
☎ 0181-570 6261, fax: 0181-569 4016
94 bedrooms; double bedroom £43-£82
Credit cards 1 2 3 5

★★★ 66% The Crown
7 London St, Chertsey
☎ (01932) 564657, fax: (01932) 570839
30 bedrooms; double B&B £58-£98
Credit cards 1 2 3 5

★★ 61% Hotel Ibis
112-114 Bath Rd, Hayes
☎ 0181-759 4888, fax: 0181-564 7894
354 bedrooms
Credit cards 1 2 3 5

Forte Posthouse
Bath Rd, Hayes
☎ 0181-759 2552, fax: 0181-564 9265
186 bedrooms; double bedroom £69

★★★★ ❀❀ 76% Cannizaro House
West Side, Wimbledon Common, London
SW19
☎ 0181-879 1464
fax: 0181-879 7338
46 bedrooms; double room £155-£220
(room only)
Credit cards 1 2 3 5

★★★★ 66% Copthorne
400 Cippenham Ln, Slough
☎ (01753) 516222, fax: (01753) 516237
219 bedrooms
Credit cards 1 2 3 5

★★★★ ❀❀ 76% Oakley Court
Windsor Road, Water Oakley, Windsor
☎ (01753) 609988
fax: (01628) 37011
92 bedrooms
Credit cards 1 2 3 5

★★★ ❀❀ 72% The Castle
High St, Windsor
☎ (01753) 851011
fax: (01753) 830244
104 bedrooms; double B&B £120
Credit cards 1 2 3 5

★★ ❀ 74% Aurora Garden
14 Bolton Av, Windsor
☎ (01753) 868686
fax: (01753) 831394
15 bedrooms
Credit cards 1 2 3 5

BED AND BREAKFAST

QQ Civic
87/89 Lampton Road, Hounslow
☎ 0181 572 5107
fax: 0181-814 0203
Close to the town centre, with a spacious
car park.
15 bedrooms; double B&B £40-£45
Credit cards 1 3

QQQ Shalimar Hotel
215-221 Staines Rd, Hounslow
☎ 0181-577 7070 & 0500 238239 (free)
fax; 0181-569 6789
Small hotel with well-equipped bedrooms.
31 bedrooms; double B&B £45-£49
Credit Cards 1 2 3 5

QQQ Longford
550 Bath Rd, Longford
☎ (01753) 682969
fax: (01753) 794189
17th-century house with period character
and good-sized bedrooms.
5 bedrooms; double B&B from £38
Credit cards 1 3

QQ Warbeck House Hotel
46 Queens Rd, Weybridge
☎ (01932) 848764
fax; (01932) 847290
Attractive Edwardian house with modestly
furnished bedrooms.
10 bedrooms

QQ The Cottage
150 High St, Hounslow
☎ 0181-897 1815
fax: 0181-897 3117
Clean and comfortable guest house
8 bedrooms; double B&B £75
Credit cards 1 3

QQ Warwick
321 Ewell Rd, Surbiton
☎ 0181-296 0516
fax: 0181-296 0517
Small guest house run by cheerful owner.
9 bedrooms; double B&B £40-£46
Credit cards 1 3

QQQ Kings Lodge
5 Kings Rd, London SW19
☎ 0181-545 0191
fax: 0181-545 0381
Bedrooms furnished to very high standard.
7 bedrooms; double B&B £59-£79
Credit cards 1 2 3 5

QQ Trochee Hotel
21 Malcolm Rd, London SW19
☎ 0181-946 1579 & 3924,
fax: 0181-785 4058
Traditional, well maintained guesthouse.
17 bedrooms; double B&B £48-£51
Credit cards 1 2 3

QQ Wimbledon Hotel
78 Worple Rd, London SW19
☎ 0181-946 9265, fax: 0181-946 9265
Detached Victorian house offering a choice
to suit everyone.
14 bedrooms
Credit cards 1 2 3 5

WHERE TO STAY

QQQ Worcester House
38 Alwyne Rd, London SW19
☎ 0181-946 1300
fax: 0181-785 4058
Choice of brightly decorated bedrooms, all equipped with modern amenities.
9 bedrooms; double B&B £57.50–£62.50
Credit cards 1 2 3 5

QQ Colnbrook Lodge
Bath Rd, Colnbrook, Slough
☎ (01753) 685958
fax: (01753) 685164
Comfortable, well equipped bedrooms with double-glazing to combat air-traffic noise.
8 bedrooms; double B&B £39–£55
Credit cards 1 3

QQ Clarence Hotel
9 Clarence Rd, Windsor
☎ (01753) 864436
fax: (01753) 857060
Centrally placed in Windsor, old building with bedrooms of variety of shapes and sizes.
21 bedrooms; double B&B £45–£52
Credit cards 1 2 3 5

QQQQ Melrose House
53 Frances Rd, Windsor
☎ (01753) 865328
fax: (01753) 865328
Elegant, detached house in residential area. Clean, well equipped bedrooms; friendly proprietor.
9 bedrooms; double B&B £50
Credit cards 1 3

WHERE TO EAT

RESTAURANTS

🏵🏵🏵 Riva
169 Church Rd, Barnes, London SW13
☎ 0181-748 0434
Regional Italian cooking in small attractive urban restaurant.
Lunch: 12-2.30
Dinner: 7-11
Credit cards 1 3

🏵🏵 Sonny's
94 Church Rd, Barnes, London SW13
☎ 0181-748 0393
fax: 0181-748 2698
Reliable imaginative modern cooking in stylish informal brasserie-type restaurant.
Lunch: 12.30-2.30; from £12.50 and à la carte
Dinner: 7.30-11; from £22.50 à la carte
Credit cards 1 3

🏵🏵 Crowthers
481 Upper Richmond Rd West, East Sheen, London SW14
☎ 0181-876 6372
Popular local restaurant with good modern cooking and a warm welcome.
Lunch: 12-2; £18.50
Dinner: 7-10; £23
Credit cards 1 2 3

🏵🏵 Le Petit Pierrot
4 The Parade, Claygate
☎ (01372) 465105
fax: (01372) 467642
Comfortable little restaurant serving French provincial-style dishes.
Lunch: 12-2.30
Dinner: 7-10.30

🏵🏵 Ayudhya
14 Kingston Hill, Kingston-upon-Thames
☎ 0181-549 5984
Thai restaurant offering a huge choice of dishes.
Lunch: 12-2.30; £18.50 à la carte
Dinner: 6.30-11; £18.50 à la carte

🏵 Dining Room
10-12 Queens Rd, Hersham
☎ (01932) 231686
Two combined cottages serving classic English dishes.
Lunch: 12-2
Dinner: 7-10.30

Leicester

The standard of racing that is held throughout the year at this Midlands venue is fairly average although fields are generally large because trainers like to introduce their inexperienced horses on the wide, galloping track.

This can get very soft during the winter, particularly in the dip in the back straight, and the testing conditions will invariably expose any runners with stamina limitations. It is also a regular occurrence to witness the jockeys bringing their mounts extremely wide into the home straight in search of better ground. In fact, the turf was once so badly cut up on the inside that a certain winner stumbled and unseated his rider just yards from the finishing line.

In summer, it can make a pleasant change to take along a picnic to the Silver Ring car park that overlooks the course, while the evening meetings are always lovely occasions. A new grandstand has recently been added to the facilities.

FURTHER INFORMATION

Leicester Racecourse Co Ltd
2 Lower Mounts, Northampton NN1 3DE
☎ (01604) 30757 or (0116) 2716515 on racedays
Fax: (01162) 711746

LOCATION AND HOW TO GET THERE

The course is adjacent to the A6, two miles south of the city centre. From the M1 leave at junction 21 and take the A46 towards Leicester. After half a mile follow signs to the Outer Ring Road/Leicester East A563.

Nearest Railway Station: Leicester; there is a connecting bus service on racedays.

ADMISSION

All classes of day ticket give access to full betting facilities, including Tote.

Day Tickets:
CLUB £13 – includes racecard and parking; access to bars, boxes and private rooms

TATTERSALLS £9 – includes racecard and parking; access to bars and restaurant

FAMILY TICKET: £22 for parking for one car and entry for 4 people.

COURSE FACILITIES

Banks:
there are no banks or cashpoint facilities on the course.

For families:
picnic area with refreshment kiosk and toilet in Silver Ring Car Park; no specific play area but a bouncy castle and climbing frame with 100m slide are provided for evening and Bank Holiday meetings.

CALENDAR OF EVENTS

January 1 – jumping	**July 22** – flat; evening meeting
January 13 – jumping	**August 5** – flat; evening meeting
January 27 – jumping	**August 10** – flat; evening meeting
February 4 – jumping	**August 19** – evening meeting
February 17 – jumping	**September 8** – flat
March 3 – jumping	**September 21** – flat
March 10 – flat	**October 12-13** – flat
April 2 – flat	**October 25-26** – flat
April 9 – flat	**November 16** – jumping
April 25	**December 3** – jumping
May 25-26 – flat	**December 9**
June 1 – flat	**December 28**– jumping
June 13 – flat; evening meeting	
July 16 – flat	

WHERE TO STAY

HOTELS

★★★★ 60% Holiday Inn
St Nicholas Circle
☎ (0116) 2531161
fax: (0116) 2513169
188 bedrooms; double room from £99
(room only)
Credit cards 1 2 3 5

★★★ ❀ 72% Belmont House Hotel
De Montfort Street, Leicester
☎ (0116) 254 4773
fax: (0116) 247 0804
75 bedrooms; double room £59.50-£93
Credit cards 1 2 3 5

★★★ 64% Hermitage
Wigston Rd
☎ (0116) 256 9955
fax: (0116) 272 0559
57 bedrooms; double room £60-£79 (room
only)
Credit cards 1 2 3 5

Forte Posthouse
Braunstone Ln
☎ (0116) 2630500, fax: (0116) 282 3623
164 bedrooms; double room £56 (room
only)
Credit cards 1 2 3 5

★★★ 66% Stage
299 Leicester Rd, Wigston Fields
☎ (0116) 288 6161, fax: (0116) 281 1874
79 bedrooms; double B&B £49-£106
Credit cards 1 2 3 5

★★★ 60% Saint James
Abbey St
☎ (0116) 251 0666, fax: (0116) 251 5183
73 bedrooms; double room £50-£62 (room
only)
Credit cards 1 2 3 5

★★ 69% Red Cow
Hinckley Rd, Leicester Forest East
☎ (0116) 238 7878
fax: (0116) 238 6539
31 bedrooms; double room £28.50-£39.50
(room only)
Credit cards 1 2 3 5

★★ 62% Old Tudor Rectory
Main St, Glenfield
☎ (0116) 291 5678, fax: (0116) 291 1416
16 bedrooms; double B&B £42.40-£60
Credit cards 1 2 3 5

★★ 61% Gables
368 London Rd
☎ (0116) 270 6969
fax: (0116) 270 6969
30 bedrooms; double B&B £45-£55
Credit cards 1 2 3 5

Around Leicester

★★ 68% Brant Inn
Leicester Rd, Groby
☎ (0116) 287 2703, fax: (0116) 232 1255
10 bedrooms; double bedroom £35-£49.95
Credit cards 1 3

★★ 65% Castle Hotel & Restaurant
Main St, Kirby Muxloe
☎ (0116) 239 5337, fax: (0116) 238 7868
21 bedrooms; double B&B £45-£60
Credit cards 1 2 3

★★★ 65% Field Head
Markfield Ln, Markfield
☎ (01530) 245454
fax: (01530) 243740
28 bedrooms; double B&B £50-£79
Credit cards 1 2 3 5

★★ 63% Charnwood
48 Leicester Rd, Narborough
☎ (0116) 286 2218, fax: (0116) 275 0119
20 bedrooms; double B&B £55
Credit cards 1 2 3

★★★ ❀ 63% Rothley Court
Westfield Ln, Rothley
☎ (0116) 237 4141, fax: (0116) 237 4483
35 bedrooms; double room from £90 (room
only)
Credit cards 1 2 3 5

★★ 63% Mill on the Soar
Coventry Rd, Sutton in the Elms
☎ (01455) 282419, fax: (01455) 285937
20 bedrooms
Credit cards 1 2 3 5

BED AND BREAKFAST

QQQ Burlington Hotel
Elmfield Av
☎ (0116) 270 5112, fax: (0116) 270 4207
Small, family-run hotel, retaining much of
its Victorian character; well maintained
bedrooms.
16 bedrooms; double B&B £44-£48
Credit cards 1 2 3

WHERE TO STAY

QQ Croft Hotel
3 Stanley Rd
☎ (0116) 270 3220, fax: (0116) 270 3220
One mile south of city centre. Dinner (by prior arrangement) offers good value for money.
26 bedrooms; double B&B £35-£42
Credit cards 1 3

QQ Scotia Hotel
10 Westcotes Dr
☎ (0116) 254 9200
Small family-run guesthouse undergoing upgrading, including refurbished lounge with licensed bar.
11 bedrooms

QQ The Stanfre House Hotel
265 London Rd
☎ (0116) 270 4294
Small, friendly, family-run guesthouse. Simply furnished, brightly decorated bedrooms.
12 bedrooms; double B&B £32

QQQQ Ambion Court Hotel
The Green, Dadlington, Hinckley
☎ (01455) 212292, fax: (01455) 213141
A pleasant conversion of red brick farm buildings.
7 bedrooms; double B&B £50-£60
Credit cards 1 3

QQQ Stoneycroft Hotel
5/7 Elmfield Av
☎ (0116) 270 7605, fax: (0116) 270 6067
Large cream-washed building in a quiet residential road.
44 bedrooms; double B&B £40-£45
Credit cards 1 2 3 5

Around Leicester

QQQQ Rutland House
61 High Street East, Uppingham
☎ (01572) 822497, fax: (01572) 822497
A comfortable house with spacious bedrooms.
4 bedrooms; double B&B £39
Credit cards 1 3

QQQQ Knaptoft House Farm & The Greenway
Bruntingthorpe Rd, Bruntingthorpe
☎ (0116) 247 8388
fax: (0116) 247 8388
Surrounded by open countryside, friendly family farm with light, cheerful bedrooms.
6 bedrooms; double B&B from £37

CAMPSITES

►►► Kilworth Caravan Park
North Kilworth
☎ (01858) 880597
South of Leicester off the A427. No tents.
Pitch price from £5 per night

WHERE TO EAT

RESTAURANTS

✿ Belmont House Hotel
De Montfort St
☎ (0116) 254 4773
fax: (0116) 247 0804
Formal dining in the Cherry restaurant and a more casual brasserie.
Lunch: 12-2
Dinner: 7-10

Lingfield Park

This pretty Surrey course known as 'leafy Lingfield' because of its beautiful countryside setting, was completely restructured a few of years ago with the addition of a ten-furlong all weather track inside the grass circuit.

This dirt surface is incredibly resilient to the vagaries of the British winter, allowing racing to continue here when other venues would be forced to abandon. The trouble is that the concept has totally failed to catch on with the public and as a result, crowds can be poor - horses almost outnumber the spectators sometimes.

Turf meetings are a completely different kettle of fish. These are much more popular and the standard of competition is also quite good. Over the jumps, there are a couple of decent cards at the beginning of December and the end of March but the highlight of the year is the Flat fixture in early May which features two important trials for the Derby and Oaks. It should also be pointed out that the course does possess some top-class facilities. The paddock and pre-parade ring are attractively sited in a natural setting among the trees and there are several fine restaurants as well as an excellent seafood bar.

FURTHER INFORMATION

The Racecourse Office
Lingfield Park, 1991 Ltd,
Lingfield, Surrey RH7 6PQ
☎ (01342) 834800; Fax:(01342) 832833

LOCATION AND HOW TO GET THERE

Leave the M25 at junction 6 and take the A22 southbound for approximately 4 miles. At Blindley Heath, after the filling station, turn sharp left onto the B2029 and continue for about 2 miles, passing through the village to reach the racecourse.

Nearest Railway Station: Lingfield; the station is a short walk from the racecourse.

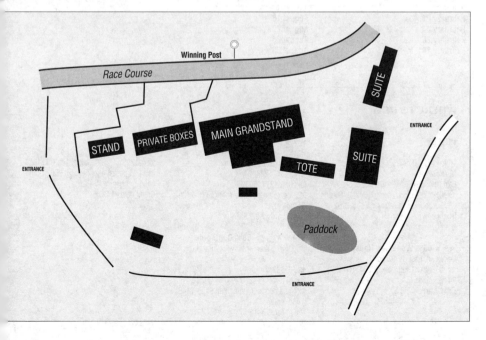

ADMISSION

All classes of day ticket give access to full betting facilities, including Tote.

Day Tickets:
There is no reduction for senior citizens, but a £2 catering voucher is given, valid on the day of issue.

CLUB £13 – £18 – access to bar, restaurant, boxes, private rooms

FAMILY £9 – access to bar, restaurant, boxes, private rooms

Annual membership: £160 – includes Club Car Park.

COURSE FACILITIES

Banks:
there are no banks or cashpoint facilities on the course

For families:
children's play area, lost children centre; creche on Saturdays

CALENDAR OF EVENTS

January 1 – jumping
January 3
January 6-8 – flat
January 10 – flat
January 13 – flat
January 15 – flat
January 17 – flat
January 20 – flat
January 22
January 24 – flat
January 27-29 – jumping on Friday
January 31
February 3 – flat
February 5-7
February 10 – flat
February 12
February 14 – flat
February 17-19
February 21 – flat
February 24 – flat
February 26 – flat
February 28 – flat

March 2 – flat
March 5 – jumping
March 19 – flat
March 21 – jumping
March 30 – jumping
April 3 – flat
April 9
May 8-9
May 13 – flat
May 23 – flat; evening meeting
May 30 – flat
June 13 – flat; evening meeting
June 20 – flat; evening meeting
June 23 – flat
June 27 – flat; evening meeting
July 9-11 – flat
July 25 – flat; evening meeting
August 1 – flat; evening meeting
August 16 – flat
August 22 – flat; evening meeting
August 25
August 29

September 8 – flat
October 2 – flat
October 26 – flat
November 9 – flat
November 12 – flat
November 17 – flat
November 24-25 – flat
November 27 – flat
December 7 – flat
December 9 – flat
December 11-12 – jumping on Saturday
December 18-19
December 21 – flat
December 29

WHERE TO STAY

HOTELS

★★★ (RED) ⊛⊛⊛ Gravetye Manor
East Grinstead
☎ (01342) 810567, fax: (01342) 810080
18 bedrooms; double room £135-£252 (room only)
Credit cards 1 3

★★★ 65% Woodbury House
Lewes Rd, East Grinstead
☎ (01342) 313657, fax: (01342) 314801
14 bedrooms
Credit cards 1 2 3 5

★★★★ 63% Copthorne Effingham Park
West Park Road, Copthorne
☎ (01342) 714994
fax: (01342) 716039
122 bedrooms; double room £115-£135 (room only)
Credit cards 1 2 3 5

★★★★⊛⊛ 68% Copthorne
Copthorne Way, nr Gatwick Airport (on A264)
☎ (01342) 714971
fax: (01342) 717375
227 bedrooms; double room £125-£145 (room only)
Credit cards 1 2 3 5

Forte Posthouse
Povey Cross Rd, Gatwick Airport
☎ (01293) 771621, fax: (01293) 771054
210 bedrooms; double room £56 (room only)
Credit cards 1 2 3 5

WHERE TO STAY

★★★ 65% Chequers Thistle
Brighton Road, Horley
☎ (01293) 786992
fax: (01293) 820625
78 bedrooms; double room from £100
(room only)
Credit cards 1 2 3 5

Travelodge
Church Rd, Lowfield Heath
☎ (01293) 533441
fax: (01293) 535369
121 bedrooms; double bedroom £from
£36.50
Credit cards 1 2 3 5

★★★ 57% The George
High St, Crawley
☎ (01293) 524215
fax: (01293) 548565
86 bedrooms
Credit cards 1 2 3 5

★★★★ 62% Le Meridien London Gatwick
North Terminal
☎ (01293) 567070, fax: (01293) 567739
456 bedrooms

★★★★ (RED) ❀❀ Ashdown Park
Wych Cross, Forest Row
☎ (01342) 824988, fax: (01342) 826206
95 bedrooms; double B&B £135–£295

★★★ (RED) ❀❀ Alexander House
East St, Turners Hill
☎ (01342) 714914, fax: (01342) 717328
15 bedrooms; double bedroom from £135
Credit cards 1 2 3 5

★★ (RED) ❀ Langshott Manor
Ladbroke Rd, Crawley
☎ (01293) 786680, fax: (01293) 783905
10 bedrooms; double B&B from £145
Credit cards 1 2 3 5

BED AND BREAKFAST

QQQQQ Bolebroke Watermill
Perry Hill, Edenbridge Rd, Hartfield
☎ (01892) 770425
fax: (01892) 770425
Charming watermill with a history dating
back to 1086.
5 bedrooms; double B&B £55–£72
Credit cards 1 2 3

QQQ Chalet
77 Massetts Rd, Horley
☎ (01293) 821666, fax: (01293) 821619
Small friendly guesthouse; beautifully clean
bedrooms with fresh decor.
6 bedrooms; double B&B from £44
Credit cards 1 3

QQQ Barnwood Hotel
Balcombe Rd, Pound Hill
☎ (01293) 425800, fax: (01293) 425808
Fully licensed hotel with a range of well-
equipped bedrooms.
35 bedrooms
Credit cards 1 2 3 5

QQQ Copperwood
Massetts Rd, Crawley
☎ (01293) 783388, fax: (01293) 420156
Appealing house with pretty, individual
bedrooms.
5 bedrooms; double B&B £35–£42
Credit cards 1 3 5

QQQQ Gainsborough Lodge
39 Massetts Rd, Horley
☎ (01293) 783982
fax: (01293) 785365
Attractive house offering comfortable en
suite bedrooms.
16 bedrooms; double B&B £44–£49
Credit cards 1 2 3 5

QQQQ The Lawn
30 Massetts Rd, Horley
☎ (01293) 775751
fax: (01293) 821803
Charming Victorian house situated close to
the town centre.
7 bedrooms
Credit cards 1 2 3 5

QQQQ Vulcan Lodge
27 Massetts Rd, Horley
☎ (01293) 771522
Stylishly furnished, individually decorated
bedrooms in 17th century farmhouse.
4 bedrooms; double B&B £42–£44
Credit cards 1 3

CAMPSITES

▶▶▶ Long Acres Farm Caravan & Camping
Newchapel Rd, Lingfield
☎ (01342) 833205 & 884307
Pitch price from £7.50 per night.

▶▶▶ Camping & Caravanning Club Site
Goldsmith Recreation Ground,
Crowborough
☎ (01892) 664827 & (01203) 694995
fax: (01203) 694886
Pitch price £9.30–£10 per night.

WHERE TO EAT

RESTAURANTS

❀ Honours Mill
87 High St, Edenbridge
☎ (01732) 866757
Generous portions of expensive, mainly
French food served in a converted watermill.
Lunch: 12-2; from £15.50
Dinner: 7-10; from £26
Credit cards 1 3

❀❀ La Bonne Auberge
Tilburstow Hill, South Godstone
☎ (01342) 892318
fax: (01342) 893435
Interesting French country cooking in a
quiet rural setting.
Lunch: 12-1.45
Dinner: 7-10
Credit cards 1 2 3 5

❀❀ Thackeray's House
85 London Rd, Royal Tunbridge Wells
☎ (01892) 511921
fax: (01892) 511921
A smart restaurant offering a good choice of
modern cooking.
Lunch: 12.30-2; £12 and à la carte
Dinner: 7-10; £24.50 and à la carte

Ludlow

Located close to the Welsh border in some pretty Shropshire countryside is this homely track in the centre of which is a nine-hole golf course. Crowds include a fair proportion of local farmers who know and love their sport and there is a tremendous country feel to the place.

This is enhanced by outlets selling freshly baked home-made food, while a more traditional sit-down meal can be obtained in the main grandstand.

All twelve or so jump meetings are held mid-week and usually feature a long-distance handicap chase as the main event. A peculiarity of the course is that six lines of coconut matting have to be put down to cover the roads that cut across it. On one infamous occasion, jockeys were alarmed to discover that they had an even trickier obstacle to negotiate in the shape of a car that had been inadvertently parked on the track! Miraculously, everyone safely avoided the vehicle. Such bloomers by officials are thankfully a thing of the past, and Ludlow is now a very professionally run course which at the same time still manages to retain its informal character.

FURTHER INFORMATION

Ludlow Race Club Ltd
Shepherd's Meadow, Eaton Bishop, Hereford
HR2 9UA
☎ (01981) 250052

LOCATION AND HOW TO GET THERE

The course is about 2 miles north of Ludlow on the B4365, just off the A49 Shrewsbury-Hereford road. From the M5 junction 6 take the A449 towards Kidderminster; turn left onto the A4025 to Stourport on Severn; leave Stourport on the B4195 Bewdley road, then turn left onto the A456. Branch right onto the A4117 and later turn right to join the Ludlow bypass. From the M54 junction 7 take the A5 towards Shrewsbury, then take the A49 southwards to Ludlow.

Nearest Railway Station: Ludlow; there is no connecting bus service to the course.

ADMISSION

Tote Credit Office available in Members' Enclosure only; Betting shop available in Members' and Tattersalls only.

Day Tickets:
MEMBERS £14 – access to bars, restaurants, private rooms and toilet for disabled racegoers

TATTERSALLS £9 – access to bar and snack bar

COURSE £4 – access to bar and snacks, railside parking and picnic area

Annual membership: £90, junior (16-21) £50

Please note: these are 1997 prices and are subject to review in 1998.

COURSE FACILITIES

Banks:
there are no banks or cashpoint facilities on the course.

For families:
picnic area with refreshment kiosk and toilets; baby changing facilities

CALENDAR OF EVENTS

January 6 – jumping	May 4
January 22	October 8
February 11	October 21
March 5	November 12
March 25	November 23
April 8	December 10
April 24 – evening meeting	December 22

WHERE TO STAY

HOTELS

★★★ 🏵🏵 69% Dinham Hall
Ludlow
☎ (01584) 876464, fax: (01584) 876019
11 bedrooms; double B&B £95-£125
Credit cards 1 2 3 5

★★★ 🏵🏵 73% Overton Grange
☎ (01584) 873500, fax: (01584) 873524
15 bedrooms; double B&B £81-£92
Credit cards 1 2 3 5

★★★ 🏵 70% The Feathers at Ludlow
Bull Ring
☎ (01584) 875261, fax: (01584) 876030
39 bedrooms; double B&B £88-£140
Credit cards 1 2 3 5

★★ 65% Dinham Weir
Dinham Bridge
☎ (01584) 874431
8 bedrooms; double B&B £65-£85
Credit cards 1 2 3 5

★★ 63% Cliffe
Dinham
☎ (01584) 872063
fax: (01584) 873991
9 bedrooms; double B&B £52-£58
Credit cards 1 2 3

Around Ludlow

★★🏵 71% Mynd House
Little Stretton, Church Stretton
☎ (01694) 722212, fax: (01694) 724180
8 bedrooms; double B&B £50-£80
Credit cards 1 2 3

★★ 65% Talbot
West St, Leominster
☎ (01568) 616347, fax: (01568) 614880
20 bedrooms; double B&B £54-£66
Credit cards 1 2 3 5

★★ 59% Royal Oak
South St, Leominster
☎ (01568) 612610, fax: (01568) 612710
18 bedrooms; double B&B £45-£55
Credit cards 1 2 3 5

★ (RED) 🏵🏵 Marsh Country
Eyton, Leominster
☎ (01568) 613952
5 bedrooms; double B&B £120
Credit cards 1 2 3 5

★★ 64% Cadmore Lodge
Tenbury Wells
☎ (01584) 810044, fax; (01584) 810044
14 bedrooms; double B&B £65-£140
Credit cards 1 3

BED AND BREAKFAST

QQQ Cecil
Sheet Rd
☎ (01584) 872442
fax: (01584) 872442
Very well maintained modern bungalow;
friendly proprietors; home cooked meals.
10 bedrooms; double B&B £38-£52
Credit cards 1 2 3

QQQQQ Number Twenty Eight
28 Lower Broad St
☎ (01584) 876996
fax: (01584) 876860
Attractive half-timbered town house;
welcoming proprietors and well equipped
bedrooms.
4 bedrooms; double B&B £50-£70

QQQ The Church
The Buttercross
☎ (01584) 872174
fax: (01584) 877146
Smart little town centre hotel. Prettily
decorated rooms with modern facilities.
8 bedrooms; double B&B £45
Credit cards 1 3

QQQQ Moor Hall
☎ (01584) 823209
fax: (01584) 823387
Georgian Palladian style house in attractive
gardens.
3 bedrooms; double B&B £37-£45

Around Ludlow

QQQQ Chadstone
Aston Munslow
☎ (01584) 841675
Modern bungalow in a small hamlet, with
views of the countryside. Friendly owners.
5 bedrooms

QQQQQ The Hills
Leysters, Leominster
☎ (01568) 750205
fax: (01568) 750205
Fifteenth-century farmhouse with old
timbers and lots of character; friendly
owners.
6 bedrooms; double B&B £46-£50
Credit cards 1 3

QQQQ Strefford Hall
Strefford
☎ (01588) 672383
fax: (01588) 672383
Imposing Victorian house with 3 spacious
bedrooms; set in its own pretty gardens.
3 bedrooms; double B&B £38

Q Compasses Hotel
Wigmore
☎ (01568) 770203
fax: (01568) 770705
Ivy-clad village inn; abundance of ceiling
beams and wall timbers.
4 bedrooms; double B&B from £36
Credit cards 1 2 3 5

CAMPSITES

► Engine & Tender Inn
Broome
☎ (01588) 660275
Northwest of Ludlow; pitch price £2-£4 per
night.

WHERE TO EAT

RESTAURANTS

❀❀ Dinham Hall
Ludlow
☎ (01584) 876464
fax: (01584) 876019
A short but imaginative menu.
Lunch: 12-2 ;£10.50
Dinner: 7-9, £27.50

❀ Feathers at Ludlow
Bull Ring
☎ (01584) 875261
fax: (01584) 876030
Good English cooking is the theme here.
Lunch: from £13.50
Dinner: 7.30-9; £16.95 and à la carte

❀❀ The Marsh Country Hotel
Eyton, Leominster
☎ (01568) 613952
A balanced menu of honest British dishes
based on quality fresh produce.
Dinner: 7-9

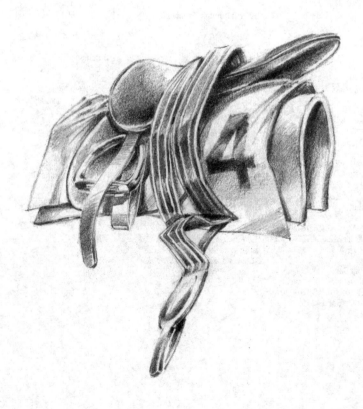

Market Rasen

Market Rasen is the sole surviving course in Lincolnshire. The lack of local competition has helped this friendly track to grow and prosper in recent times so that meetings are always well attended even though its location is fairly isolated. The grandstand has undergone a steady programme of improvements and offers some of the best viewing that can be found on any racecourse.

There is a wide selection of bars and restaurants, with the standard of catering being exceptionally high. It is also an excellent venue for families, as there is a particularly good children's playground which should keep the youngsters occupied.

The racing is over the jumps on a sharp oval circuit. Most of the fences are relatively soft although the second last is a notorious exception, causing all manner of mishaps in recent years. Fixtures take place here throughout the National Hunt season and sizeable crowds are always in evidence on Boxing Day and Easter Monday. Easily the most popular occasions, though, are the summer Saturday evening meetings, so make sure to book ahead.

FURTHER INFORMATION

The Racecourse Office
Market Rasen Racecourse Ltd, Legsby Road,
Market Rasen, Lincs LN8 3EA
Telephone (01673) 843434
Fax: (01673) 844532

LOCATION AND HOW TO GET THERE

The course is in Legsby Road, Market Rasen and is reached via the A46 and the A631.
Nearest Railway Station: Market Rasen; there is no connecting bus service to the course.

ADMISSION

All classes of day ticket give access to full betting facilities, including Tote.

Day Tickets:
Accompanied children under 16 are admitted free.

MEMBERS £12.50 evening meetings and Bank Holidays – access to à la carte restaurant, champagne and seafood bar, members' bar, boxes.

TATTERSALLS £8.50 – access to pre-parade and parade rings and winners' enclosure, bars, snack bars, information kiosk and facilities for disabled racegoers.

SILVER RING £5 – access to bars, fish and chip restaurant, toilets for disabled racegoers

Annual membership: £95 single, £165 dual (husband and wife) £55 junior (16-24 years)

COURSE FACILITIES

Banks:
there are no banks or cashpoint facilities on the course.

For families:
picnic area, children's play area

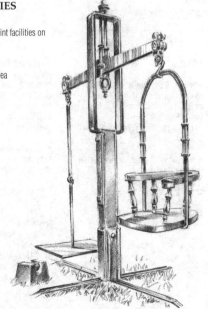

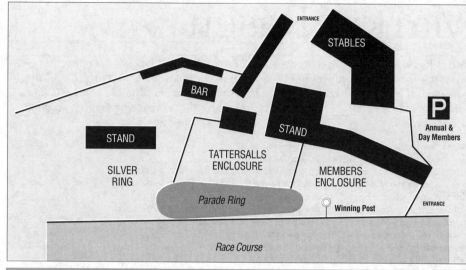

CALENDAR OF EVENTS

January 8
February 14
March 13
April 13
April 25
May 30 – evening meeting
June 12-13 – evening meeting on Friday
July 3
July 25
August 1 – evening meeting

August 8
August 22 – evening meeting
September 19
October 4
October 24
November 14
November 24
December 10
December 26

WHERE TO STAY

HOTELS

★★★★ 63% The White Hart
Bailgate, Lincoln
☎ (01522) 526222
fax: (01522) 531798
48 bedrooms; double bedroom £105-£110
Credit cards 1 2 3 5

★★★ 64% Washingborough Hall
Country House
Church Hill, Washingborough
☎ (01522) 790340
fax: (01522) 792936
14 bedrooms; double B&B £79-£91
Credit cards 1 2 3 5

Forte Posthouse
Eastgate
☎ (01522) 520341
fax: (01522) 510780
70 bedrooms; double room from £99 (room only)
Credit cards 1 2 3 5

★★ 69% Hillcrest
15 Lindum Ter
☎ (01522) 510182
fax: (01522) 510182
17 bedrooms; double B&B £65-£67
Credit cards 1 2 3

Travel Inn
Lincoln Rd, Cantwick Hill, Lincoln
☎ (01522) 525216
fax: (01522) 542521
40 bedrooms; double bedroom £36.50

★★ 67% Castle
Westgate
☎ (01522) 538801
fax: (01522) 575457
19 bedrooms; double B&B £65-£75
Credit cards 1 3

★★★ 64% Beaumont
Victoria Rd, Louth
☎ (01507) 605005
fax: (01507) 607768
17 bedrooms; double room £60-£75 (room only)
Credit cards 1 2 3

WHERE TO STAY

BED AND BREAKFAST

QQQ The Old Vicarage
School Ln, Hainton
☎ (01507) 313660
Quiet, relaxing guesthouse, friendly
proprietors, brightly decorated bedrooms.
3 bedrooms; double B&B £35

QQQQ D'Isney Place Hotel
Eastgate, Lincoln
☎ (01522) 538881
fax: (01522) 511321
Georgian town house; excellent spacious
bedrooms, furnished in period style
18 bedrooms; double B&B £69
Credit cards 1 2 3 5

QQQQ Carline
1-3 Carline Rd, Lincoln
☎ (01522) 530422
Good quality accommodation; attractive,
comfortable bedrooms.
12 bedrooms; double B&B £34-£40

QQQQ Minster Lodge Hotel
3 Church Ln, Lincoln
☎ (01522) 513220, fax: (01522) 513220
Located in the upper part of the city, with
high standards of housekeeping.
6 bedrooms; double B&B £50-£60
Credit cards 1 3

QQQQ Greenfield Farm
Horncastle
☎ (01507) 578457
3 bedrooms; double B&B £38-£40

QQQ Tennyson Hotel
7 South Park, Lincoln
☎ (01522) 521624
fax: (01522) 521624
Extremely well kept, comfortable
guesthouse.
8 bedrooms; double B&B £40
Credit cards 1 2 3 5

CAMPSITES

**►►► Walesby Woodlands Caravan
Park**
Walesby Rd, Market Rasen
☎ (01673) 843285
Pitch price from £6.50 per night.

►►► Racecourse Caravan Park
Legsby Rd, Market Rasen
☎ (01673) 842307 & 843434
fax: (01673) 844532
One mile southeast of town centre off
A63 Louth road.

WHERE TO EAT

RESTAURANTS

❀ Wig & Mitre
29 Steep Hill, Lincoln
☎ (01522) 535190
fax: (01522) 532402
English food, ranging from light to
substantial,served in a convivial medieval
inn.
Lunch: £18.50 à la carte
Dinner: Last dinner 11pm

❀❀ Kenwick Park Hotel
Louth
☎ (01507) 608806
fax: (01507) 608027
Golfing hotel with extensive leisure
facilities, serving sound modern cooking.

Musselburgh

Until recently called Edinburgh, the site of this racecourse is some eight miles to the east of Scotland's capital city. Its location, the the sea-shore whose beaches overlook the Firth of Forth, usually helps to protect the course from extremes of weather and racing is rarely abandoned here.

Indeed, it has even been known for a meeting to go ahead when neighbouring areas are completely covered under a blanket of snow, so favoured by a mild climate is this coastal venue. The sharp mile and a quarter oval circuit is very level, suiting front-runners who accordingly have an excellent record at the track. It was originally devoted solely to Flat racing until the decision was taken to develop it into a dual purpose course with the successful introduction of jump meetings in the 1980s. Admission charges are cheap compared to most southern racetracks, and a recent addition is the Queen's Hospitality Stand.

FURTHER INFORMATION

Lothian Racing Syndicate Ltd
Racecourse Office, 2 Whitletts Road
Ayr KA8 0JE
☎ (01292) 264179 or (01620) 827332
Fax: (0131) 6532083

LOCATION AND HOW TO GET THERE

The course is east of the city at Musselburgh, off the A1. Leave the M8 at junction 2, take the A8 towards Edinburgh, then follow the ring road. **Nearest Railway Station:** Musselburgh; there is no connecting bus service to the course.

ADMISSION

All classes of day ticket give access to full betting facilities, including Tote Accompanied children under 16 free.

Day Tickets:
CLUB £12 – access to bar, restaurant, private rooms

GRANDSTAND £6, senior citizens £3 – access to bar, restaurant and snack bar Reductions for groups of 10 or more, booked in advance.

Annual membership: £100; ladies £70; juniour £50; disabled half price.

COURSE FACILITIES

Banks:
there are no banks or cashpoint facilities on the course

For families:
picnic area; children play area; lost children centre

CALENDAR OF EVENTS

January 3 – jumping
January 7 – jumping
January 16 – jumping
February 3 – jumping
February 18 – jumping
February 28
April 9 – flat
May 1 – flat
May 6 – flat
May 18 – flat; evening meeting
May 30 – evening meeting
June 15 – flat

June 22 – flat
June 29 – flat; evening meeting
July 6 – flat
August 19 – flat
August 27 – flat
September 14 – flat
September 27
November 4 – flat
December 15 – jumping
December 29 – jumping

WHERE TO STAY

HOTELS

★★★★★🏵🏵🏵 70% Sheraton Grand
1 Festival Sq
☎ 0131-229 9131, fax: 0131-228 4510
261 bedrooms; double bedroom £157-£225
Credit cards 1 2 3 5

★★★★★🏵🏵 66% Caledonian
Princes St
☎ 0131-459 9988
fax: 0131-225 6632
236 bedrooms; double bedroom £209-£325
Credit cards 1 2 3 5

★★★★★🏵🏵 71% Balmoral
Princes St
☎ 0131-556 2414
fax: 0131-557 8740
186 bedrooms; double bedroom £150-£245
Credit cards 1 2 3 5

★★★★🏵 67% Carlton Highland
North Bridge
☎ 0131-556 7277
fax: 0131-556 2691
197 bedrooms; double B&B £176-£205
Credit cards 1 2 3 5

★★★★🏵72% George Inter-Continental
19-21 George St
☎ 0131-225 1251, fax: 0131-226 5644
195 bedrooms; double bedroom £115-£190
Credit cards 1 2 3 5

★★★🏵 71% Channings
South Learmonth Gardens
☎ 0131-315 2226, fax: 0131-332 9631
48 bedrooms; double B&B £125-£175
Credit cards 1 2 3 5

★★★ 70% King James
107 Leith St
☎ 0131-556 0111
fax: 0131-557 5333
143 bedrooms; double B&B £110-£175
Credit cards 1 2 3 5

★★★★ 🏵🏵 The Howard
Great King St
☎ 0131-557 3500
fax: 0131-557 6515
15 bedrooms; double B&B £195
Credit cards 1 2 3 5

★★★ 64% Barnton Thistle
Queensferry Rd, Barnton
☎ 0131-339 1144
fax: 0131-339 5521
50 bedrooms; double room £100-£115
(room only)
Credit cards 1 2 3 5

★★★ 69% Bruntsfield
69/74 Bruntsfield Place
☎ 0131-229 1393
fax: 0131-229 5634
50 bedrooms; double bedroom £79-£130
Credit cards 1 2 3 5

★★★ 64% Roxburghe
Charlotte Square
☎ 0131-225 3921
fax: 0131-220 2518
75 bedrooms; double B&B £75-£145
Credit cards 1 2 3 5

★★★ 67% Edinburgh Capital Moat House
Clermiston Rd
☎ 0131-535 9988
fax: 0131-334 9712
111 bedrooms; double bedroom £75-£125
Credit cards 1 2 3 5

★★★ 67% Braid Hills
134 Braid Rd, Braid Hills
☎ 0131-447 8888
fax: 0131-452 8477
68 bedrooms
Credit cards 1 2 3 5

Hilton National Edinburgh
69 Belford Rd
☎ (0131)332 2545
fax: (0131) 332 3805
144 bedrooms; double bedroom £110-£150
Credit cards 1 2 3 5

★★★ 63% Holiday Inn Garden Court
107 Queensferry Road
☎ (0131) 332 2442
fax: (0131) 332 3408
119 bedrooms
Credit cards 1 2 3 5

★★★ 58% Old Waverley
Princes St
☎ 0131-556 4648
fax: 0131-557 6316
66 bedrooms; double B&B £144-£152
Credit cards 1 2 3 5

★★ 65% Murrayfield
18 Corstorphine Rd
☎ 0131-337 1844, fax: 0131-346 8159
33 bedrooms
Credit cards 1 2 3 5

Around Edinburgh

★★ 63% Eskbank Hotel
29 Dalhousie Rd, Dalkeith
☎ 0131-663 3234, fax: 0131-660 4347
16 bedrooms; double B&B £60-£80
Credit cards 1 2 3 5

BED AND BREAKFAST

QQ The Adria Hotel
11-12 Royal Ter
☎ 0131-556 7875
Relaxed spacious atmosphere, offering spacious accommodation.
24 bedrooms

QQQQ Brunswick Hotel
7 Brunswick St
☎ 0131-556 1238
fax: 0131-557 1404
Family-run guesthouse with pleasant, well decorated bedrooms.
11 bedrooms; double B&B £50-£90
Credit cards 1 2 3

QQQQ Ellesmere House
11 Glengyle Ter
☎ 0131-229 4823
fax: 0131-229 5285
Delightful, cheery proprietor and spacious, individually decorated bedrooms.
6 bedrooms; double B&B £40-£60

WHERE TO STAY

QQQQQ Drummond House
17 Drummond Place
☎ 0131-557 9189
fax 0131-557 9189
No smoking accommodation in elegant town house.
3 bedrooms
Credit cards 1 3

QQQ Greenside Hotel
9 Royal Ter
☎ 0131-557 0022
fax: 0131-557 0022
Friendly, family-run hotel offering good-value bed and breakfast.
14 bedrooms; double B&B £40-£70
Credit cards 1 2 3 5

QQQQ International
37 Mayfield Gardens
☎ 0131- 667 2511
fax: 0131- 667 1112
Friendly atmosphere and good value bed and breakfast accommodation.
7 bedrooms

QQQ The Newington
18 Newington Rd
☎ 0131-667 3356
Delightful accommodation with lots of character.
8 bedrooms

QQQ Ravensnuek
11 Blacket Av
☎ 0131-667 5347
fax: 0131-667 5347
A tastefully restored semi-detached Victorian house in a quiet avenue on the south side of the city.
7 bedrooms
Credit cards 1 2 3

QQQ Meadows Guest House
17 Glengyle Terrace
☎ 0131-229 9559
fax: 0131-229 2226
A relaxed, comfortable guest house in a residential area.
6 bedrooms
Credit cards 1 2 3

QQQ Elder York Guest House
38 Elder St
☎ 0131-556 1926
Well-decorated bedrooms and good breakfasts.
13 bedrooms

QQQ Terrace Hotel
37 Royal Terrace
☎ 0131-556 3423, fax; 0131-556 2520
Fashionable Georgian town house with well-maintained bedrooms and hearty breakfasts.
14 bedrooms; double B&B £43-£70
Credit cards 1 3

Q Halcyon Hotel
8 Royal Terrace
☎ 0131-556 1033
fax: 0131-556 1032
Good value, practical accommodation just east of city centre.
16 bedrooms

QQQ Salisbury View Hotel
64 Dalkeith Rd
☎ 0131-667 1133
fax: 0131-667 1133
Accommodation throughout is tastefully decorated and fitted with comfort in mind.
8 bedrooms; double B&B £52-£64
Credit cards 1 3 4 5

QQQ Stra'ven
3 Brunstane Rd North, Joppa
☎ 0131-669 5580
fax: 0131 657 2517
Fine semi-detached Victorian house close to beach and 3 miles east of city centre.
7 bedrooms

QQQQ Stuart House
12 East Claremont St
☎ 0131-557 9030, fax: 0131-557 0563
North of city; well appointed bedrooms.
7 bedrooms; double B&B £60-£78
Credit cards 1 2 3

QQQ Classic House
50 Mayfield Road
☎ 0131-667 5847
fax: 0131-662 1016
A popular 16th-century inn, carefully restored with exposed brickwork and beams.
4 bedrooms; double B&B £40-£60
Credit cards 1 3 5

Around Edinburgh

QQQ Olde Original Rosslyn
4 Main St, Roslin
☎ 0131-440 2384
fax: 0131-440 2514
Attractive village inn, 7 miles from Edinburgh;
pretty well appointed bedrooms.
6 bedrooms
Credit cards 1 2 3 5

CAMPSITES

►►►► Mortonhall Caravan Park
38 Mortonhall Gate, Frogston Rd East
☎ 0131-664 1533, fax; 0131-664 5387
On the south side of Edinburgh, a large site with high standards; pitch price £7.75-£12 per night

►►►► Drum Mohr Caravan Park
Levenhall
☎ 0131-665 6867
fax: 0131-653 6859
Attractive park 2 miles east of Musselburgh between A198 and B1348; pitch price £7.50-£8.50 per night

►►► Fordel
Lauder Rd, Dalkeith
☎ 0131-663 3046
fax: 0131-663 8891
Small site on A68; pitch price £7-£12.50 per night

WHERE TO EAT

RESTAURANTS

❀❀ L'Auberge
56 Saint Mary St, Edinburgh
☎ 0131-556 5888
Elegant, stylish food – and good value at lunchtime.
Lunch: 12-2
Dinner: 7-9.30

❀❀❀ Martins
70 Rose St, North Lane, Edinburgh
☎ 0131-225 3106
Great warmth and friendliness, and satisfying modern British food with an organic emphasis.
Lunch: 12-2
Dinner: 7-10

❀❀❀ Atrium
Cambridge St
☎ 0131-228 8882
Modern Scottish cooking in avant-garde setting.
Lunch: 12-2.30
Dinner: 6-9.30

❀❀ Duck's at Le Marche Noir
2/4 Eyre Place
☎ 0131-558 1608
Mainly contemporary French dishes.
Lunch: 12-2.30
Dinner: 7-10

❀❀ The Vintners Room
The Vaults, 87 Giles St, Leith
☎ 0131-554 6767
fax: 0131-467 7130
Confident, highly enjoyable provincial French and modern cooking in atmospheric, relaxed period setting.
Lunch: 12-3.30; £13 and à la carte
Dinner: 6-12; £25 à la carte

❀❀ Caledonian
Princes St
☎ 0131-459 9988
fax: 0131-225 6632
A elegant hotel with a choice of two restaurants.
Dinner: 7.30-10.30, £35 and à la carte

❀❀ No.1 The Restaurant
Balmoral Hotel, Princes St
☎ 0131-556 2414; fax: 0131-557 3747
Scottish cooking of international standard.
Lunch 12-2.30; £19.95 and à la carte
Dinner: 7-10.30; £29.50 and à la carte

❀ Carlton Highland
North Bridge
☎ 0131-556 7277; fax: 0131-556 2691
A range of Scottish and international dishes.
Lunch: 12-2.30; from £14.50 and à la carte
Dinner: 7-10.30, £21.50 and à la carte

❀ George Inter-Continental
19-21 George St
☎ 0131-459 2506
fax: 0131-226 5644
French-style dishes made from good Scottish produce.
Lunch: from £17.95 and à la carte
Dinner: from £17.95 and à la carte

PUBS

The Tattler
23 Commercial Street, Leith
☎ 0131-554 9999
fax: 0131-226 5936
A pleasant and cosy pub near the harbour and river. Range of real ales and excellent wine list. Bar menu includes good fish dishes. Children are permitted into pub, but not allowed to stand at the bar.
Principal beers: Burton, Tetley, Carlsberg
Open: all day, every day
Bar food: 12.30-2pm, 6-10pm
Saturday and Sunday 12-10pm
Restaurant: hours as bar food

Newbury

This is one of the foremost racing venues in this country and it is very rare for anyone to leave this wonderful course disappointed. Newbury caters for virtually every requirement with some superb facilities in the Berkshire Stand.

The terrific range of restaurants would do justice to a first-rate hotel and there are also plenty of stalls selling seafood and snacks for those who want a quicker bite to eat. Another major advantage here is the almost unparalleled view of the action that can be obtained from the top of stands. However, be warned that the town of Newbury continues to suffer from traffic congestion, so either set off early or go by train.

The wide oval track finds almost universal favour among trainers and consequently runners tend to be of the highest quality at the 28 or so fixtures that are held here under both codes. The list of important races is long, but a couple that warrant a special mention are the Dubai Duty Free Fred Darling and Tripleprint Greenham Stakes, both important Classic trials that are run at a two-day meeting in mid-April. Over the jumps, the Tote Gold Trophy in February is always a competitive contest, but the course really saves the best to last in the shape of the Hennessy Gold Cup in late November, one of the most prestigious handicap chases of the entire season. A new addition is the Dubai Duty Free International Raceday on the first day of the September Festival.

FURTHER INFORMATION

Newbury Racecourse
Newbury, Berkshire RG14 7NZ
☎ (01635) 40015/41485; fax:(01635) 528354

LOCATION AND HOW TO GET THERE

The course is in the town, just off the A34. Racegoers from the London direction should leave the M4 at junction 12 (Theale) and continue to Newbury on the A4; those from the west should leave at junction 13 and continue south on the A34. **Nearest Railway Station:** Newbury Racecourse; the station is a few yards from the course and has a special raceday timetable. Produce your ticket and get a £2 discount to Members (except Hennessy Day). By air: the racecourse has a landing strip suitable for light aircraft on race days.
☎ (01635) 40015.

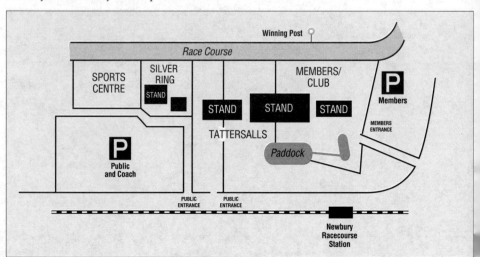

ADMISSION

All classes of day ticket give access to full betting facilities, including Tote.

Day Tickets:
Accompanied children under 17 admitted free; senior citizens half price in Silver Ring; parking free, except Picnic Car Park.

MEMBERS OR CLUB £14 – £17, £25 for Hennessy Cognac Gold Cup Day; Seat £5 on Feature and Premium Days – access to Berkshire Stand, Hampshire Stand, paddock, winners enclosure, saddling up boxes, bars, restaurants, lift and wheelchair viewing for disabled racegoers.

TATTERSALLS £8 – £10, £12 on Hennessy Cognac Gold Cup Day – access to paddock and winners' enclosure, stepped viewing and 2nd floor viewing deck on Berkshire Stand, bars, grill room, fish bar, and other refreshments, large private room for hire

SILVER RING £4, £5 on Hennessy Cognac Gold Cup Day – access to viewing within last furlong before winning post, parking beside rails, bars, refreshments.

PICNIC CAR PARK £3, £4 on Hennessy Cognac Gold Cup Day – access as Silver Ring.

Annual membership: Single £175, double £320 to include one non-transferable badge and one transferable badge; junior member £80; annual bench reservation £60; annual seat reservation £50 – includes car park label and reciprocal arrangements with certain other courses, including Arlington International Racecourse, Chicago. Joining fee £25.

COURSE FACILITIES

Banks:
There are no banks or cashpoint facilities on the course.

For families:
Picnic area with refreshment kiosk and toilets, children's play area, baby changing facilities, lost children centre; Rocking Horse Nursery provides creche for patrons of Club, Tattersalls and Silver Ring.

CALENDAR OF EVENTS

January 2-3 – jumping
February 13-14 – jumping; includes Tote Gold Trophy and Game Spirit Steeple Chase on Saturday
March 6-7 – jumping
March 27-28 – jumping
April 17-18 – flat; includes Dubai Duty Free Fred Darling Stakes, Lanes End John Porter Stakes, Tripleprint Greenham Stakes and Ladbroke Spring Cup
May 15-16 – flat; includes Juddmonte Lockinge Stakes, Vodafone Group Fillies Trial Stakes, Quantel Aston Park Stakes, London Gold Cup and Winchester Stakes
May 27 – evening meeting; flat
June 11 – flat; includes Kingsclere Stakes, Ballymacoll Stud Stakes
July 12 – flat
July 17-18 – flat; includes Ruinart Hackwood Stakes, Weatherbys Super Sprint and Rose Bowl Stakes
August 14-15 – flat; includes Grosvenor Casinos Hungerford Stakes and Tripleprint Geoffrey Freer Stakes
September 17-19 – flat; includes Mill Reef Stakes
October 23-24 – flat
November 11-12 – jumping
November 29-30 – jumping; Hennessy Cognac Gold Cup Meeting

WHERE TO STAY

HOTELS

★★★★⚜⚜ 78% Donnington Valley
Old Oxford Rd, Donnington
☎ (01635) 551199, fax: (01635) 551123
58 bedrooms; double room £90-£130
Credit cards 1 2 3 5

★★★ 61% Millwaters
London Rd
☎ (01635) 528838
fax: (01635) 523406
30 bedrooms; double room £50-£90
Credit cards 1 2 3 5

★★★ 61% The Chequers
Oxford St
☎ (01635) 38000
fax: (01635) 37170
56 bedrooms; double room £80
Credit cards 1 2 3 5

Around Newbury

★★★ ⚜⚜ Hollington Country House
Woolton Hill, nr Highclere
☎ (01635) 255100
fax: (01635) 255075
20 bedrooms; double B&B £120
Credit cards 1 2 3 5

Hilton National Newbury
Pinchington
☎ (01635) 529000
fax: (01635) 529337
109 bedrooms; double bedroom £78-£102

★★ 65% Three Swans
117 High St, Hungerford
☎ (01488) 682721
fax: (01488) 681708
15 bedrooms; double room£70
Credit cards 1 2 3 5

★★★ ⚜ 68% Esseborne Manor
Hurstbourne Tarrant
☎ (01264) 736444
ax: (01264) 736725
12 bedrooms
Credit cards 1 2 3 5

★★★★ ⚜⚜ 72% Regency Park
Bowling Green Rd, Thatcham
☎ (01635) 871555
fax: (01635) 871571
50 bedrooms; double room £99-£110
(room only)
Credit cards 1 2 3 5

★★ ⚜⚜⚜ 76% Royal Oak
The Square, Yattendon
☎ (01635) 201325
fax: (01635) 201926
5 bedrooms; double B&B from £95
Credit cards 1 2 3 4 5

BED AND BREAKFAST

QQQ Marshgate Cottage Hotel
March Ln, Hungerford
☎ (01488) 682307
fax: (01488) 685475
Cosy bedrooms and public areas full of
character; informal friendly atmosphere.
9 bedrooms; double B&B £48.50
Credit cards 1 2 3

QQQQ Lodge Down
The Woodlands, Lambourne
☎ (01672) 540304
fax: (01672) 540304
Attractive farmhouse in tranquil countryside
with period furnished bedrooms.
3 bedrooms; double B&B from £45

WHERE TO EAT

RESTAURANTS

⚜⚜⚜ Royal Oak
The Square, Yattendon
☎ (01635) 201325
fax: (01635) 201926
A good range of carefully cooked dishes in
a lovely old village inn.
Lunch: 11-2.30
Dinner: 7-10

⚜⚜ Hollington House
Woolton Hill, Newbury
☎ (01635) 255100
Enjoyable cooking in a delightfully friendly
atmosphere.
Lunch: 12-2; from £19 and à la carte
Dinner: 7-9.30; £39 à la carte

⚜ Esseborne Manor
Hurstbourne Tarrant
☎ (01264) 736444
fax: (01264) 736725
Good-value menus offering a range of
traditional dishes.
Lunch: 12-2.30; from £13 and à la carte
Dinner: 7-9.30; £17 and à la carte

⚜⚜ Regency Park
Bowling Green Rd, Thatcham
☎ (01635) 871555
Excellent fresh cooking of modern
English/French cuisine.
Lunch: 12-2.30
Dinner: 7-10.30

⚜ Romans
Little London Rd, Silchester
☎ (01189) 700421
English/French cuisine featuring
imaginative dishes.
Lunch: 12-2, from £18
Dinner: 7-9.30, from £18

⚜⚜⚜ The Dew Pond
Old Burghclere
☎ (0163527) 408
Reasonably priced, imaginative use of local
ingredients in an off-the-beaten-path
location.
Dinner: 7-10; £23
Credit cards 1 3

WHERE TO EAT

PUBS

Bell Inn
Aldworth
☎ (01635) 578272
Established in 1314 and run by the same family for some 200 years, this fascinating pub is remarkably unchanged, with stone floors and huge fireplaces. There is an attractive garden, backing onto open fields. Draught beers include Arkell Bitter, Badger Best, Morrell Dark Mild, Hook Norton Best and Kingsdown Bitter; bar food is simple – hot crusty rolls with various fillings – but very popular. Children are welcome.
Open: 11am-3pm, 6-11pm; Sunday 12-3pm, 7-10.30pm; closed Monday, except Bank Holidays
Bar food: as opening times

Bell
Lambourn Rd, Boxford
☎ (01488) 38721
Roomy pub dating back to Tudor times with an attractive garden. Beers include Whitbread Best Bitter, Flowers Original, Boddington Bitter and Wadworth 6X and there is a reasonable list of French and German wines. Daily blackboard specials can be eaten in the bar or the small restaurant. Children are welcome. Occasional jazz evenings when the races are on.
Open: 11am-2.30pm, 6-11pm (closes 10.30pm on Sunday)
Bar food: as opening hours
Restaurant: as opening hours

Pot Kiln
Frilsham, nr Yattendon
☎ (01635) 201366
Secluded 17th-century pub in traditional style. Beers include Arkell, Morland Bitter or West Berkshire and menu includes vegetarian dishes, but on Sunday and Tuesday, only rolls are available. Children are welcome.
Open: 12-3pm, 6.30-11pm; Closed Tues morning
Bar food: 12-2pm, 7-9.30pm

Swan
East Ilsley
☎ (01635) 281238
fax: (01635) 281791
Roomy 16th-century coaching inn in peaceful village location. Beers include Morlands or Old Speckled hen and the menu includes traditional favourites. There is a spacious garden with play area and children are welcome in the pub.
Open: 10.30am-2.30pm, 6-11pm
Bar food: 12-2pm, 6-10pm
Restaurant: as opening hours
Accommodation: double B&B £48-£50

Dundas Arms
53 Station Rd, Kintbury
☎ (01488) 658263 ; fax: (01488) 658559
This charming pub is right beside the Kennet and Avon canal, with lots of tables and chairs by the water's edge. Beers include Morland Original, Spitfire and Charles Wells Bombadier and the menu is varied and interesting. Children are welcome.
Open: 11am-2.30pm, 6.-11pm
Bar food: 12-2pm, 7-9pm, but no food on Sunday or on Monday evening.
Accommodation: double B&B £65-£70

Bull
Stanford Dingley
☎ (01734) 744409
This delightful village inn, dating from the 15th century, offers above average bar food and a friendly welcome. Beers include Brakspear Ordinary and Bass Charrington. Children are welcome and there is outdoor seating.
Open: Tuesday to Saturday 12-3pm, 7-11pm; Sunday 12-3pm, 7-10.30pm
Bar food: as opening hours

Harrow
West Ilsley
☎ (01635) 28260
An imaginative menu of country dishes, including a renowned rabbit pie, are on offer here together with beers such as Morland Original, Old Masters and Old Speckled Hen. The building is very old, with lots of character in the comfortable bar, and there is a pleasant garden.
Open: 11am-3pm, 6-11pm; Sunday 12-3pm, 7-10.30pm
Bar food: 12-2.15pm, 6-9.15pm; Sunday 12-2.15pm, 7-9.15pm

Newcastle

Like most things in life, the Geordies are passionate about their racing, and well-backed favourites are sure to receive plenty of vocal encouragement from the stands at the northeast venue.

Known locally as Gosforth Park, the course is one of many whose facilities have been significantly upgraded in recent times, a particularly necessary improvement here as it used to be a fairly depressing site. The whole place is much brighter now, thanks to an extensive programme of refurbishment and redevelopment following the aquisition of the course by chairman Stan Clarke in 1994.

Decent racing is to be found at all times of the year. The highlight of the summer is the Saturday fixture in late June featuring the Northumberland Plate, an extremely valuable two-mile handicap. Loads of runners make the long journey up from their southern training centres to participate, resulting in a huge field and open betting market. Jumping fans, meanwhile, get the chance to see some of the top hurdlers in action in the Fighting Fifth, one of the major early season trials for the Champion Hurdle.

FURTHER INFORMATION

High Gosforth Park plc
High Gosforth Park, Newcastle upon Tyne
NE3 5HP
☎ 0191-236 2020

LOCATION AND HOW TO GET THERE

The course is north of the city, beyond Gosforth and is easily accessible from the A1; from the A19 northbound, about 4 miles beyond North Shields, turn left onto the A1056, crossing the A189 to reach the course.

Nearest Railway Station: Newcastle Central; from here transfer to Metro train to Regent Centre or Four Lane End stations, from where free buses or taxis run to the course.

ADMISSION

CLUB £12-£20 - access to restaurant and bar. Members also admitted free to Uttoxeter

TATTERSALLS £10 - access to restaurant, bar, snack bar, fast food

SILVER RING £4 - access to snacks, bar and fast food

COURSE FACILITIES

Banks:
there are no banks or cashpoint facilities on the course.

For families:
picnic area

CALENDAR OF EVENTS

January 17 – jumping	**July 27** – flat
February 9 – jumping	**August 2** – flat
February 21 – jumping	**August 5** – flat
March 2 – jumping	**August 31** – flat
March 21 – jumping	**September 8**
March 23 – jumping	**September 30**
March 31 – flat	**October 21** – flat
April 13	**October 30**
May 4 – flat	**November 13** – jumping
May 21 – flat	**November 28** – jumping; 'Fighting Fifth' Hurdle
June 3 – flat	**December 1** – jumping
June 25-27 – flat; evening meeting on Friday	**December 14** – jumping
July 25 – flat; Beeswing Stakes	

WHERE TO STAY

HOTELS

★★★★ ❀ 75% Swallow Gosforth Park
High Gosforth Park, Gosforth
☎ 0191-236 4111
fax: 0191-236 8192
178 bedrooms; double B&B £85-£135
Credit cards 1 2 3 5

★★★★ ❀ 72% The Copthorne
The Close, Quayside
☎ 0191-222 0333
fax: 0191-230 1111
156 bedrooms; double room £99 (room only)
Credit cards 1 2 3 5

★★★ 62% County Thistle
Neville St
☎ 0191-232 2471
fax: 0191-232 1285
115 bedrooms; double room from £84 (room only)
Credit cards 1 2 3 5

Forte Posthouse
New Bridge St
☎ 0191-232 6191
fax: 0191-261 8529
166 bedrooms; double room £79-£89 (room only)
Credit cards 1 2 3 5

★★★ 62% Novotel
Ponteland Rd, Kenton
☎ 0191-214 0303
fax: 0191-214 0633
126 bedrooms; double bedroom £69
Credit cards 1 2 3 5

★★★ ❀ 66% Swallow
Newgate Arcade
☎ 0191-232 5025
fax: 0191-232 8428
93 bedrooms; double B&B £70-£105
Credit cards 1 2 3 5

★★★ 62% New Kent Hotel
Osborne Rd
☎ 0191-281 1083, fax: 0191-281 3369
32 bedrooms
Credit cards 1 2 3 5

★★★★ ❀❀❀ 78% Vermont
Castle Garth
☎ 0191-233 1010, fax: 0191-233 1234
101 bedrooms; double bedroom £89-£135
Credit cards 1 2 3 5

★★★ 69% Imperial Swallow
Jesmond Rd
☎ 0191-281 5511
fax: 0191-281 8472
122 bedrooms; double B&B £70-£105
Credit cards 1 2 3 5

★★★ 61% Hospitality Inn
64 Osborne Rd, Jesmond
☎ 0191-281 7881
fax: 0191-281 6241
89 bedrooms; double B&B from £76-£97
Credit cards 1 2 3 5

★★ 64% Cairn
97/103 Osborne Road, Jesmond
☎ 0191-281 1358
fax: 0191-281 9031
50 bedrooms; double B&B £50-£70
Credit cards 1 2 3 5

Around Newcastle

★★★ 65% Quality Friendly Hotel
Witney Way, Boldon Business Park, Boldon
☎ 0191-519 1999
fax: 0191-519 0655
82 bedrooms; double room £92 (room only)
Credit cards 1 2 3 4 5

★★ 63% Bay
Front St, Cullercoats
☎ 0191-252 3150
17 bedrooms
Credit cards 1 2 3 5

Travelodge
Leam Ln, Wardley, Whitemare Pool, Felling
☎ 0191-438 3333
fax: 0191-438 3333
41 bedrooms; double room £36.50 (room only)
Credit cards 1 2 3

★★★ 68% Swallow
High West St, Gateshead
☎ 0191-477 1105
fax: 0191-478 7214
103 bedrooms; double B&B £95-£105
Credit cards 1 2 3 5

★★ ❀ 74% Eslington Villa
8 Station Rd, Low Fell, Gateshead
☎ 0191-487 6017
fax: 0191-420 0667
12 bedrooms; double B&B £40-£64.50
Credit cards 1 2 3 5

★★★ 64% Airport Moat House
Woolsington
☎ (0191) 401 9988
fax: (01661) 860157
100 bedrooms; double bedroom £80-£115
Credit cards 1 2 3 5

★★★★ 61% Holiday Inn
Great North Rd, Seaton Burn
☎ 0191-201 9988
fax: 0191-236 8091
150 bedrooms; double room £108.50-£134 (room only)
Credit cards 1 2 3 5

★★★ 64% Sea
Sea Rd, South Shields
☎ 0191-427 0999
fax: 0191-454 0500
33 bedrooms; double B&B £80
Credit cards 1 2 3 5

★★★ 61% Park
Grand Pde, Tynemouth
☎ 0191-257 1406
fax: 0191-257 1716
49 bedrooms; double B&B £63-£67
Credit cards 1 2 3 5

WHERE TO STAY

★★★ 71% Gibside Arms
Front St, Whickham
☎ 0191-488 9292
fax: 0191-488 8000
45 bedrooms; double room £45-£64
Credit cards 1 2 3 5

★★ 65% High Point
The Promenade, Whitley Bay
☎ 0191-251 7782, fax: 0191-251 6318
14 bedrooms; double B&B £55-£65
Credit cards 1 2 3 5

★★★ 64% Windsor
South Pde, Whitley Bay
☎ 0191-251 8888, fax: 0191-297 0272
64 bedrooms; double B&B £55-£70
Credit cards 1 2 3 5

★★ 62% Park Lodge Hotel
160-164 Park Av, Whitley Bay
☎ 0191-253 0288
fax: 0191-297 1006
16 bedrooms; double B&B £45-£60
Credit cards 1 2 3 5

★★ 52% Holmedale
106 Park Av, Whitley Bay
☎ 0191-251 3903 & 0191-253 1162,
fax: 0191-253 0053
18 bedrooms
Credit cards 1 2 3 5

★ 61% Cavendish
51 Esplanade, Whitley Bay
☎ 0191-253 3010
11 bedrooms; double B&B £25-£35
Credit cards 1 3

BED AND BREAKFAST

QQQ Chirton House Hotel
46 Clifton Rd
☎ 0191-273 0407
Individually decorated bedrooms; cosy bar
and comfortable lounges.
11 bedrooms; double B&B £34-£44
Credit cards 1 3

QQ The George Hotel
88 Osborne Rd, Jesmond
☎ 0191-281 4442, fax: 0191-281 8300
14 bedrooms
Credit cards 1 2 3 5

Around Newcastle

QQQQQ Hope House
47 Percy Gardens, Tynemouth
☎ 0191-257 1989
fax: 0191-257 1989
Antiques feature in all rooms in this
spacious Victorian house overlooking the
sea.
3 bedrooms
Credit cards 1 2 3 5

QQQ Marlborough Hotel
20-21 East Pde, Central Promenade,
Whitley Bay
☎ 0191-251 3628
fax: 0191-251 3628
Family-owned hotel with spacious
accommodation.
15 bedrooms; double B&B £45-£50
Credit cards 1 2 3

QQQ York House Hotel
30 Park Pde, Whitley Bay
☎ 0191-252 8313
fax: 0191-251 3953
Family-run guesthouse offering sound
accommodation.
8 bedrooms
Credit cards 1 2 3

QQQ Cherrytree House
35 Brook St, Whitley Bay
☎ 0191-251 4306
Close to the seafront; neat accommodation
and friendly service.
4 bedrooms

QQ Bush Blades Farm
Harperley, Stanley
☎ (01207) 232722
Large detached house with three pleasant
bedrooms
3 bedrooms; double B&B £32-£37

CAMPSITES

►►► Derwent Park Caravan Site
Rowlands Gill
☎ (01207) 543383
fax: (01207) 543383
Southwest of Newcastle

►► Lizard Lane Caravan & Camping Site
Lizard Ln, South Shields
☎ 0191-454 4982 & 455 7411
fax: 0191-427 0469
Two miles south of town centre on A183
Sunderland road; pitch price from £8.10 per
night

►► Sandhaven
Bents Park Rd, South Shields
☎ 0191-454 5594 & 455 7411
fax: 0191-427 0469
Situated on A183; pitch price from £7.90
per night

►►► Bobby Shafto Caravan Park
Cranberry Plantation, Beamish
☎ 0191-370 1776
A tranquil, rural site

WHERE TO EAT

RESTAURANTS

✿✿✿ 21 Queen Street
Quayside
☎ 0191-222 0755
fax: 0191-230 5875
A busy, modern restaurant serving a
fashionably eclectic mix of food cooked with
great style.
Lunch: 12-2; from £14.50
Dinner: 7-10.30; from £31.30 a la carte
Credit cards 1 2 3 5

✿✿ Fishermans Lodge
Jesmond Dene, Jesmond,
☎ 0191-281 3281
fax: 0191-281 6410
A speciality seafood restaurant serving
light, modern dishes in an elegant setting.
Lunch: 12-4; £17.80 and a la carte
Dinner: 7-1am; £28.50 and a la carte
Credit cards 1 2 3 5

✿✿ Courtneys
5-7 The Side
☎ 0191-232 5537
Lunch 12-2; from £13 and a la carte
Dinner 7-10.30; from £24 a la carte
Credit cards 1 2 3

✿✿ Forsters
2 St Bedes, Station Rd, Boldon
☎ 0191-519 0929
One of the north's leading restuarants,
serving light modern cooking.
Dinner: 7-10; £17 and a la carte

✿✿✿ Vermont
Castle Garth
☎ 0191-233 1010
Superbly cooked and presented food in a
delightful hotel.
Dinner: £20

✿ Fisherman's Wharf
15 The Side
☎ 0191-232 1057
A predominantly seafood restaurant using
only the best supplies.
Lunch: 12-2; from £10 and a la carte
Dinner: £25 a la carte

✿ Copthorne
The Close, Quayside
☎ 0191-222 0333
Well-presented French dishes with some
elaborate combinations
Dinner: 7.30-10.15, from £30 a la carte

PUBS

Shiremoor House
Middle Engine Lane, New York, North
Shields
☎ 0191-257 6302
An imaginative conversion of an old stone
farm building now houses this pleasant pub
offering good value meals which are both
substantial and interesting. Beers include
Stones, Theakstons, Courage Directors and
draught Bass. Children are allowed in
granary and restaurant only.
Open: 11am-11pm; Sunday 12-3pm, 7-
10.30pm
Bar food: 12-2.30pm, 6-9.30pm (7-9.30pm
on Sunday)
Restaurant: 12-1.30pm, 7-8.30pm

Black Bull
Matfen
☎ (01661) 886330
Attractive stone village-centre pub offering a
wide choice of good-value food. Real ale
includes Newcastle & Scottish and a guest
beer. Children are allowed in family room
and restaurant only.
Open: 11am-3pm, 6-11pm; Sunday 12-
3pm, 7-10.30pm
Bar food: 12-2pm, 6.30-9.30pm
Restaurant: 12-2pm, 7-9.30pm

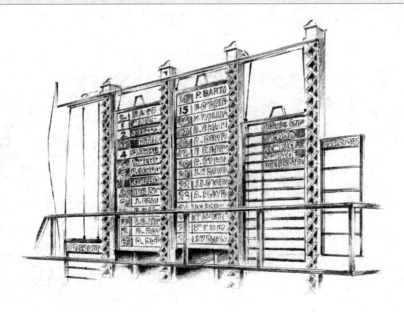

Newmarket

Acknowledged as the 'Horseracing Capital of the World', Newmarket has been the home of the sport of Kings since 1605, when James I and his nobles established racing on the springy turf of Newmarket Heath.

There are two racecourses here - The Rowley Mile, named after King Charles II's favourite hack, Rowley, and the July Course, one of the most beautiful racecourses in the world. Racing on the Rowley Mile is divided into a spring and an autumn session, the spring session featuring the first two classics of the season - the 1000 and 2000 Guineas Stakes. The July Course takes over for the summer months, beginning with the important three-day July Meeting, featuring the TNT International Aviation July Cup, a Group 1 international race which is the most valuable six furlong race in Europe. There are also several very popular evening meetings throughout the year, with a barbeque and live entertainment by top performers immediately after the last race.

FURTHER INFORMATION

Newmarket Racecourses Trust
Westfield House, The Links, Newmarket
CB8 0TG ☎ (01638) 663482; Fax:(01638) 663044

THE NATIONAL HORSERACING MUSEUM

The story of the development of horseracing is told in this museum's five permanent galleries. There is a collection of videos of classic races and displays are changed each year.

Open: end of Mar to beginning of Dec, 10am-5pm Tue to Sat, 12-4pm Sun (10-5 on Sun in Jul and Aug); closed Mon, except during Jul and Aug and Bank Hols. Admission: £3.30, £2 senior citizens, £1 children.

THE NATIONAL STUD

This is one of the most prestigious centres of racehorse breeding and tours are available to visitors, taking in modern purpose-built stable units and, of course, some of the racing stars of the past and the future.

Open: by appointment only: 27 March to 30 Sept plus October race days, Mon to Fri 11.15am and 2.30pm, also Sat mornings when there is racing at Newmarket and most Suns at 2.30pm.
Admission: £3.50, £2.50 for senior citizens, students and children over 5. ☎ (01638) 663464 during office hours

LOCATION AND HOW TO GET THERE

The course is on the western edge of the town. From the M11 (south), take the A11 at junction 9, then at the start of the Newmarket bypass (A45) turn right onto the A1304; from the A1 take the A45 eastwards. **Nearest Railway Station:** Newmarket (unmanned halt) or Cambridge; there is a free bus service to and from Newmarket station, and a service from Cambridge station.

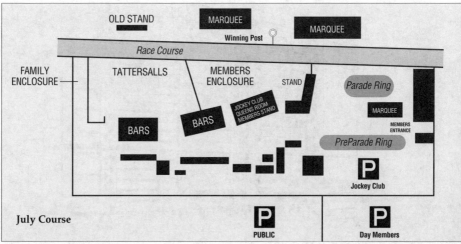

July Course

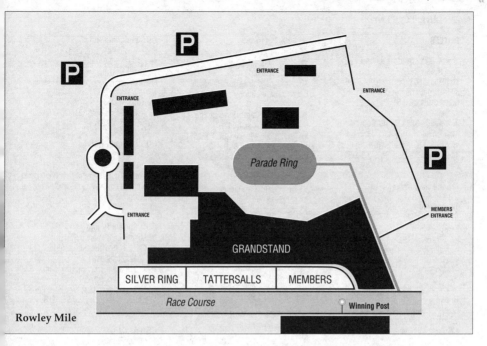

Rowley Mile

ADMISSION

All classes of day ticket give access to full betting facilities, including Tote.

Day Tickets:

MEMBERS £15 normal days, £20 July Meeting, £20 for 1000 Guineas, £23 for 2000 Guineas, William Hill Cambridgeshire and Tote Cesarewitch Days - access to restaurants, bars, private boxes and luncheon rooms. Discounts for Senior citizens & 16-25 year olds

GRANDSTAND AND PADDOCK £10 normal days, £12 special days as listed above - access to bars, snacks and fast food

SILVER RING (FAMILY ENCLOSURE ON JULY COURSE) £3 July Course, £3 Rowley Mile, £5 for special days (see Members Enclosure details) - access to bars, snacks, fast food, childrens supervised adventure playground

Annual membership: £185, £75 juniors

COURSE FACILITIES

Banks:
there are no bank or cashpoint facilities on the course.

For families:
picnic area with refreshment kiosk and toilets in the Family Enclosure on the July Course; children's play area, lost children centre, zoo, pony rides.

CALENDAR OF EVENTS

April 14-16 – Craven Meeting
May 1-3 – includes 1000 Guineas, 2000 Guineas and The Jockey Club Stakes
May 15
May 30
June 6 – evening meeting
June 19 – evening meeting
June 26-27
July 7-9
July 17-18 – Evening Meeting on Friday, Food Brokers Trophy on Saturday
July 24 – evening meeting

July 31-August 1 – evening meeting on Friday
August 7-8 – evening meeting on Friday
August 28-29 – includes the Hopeful Stakes
September 29
October 1-3
October 15-17
October 30-31

WHERE TO STAY

HOTELS

★★★ 72% Bedford Lodge
Bury Road
☎ (01638) 663175, fax: (01638) 667391
56 bedrooms; double B&B £97-£187
Credit cards 1 2 3 5

★★★ ⏣ 68% Heath Court
Moulton Rd
☎ (01638) 667171, fax: (01638) 666533
44 bedrooms; double B&B £65-£95
Credit cards 1 2 3 5

Around Newmarket

Travelodge
A11, Barton Mills
☎ (01638) 717675
fax: (01638) 717675
32 bedrooms; double room £36.50 (room only)
Credit cards 1 2 3

★★★★ ⏣ 66% Cambridge Garden House
Granta Place, Mill Ln, Cambridge
☎ (01223) 259988, fax: (01223) 316605
118 bedrooms; double bedroom £145-£185
Credit cards 1 2 3 5

★★★★ 64% Holiday Inn
Downing St, Cambridge
☎ (01223) 464466, fax: (01223) 464440
199 bedrooms; double room from £125
Credit cards 1 2 3 5

★★★★ 60% University Arms
Regent St, Cambridge
☎ (01223) 351241, fax: (01223) 461319
115 bedrooms; double B&B £80-£140
Credit cards 1 2 3 5

★★★ 72% Gonville
Gonville Pl, Cambridge
☎ (01223) 366611; fax: (01223) 315470
64 bedrooms; double B&B from £101
Credit cards 1 2 3 5

★★★ 66% Royal Cambridge
Trumpington St, Cambridge
☎ (01223) 351631
fax: (01223) 352972
46 bedrooms; double B&B £95-£120
Credit cards 1 2 3 5

★★★ ⏣ 66% Lamb
2 Lynn Rd, Ely
☎ (01353) 663574, fax: (01353) 662023
32 bedrooms; double B&B £80-£100
Credit cards 1 2 3 5

★ 62% Nyton
7 Barton Rd, Ely
☎ (01353) 662459
fax: (01353) 666217
10 bedrooms; double B&B £50-£60
Credit cards 1 2 3 5

★★⏣ 71% Cambridge Lodge
Huntingdon Rd, Cambridge
☎ (01223) 352833, fax: (01223) 355166
11 bedrooms; double B&B £70
Credit cards 1 2 3 5

★★ 68% Centennial
63-71 Hills Rd, Cambridge
☎ (01223) 314652, fax: (01223) 315443
39 bedrooms; double B&B £77-£90
Credit cards 1 2 3 5

★★ ⏣ 71% Arundel House
53 Chesterton Rd, Cambridge
☎ (01223) 367701
fax: (01223) 367721
105 bedrooms; double B&B £57-£89
Credit cards 1 2 3 5

★★★ 64% Smoke House Inn
Beck Row, Mildenhall
☎ (01638) 713223 & 0800 507050 (free)
fax: (01638) 712202
104 bedrooms; double B&B £90
Credit cards 1 2 3 5

★★★ ⏣ 67% Riverside
Mill St, Mildenhall
☎ (01638) 717274
fax: (01638) 715997
20 bedrooms; double B&B £80-£92
Credit cards 1 2 3 5

★★★ ⏣ 72% Swynford Paddocks
Six Mile Bottom
☎ (01638) 570234, fax: (01638) 570283
15 bedrooms; double B&B £122-£152
Credit cards 1 2 3 5

BED AND BREAKFAST

QQQ Helen Hotel
167-169 Hills Rd, Cambridge
☎ (01223) 246465
fax: (01223) 214406
About a mile east of the city centre; well equipped accommodation of a good standard, run by friendly Italian couple.
27 bedrooms
Credit cards 1 2 3 5

QQQ Lensfield Hotel
53 Lensfield Rd, Cambridge
☎ (01223) 355017
fax: (01223) 312022
Friendly, family run hotel on the ring road with a restaurant offering English, French and Greek dishes.
36 bedrooms: double B&B £52-£58
Credit cards 1 2 3 5

QQQ Sorrento Hotel
196 Cherry Hinton Rd, Cambridge
☎ (01223) 243533, fax: (01223) 213463
Welcoming guesthouse with well equipped accommodation and a well-stocked bar.
24 bedrooms
Credit cards 1 2 3 5

QQQ Suffolk House
69 Milton Rd, Cambridge
☎ (01223) 352016
fax: (01223) 566816
Fresh, attractive bedrooms and high standards of housekeeping are offered at this hotel to the north of the city centre.
11 bedrooms; double B&B £50-£68
Credit cards 1 2 3

QQQ Assisi
193 Cherry Hinton Rd, Cambridge
☎ (01223) 211466 & 246648
fax: (01223) 412900
East of the city centre; well equipped accommodation and friendly atmosphere.
17 bedrooms; double B&B £39-£42
Credit cards 1 2 3

QQ Avimore
310 Cherry Hinton Rd, Cambridge
☎ (01223) 410956
fax: (01223) 410956
Small, family run guesthouse near the ring road. Evening meals available with prior notice.
6 bedrooms; double B&B £38-£42
Credit cards 1 3 5

QQ Benson House
24 Huntingdon Rd, Cambridge
☎ (01223) 311594; fax: (01223) 510744
Modest, rather compact bedrooms; close to the city centre on the A604.
5 bedrooms

QQ Bon Accord House
20 St Margarets Sq, Cambridge
☎ (01223) 411188
In a quiet cul-de-sac off the Cherry Hinton road; comfortable accommodation; no smoking.
9 bedrooms
Credit cards 1 3

WHERE TO STAY

QQQ Brooklands
95 Cherry Hinton Rd, Cambridge
☎ (01223) 242035
fax: (01223) 242035
Cosy, family run guesthouse with pretty
bedrooms and comfortable lounge.
5 bedrooms; double B&B £38-£45
Credit cards 1 2 3 5

QQQ Cristina's
47 St Andrews Rd, Cambridge
☎ (01223) 365855 & 327700
fax: (01223) 365855
North of the city centre; bright, clean
accommodation and helpful proprietors.
6 bedrooms

QQQ Fairways
141-143 Cherry Hinton Rd, Cambridge
☎ (01223) 246063, fax: (01223) 212093
Good standard of accommodation, and
always improving range of facilities; bar
meals and small a la carte selection
available in the evening.
15 bedrooms; double B&B £37-£48
Credit cards 1 3

QQQQ De Freville House
166 Chesterton Rd, Cambridge
☎ (01223) 354993, fax: (01223) 321890
Friendly atmosphere in a Victorian house
maintained in its original style; pleasant
basement dining room.
9 bedrooms; double B&B £38-£45

QQQ Hamilton Hotel
156 Chesterton Rd, Cambridge
☎ (01223) 365664
fax: (01223) 314866
Popular, good-value accommodation with a
range of services including bar, snacks and
bar meals.
18 bedrooms
Credit card 1 2 3 5

QQ Hill Farm
Kirtling
☎ (01638) 730253
Traditional 16th-century farmhouse with
modern exterior and comfortable
accommodation.
3 bedrooms; double B&B £40

QQ Hamden
89 High Street, Cherry Hinton, Cambridge
☎ (01223) 413263
fax: (01223) 245960
No-smoking guest house run by friendly
Italian owners.
5 bedrooms; double B&B £40-£45

CAMPSITES

►►► Camping and Caravanning Club Site
19 Cabbage Moor, Great Shelford
☎ (01223) 841185 & (01203) 694995
fax: (01203) 694886
Attractive site with good landscaping; pitch
price £9.30-£10 per night.

WHERE TO EAT

RESTAURANT

❀❀❀ Midsummer House
Midsummer Common, Cambridge
☎ (01223) 369299
Excellent food in a charming restaurant with
four distinctive dining rooms; you would be
well advised to book in advance - and get
directions.
Last lunch: 12.30-1.45; £23 and à la carte
Last dinner: 7-10; £45 and à la carte
Credit cards 1 2 3 5

❀ Cambridge Lodge
139 Huntingdon Rd, Cambridge
☎ (01223) 352833
An imaginative range of dishes.
Lunch: 12-1.45, £15.95 and à la carte
Dinner: 7-9.15; £19.95 and à la carte

❀ Old Fire Engine House
25 St Mary's St, Ely
☎ (01353) 662582
A well-established English restaurant.
Lunch: 12-2, from £21 à la carte
Dinner: 7.30-9; from £21 à la carte

❀ Swynford Paddocks
Six Mile Bottom
☎ (01638) 570234
Imaginative country Irish and French
cuisine.
Lunch: 12-2; £25 à la carte
Dinner: 7-8.30;£25 and à la carte

PUBS

Plough & Fleece
High Rd, Horningsea
☎ (01223) 860795
A 300-year-old pub on the edge of the
village with beams, quarry tiles and a
collection of farm implements. Excellent
home-made food is on offer and beers
include Greene King IPA and Abbott Ale.
Open: 11am-2.30pm, 7-11pm; Sunday 12-
2pm, 7-10.30pm
Bar food: 12-2pm, 7-9.30pm (except Sun-
Mon evening); Sunday 12-1.30pm
Restaurant: 12-2pm, 7-9.30pm; Sunday 12-
1.30pm; (closed Sun-Mon evening.)

Free Press
Prospect Row, Cambridge
☎ (01223) 368337
fax: (01223) 353797
This town pub has engagingly old-
fashioned decor with cricketing and rowing
memorabilia. Good traditional dishes are
served and beers include Green King IPA
and Abbott Ale. There is a sunny patio and
small garden. Children welcome anywhere.
Open: 12-2.30pm, 6-11pm; weekend 12-
3pm, 6-11pm
Bar food: 12-2pm, 6-9pm

Newton Abbot

This is a friendly little West Country course (the furthest west in England) where a high priority has been placed on the creation of a pleasant, laid-back atmosphere. It makes no pretensions to being a glamorous, up-market track; instead, there is an unassuming, down-to-earth feel and it is all the better for that.

The quality of racing may perhaps suffer as a result, but prize money has been substantially boosted in recent seasons and the standard of competition is getting better all the time. In particular, champion trainer Martin Pipe is always a great supporter of meetings here and his runners always merit respect.

August and September are Newton Abbot's busiest time of the year with a cluster of fixtures scheduled during those late summer months in order to attract holiday-makers from the nearby Torbay resorts. Entrance fees are amongst the lowest in the land and it is one of a small band of courses which does not have a separate Members enclosure, presumably due to its lack of space. Facilities are closely grouped together with only a short walk from the paddock to the stands, while the tight track provides excellent viewing and means binoculars are not essential.

All in all, it is well worth paying a visit if taking a holiday in the area.

FURTHER INFORMATION

Newton Abbot Races Ltd
The Racecourse, Kingsteignton Rd
Newton Abbot, Devon TQ12 3AF
☎ (01626) 53235; Fax:(01626) 336972

LOCATION AND HOW TO GET THERE

The course is between Newton Abbot and Kingsteignton. From the end of the M5 continue south, taking the A380 towards Torbay. The Newton Abbot turn-off is thirteen miles from the end of the motorway.
Nearest railway station: Newton Abbot 0.5 mile away.

ADMISSION

Day tickets:
Paddock £10

COURSE £5 - access to restaurants, bars

transfers: Course to Paddock £5

COURSE FACILITIES

Banks:
there are no banks or cashpoint facilities on the course

For families:
picnic area; lost children centre

CALENDAR OF EVENTS

March 9 – jumping
March 18 – jumping
April 11 – jumping
May 1 – jumping
May 20 – jumping; evening meeting
June 6
June 20
June 27 – evening meeting
July 6 – evening meeting
July 30 – evening meeting
August 3 – jumping
August 16 – jumping
August 31 – jumping
September 2 – jumping
September 10 – jumping
October 12
November 4 – jumping
November 17 – jumping

December 1 – jumping
December 14 – jumping
December 26 – jumping

WHERE TO STAY

HOTELS

Around Newton Abbot

★★★ ❀❀❀ **74% Holne Chase**
Ashburton
☎ (01364) 631471f
ax: (01364) 631453
14 bedrooms; double B&B £115-£150
Credit cards 1 2 3 5

★★ **71% Dartmoor Lodge**
Peartree Cross, Ashburton
☎ (01364) 652232
fax: (01364) 653990
30 bedrooms
Credit cards 1 2 3

★★ **60% Norcliffe**
7 Babbacombe Downs Rd, Babbacombe
☎ (01803) 328456
fax: (01803) 328023
27 bedrooms; double B&B & dinner £50-£75
Credit cards 1 3

★ **68% Ashley Rise**
18 Babbacombe Rd, Babbacombe
☎ (01803) 327282
25 bedrooms; double B&B £32-£40

★★★ ❀❀ **70% Edgemoor**
Haytor Rd, Bovey Tracey
☎ (01626) 832466
fax: (01626) 834760
17 bedrooms; double B&B £75-£90
Credit cards 1 2 3 5

★★ **63% Riverside Inn**
Fore St, Bovey Tracey
☎ (01626) 832293
fax: (01626) 833880
10 bedrooms; double B&B £39.50
Credit cards 1 3

★★ **65% Coombe Cross**
Coombe Cross, Bovey Tracey
☎ (01626) 832476
ax: (01626) 835298
26 bedrooms; double B&B £68
Credit cards 1 2 3 5

★★★ **67% Langstone Cliff**
Dawlish Warren, Dawlish
☎ (01626) 865155
fax: (01626) 867166
64 bedrooms
Credit cards 1 2 3 5

★★ **69% Fairwinds**
Kennford
☎ (01392) 832911
fax: (01392) 832911
8 bedrooms; double B&B £49-£52
Credit cards 1 3

★★★★ **62% Manor House**
Moretonhampstead
☎ (01647) 440355, fax: (01647) 440961
89 bedrooms; double B&B £110
Credit cards 1 2 3 5

★★ **74% The White Hart**
The Square, Moretonhampstead
☎ (01647) 40406, fax: (01647) 40565
20 bedrooms; double B&B from £65
Credit cards 1 2 3 5

★★★ **68% Redcliffe**
Marine Dr, Paignton
☎ (01803) 526397, fax: (01803) 528030
59 bedrooms; double B&B £84-£108
Credit cards 1 2 3

★★★ **59% The Palace**
Esplanade Rd, Paignton
☎ (01803) 555121, fax: (01803) 527974
52 bedrooms; double room £75
Credit cards 1 2 3 5

★★ **64% Sunhill**
Alta Vista Rd, Paignton
☎ (01803) 557532, fax: (01803) 663850
30 bedrooms
Credit cards 1 2 3

★★ **68% Preston Sands**
10/12 Marine Pde, Paignton
☎ (01803) 558718
fax: (01803) 522875
31 bedrooms; double B&B £42-£50
Credit cards 1 2 3

★★ **65% Dainton**
95 Dartmouth Rd, Three Beaches,
Goodrington, Paignton
☎ (01803) 550067
fax: (01803) 666339
11 bedrooms; double B&B from £54
Credit cards 1 2 3

WHERE TO STAY

★ **62% South Sands**
Alta Vista Rd, Paignton
☎ (01803) 557231 & 529947
fax: (01803) 529947
19 bedrooms; double B&B £40–£60
including dinner
Credit cards 1 3

★★●●● **68% Sea Trout Inn**
Staverton
☎ (01803) 762274, fax: (01803) 762506
10 bedrooms; double B&B £48–£63
Credit cards 1 2 3

★★ **68% Ness House**
Marine Dr, Shaldon, Teignmouth
☎ (01626) 873480, fax: (01626) 873486
12 bedrooms; double B&B £70–£85
Credit cards 1 2 3

★★ **65% Belvedere**
Parnpark Rd, Teignmouth
☎ (01626) 774561
13 bedrooms; double B&B £40–£45
Credit cards 1 2 3

★ **67% Glenside**
Ringmoor Rd, Shaldon, Teignmouth
☎ (01626) 872448
10 bedrooms; double B&B £36–£50

★★★★★ ● **64% The Imperial**
Park Hill Rd, Torquay
☎ (01803) 294301
fax: (01803) 298293
167 bedrooms; double bedroom £95–£145
Credit cards 1 2 3 5

★★★★ **65% Palace**
Babbacombe Rd, Torquay
☎ (01803) 200200
fax: (01803) 299899
140 bedrooms; double B&B £100–£150
Credit cards 1 2 3 5

★★★★ ● **65% Grand**
Sea Front, Torquay
☎ (01803) 296677, fax: (01803) 213462
112 bedrooms; double B&B £110–£170
Credit cards 1 2 3 5

★★★ ●● **73% Orestone Manor**
Rockhouse Ln, Maidencombe
☎ (01803) 328098
fax: (01803) 328336
18 bedrooms; double B&B £110–£150
Credit cards 1 2 3 5

★★★ ● **77% Corbyn Head**
Torquay Rd, Sea Front, Livermead, Torquay
☎ (01803) 213611
fax: (01803) 296152
51 bedrooms; double B&B £80–£140
Credit cards 1 2 3 5

★★★ **68% Abbey Lawn Hotel**
Scarborough Rd, Torquay
☎ (01803) 299199
fax: (01803) 291460
56 bedrooms; double B&B £86
Credit cards 1 2 3 5

★★★ **70% Livermead Cliff**
Torbay Rd, Torquay
☎ (01803) 299666 & 292881,
fax: (01803) 294496
64 bedrooms; double B&B £65–£118
Credit cards 1 2 3 5

★★★ **66% Belgrave**
Seafront, Torquay
☎ (01803) 296666, fax: (01803) 211308
68 bedrooms
Credit cards 1 2 3 5

★★★ **62% Kistor**
Belgrave Rd, Torquay
☎ (01803) 212632, fax: (01803) 293219
56 bedrooms; double B&B £56–£80
Credit cards 1 2 3

★★★ **66% Toorak**
Chestnut Av, Torquay
☎ (01803) 291444, fax: (01803) 291666
91 bedrooms; double B&B £90–£118
including dinner
Credit cards 1 2 3 5

★★★ **59% Devonshire**
Parkhill Rd, Torquay
☎ (01803) 291123, fax: (01803) 291710
71 bedrooms
Credit cards 1 3 5

★★★ **65% Livermead House**
Torbay Rd, Torquay
☎ (01803) 294361
fax: (01803) 200758
64 bedrooms; double B&B £80–£116
Credit cards 1 2 3 5

★★ **67% Coppice**
Babbacombe Rd, Torquay
☎ (01803) 297786
fax: (01803) 211085
40 bedrooms

★★ **66% Frognel Hall**
Higher Woodfield Rd, Torquay
☎ (01803) 298339
fax:(01803) 215115
28 bedrooms; double B&B £38–£56
Credit cards 1 3

★★ **64% Burlington**
462-466 Babbacombe Rd, Torquay
☎ (01803) 294374, fax: (01803) 200189
55 bedrooms; double B&B £40–£80
Credit cards 1 3

★★ **65% Gresham Court**
Babbacombe Rd, Torquay
☎ (01803) 293007 & 293658
fax: (01803) 215951
30 bedrooms; double B&B £44–£58
Credit cards 1 3

★★ **65% Red House**
Rousdown Rd, Chelston, Torquay
☎ (01803) 607811, fax: (01803) 200592
10 bedrooms; double B&B £44–£56
Credit cards 1 3

★★ **69% Albaston House**
27 St Marychurch Rd, Torquay
☎ (01803) 296758
13 bedrooms; double B&B £64–£66
Credit cards 1 3 5

★★ **66% Oscar's Hotel & Restaurant**
56 Belgrave Rd, Torquay
☎ (01803) 293563
fax: (01803) 296685
12 bedrooms; double bedroom £39-£60
Credit cards 1 3

WHERE TO STAY

★★ 62% Seascape
8-10 Tor Church Rd, Torquay
☎ (01803) 292617
62 bedrooms; double B&B £38-£62
including dinner
Credit cards 1 3

★★ 66% Bute Court
Belgrave Rd, Torquay
☎ (01803) 293771
fax: (01803) 213429
48 bedrooms
Credit cards 1 2 3 5

★★ 58% Roseland
Warren Rd, Torquay
☎ (01803) 213829
fax: (01803) 291266
35 bedrooms; double B&B £70-£90
Credit cards 1 3

★★ 64% Hotel Sydore
Meadfoot Rd, Torquay
☎ (01803) 294758
fax: (01803) 294489
13 bedrooms; double B&B £37-£54
Credit cards 1 2 3 5

★★ 63% Bancourt
Avenue Rd, Torquay
☎ (01803) 295077
fax: (01803) 201114
40 bedrooms
Credit cards 1 3 5

★★ 66% Hotel Balmoral
Meadfoot Sea Rd, Torquay
☎ (01803) 293381 & 299224
fax: (01803) 299224
24 bedrooms; double B&B £50
Credit cards 1 2 3

★★ 61% Carlton
Falkland Rd, Torquay
☎ (01803) 291555
fax: (01803) 291666
32 bedrooms
Credit cards 1 2 3

★★ 66% Shelley Court
Croft Rd, Torquay
☎ (01803) 295642
fax: (01803) 215793
28 bedrooms; double B&B £36-£56
including dinner
Credit cards 1 3 5

★ 63% Westwood
111 Abbey Rd, Torquay
☎ (01803) 293818
fax: (01803) 293818
26 bedrooms; double B&B £32-£42
Credit cards 1 3

★ 64% Sunleigh
Livermead Hill, Torquay
☎ (01803) 607137
20 bedrooms; double B&B £44-£70
including dinner
Credit cards 1 2 3 5

★★ 62% Royal Seven Stars
Totnes
☎ (01803) 862125 & 863241,
fax: (01803) 867925
18 bedrooms; double B&B £54-£62
Credit cards 1 3 5

BED AND BREAKFAST

QQQQ Gages Mill
Buckfastleigh Rd, Ashburton
☎ (01364) 652391
Former 14th-century wool mill; warm,
relaxed, cosy atmosphere.
8 bedrooms; double B&B £44-£46

QQQQ East Burne Farm
Bickington
☎ (01626) 821496
fax: (01626) 821105
Grade II listed medieval house full of
character.
3 bedrooms; double B&B £42-£50

QQ Blenheim Hotel
Brimley Rd, Bovey Tracey
☎ (01626) 832422
Fine detached Victorian property.
5 bedrooms; double B&B £54-£56

QQQ Furzeleigh Mill Country Hotel
Dart Bridge, Buckfast
☎ (01364) 643476
fax: (01364) 643476
A 16th-century converted mill house in a
pleasant rural spot.
15 bedrooms
Credit cards 1 2 3 5

QQ Dartbridge Manor
20 Dartbridge Rd, Buckfastleigh
☎ (01364) 643575
Four hundred year old manor house full of
character and charm.
10 bedrooms; double B&B from £35

QQQQ Clennon Valley Hotel
1 Clennon Rise, Paignton
☎ (01803) 550304
fax: (01803) 550304
Brightly decorated bedrooms, several of
which offer family accommodation.
10 bedrooms; double B&B £38-£42
Credit cards 1 3

QQQ Danethorpe Hotel
23 St Andrews Rd, Paignton
☎ (01803) 551251
fax: (01803) 557075
Short walk from the seafront and harbour;
nicely equipped bedrooms.
10 bedrooms
Credit cards 1 2 3

WHERE TO STAY

QQQ Redcliffe Lodge Hotel
1 Marine Dr, Paignton
☎ (01803) 551394
fax: (01803) 551394
Beside the safe, sandy beach and green;
relaxed atmosphere.
17 bedrooms
Credit cards 1 3

QQQ St Weonard's Private Hotel
12 Kernou Rd, Paignton
☎ (01803) 558842
Close to town centre; warm and welcoming.
8 bedrooms; double B&B £30-£36
Credit cards 1 3

QQQ The Sealawn Hotel
Sea Front, 20 Esplanade Rd, Paignton
☎ (01803) 559031
Four-storey establishment affording views
across the greens to the sea.
12 bedrooms; double B&B £40-£48

QQQ Torbay Sands Hotel
16 Marine Pde, Preston Sea, Paignton
☎ (01803) 525568
Hospitable atmosphere, with panoramic
views of the bay.
13 bedrooms
Credit cards 1 3

QQQQ Fonthill
Torquay Rd, Shaldon, Teignmouth
☎ (01626) 872344
fax: (01626) 872344
The Graeme family warmly welcome non-
smoking guests to their home.
3 bedrooms; double B&B £48-£52

QQQ Hill Rise Hotel
Winterbourne Rd, Teignmouth
☎ (01626) 773108
Edwardian house offering light, airy
accommodation.
8 bedrooms; double B&B £26-£30

QQQQQ Thomas Luny House
Teign St, Teignmouth
☎ (01626) 772976
Bedrooms furnished with great flair and
thoughtful touches. Restored to its 18th-
century style.
4 bedrooms; double B&B £60-£70

QQQQ Glenorleigh Hotel
26 Cleveland Rd, Torquay
☎ (01803) 292135
fax: (01803) 292135
This friendly family holiday hotel has won
many awards, both for its hospitality and for
its beautifully kept gardens.
16 bedrooms; double B&B £32-£50
Credit cards 1 3

QQQQ Kingston House
75 Avenue Rd, Torquay
☎ (01803) 212760
Cheerful hosts; high standard of
accommodation; delightful place to stay.
6 bedrooms; double B&B £28-£35
Credit cards 1 3 5

QQQQ The Berburry Hotel
64 Bampfylde Rd, Torquay
☎ (01803) 297494
fax: (01803) 215902
Well equipped, pretty bedrooms; friendly
and attentive service.
10 bedrooms; double B&B £40-£56
Credit cards 1 3

QQQ Braddon Hall Hotel
Braddons Hill Rd East, Torquay
☎ (01803) 293908
High standard accommodation and a warm
welcome are offered here.
12 bedrooms; double B&B £32-£40

QQQ Chesterfield Hotel
62 Belgrave Rd, Torquay
☎ (01803) 292318
fax: (01803) 293676
Four minutes walk from the seafront and
gardens.
12 bedrooms; double B&B £30-£40
Credit cards 1 3

QQQ Craig Court Hotel
10 Ash Hill Rd, Castle Circus, Torquay
☎ (01803) 294400
Victorian detached house with views of
Torquay and beyond. Narrow gauge railway
track in the garden.
10 bedrooms

QQQ Cranborne Hotel
58 Belgrave Rd, Torquay
☎ (01803) 298046
fax: (01803) 298046
A regular award winner; food, puddings in
particular, are of a good standard.
12 bedrooms; double B&B £30-£48
Credit cards 1 3

QQQ Cranmore
89 Avenue Rd, Torquay
☎ (01803) 298488
Bedrooms are well equipped and have
orthopaedic beds.
8 bedrooms
Credit cards 1 2 3 5

QQQ Elmdene Hotel
Rathmore Rd, Torquay
☎ (01803) 294940
11 bedrooms; double B&B £32-£42
Credit cards 1 3

WHERE TO STAY

QQQ Grosvenor House Hotel
Falkland Rd, Torquay
☎ (01803) 294110
Small, friendly and comfortable hotel.
10 bedrooms
Credit cards 1 3

QQQ Hotel Trelawney
48 Belgrave Rd, Torquay
☎ (01803) 296049
fax: (01803) 296049
Bright and airy bedrooms are all en suite.
14 bedrooms
Credit cards 1 3 5

QQ Lindum Hotel
Abbey Rd, Torquay
☎ (01803) 292795
fax: (01803) 299358
Long-established, centrally situated hotel
with nicely furnished bedrooms.
20 bedrooms

QQQ Seaway Hotel
Chelston Rd, Torquay
☎ (01803) 605320
A spacious Victorian house with
comfortable lounge and bar.
14 bedrooms
Credit cards 1 3

QQQQ Westgate Hotel
Falkland Rd, Torquay
☎ (01803) 295350
fax: (01803) 295350
This relaxed and friendly holiday hotel has
comfortable bedrooms.
13 bedrooms
Credit cards 1 3

CAMPSITES

►►►► Ashburton Caravan Park
Waterleat, Ashburton
☎ (01364) 652552
Off the A38 west of Newton Abbot; pitch
price from £7-£9 per night.

►►►► Lemonford Caravan Park
Bickington
☎ (01626) 821242
West of Exeter off the A382; pitch price £6-
£8 per night.

►►► Galmpton Park Camping Site
Greenway Rd, Brixham
☎ (01803) 842066
Overlooking the River Dart; pitch price from
£6.50 per night.

►►► Hillhead Holiday Camp
Brixham
☎ (01803) 853204
On B3205 between Brixham and Kingswear.

► Beara Farm Campsite
Colston Rd, Buckfastleigh
☎ (01364) 642234
Off the A38; pitch price from £4 per night.

►►►►► Finlake Leisure Park
Chudleigh
☎ (01626) 853833
fax: (01626) 854031
North of Newton Abbot; pitch price from £7
per night.

►►► Holmans Wood Tourist Park
Harcombe Cross, Chudleigh
☎ (01626) 853785
North of Newton Abbot; pitch price from
£8.35 per night.

►►►► Cofton Country Holiday Park
Dawlish
☎ (01626) 890111
fax: (01626) 891572
South of Exeter on A379; pitch price £5-
£9.50 per night.

►►►► Kennford International Caravan Park
Kennford
☎ (01392) 833046
fax: (01392) 833046
Just west of Exeter off the A38; pitch price
from £8.50 per night.

►►►► Dornafield
Dornafield Farm, Newton Abbot
☎ (01803) 812732
fax: (01803) 812032
Situated off the A381; pitch price £6-£10.50
per night.

►►►► Stover International Caravan Park
Lower Staple Hill, Newton Abbot
☎ (01626) 821446
Situated off the A382; pitch price £7.15-
£11.15 per night.

►►►►► Beverley Parks Caravan & Camping Park
Goodrington Rd, Paignton
☎ (01803) 843887
fax: (01803) 845427

►►►► Byslades Camping Park
Totnes Rd, Paignton
☎ (01803) 555072
fax: (01803) 555072
Pitch price from £4.50 per night.

WHERE TO STAY

►►►► **Grange Court Holiday Centre**
Grange Rd, Paignton
☎ (01803) 558010
fax: (01803) 663336
Pitch price from £8.25 per night.

►►►► **Widend Camping Park**
Berry Pomeroy Rd, Marldon, Paignton
☎ (01803) 550116
Pitch price from £7 per night

►►► **Marine Park Holiday Centre**
Grange Rd, Paignton
☎ (01803) 843887
fax: (01803) 845427
Pitch price £7–£11.50 per night.

►►►► **Ramslade Touring Park**
Stoke Rd, Stoke Gabriel
☎ (01803) 782575
fax: (01803) 782828
Between Paignton and Stoke Gabriel; pitch price £7.50–£10 per night.

WHERE TO EAT

RESTAURANTS

⊛⊛ **The Table**
135 Babbacombe Rd, Torquay
☎ (01803) 324292
Fresh, honest cooking in a small restaurant on the outskirts of town.
Lunch: 12.15-1.45; £11.85
Dinner: 7.15-9.45; £26.50
Credit cards 1 3

⊛⊛ **River House**
The Strand, Lympstone
☎ (01395) 265147
Fine cuisine in one of Devon' best restaurants.
Lunch: 12-1.30; £28.95 and à la carte
Dinner: from £28.95 and à la carte

⊛⊛⊛ **Carved Angel**
2 South Embankment, Dartmouth
☎ (01803) 832465
An emphasis on French and Mediterranean cooking.
Lunch: 12.30-2.30, from £29 and à la carte
Dinner: 7-9.30, from £45 and à la carte

⊛⊛⊛ **Holne Chase**
Newton Abbott
☎ (01364) 631471
A unique family-run hotel in a hunting lodge.
Lunch: 12-2; £20 and à la carte
Dinner: 7-9; £25 and à la carte

⊛⊛ **Orestone Manor**
Rockhouse Lane, Maidencombe, Torquay
☎ (01803) 328098
Some elaborate Anglo-French cooking
Lunch: 12-1.30; £14.50
Dinner: 6.30-9; £25.50

⊛ **The Imperial**
Park Hill Rd, Torquay
☎ (01803) 294301
Classical French cuisine with seasonal dishes
Lunch: 12.30-2.30
Dinner: 6.30-9.30; £27.50 and à la carte

⊛⊛ **Edgemoor**
Haytor Rd, Bovey Tracey
☎ (01626) 832466
Food prepared with flair and imagination
Lunch: 12-2
Dinner: 7-9.30; £22.50

PUBS

See under Exeter Racecourse – Where to Eat.

Nottingham

A pretty bleak picture used to be painted of this Midlands course, but much work has been carried out to correct that image in recent times and its great potential is finally beginning to be realised.

For instance, a new grandstand has risen phoenix-like from the ashes after a previous structure was ravaged by fire in an arson attack a few years back. This has led to a significant improvement in the facilities that are on offer to patrons with the result that there is a far jollier atmosphere about the place nowadays.

The track itself is one of the fairest in the country and there can be few excuses for beaten horses here. Many of the top Newmarket trainers, most notably Henry Cecil, take advantage of the wide, galloping circuit to introduce some of their better unraced two-year-olds and there is always the possibility that a new star will be born at one of the late season Flat meetings. Nottingham also has a rich jumping history as the site of former jockey Stan Mellor's 1000th winner over the sticks. Now retired, he was the first National Hunt jockey ever to reach that figure and the feat is suitably commemorated with a race named in his honour. Nottingham not longer stages National Hunt racing, so this commemorative race is a flat one nowadays.

FURTHER INFORMATION

Nottingham Racecourse Co Ltd
Colwick Park, Colwick Road, Nottingham NG2 4BE
☎ (0115) 9580620

LOCATION AND HOW TO GET THERE

The course is on the southwestern edge of Nottingham, on the B686 at Colwick. From the M1 junction 25, take the A52 east; from the A1 south take the A52 west, or from the north take the A46 from Newark to join the A52, then continue west.
Nearest Railway Station: Nottingham; there is no connecting bus service to the course.

ADMISSION

All classes of day ticket give access to full betting facilities, including Tote.

Day Tickets:
CENTENARY STAND £12 - access to bar, light snacks, boxes, balcony viewing, facilities for disabled racegoers

TATTERSALLS £8 - access to bar, restaurant, roof-top bar, private rooms

SILVER RING £4 - access to paddock bar and light snacks

Annual membership: £120 single, £200 double

(Please note: the above are 1997 prices and are subject to review in 1998.)

COURSE FACILITIES

Banks:
there are no banks or cashpoint facilities on the course

For families:
picnic area with toilets; children's play area (unsupervised)

CALENDAR OF EVENTS

March 31 – flat	**July 24** – flat; evening meeting
April 7 – flat	**August 12** – flat; evening meeting
April 13 – flat	**August 29** – flat; evening meeting
April 20 – flat	**September 14** – flat
April 28 – flat	**September 26** – flat
May 8 – flat	**September 28** – flat
May 16 – flat	**October 6** – flat
May 22 – flat	**October 14** – flat
June 8 – flat	**October 21-22** – flat
June 17 – flat; evening meeting	**October 29** – flat
June 22 – flat	**November 2** – flat
July 4 – flat; evening meeting	
July 18 – flat	

WHERE TO STAY

HOTELS

★★★★ 63% Nottingham Royal Moat House
Wollaton St
☎ (0115) 936 9988
fax: (0115) 947 5888
201 bedrooms; double room £129 (room only)
Credit cards 1 2 3 5

Forte Posthouse
Saint James's St, Nottingham
☎ (0115) 947 0131
fax: (0115) 948 4366
130 bedrooms; double room £49.50–£79
Credit cards 1 2 3 5

★★★ 65% Nottingham Gateway
Cinderhill
☎ (0115) 979 4949
fax: (0115) 979 4744
108 bedrooms; double £42–£70
Credit cards 1 2 3 5

★★★ 68% Nottingham Moat House
Mansfield Rd,
☎ (0115) 935 9988
fax: (0115) 969 1506
172 bedrooms; double room from £110 (room only)
Credit cards 1 2 3 5

★★★ 61% Swan Hotel & Restaurant
84-90 Radcliffe Rd, West Bridgford
☎ (0115) 981 4042
fax: (0115) 945 5745
31 bedrooms; double B&B £50–£65
Credit cards 1 2 3 5

★★★ 63% Rutland Square
St James St
☎ (0115) 941 1114
fax: (0115) 941 0014
105 bedrooms ; double room £70–£83 (room only)
Credit cards 1 2 3 5

★★★ 64% Holiday Inn Garden Court
Castle Marina Park
☎ (0115) 993 5000
fax: (0115) 993 4000
100 bedrooms; double room £55–£84 (room only)
Credit cards 1 2 3 5

★★ 64% The Stage
Gregory Boulevard
☎ (0115) 960 3261
fax: (0115) 969 1040
58 bedrooms; double B&B £49–£54.50

★★★ 65% Westminster Hotel
312 Mansfield Rd, Carrington
☎ (0115) 955 5000, fax: (0115) 955 5005
56 bedrooms; double bedroom £60-90
Credit cards 1 2 3 5

★★ 65% Rufford
52 Melton Road, West Bridgford,
☎ (0115) 981 4202, fax: (0115) 945 5801
35 bedrooms; double B&B £45–£54
Credit cards 1 2 3 5

★★ 70% Priory
Derby Rd, Wollaton Vale
☎ (0115) 922 1691
fax: (0115) 925 6224
31 bedrooms; double B&B £54–£73
Credit cards 1 2 3 5

★★ 63% Balmoral
55-57 Loughborough Rd, West Bridgford
☎ (0115) 945 5020, fax: (0115) 955 2991
31 bedrooms; double B&B £45
Credit cards 1 2 3 5

★★★ 58% Tudor Court
Gypsy Ln, Draycott
☎ (01332) 874581, fax: (01332) 873133
30 bedrooms
Credit cards 1 2 3 5

★★ 66% Unicorn
Gunthorpe Bridge, Gunthorpe
☎ (0115) 966 3612, fax: (0115) 966 4801
16 bedrooms
Credit cards 1 2 3 5

★★ ✿ 71% Langar Hall
Langar
☎ (01949) 860559, fax: (01949) 861045
12 bedrooms; double B&B £85–£200
Credit cards 1 2 3 5

★★★ 62% Novotel
Bostock Ln, Long Eaton
☎ (0115) 946 5111
fax: (0115) 946 5900)
105 bedrooms; double bedroom £59.50
Credit cards 1 2 3 5

★★ 61% Europa
20-22 Derby Rd, Long Eaton
☎ (0115) 972 8481
fax: (0115) 946 0229
15 bedrooms; double B&B £39–£43
Credit cards 1 2 3 5

Forte Posthouse
Bostocks Ln, Sandiacre
☎ (0115) 939 7800, fax: (0115) 949 0469
91 bedrooms; double room £43–£59 (room only)
Credit cards 1 2 3 5

★★ 64% The Haven
Grantham Rd, Whatton
☎ (01949) 850800, fax: (01949) 851454
33 bedrooms; double B&B £48
Credit cards 1 2 3

BED AND BREAKFAST

QQQ Royston Hotel
326 Mansfield Rd, Sherwood
☎ (0115) 962 2947
On the A60 out of the city; bedrooms individually furnished with care and attention.
12 bedrooms
Credit cards 1 2 3 5

QQQ Grantham Hotel
24-26 Radcliffe Rd, West Bridgford
☎ (0115) 981 1373
fax: (0115) 981 8657
Rooms are neat and well equipped.
22 bedrooms; double B&B £40–£42
Credit cards 1 2 3

QQQQ Hall Farm House
Gonalston
☎ (0115) 966 3112
Guests are treated as family friends at this 18th-century farmhouse.
3 bedrooms

QQ P & J Hotel
277-279 Derby Rd, Lenton
☎ (0115) 978 3998
fax: (0115) 978 3998
Small commercial hotel converted from a Victorian house.
19 bedrooms
Credit cards 1 2 3 5

WHERE TO STAY

Around Nottingham

QQ Fairhaven Private Hotel
19 Meadow Rd, Beeston
☎ (0115) 922 7509
A clean modest hotel on the edge of town.
12 bedrooms; double B&B £30-£42

QQ Station Hotel
Station Rd, Hucknall
☎ (0115) 963 2588
Victorian public house, considerably
modernised and with spacious bedrooms.
6 bedrooms
Credit cards 1 3

CAMPSITES

►►► Thornton's Holt Camping Park
Stragglethorpe, Radcliffe on Trent
☎ (0115) 933 2125 & 933 4204
fax: (0115) 933 3318
Five miles south of A52, 2 miles north of
A46; pitch price from £6.50

**►►► Shardlow Marina Caravan
Park**
London Rd, Shardlow
☎ (01332) 792832
fax: (01332) 792832
Part of a large marina complex; pitch price
from £6.50 per night

WHERE TO EAT

RESTAURANTS

Sonny's
3 Carlton St, Hockley
☎ (0115) 9473041
Lunch: 12-2.30
Dinner: 7-10.30

Langar Hall
Langar
☎ (01949) 860559
Short carte of classic British dishes with a
Mediterranean influence.
Lunch: 12-2
Dinner: 7.30-9.30

PUBS

Ye Olde Trip to Jerusalem
Brewhouse Yard
☎ (0115) 947 3171
fax: (0115) 950 1185
Originally the brewhouse for Nottingham
Castle and a pub since 1189 (catering then
for crusaders), this is certainly a place worth
visiting, though it could be full of tourists.
There are three real ales, an interesting
range of whiskies and limited bar food.
Children are not permitted inside the pub.
Open: 11am-11pm; Sunday 12-10.30pm
Bar food: 12-6pm

Around Nottingham

Cross Keys
Epperstone, nr Southwell
☎ (0115) 966 3033
A good village 'local' atmosphere prevails at
this popular old inn. The food is home
cooked and pies are particularly popular.
Kimberley Classic Ale is dispensed from a
handpump; there are also cask conditioned
bitter and mild and a good range of single
malt whiskies. Children are welcome in the
family room and there is a spacious lawned
garden.
Open: 11.45am-2.30pm, 6-11pm; Sunday
12-2.30pm, 7-10.30pm. Closed Monday
lunchtime.
Bar food:

Reindeer Inn
Main St, Hoveringham, nr Southwell
☎ (0115) 966 3629
Food and wine are taken seriously at this
17th-century inn overlooking the cricket
pitch, with some excellent choices available
to discerning evening diners. The lunchtime
snack menu is imaginative too and, as well
as Marstons Bitter, Pedigree and a guest
beer, there are quality wines and unusual
whiskies to enjoy. Children not permitted in
public bar.
Open: 12-3pm, 5-11pm (opens 5.30pm on
Monday); Sunday 12-3pm, 7-10.30pm.
Closed Monday lunchtime except Bank
Holidays
Bar food: Tuesday to Saturday 12-2pm;
Sunday 12-3pm
Restaurant: Tuesday to Saturday 7-9.30pm

Star Inn
Melton La, West Leake
☎ (01509) 852233
Choose between the traditionally furnished
main bar, decorated with various rural
implements, or the modernised and
comfortable lounge bar. The pub is noted
for its well kept draught Bass and Theakston
ales and for a good-value cold table at
lunchtime. A home-made hot dish is usually
available. Children are welcome in eating
areas and there are picnic tables outside.
Open: 11-2.30pm, 6-11pm; Sunday 12-
3pm, 7-10.30pm
Bar food: Tuesday-Saturday 12.30-2pm,
6.30-8.30pm

Perth Hunt

For anyone seeking to combine a break in the countryside with some exciting National Hunt racing, Perth offers the perfect solution. This beautiful Tayside area has an abundance of alternative leisure activities with an ample choice of top-class golf courses and some superb salmon and trout fishing in the near vicinity.

The fixture list has been carefully designed with the needs of holiday-makers in mind, so that all the meetings last for at least two days and are scheduled to avoid the depths of winter. Instead, they are run at the beginning of the jumps season (from August to September) and at the end (April to June). The pick of the bunch is the three-day Perth Festival Meeting in late April, a truly wonderful occasion.

The racecourse could hardly have been situated in a more alluring setting, hidden away among the picturesque woodland of Scone Park. Although the trees may occasionally obscure viewing, this is a very small price to pay considering the marvellous backdrop that they form and the intimate atmosphere that they help to create. There is always a tremendously warm welcome extended to any visitors and a trip to this delightful track, the most northerly in Britain, can not be too highly recommended.

FURTHER INFORMATION

The Perth Hunt
Perth Racecourse, Scone Palace Park PH2 6BB
☎ (01738) 551597

LOCATION AND HOW TO GET THERE

The course is situated in Scone Palace Park, Perth. Follow signposts from the A93 north of Perth. **Nearest Railway Station:** Perth; there is a bus service from Perth to the course on racedays.

ADMISSION

All classes of day ticket give access to full betting facilities, including Tote.

Day Tickets:

CLUB £12 - access to bars, restaurant, private rooms

TATTERSALLS AND PADDOCK £7, senior citizens £4 - access to bars and snacks

COURSE £2 - access to mobile food trailer and picnic area. No bar.

Annual membership: £70 (requires a proposer and a seconder)

COURSE FACILITIES

Banks:
there are no banks or cashpoint facilities on the course.

For families:
picnic area with refreshment kiosk and toilets.

CALENDAR OF EVENTS

April 22-24 – Spring Festival Meeting
May 13-14 – evening meeting on Wednesday
June 4-5 – evening meeting on Friday
August 21-22
September 23-24

WHERE TO STAY

HOTELS

★★★ ❀❀ **74% Murrayshall Country House Hotel & Golf Course**
New Scone
☎ (01738) 551171
fax: (01738) 552595
27 bedrooms; double B&B £90-£120
Credit cards 1 2 3 5

★★★ ❀ **72% Parklands**
St Leonards Bank
☎ (01738) 622451, fax: (01738) 622046
14 bedrooms; double B&B £80-£135
Credit cards 1 2 3

★★★ ❀ **69% Huntingtower**
Crieff Rd, Almondbank
☎ (01738) 583771, fax: (01738) 583777
35 bedroom; double B&B £45-£95
Credit cards 1 2 3 5

★★★ **62% Queens Hotel**
Leonard St
☎ (01738) 442222, fax: (01738) 638496
51 bedrooms; double B&B £64-£102
Credit cards 1 2 3 5

★★★ **63% Lovat**
90 Glasgow Rd
☎ (01738) 636555
fax: (01738) 643123
30 bedrooms; double B&B £82-£92
Credit cards 1 2 3 5

★★★ **61% The Royal George**
Tay St
☎ (01738) 624455, fax: (01738) 630345
42 bedrooms
Credit cards 1 2 3 5

★★ **68% Isle of Skye Toby**
Queen's Bridge, Dundee Rd
☎ (01738) 624471
fax: (01738) 622124
47 bedrooms; double B&B £57-£66
Credit cards 1 2 3 5

★★★ **60% Quality Station**
Leonard St
☎ (01738) 624141
fax: (01738) 639912
70 bedrooms; double bedroom £71-£81
Credit cards 1 2 3 5

Around Perth

★★★ ❀❀ **78% Ballathie House**
Kinclaven
☎ (01250) 883268, fax: (01250) 883396
27 bedrooms; double B&B £120-£180
Credit cards 1 2 3 5

★★ ❀ **65% The Tayside**
Mill St, Stanley
☎ (01738) 828249, fax: (01738) 827216
16 bedrooms; double B&B £42-£45
Credit cards 1 3

BED AND BREAKFAST

QQQQ Ardfern House
15 Pitcullen Crescent
☎ (01738) 637031
2 bedrooms

QQQ Clark Kimberley
57-59 Dunkeld Rd
☎ (01738) 637406
fax: (01738) 643983
Friendly guesthouse offering high standard of accommodation.
8 bedrooms

QQQ Clunie
12 Pitcullen Crescent
☎ (01738) 623625
A short way from town centre; friendly with mainly modern bedrooms.
7 bedrooms; double B&B from £32
Credit cards 1 3

QQQQ Kinnaird
5 Marshall Place
☎ (01738) 628021
Overlooking a park; attractively decorated bedrooms.
7 bedrooms, Credit cards 1 3

QQ The Gables
24 Dunkeld Rd
☎ (01738) 624717
fax: (01738) 624717
A cheerful, informal family guest house.
7 bedrooms
Credit cards 1 3

QQQ Pitcullen
17 Pitcullen Crescent
☎ (01738) 626506 ; fax:(01738) 628265
Well-maintained semi-detached villa.
3 bedrooms
Credit cards 1 3

QQQQ Park Lane
17 Marshall Place
☎ (01738) 637218, fax: (01738) 643519
Comfortable, nicely appointed bedrooms; a few minutes' walk from the city centre.
6 bedrooms; double B&B £38-£44
Credit cards 1 3

Around Perth

QQQ Craighall Farm
Forgandenny
☎ (01738) 812415
fax: (01738) 812415
Modern bungalow admist peaceful countryside.
3 bedrooms

CAMPSITE

►►►► **Erigmore House Holiday Park**
Birnam
☎ (01350) 727236
fax: (01350) 728636
Situated on B898 north of Perth; pitch price from £9 per night.

►►► **Camping and Caravanning Club Site**
Scone Racecourse, Scone
☎ (01738) 552323 & (01203) 694995
A sheltered site adjacent to the racecourse; pitch price £9.40-£10.20 per night.

►►►► **Cleeve Caravan Park**
Glasgow Rd
☎ (01738) 639521
fax: (01738) 441690
Pitch price £5-£8.20 per night.

WHERE TO EAT

RESTAURANTS

❀ **Number Thirty Three Seafood Restaurant**
33 Saint George St, Perth
☎ (01738) 633771
Small, popular restaurant offering fresh, carefully cooked seafood.
Lunch: 12-2.30
Dinner: 7-9.30
Credit cards 1 2 3

Plumpton

Set on the side of a steep hill, this undulating National Hunt track is one of the sharpest in the country. The oblong-shaped circuit has a circumference of just nine furlongs and the extremely tight bends require a handy type of horse as opposed to a long-striding galloper who will find it difficult to negotiate the turns.

The fences in the back straight are all located on a downhill stretch and, when the ground is riding firm, as it generally does during the early and late season meetings, these are tackled at a breakneck pace. This inevitably leads to plenty of thrills and spills and the track has been rather unfairly nicknamed by jockeys as 'The Wall of Death'.

Even though the quality of racing may remain low, a good day out should be had by all thanks to the strenuous efforts that the management of the course have made to try and upgrade facilities. Over a million pounds was spent on the new stand alone, and the restaurant and bar areas are now much more spacious following recent expansions. Another good point about this venue is its easy accessibility from London by rail. On race days, trains on the Victoria-Brighton line stop at Plumpton station which is just a short walk from the track.

FURTHER INFORMATION

Pratt & Company
11 Boltro Road, Haywards Heath, Sussex
RG16 1BP

LOCATION AND HOW TO GET THERE

The course is between Lewes and Haywards Heath, about eight miles from Brighton. From the south coast approach via the A27 and the A273; from London take the M23 then either the A23, A273 or B2112.
Nearest Railway Station: Plumpton, adjacent to the racecourse.

ADMISSION

All classes of day ticket give access to full betting facilities, including Tote.

Day Tickets:

CLUB £13 - access to bars, restaurant and hot food bar

TATTERSALLS AND PADDOCK £9 - access to bars, seafood bar, hot food bar, mobile catering, boxes and private rooms

CENTRE OF COURSE £5 - access to bar, mobile catering and picnic area

Annual membership: £100, plus £10 for car badge, if required

Parking: £1; picnic area parking in centre of course £4 per car plus £4 per occupant

(Please note: The above are 1997 prices and are subject to review in 1998)

COURSE FACILITIES

Banks:
there are no banks or cashpoint facilities on the course.

For families:
picnic area with refreshment kiosk and toilets; children's play area on Bank Holidays and August Meeting only.

CALENDAR OF EVENTS

January 12 – jumping	**October 19** – jumping
February 2 – jumping	**November 2** – jumping
February 16 – jumping	**November 16** – jumping
March 2 – jumping	**December 8** – jumping
March 16 – jumping	**December 30** – jumping
March 26 – jumping	
April 11 – jumping	
April 13 – jumping	
April 29 – jumping	
September 14 – jumping	
October 8 – jumping	

WHERE TO STAY

HOTELS

★★★ 71% Old Ship
Kings Rd, Brighton
☎ (01273) 329001
fax: (01273) 820718
152 bedrooms; double B&B £52-£110
Credit cards 1 2 3 5

★★★ 65% Imperial
First Av, Brighton
☎ (01273) 777320
fax: (01273) 777310
76 bedrooms; double B&B £61-£90
Credit cards 1 2 3 5

★★★ 58% Sackville
Kingsway, Brighton
☎ (01273) 736292
fax: (01273) 205759
45 bedrooms
Credit cards 1 2 3 5

★★★★★ 63% Grand
Kings Rd, Brighton
☎ (01273) 321188, fax: (01273) 202694
200 bedrooms; double B&B £150-£270
Credit cards 1 2 3 5

★★★★ ❀ 68% Brighton Thistle
Kings Rd, Brighton
☎ (01273) 206700
fax: (01273) 820692
204 bedrooms; double room £145-£170
Credit cards 1 2 3 5

★★★ 63% Brighton Oak
West St, Brighton
☎ (01273) 220033
fax: (01273) 778000
138 bedrooms; double bedroom £62-£105
Credit cards 1 2 3 5

★★ 60% St Catherines Lodge
Seafront, Kingsway, Brighton
☎ (01273) 778181
fax: (01273) 774949
50 bedrooms; double B&B £40-£65
Credit cards 1 2 3 5

★★★ ❀❀ 76% Ockenden Manor
Ockenden Ln, Cuckfield
☎ (01444) 416111
fax: (01444) 415549
22 bedrooms; double B&B £105
Credits cards 1 2 3 5

★★★ 65% The Birch
Lewes Rd, Haywards Heath
☎ (01444) 451565
fax: (01444) 440109
53 bedrooms
Credit cards 1 2 3 5

★★★ ❀❀ 77% Shelleys
High St, Lewes
☎ (01273) 472361
fax: (01273) 483152
19 bedrooms; double bedroom £106-£195
(room only)
Credit cards 1 2 3 5

★★★ 68% White Hart
55 High St, Lewes
☎ (01273) 476694
fax: (01273) 476695
52 bedrooms
Credit cards 1 2 3 5

BED AND BREAKFAST

QQQQ Adelaide Hotel
51 Regency Square, Brighton
☎ (01273) 205286
fax: (01273) 220904
Freshly decorated and tastefully furnished
bedrooms with welcoming proprietors.
12 bedrooms; double B&B £62-£78
Credit cards 1 2 3 5

QQQ Allendale Hotel
3 New Steine, Brighton
☎ (01273) 675436
fax: (01273) 602603
Charming proprietors and smart, modern
bedrooms, exceptionally well equipped.
13 bedrooms
Credit cards 1 2 3 5

QQQ Ambassador Hotel
22 New Steine, Brighton
☎ (01273) 676869, fax: (01273) 689988
Family-run hotel offers of a range of neat,
well equipped bedrooms.
10 bedrooms; double B&B £42-£65
Credit cards 1 2 3 5

QQQQ Arlanda Hotel
20 New Steine, Brighton
☎ (01273) 699300
fax: (01273) 600930
Regency-style house offers a mixed style of
accommodation.
12 bedrooms; double B&B £46-£80
Credit cards 1 2 3 5

QQQQ Ascott House Hotel
21 New Steine, Marine Pde, Brighton
☎ (01273) 688085
fax: (01273) 623733
Small personally run hotel close to the
seafront, offering bright, freshly decorated
bedrooms.
12 bedrooms; double B&B £40-£80
Credit cards 1 2 3 5

WHERE TO STAY

QQQ Ainsley House Hotel
28 New Steine
☎ (01273) 605310
fax: (01273) 688604
Charming Regency terraced house
overlooking the sea.
11 bedrooms; double B&B £48-£68
Credit cards 1 2 3 5

QQQ Gullivers
10 New Steine, Brighton
☎ (01273) 695415
fax: (01252) 372774
Attractive bedrooms feature in this Regency
residence close to the seafront.
9 bedrooms; double B&B £38-£54
Credit cards 1 2 3 5

QQQ New Steine Hotel
12a New Steine, Marine Pde, Brighton
☎ (01273) 681546
Smart, comfortable accommodation.
11 bedrooms; double B&B £40-£49

QQQ Alvia Hotel
36 Upper Rock Gardens
☎ (01273) 682939
fax: (01273) 682939
Ideally positioned for easy access to the
seafront
10 bedrooms; double B&B £38-£50
Credit cards 1 2 3 5

QQQ Trouville Hotel
11 New Steine, Marine Pde, Brighton
☎ (01273) 697384
Seafront, family-run guesthouse offering
freshly decorated bedrooms.
9 bedrooms; double B&B £38-£49
Credit cards 1 2 3

QQQQ The Twenty One
21 Charlotte St, Marine Pde, Brighton
☎ (01273) 686450
fax: (01273) 695560
Exceptionally well equipped bedrooms,
each with its own charm.
6 bedrooms
Credit cards 1 2 3

QQQQQ Fairseat House
Newick, Lewes
☎ (01825) 722263
fax: (01825) 722263
An elegant Edwardian house, furnished
with antiques.
3 bedrooms; double B&B £44-£85
Credit cards 3

QQQQ Nightingales
The Avenue, Kingston, Lewes
☎ (01273) 475673
fax: (01273) 475673
A modern family bungalow with well-
furnished bedrooms
2 bedrooms; double B&B £40-£50
Credit cards 1 2 3

QQQQ Amblecliff Hotel
35 Upper Rock Gardens, Brighton
☎ (01273) 681161 & 676945
fax: (01273) 676945
Bright individually furnished
accommodation.
8 bedrooms; double B&B £40-£60
Credit cards 1 2 3

QQ Harbour View
22 Mount Rd, Newhaven
☎ (01273) 512096
Situated on eastern edge of town with a
relaxed atmosphere
3 bedrooms

QQ Braemar House
Steyning Rd, Rottingdean
☎ (01273) 304263
Family run guesthouse offering simple but
well kept accommodation.
15 bedrooms; double B&B £30-£35

WHERE TO EAT

RESTAURANTS

🍲🍲 Langan's Bistro
1 Paston Place, Brighton
☎ (01273) 606933
fax: (01273) 675686
Down to earth and flavoursome cooking in a
relaxed friendly atmosphere.
Lunch 12-2.15
Dinner 7-10.15

🍲🍲 Whyte's
33 Western St, Brighton
☎ (01273) 776618
Cosy, small restaurant near the seafront,
serving sound, honest cooking in French
and English styles.
Dinner: 7-10

🍲🍲 Black Chapati
12 Circus Parade, New England Rd,
Brighton
☎ (01273) 699011
Charming restaurant serving an eclectic
blend of cooking styles.
Lunch:12-2
Dinner: 7-10.30

🍲 Brighton Thistle
Kings Rd, Brighton
☎ (01273) 206700
A very formal French restaurant in a smart
seafront hotel.
Lunch:12-2; from £17.50
Dinner: 7-10; from £17.50

🍲🍲 Quentin's
42 Western Rd, Hove
☎ (01273) 822734
Combined modern English, Mediterranean
and Oriental dishes.
Lunch:12-2.30; from £4.95 and à la carte
Dinner: 7-10.30; from £16 à la carte

Pontefract

Despite its close proximity to the urbanisation around Leeds, Castleford and Featherstone, Pontefract remains very much a country setting and is therefore an ideal place to take a break from city life during the summer.

Yet, at the same time, it could hardly be easier to reach as the course is situated within a stone's throw of the M62. This is an unpretentious venue which upholds the traditional values of its county in providing good, solid entertainment at a working man's price. To that end, facilities are compact and offer decent value for money. The track itself is a very stiff and unusually lengthy two-mile circuit with a tremendous emphasis being placed on stamina in long-distance contests. Indeed, of the courses that are devoted solely to Flat racing, it is probably the most testing in Britain. Early speed is still a vital ingredient for sprinters who run here, however, as there is a sharp bend in the track about two and a half furlongs from the finish and many lengths will be saved by gaining a good early position close to the rails. Consequently, a low draw on the inside is almost always a huge advantage.

FURTHER INFORMATION

Pontefract Park Race Co Ltd
33 Ropergate, Pontefract WF8 1LE
☎ (01977) 703224

LOCATION AND HOW TO GET THERE

The course is on the north of the town in Pontefract Park, adjoining the M62. Leave the motorway at junction 32 and take the A539 towards Pontefract. **Nearest Railway Station:** Pontefract Monkhill or Pontefract Baghill; there is no connecting bus service - Monkhill adjoins the park gates and Baghill is just half a mile away.

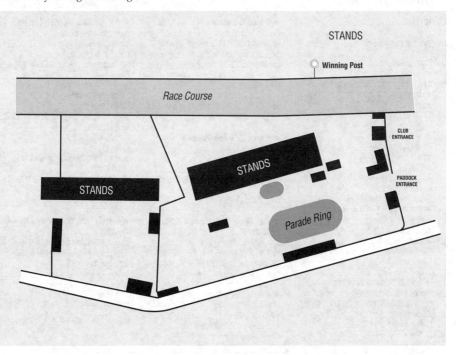

ADMISSION

All classes of day ticket give access to full betting facilities, including Tote.

Day tickets:
Accompanied children under 16 are admitted free to all enclosures. No dogs allowed, except in car in Third Ring/Car park.

CLUB £12 - access to restaurant, bars, private rooms, seating in the stands

PADDOCK/TATTERSALLS £8 - access to self-service restaurant, bars, course betting office, betting ring, parade ring, unsaddling enclosure

SILVER RING/2ND ENCLOSURE £3.50 - access to cafeteria, bars, course betting office, betting ring

THIRD RING/CAR PARK £2, or £5 for car and up to four occupants - access to viewing stand (part of 2nd grandstand), cafeteria, bar, betting ring

Annual membership: £105, joint (husband and wife) £140, junior (under 21) £50
(Please note: All prices are 1997 and are subject to revision in 1998)

COURSE FACILITIES

Banks:
there are no banks or cashpoint facilities on the course.

For families:
picnic area with refreshment kiosk and toilets; children's play area and creche (evenings and school holidays only) in Third Ring; lost children centre.

CALENDAR OF EVENTS

April 15	June 29	October 5
April 21	July 7	October 19
April 27	July 17 – evening meeting	
May 22 – evening meeting	August 5	
June 2	August 16	
June 8	August 25	
June 15	September 24	

WHERE TO STAY

HOTELS

Around Pontefract

Travelodge
Ferrybridge Service Area
☎ Central reservations (0800) 850950
35 bedrooms; double room £35-£50 (room only)
Credit cards 1 2 3 5

★★ 66% Owl
Main Rd, Hambleton
☎ (01757) 228374
fax: (01757) 228125
15 bedrooms; double B&B £55
Credit cards 1 2 3 5

★★★★ 68% Holiday Inn
Wellington St, Leeds
☎ (0113) 244 2200
fax: (0113) 244 0460
125 bedrooms
Credit cards 1 2 3 5

★★★ 72% Waterton Park
Walton Hall, The Balk, Walton, Wakefield
☎ (01924) 257911, fax: (01924) 240082
43 bedrooms
Credit cards 1 2 3 5

★★★ 65% Swallow
Queens St, Wakefield
☎ (01924) 372111, fax: (01924) 383648
64 bedrooms; double B&B £49-£99
Credit cards 1 2 3 5

Campanile
Monckton Rd, Wakefield
☎ (01924) 201054, fax: (01924) 201055
77 bedrooms

★★★★ 69% The Queen's
City Square, Leeds
☎ (0113) 243 1323
fax: (0113) 242 5154
190 bedrooms; double room £85 (room only)
Credit cards 1 2 3 5

★★★ ❀❀ 79% Haley's Hotel & Restaurant
Shire Oak Rd, Headingley
☎ (0113) 278 4446, fax: (0113) 275 3342
22 bedrooms; double B&B £90-£150
Credit cards 1 2 3 5

★★★ 62% Parkside
Park Road, Pontefract
☎ (01977) 709911, fax: (01977) 701602
28 bedrooms; double room £65
Credit cards 1 2 3 5

★★★ ❀ 69% Merrion Thistle
Merrion Centre, Leeds
☎ (0113) 243 9191
fax: (0113) 242 3527
109 bedrooms; double bedroom £64-£99
Credit cards 1 2 3 5

Forte Posthouse
South Milford
☎ (01977) 682711, fax: (01977) 685462
95 bedrooms
Credit cards 1 2 3 5

★★★ 68% Monk Fryston Hall
Monk Fryston
☎ (01977) 682369, fax: (01977) 683544
28 bedrooms; double B&B £98-£105
Credit cards 1 2 3

★★★ ❀ 71% Wentbridge House
Wentbridge
☎ (01977) 620444, fax: (01977) 620148
12 bedrooms; double B&B £62-£99
Credit cards 1 2 3 5

WHERE TO STAY

Travelodge
M1, Woolley Edge Motorway Service Area
☎ (0800) 850950 Central Reservations
31 bedrooms; double bedroom £35-£50
Credit cards 1 2 3 5

BED AND BREAKFAST

QQQ Ash Mount Hotel
22 Wetherby Road, Oakwood, Leeds
☎ (0113) 265 8164
fax: (0113) 265 8164
Attractive stone-built house; smart rooms,
comfortable and pleasantly furnished.
11 bedrooms; double B&B from £44
Credit cards 1 3

QQQ Merevale Hotel
16 Wetherby Rd, Oakwood, Leeds
☎ (0113) 265 8933
fax: (0113) 265 8933
Large detached house. Bedrooms of various
sizes all coordinated with crisp duvets.
14 bedrooms; double B&B £38-£45
Credit cards 1 3

QQQ Trafford House & Budapest Hotel
18 Cardigan Road, Headingley, Leeds
☎ (0113) 275 2034 & 275 6637
fax: (0113) 274 2422
Victorian house; accommodation is well
furnished and comfortable.
18 bedrooms; double B&B £36
Credit cards 1 3

QQQQ Stanley View
226/228 Stanley Rd, Wakefield
☎ (01924) 376803
fax: (01924) 369123
Modern bedrooms that are bright and cosy.
10 bedrooms; double B&B £30-£34
Credit cards 1 3

CAMPSITES

►► Roundhay Park
Elmete Lane, off Wetherby Road
☎ (0113) 265 2354 & 266 1850
fax: (0113) 237 0077
On a south-facing hill, 3.5 miles from city
centre; pitch price £7.50-£8 per night.

WHERE TO EAT

RESTAURANTS

◉◉ Brasserie Forty Four
42-44 The Calls
☎ (0113) 2343232, fax: (0113) 2343332
Fun place to eat with quality food at a
reasonable price.
Lunch: 12-2
Dinner: 7-10.30
Credit cards 1 2 3

◉◉ Armstrongs
102 Dodworth Rd, Barnsley
☎ (01226) 240113
Interesting continental dishes made frrom
Mediterranean ingredients
Lunch: 12-2
Dinner: 7-9.30

◉◉ Leodis Brasserie
Victoria Mill, Sovereign St, Leeds
☎ (0113) 2421010
A smart brasserie offering an imaginative
range of dishes.
Lunch: 12-2; £11.95 and à la carte
Dinner: 7-10; £11.95 and à la carte

PUBS

Kings Arms
Heath Common, Kirkthorpe
☎ (01924) 377527
In a converted stables, this friendly and well
kept pub includes some of its own brew
among the range of draught beers. The food
is impressive in quality and size. There is
one room where children area allowed and
there is a garden.
Open: 11am-3pm, 6-11pm; Sunday 12-
3pm, 7-10.30pm
Bar food: 12-2pm, 7-9.30pm; Sunday 12-2
Restaurant: as bar food times

The Chequers Inn
Claypit La, Ledsham
☎ (01477) 683135
fax: (01477) 685921
Ivy-clad pub dating from the 16th century
with wood panelling and old beams inside.
There is a good range of draught beers, a
wine list and a simple range of bar food.
There are two rooms where children are
allowed.
Open: Monday to Friday 11am-5pm, 5.30-
11pm; Saturday 11am-11pm; closed
Sunday
Bar food: 12-2.15pm, 6.30-9.15pm

Redcar

Set in the midst of the industrial heartland of the northeast of England, the racecourse at Redcar stands out like a green oasis. It is to be found just to the south of the town which is located a few miles away from Middlesbrough, close to the North Sea.

In the old days, races were originally held on the nearby beaches, but now they take place on the narrow, left-handed track. The oval circuit has a long run-in of five furlongs which also forms part of the straight mile course where horses drawn high are greatly favoured.

This venue has really come to prominence in recent years thanks to the efforts of its owner, Lord Zetland, widely regarded as one of the Jockey Club's more radical thinkers. He introduced a completely new two-year-old event, which is run at a televised meeting in late October and carries over £100,000 in prize money. This huge sum explains why the contest regularly attracts many of the season's leading juveniles. Another feature race is the Tote Zetland Gold Cup, a prestigious and valuable handicap that is held towards the end of May. The facilities here have recently been improved and now include the Crow's Nest Restaurant, new executive boxes, and a 'Classic Suite', which can be hired.

FURTHER INFORMATION

The Racecourse
Redcar, Cleveland TS10 2BY
☎ (01642) 484068; Fax: (01642) 488272

LOCATION AND HOW TO GET THERE

Redcar is on the northeast coast, eight miles east of Middlesbrough. From the A1 take the A168, then the A19 and finally the A174 to Redcar. **Nearest Railway Station:** Redcar Central; the course is a five-minute walk from the station.

ADMISSION

All classes of day ticket give access to full betting facilities, including Tote

Day Tickets:

CLUB £12 - access to bars, restaurant, snack areas, private rooms and boxes

TATTERSALLS £8, senior citizens £3.50 - access to bars, self-service restaurant, snack areas

COURSE £2.50, senior citizens £1.25 - access to bar and cafeteria
(Please note: The above prices are subject to change during 1998)

Annual membership: £95 single, £140 joint (husband and wife), £40 junior (under 21)
(Please note: The above are 1997 prices and are subject to review in 1998)

COURSE FACILITIES

Banks:
there are no banks or cashpoint facilities on the course.

For families:
picnic area with refreshment kiosk and toilets; children's play area.

CALENDAR OF EVENTS

April 30 – flat
May 11 – flat
May 25-26 – includes the Tote Zetland Gold Cup
June 9
June 19-20
July 1
July 18 – evening meeting
July 25 – evening meeting

August 8-9
August 29 – flat; evening meeting
September 25
October 6
October 17 – includes Comcast Teesside Two-Year Old Trophy
October 27
November 2

WHERE TO STAY

HOTELS

★★★ ⊕ 69% Grinkle Park
Easington
☎ (01287) 640515
fax: (01287) 641278
20 bedrooms; double B&B £69-£84
Credit cards 1 2 3 5

★★ 66% Ryedale Moor
3 Beaconsfield St, Headland, Hartlepool
☎ (01429) 231436
fax: (01429) 863787
14 bedrooms; double B&B £48
Credit cards 1 2 3 5

★★ 60% Marton Way Toby
Marton Rd, Middlesbrough
☎ (01642) 817651
fax: (01642) 829409
53 bedrooms; double B&B £45-£49
Credit cards 1 2 3 5

★ 68% The Grey House
79 Cambridge Rd, Linthorpe,
Middlesborough
☎ (01642) 817485
fax: (01642) 817485
9 bedrooms; double B&B £46-£50
Credit cards 1 3

★★★ 62% The Grand
Swainson St, Hartlepool
☎ (01429) 266345
fax; (01429) 265217
47 bedrooms
Credit cards 1 2 3 5

★★★★ 66% Swallow
10 John Walker Sq, Stockton-on-Tees
☎ (01642) 679721
fax; (01642) 601714
125 bedrooms; double B&B £60-£125
Credit cards 1 2 3 5

★★★ 59% Billingham Arms
The Causeway, Billingham, Stockton-on-
Tees
☎ (01642) 553661 & 360880
fax; (01642) 552104
69 bedrooms
Credit cards 1 2 3 5

Forte Posthouse
Low Lane, Stainton Village, Thornaby,
Stockton-on-Tees
☎ (01642) 591213
fax; (01642) 594989
135 bedrooms

BED AND BREAKFAST

QQQ Claxton Hotel
196 High St
☎ (01642) 486745
fax: (01642) 486522
Well established hotel providing well
appointed accommodation.
27 bedrooms; double B&B £35-£37

QQQ Royal Oak Hotel
123 High St., Great Ayton
☎ (01642) 722361 & 723270
fax: (01642) 724047
An 18th-century coaching inn which has
historical associations with Captain Cook;
well furnished bedrooms.
5 bedrooms
Credit cards 1 3 5

QQQQ The Edwardian Hotel
72 Yarm Rd, Stockton-on-Tees
☎ (01642) 615655
Carefully furnished house with homely
bedrooms.
6 bedrooms
Credit cards 1 3

QQQ Fox and Hounds
Slapewath, Guisborough
☎ (01287) 632964
fax: (01287) 610778
Modern bedrooms in a popular hotel.
15 bedrooms; double B&B from £45
Credit cards 1 2 3 5

QQQQ Manor House Farm
Ingleby Greenhow
☎ (01642) 722384
18th-century farmhouse offering spacious,
comfortable accommodation.
3 bedrooms; double B&B £73-£82
including dinner

CAMPSITE

►►► Tockett's Mill Caravan Park
Skelton Rd, Guisborough
☎ (01287) 610182
fax: (01287) 610182
South of Redcar; pitch price from £8 per
night.

WHERE TO EAT

RESTAURANTS

⊕ Krimo's
8 The Front, Seaton Carew, Hartlepool
☎ (01429) 266120
Some of the best Mediterranean food on the
northeast coast.
Lunch: 12-1.30
Dinner: 7-9.30
Credit cards 1 3

⊕ Grinkle Park
Saltburn-by-the-sea,Easington
☎ (01287) 640515
Meticulously presented English/French
cooking of a high quality.
Lunch: 12-1.45
Dinner: 7-9

⊕ Parkmore
636 Yarm Rd, Eaglescliffe, Stockton-on-
Tees
☎ (01642) 786815
International cuisine in a popular hotel.
Lunch: 12-2
Dinner: 7-9.45

PUBS

The Ship
Saltburn
☎ (01287) 622361
Gloriously situated on the beach with high
cliffs beyond and views across the beautiful
bay, this very pretty Tetleys pub offers a
range of dishes to suit all tastes.
Open: 11am-3pm, 6-11pm; Sunday 12-
3pm, 7-10.30pm
Bar food: as opening times
Restaurant: evenings only

Ripon

This is one of the most aesthetically pleasing venues in Britain. Located among the beautiful Yorkshire Dales, it is a really lovely site to spend a day at the races. Great care has been taken to make the racecourse buildings look appealing to the eye and colourful flower-beds of many hues adorn the grounds.

There is an extensive range of bars and restaurants, while children are well catered for with a pair of playgrounds. This encourages lots of families to attend during the school holidays, creating a lively, happy atmosphere.

Flat racing is held throughout the spring and summer with a large number of the meetings being concentrated in August. The quality of competition is particularly good during this month and included among the races is the course's annual feature event, the Great St Wilfrid Handicap. This is a fiercely contested six-furlong sprint that draws runners from all over the country. The oval circuit has a large circumference of more than one and a half miles, but it is regarded as being a sharp track because of the slightly cramped bends. There are also minor surface undulations in the home straight, with a pronounced dip about a furlong from the finish.

FURTHER INFORMATION

Ripon Race Company Ltd
P O Box 1, Ripon HG4 1DS
☎ (01765) 602156; fax: (01765) 690018

LOCATION AND HOW TO GET THERE

The course is two miles from the centre of Ripon on the B6265. The M1 ends in Leeds, to the south, from where you can continue north on the A61, through Harrogate to Ripon. To avoid the centre of Leeds, leave the M1 at junction 42, taking the M62 eastbound to junction 30, then take the A642 northwards to connect with the A1 beyond Garforth. Leave the A1 at the Walshford intersection and take the A road parallel to the A1(M), then the B6265 near Kirby Hill. **Nearest Railway Station:** Harrogate; there is a bus service from Harrogate to the centre of Ripon, which is about 1 mile from the course

ADMISSION

All classes of day ticket give access to full betting facilities, including Tote. Children under 16 admitted free if accompanied by paying adult

Day tickets:

CLUB £12 - access to restaurant, bar, boxes and private rooms

TATTERSALLS £8 - access to restaurants, bars, private rooms and fast food

SILVER RING £4 - access to restaurant, bar, ice cream

COURSE £2.50, or £8 for a car and up to four occupants - access to bar, snack bar and mobile refreshment outlets

Annual membership: £75 single, £115 joint (husband and wife), £50 junior (under 21)

COURSE FACILITIES

Banks:
there are no banks or cashpoint facilities on the course

For families:
picnicking is permitted anywhere, but the Course enclosure is the only one where you can do so from your car; children's play areas in Silver Ring and Course enclosures; no lost children centre, but one of the ambulance rooms is used for this purpose; free car parking

CALENDAR OF EVENTS

April 8 – flat
April 16 – flat
April 25 – flat
May 17
May 27 – evening meeting
June 17-18 – evening meeting on Wednesday
July 6 – evening meeting

July 18
August 3
August 15 – includes William Hill Great St Wilfred Handicap Stakes
August 22
August 31
September 1

WHERE TO STAY

HOTELS

★★★ 67% Ripon Spa
Park St
☎ (01765) 602172
fax: 01765 690770
40 bedrooms; double B&B £75-£95
Credit cards 1 2 3 5

★★ 61% Unicorn
Market Place
☎ (01765) 602202
fax: (01765) 690734
33 bedrooms
Credit cards 1 2 3 5

Around Ripon

★★★ 70% Aldwark Manor
Aldwark
☎ (01347) 838146, fax: (01347) 838867
20 bedrooms
Credit cards 1 2 3 5

★★★ 62% Crown
Horsefair, Boroughbridge
☎ (01423) 322328
fax: (01423) 324512
42 bedrooms; double B&B £70-£90
Credit cards 1 2 3 5

★★★ 67% Rose Manor
Horsefair, Boroughbridge
☎ (01423) 322245, fax: (01423) 324920
17 bedrooms; double B&B £94-£99 (room only)
Credit cards 1 2 3 5

★★ 66% Bay Horse Inn & Motel
Burnt Yates
☎ (01423) 770230
16 bedrooms
Credit cards 1 3

★★★★ 65% Harrogate Moat House
Kings Rd, Harrogate
☎ (01423) 849988,
fax: (01423) 524435
214 bedrooms; double room £78-£134
Credit cards 1 2 3 5

★★★★ 61% The Majestic
Ripon Rd, Harrogate
☎ (01423) 568972
fax: (01423) 502283
156 bedrooms; double room £65-£100 (room only)
Credit cards 1 2 3 5

★★★ 70% Grants
3-13 Swan Rd
☎ (01423) 560666
fax: (01423) 502550
42 bedrooms
Credit cards 1 2 3 5

★★★ 🏵🏵 68% White House
10 Park Pde, Harrogate
☎ (01423) 501388
fax: (01423) 527973
11 bedrooms; double B&B £90-£135
Credit cards 1 2 3 5

★★★ 65% St George Swallow
1 Ripon Rd, Harrogate
☎ (01423) 561431
fax: (01423) 530037
92 bedrooms; double B&B £110-£125
Credit cards 1 2 3 5

★★★ 61% The Crown
Crown Place, Harrogate
☎ (01423) 567755
fax: (01423) 502284
121 bedrooms
Credit cards 1 2 3 5

★★★ 🏵 65% Studley
Swan Rd, Harrogate
☎ (01423) 560425
fax: (01423) 530967
36 bedrooms
Credit cards 1 2 3 5

★★★ 61% Hospitality Inn
Prospect Place, West Park, Harrogate
☎ (01423) 564601
fax: (01423) 507508
71 bedrooms; double room £80-£95 (room only)
Credit cards 1 2 3 5

★★ 🏵 68% Harrogate Brasserie Hotel & Bar
28-30 Cheltenham Pde, Harrogate
☎ (01423) 505041
fax: (01423) 530920
14 bedrooms
Credit cards 1 3 5

★★ 70% The Manor
3 Clarence Dr, Harrogate
☎ (01423) 503916
fax: (01423) 568709
17 bedrooms; double B&B £62-£89
Credit cards 1 3

★★ 70% Ascot House
53 Kings Rd, Harrogate
☎ (01423) 531005
fax: (01423) 503523
19 bedrooms; double B&B £69-£100
Credit cards 1 2 3 5

★★ 67% Abbey Lodge
29-31 Ripon Rd, Harrogate
☎ (01423) 569712
fax: (01423) 530570
19 bedrooms; double B&B from £55-£59
Credit cards 1 2 3

★★ 69% Green Park
Valley Dr, Harrogate
☎ (01423) 504681
fax: (01423) 530811
43 bedrooms; double B&B £65-£83
Credit cards 1 2 3 5

★★★ 68% Imperial
Prospect Place, Harrogate
☎ (01423) 565071
fax: (01423) 500082
85 bedrooms; double B&B from £90
Credit cards 1 2 3 5

★★ 64% Valley
93-95 Valley Dr, Harrogate
☎ (01423) 504868
fax: (01423) 531940
15 bedrooms; double B&B £52-£65
Credit cards 1 2 3 5

★ 72% Britannia Lodge
16 Swan Rd, Harrogate
☎ (01423) 508482
fax: (01423) 526840
12 bedrooms; double B&B £54-£75
Credit cards 1 2 3

WHERE TO STAY

★ **70% Gables**
2 West Grove Rd, Harrogate
☎ (01423) 505625, fax: (01423) 561312
9 bedrooms; double B&B £55-£70
Credit cards 1 3

★ **67% Grafton**
1-3 Franklin Mount, Harrogate
☎ (01423) 508491, fax: (01423) 523168
17 bedrooms; double B&B £54-£68
Credit cards 1 2 3 5

★ **69% Alvera Court**
76 Kings Rd, Harrogate
☎ (01423) 505735, fax: (01423) 507996
12 bedrooms
Credit cards 1 3

★ **67% The Croft**
42-46 Franklin Rd, Harrogate
☎ (01423) 563326
fax: (01423) 530733
13 bedrooms; double B&B £52
Credit cards 1 2 3 5

★★★ ❀ **70% Dower House**
Bond End, Knaresborough
☎ (01423) 863302
fax: (01423) 867665
32 bedrooms; double B&B £75-£100
Credit cards 1 2 3 5

★★★ ❀ **76% Hob Green**
Markington
☎ (01423) 770031
fax: (01423) 771589
12 bedrooms; double B&B £90
Credit cards 1 2 3 5

★★ **65% Nags Head Country Inn**
Pickhill
☎ (01845) 567391
fax: (01845) 567212
15 bedrooms
Credit cards 1 3

★★ ❀ **71% Sheppard's**
Church Farm, Front St, Sowerby, Thirsk
☎ (01845) 523655
fax: (01845) 524720
8 bedrooms; double B&B £75-£85
Credit cards 1 3

★★ **62% Three Tuns Hotel**
Market Place, Thirsk
☎ (01845) 523124
fax: (01845) 526126
11 bedrooms; double B&B £50-£60
Credit cards 1 2 3 5

★ **60% Old Red House**
Station Rd, Thirsk
☎ (01845) 524383
10 bedrooms; double B&B £32-£36
Credit cards 2 3 5

★★ **68% The Angel Inn**
Long St, Topcliffe
☎ (01845) 577237
fax: (01845) 578000
15 bedrooms; double B&B £59-£50
Credit cards 1 3

BED AND BREAKFAST

QQQQ The Crown
Roecliffe, Boroughbridge
☎ (01423) 322578
fax: (01423) 324060
Delightful country inn with attractive
modern bedrooms that are furnished and
decorated to high standard.
12 bedrooms
Credit cards 1 3

QQQQ Alexa House & Stable Cottages
26 Ripon Rd, Harrogate
☎ (01423) 501988
fax: (01423) 504086
Yorkshire hospitality in very congenial
surroundings; high standard throughout.
13 bedrooms; double B&B £55-£65
Credit cards 1 3

QQQQ Acacia Lodge
21 Ripon Rd, Harrogate
☎ (01423) 560752
fax: (01423) 503725
A few minutes walk from the town centre;
very attractively furnished and decorated
throughout.
5 bedrooms; double B&B £48-£68

QQQQ Ashley House Hotel
36-40 Franklin Rd, Harrogate
☎ (01423) 507474, fax: (01423) 560858
Attractive, friendly hotel with very well
equipped bedrooms.
17 bedrooms; double B&B £50-£70
Credit cards 1 2 3 5

QQQQ Bay Tree
Aldfield, Ripon
☎ (01765) 620394; fax: (01765) 620394
6 bedrooms; double B&B £40-£45
Credit cards 1 3

QQQ Ashwood House
7 Spring Grove, Harrogate
☎ (01423) 560081
fax: (01423) 527928
Bedrooms are mostly spacious and
comfortable.
9 bedrooms; double B&B £46-£50

QQQQ Delaine Hotel
17 Ripon Rd, Harrogate
☎ (01423) 567974
fax: (01423) 561723
Family-run Victorian house with tastefully
decorated bedrooms and attractive flower
gardens.
10 bedrooms
Credit cards 1 2 3

QQQ Glenayr
19 Franklin Mount, Harrogate
☎ (01423) 504259
fax: (01423) 504259
Tastefully decorated and pleasantly
furnished with freshly prepared home-
cooked dinners.
6 bedrooms
Credit cards 1 2 3 5

QQQ Wharfedale House
28 Harlow Moor Dr, Harrogate
☎ (01423) 522233
Immaculate hotel situated in pleasant
location and providing well appointed
bedrooms.
8 bedrooms

QQQQ Quality Kimberley Hotel
11-19 Kings Road, Harrogate
☎ (01423) 505613
fax: (01423) 530270
A large refurbished hotel with well-
furnished bedrooms.
49 bedrooms
Credit cards 1 2 3 5

WHERE TO STAY

QQQ Wynnstay House
60 Franklin Rd, Harrogate
☎ (01423) 560476
fax: (01423) 562539
Very comfortable, with particularly well appointed bedrooms.
5 bedrooms; double B&B £46
Credit cards 1 3

QQQ Newton House Hotel
5/7 York Place, Knaresborough
☎ (01423) 863539, fax: (01423) 869748
Lovely Grade II listed house with individually decorated, spacious bedrooms.
12 bedrooms; double B&B £50-£60
Credit cards 1 3

QQQ The Villa
47 Kirkgate, Knaresborough
☎ (01423) 865370
fax: (01423) 867740
Beautifully situated high above the River Nidd; bedrooms are furnished in period style.
6 bedrooms

QQQQ Bank Villa
Masham
☎ (01765) 689605
Well established, popular guesthouse offering personal service.
7 bedrooms; double B&B £39

CAMPSITES

Around Ripon

►►►► Allerton Park Caravan Site
Allerton Mauleverer, Allerton Park
☎ (01423) 330569
Quarter of a mile east of the A1, off the A59; pitch price £8-£11 per night

►► Church Farm
Knaresborough Rd, Bishop Monkton
☎ (01765) 677405
South of Ripon off the A61; pitch price from £4 per night

►►► Shaws Trailer Park
Knaresborough Rd
☎ (01423) 884432 & 883622
On the A59 Harrogate-Knaresborough road; pitch price from £5.50 per night.

►►► Sleningford Water Mill Caravan Site
North Stanley
☎ (01765) 635201
Adjacent to River Ure and A6108; pitch price £6.50-£10.50 per night

►►►► Ripley Caravan Park
Knaresborough Rd, Ripley
☎ (01423) 770050
fax: (01423) 770050
On B6165 south of Ripley; pitch price from £5.50 per night.

►►► Sowerby Caravan Park
Sowerby, Thirsk
☎ (01845) 522753
Off A168 half a mile south; pitch price from £5.75 per night.

►►► Woodhouse Farm Caravan & Camping Park
Winksley
☎ (01765) 658309
fax: (01765) 658882
Six miles west of Ripon off B6265; pitch price £7.50-£9 per night.

WHERE TO EAT

RESTAURANTS

❀ Grundy's
21 Cheltenham Crescent, Harrogate
☎ (01423) 502610
Bright flavours, unusual combinations and an admirable wine list.
Lunch not served
Dinner: 6.30-10
Credit cards 1 2 3 5

❀ The Bistro
1 Montpellier Mews, Harrogate
☎ (01423) 530708
Ambitious and accomplished cooking in a small mews restaurant.
Lunch 12-2
Dinner: 7-9.30
Credit cards 1 3

❀ Sportsman's Arms
Wath-in-Nidderdale, Pateley Bridge
☎ (01423) 711306
Generously proportioned dishes based on fresh local produce.
Lunch: 12-2.30
Dinner: 7-10

❀ Hob Green
Markington
☎ (01423) 770031
A delightful country house serving excellent cooking
Lunch: 12-1.45
Dinner: 7-9.30

PUBS

Buck Inn
Thornton Watlass
☎ (01677) 422461
fax: (01677) 422447
The original old stone bar dates from the 17th century and is very cosy. An interesting range of meals is offered and beers include Theakstons, John Smiths, Beamish and Black Sheep as well as a weekly guest beer. Whisky drinkers can choose between 45 single malts.
Open: 11am-2.30pm, 6-11pm; Saturday 11-11; Sunday 12-10.30pm
Bar food: 12-2pm, 6.30-9.30pm

Royal Windsor

A picturesque course which is situated in 165 acres of beautiful Berkshire countryside next to the banks of the River Thames. Loose horses have been known to go for a dip and one jockey even had to be saved from drowning after being carted into the water.

On a more practical note, those wishing to arrive at the track in style can do so by taking the river bus during the summer.

Meetings are predominantly on the Flat, though not exclusively, and particularly popular are the ones run on Monday evenings in mid-summer. These always attract large cosmopolitan crowds spanning the whole social spectrum. This creates the lively and entertaining atmosphere that makes Windsor such a unique and appealing venue. This is one of the two figure-of-eight tracks in Britain (the other is Fontwell) and an excellent close-up of the start of races over one and a half miles can be obtained by walking across to the centre of the course. Viewing is rather restricted from the main stands, however, especially in the Members Enclosure.

FURTHER INFORMATION

The Racecourse Office
Windsor Racecourse, Maidenhead Road
Windsor, Berks SL4 5JJ
Telephone (01753) 864726

LOCATION AND HOW TO GET THERE

The course is by the River Thames, two miles from central Windsor on the A308. From the M4 junction 6 take the A355 to Windsor, cross the river, take slip road to A308 and follow signs.

Nearest Railway Stations: Windsor and Eton Riverside; there are frequent services from Waterloo; from both stations head for the Barry Avenue Promenade close to Windsor Bridge, from where there is a connecting riverboat service to and from the course on racedays.

Helicopter landing and take off facilities are available - telephone the secretary (01753) 865234 for advance permission.

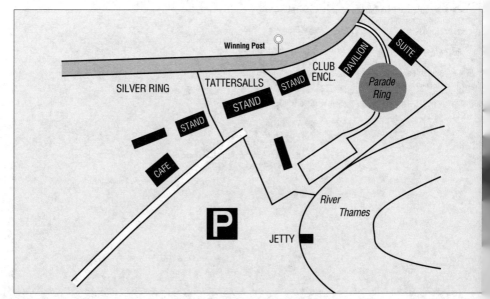

ADMISSION

Children and wheelchair users are admitted free of charge to all enclosures.

Day Tickets:

CLUB ENCLOSURE £14 - access to paddock and parade ring, grandstand with some seating available, restaurant, bars, private boxes overlooking course and paddock, champagne bar, facilities for disabled; Tote, Tote bookmakers shop and credit only.

TATTERSALLS AND PADDOCK £10 - access to paddock and parade ring, viewing from terraces, bars, snack bars, facilities for disabled racegoers; Tote, Tote bookmakers

shop and credit only.

SILVER RING £4 - access to viewing from terraces, Tote, bars, cafeteria, snack bars, picnic area, facilities for disabled racegoers; Tote only

PICNIC AREA £12 per car, including all occupants

Annual membership: £120 includes 23 racedays and 6 reciprocal days at other courses

COURSE FACILITIES

Banks:
there are no banks or cashpoint facilities on the course.

For families:
picnic area with refreshment kiosk and toilets in Silver Ring for all summer (flat) meetings and Saturdays and Bank Holidays in National Hunt season; children's play area; creche; baby changing facilities; lost children centre.

CALENDAR OF EVENTS

January 1 – jumping	**July 6** – evening meeting
January 21 – jumping	**July 13** – evening meeting
January 26 – jumping	**July 20** – evening meeting
February 4 – jumping	**July 27** – evening meeting
February 21 – jumping	**August 3** – flat; evening meeting
May 11 – flat; evening meeting	**August 10**
May 18 – flat; evening meeting	**August 17** – flat
June 1 – flat; evening meeting	**August 29** – evening meeting – Winter Hill Stakes
June 8 – evening meeting	**November 14** – jumping
June 15 – evening meeting	**November 23** – jumping
June 22 – evening meeting	**December 3** – jumping
June 29 – evening meeting	

WHERE TO STAY

HOTELS

★★★★ ❀❀ 76% Oakley Court
Windsor Rd, Water Oakley
☎ (01753) 609988
fax: (01628) 37011
92 bedrooms; double bedroom £140–£205 (room only)
Credit cards 1 2 3 5

★★★ ❀❀❀ 72% The Castle
High St
☎ (01753) 851011
fax: (01753) 830244
104 bedrooms
Credit cards 1 2 3 5

★★ ❀ 74% Aurora Garden
14 Bolton Av
☎ (01753) 868686
fax: (01753) 831394
15 bedrooms
Credit cards 1 2 3 5

Around Windsor

★★★★ ❀ 68% Berystede
Bagshot Rd, Sunninghill
☎ (01344) 23311
fax: (01344) 872301
91 bedrooms
Credit cards 1 2 3 5

★★ 72% Highclere
19 Kings Rd, Sunninghill
☎ (01344) 25220
fax: (01344) 872528
11 bedrooms; double B&B £70–£85.
Credit Cards 1 2 3

★★★★ (Red) ❀❀❀ Pennyhill Park
London Rd, Bagshot
☎ (01276) 471774
fax: (01276) 473217
76 bedrooms
Credit Cards 1 2 3 5

★★★ 72% Stirrups Country House
Maidens Green, Winkfield, Bracknell
☎ (01344) 882284
fax: (01344) 882300
24 bedrooms; double bedroom from £70 (room only)
Credit Cards 1 2 3 5

★★★ ❀ 68% Burnham Beeches Moat House
Grove Road, Burnham
☎ (01628) 429955
fax: (01628) 603994
75 bedrooms; double bedroom £110–£180 (room only)
Credit Cards 1 2 3 4 5

★★★★ ❀ 70% Runnymede
Windsor Rd, Egham
☎ (01784) 436171
fax: (01784) 436340
171 bedrooms; double room £92–£175 (room only)
Credit Cards 1 2 3 5

WHERE TO STAY

★★★★ 64% The Excelsior
Bath Rd, West Drayton
☎ 0181-759 6611
fax: 0181-759 3421
828 bedrooms
Credit cards 1 2 3 5

★★★★ 70% London Heathrow Hilton
Terminal 4, Heathrow Airport
☎ 0181-759 7755
fax: 0181-759 7579
400 bedrooms; double bedroom from £176
Credit cards 1 2 3 5

★★★ 67% Courtyard by Marriott
Church St, Chalvey, Slough
☎ (01753) 551551
fax; (01753) 553333
148 bedrooms; double bedroom £53-£90

★★★★ 66% The Copthorne
400 Cippenham Lane, Slough
☎ (01753) 516222, fax; (01753) 516237
219 bedrooms
Credit cards 1 2 3 5

★★★★ 67% Forte Crest Heathrow
Sipson Road, West Drayton
☎ 0181-759 2323
fax: 0181-897 8659
569 bedrooms
Credit cards 1 2 3 5

★★★★ ❀ 73% Holiday Inn Crowne Plaza
Stockley Rd, West Drayton
☎ (01895) 445555
fax: (01895) 445122
374 bedrooms; double room from £140
(room only)
Credit cards 1 2 3 5

★★★★ 69% Ramada
Bath Rd, Heathrow Airport
☎ 0181-897 6363
fax: 0181-897 1113
638 bedrooms
Credit cards 1 2 3 5

Forte Posthouse
Bath Rd, Heathrow Airport
☎ 0181-759 2552
fax: 0181-564 9265
186 bedrooms; double room from £69
(room only)
Credit cards 1 2 3 5

★★★ ❀ 64% Ye Olde Bell
Hurley, Maidenhead
☎ (01628) 825881, fax: (01628) 825939
36 bedrooms
Credit cards 1 2 3 5

★★★★ ❀❀❀ 78% Fredrick's
Shoppenhangers Rd, Maidenhead
☎ (01628) 635934
fax: (01628) 771054
37 bedrooms; double B&B £188-£198
Credit Cards 1 2 3 5

★★★ 66% Thames Riviera
At the Bridge, Maidenhead
☎ (01628) 74057
fax: (01628) 776586
52 bedrooms; double B&B £80-£95
Credit Cards 1 2 3 5

★★★★ ❀ 69% The Compleat Angler
Marlow Bridge, Marlow
☎ (01628) 484444
fax: (01628) 486388
62 bedrooms; double room £150-£195
(room only)
Credit cards 1 2 3 5

★★★ 70% The Thames Lodge
Thames St, Staines
☎ (01784) 464433, fax: (01784) 454858
44 bedrooms; double bedroom £55-£110
(room only
Credit cards 1 2 3 5

★★★★★ ❀❀❀❀ (RED) Cliveden
Taplow, signposted from all directions
☎ (01628) 668561
fax: (01628) 661837
39 bedrooms; double room £230-£410
Credit cards 1 2 3 5

★★ ❀ 68% Chequers Inn
Kiln Ln, Wooburn Common
☎ (01628) 529575, fax: (01628) 850124
17 bedrooms; double B&B £72.50-£100
Credit cards 1 2 3

BED AND BREAKFAST

QQ Clarence Hotel
9 Clarence Rd
☎ (01753) 864436, fax: (01753) 857060
Centrally placed historic hotel offering
attractive and well coordinated rooms.
21 bedroom; double B&B £44-£52
Credit cards 1 2 3 5

Around Windsor

QQQ Longford Guest House
550 Bath Rd, Longford, Heathrow Airport
☎ (01753) 682969
fax: (01753) 794189
5 bedrooms; double B&B from £39
Credit cards 1 3

Q Shepiston Lodge
31 Shepiston Lane, Hayes
☎ 0181-573 0266 or 569 2356
fax: 0181-569 2536
Small guest house close to Heathrow
Airport
13 bedrooms; double B&B from £41.50
Credit cards 1 2 3 5

QQ The Cottage
150 High St, Cranford, Heathrow Airport
☎ 0181-897 1815
fax: 0181-897 3117
Clean, comfortable, well-maintained
accommodation.
7 bedrooms; double B&B from £55
Credit cards 1 3

QQQ Bridgettine Convent
Fulmer Common Rd, Iver Heath
☎ (01753) 662073 & 662645
fax: (01753) 662172
Very attractive Tudor-style timbered house
where peace and tranquility are assured.
13 bedrooms; double B&B £36-£40

QQQQ Holly Tree House
Burford Close, Marlow Bottom, Marlow
☎ (01628) 891110, fax: (01628) 481278
Large modern detached property; tastefully
decorated bedrooms have every facility.
5 bedrooms; double B&B £69.50-£79.50
Credit cards 1 2 3

WHERE TO STAY

QQ Colnbrook Lodge
Bath Rd, Colnbrook, Slough
☎ (01753) 685958
fax: (01753) 685164
Comfortable and well equipped detached
house on the edge of the village.
8 bedrooms; double B&B £39-£55
Credit cards 1 3

CAMPSITES

►►► Highclere Farm Country Touring Park
Newbarn Lane, Seer Green, Chalfont St
Giles
☎ (01494) 874505 & 875665
fax: (01494) 875238
Pitch prices from £7.50 per night

WHERE TO EAT

RESTAURANTS

❀❀❀❀ Waterside
River Cottage, Ferry Rd, Bray
☎ (01628) 20691
Excellent French cuisine prepared by
Michael Roux in picturesque riverside
setting.
Lunch: 12-2
Dinner: 7-10
Credit cards 1 3 5

❀ Jade Fountain
38 High St, Sunninghill
☎ (01344) 27070
Smart and friendly Chinese restaurant
offering high standard Chinese cuisine.
Lunch: 12-1.50
Dinner: 6-10
Credit cards 1 2 3 5

❀ Aurora Garden
14 Bolton Ave, Windsor
☎ (01753) 868686
Fresh and flavoursome dishes served in a
small hotel restaurant.
Lunch: 12-2; £13.95 and à la carte
Dinner; 7-9; £13.95 and à la carte

❀❀ McClements Restaurant
2 Whitton Rd, Twickenham
☎ 0181-744 9610
An interesting variety of mainly rustic
French cooking.
Lunch: 12-2.30
Dinner; 7-11

Salisbury

Salisbury may be better known for its awe-inspiring cathedral, but it is also home to an extremely attractive and popular racecourse. Around a dozen fixtures are scheduled here annually and a good standard of racing is maintained during the entire Flat season.

July and August see the highest attendances, especially at the marvellous evening meetings. The facilities are top-notch and this is one course where it is well worth paying a little extra for the added privileges of the Members enclosure - the restaurant and bar are particularly good in this section.

The wide track rises steadily throughout and there is a right-handed elbow in it, five furlongs from the finish. The course is used by many of the top trainers to introduce and educate their best two-year-olds, so there is usually a smattering of potentially smart youngsters on view. It is appropriate, then, that the highlight of the year is a contest restricted to juveniles, the Champagne Stakes, which is run towards the end of June. A man whose horses it usually pays to follow here is local handler Richard Hannon. He became champion trainer for the first time in the early nineties and normally sends a strong raiding party down from his nearby base on the edge of Salisbury Plain.

FURTHER INFORMATION

Salisbury Racecourse
Netherhampton, Salisbury, Wiltshire SP2 8PN
☎ (01722) 326461/327327

LOCATION AND HOW TO GET THERE

The course is 3.5 miles southwest of Salisbury off the A3094 Netherhampton road. From the A303, take the A30 to Salisbury, continue on the A30 to the west of Salisbury, then take the A3094 to Netherhampton.
Nearest Railway Station: Salisbury; there is a connecting bus service to the course on racedays.

ADMISSION

All classes of day ticket give access to full betting facilities, including Tote.

Day Tickets:

MEMBERS £13 - access to restaurant, bars, boxes, private rooms

TATTERSALLS £9 - access to bars and Tote betting shop
COURSE £4 - access to bar

Annual membership: £95 single, £190 double

COURSE FACILITIES

Banks:
there are no banks or cashpoint facilities on the course.

For families:
children's play area during July and August meetings only.

CALENDAR OF EVENTS

May 3
May 14
June 9-10
June 24-25 – includes Gibbs Mew Bibury Stakes & Champagne Stakes
July 11
July 17 – evening meeting
July 31 – evening meeting
August 7
August 12 – includes Upavon Stakes
August 20
September 3 – EBF Lochsong Stakes
September 30

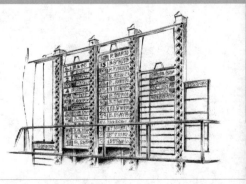

WHERE TO STAY

HOTELS

★★★ 69% Rose & Crown
Harnham Rd, Harnham
☎ (01722) 399955
fax: (01722) 339816
28 bedrooms; double bedroom £130
Credit cards 1 2 3 5

★★★ 68% Red Lion
Milford St
☎ (01722) 323334, fax: (01722) 325756
54 bedrooms; double bedroom £115-£125
Credit cards 1 2 3 5

★★★ ⚜ 73% The White Hart
Saint John St
☎ (01722) 327476, fax: (01722) 412761
68 bedrooms
Credit cards 1 2 3 5

★★ 55% The Trafalgar
33 Milford St
☎ (01722) 338686, fax: (01722) 414496
18 bedrooms; double B&B £49.50-£65.50
Credit cards 1 2 3 5

★★ 68% King's Arms
9-11 Saint John's St
☎ (01722) 327629, fax: (01722) 414246
15 bedrooms; double B&B £58-£78
Credit cards 1 2 3 5

★★★ ⚜ 74% Milford Hall
206 Castle St
☎ (01722) 417411, fax: (01722) 419444
35 bedrooms; double B&B £60-£75
Credit cards 1 2 3 5

★★ ⚜⚜⚜ 79% Howard's House
Teffont Evias
☎ (01722) 716392, fax: (01722) 716820
9 bedrooms; double B&B £95-£135
Credit cards 1 2 3 5

Around Salisbury

Travelodge
Amesbury
☎ (01980) 624966
fax: (01980) 624966
32 bedrooms; double room £34.95-£49.95
(room only)
Credit cards 1 2 3

★★ ⚜ 67% Ashburn Hotel & Restaurant
Damerham Rd, Fordingbridge
☎ (01425) 652060
fax: (01425) 652150
20 bedrooms; double B&B £72-£82
Credit cards 1 2 3

BED AND BREAKFAST

QQQ Byways House
31 Fowlers Rd
☎ (01722) 328364, fax: (01722) 322146
Victorian house which is attractively
decorated, comfortably furnished and has
well equipped bedrooms.
23 bedrooms; double B&B from £39-£53
Credit cards 1 3

QQQQ Cricket Field Cottage
Skew Bridge, Wilton Rd
☎ (01722) 322595
fax: (01722) 322595
Well appointed, en suite bedrooms are
offered in this modernised gamekeeper's
cottage.
14 bedrooms; double B&B £45

QQQQ The Old House
161 Wilton Rd
☎ (01722) 333433
fax: (01722) 416144
Full of character with exposed beams and
brick walls; furnished and decorated in
country-cottage style.
7 bedrooms; double B&B from £38-£45

QQQ Glen Lyn
6 Bellamy Ln, Milford Hill
☎ (01722) 327880
fax: (01722) 327880
Substantial Victorian property a few minutes
walk from the city centre.
6 bedrooms; double B&B £37-£42

QQQQ The Edwardian Lodge
59 Castle Rd
☎ (01722) 413329
fax: (01722) 503105
Fine house with spacious rooms
7 bedrooms; double B&B £38-£44

QQQ Hayburn Wyke
72 Castle Rd
☎ (01722) 412627
fax: (01722) 412627
Close to the cathedral; clean and bright
accommodation.
6 bedrooms; double B&B £36-£42

QQQ Leena's
50 Castle Rd
☎ (01722) 335419
fax: (01722) 335419
Small guesthouse with friendly, relaxed
atmosphere.
6 bedrooms; double B&B £36-£41

QQ Richburn
23/25 Estcourt Road
☎ (01722) 325189
Detached Victorian family home with clean
and comfortable accommodation
10 bedrooms; double B&B £32-£42

QQ Holmhurst
Downton Rd
☎ (01722) 410407
fax: (01722) 323164
Detached red-brick family home; bedrooms
are simply appointed and comfortable.
6 bedrooms; double B&B £34-£40

QQ Swaynes Firs Farm
Coombe Bissett
☎ (01725) 519240
Friendly farmhouse seven miles from
Salisbury on the A354 Blandford road.
3 bedrooms; double B&B £40

QQQ Warren
15 High St, Downton
☎ (01725) 510263
A 15th-century house, lovingly furnished;
bedrooms are clean and fresh flowers add
colour.
6 bedrooms; double B&B £40-£45

WHERE TO STAY

CAMPSITES

►►► Coombe Nurseries Touring Park
Race Plain, Netherhampton, Salisbury
☎ (01722) 328451
Pitch price from £5 per night.

►►►► New Forest Country Holidays
Sandy Balls Estate Ltd, Godshill
☎ (01425) 653042
Situated south of Salisbury near New Forest; pitch price £7-£17 per night.

►►► Stonehenge Touring Park
Orcheston, Shrewton
☎ (01980) 620304
fax: (01980) 621121
Four miles from Stonehenge; pitch price from £6.25 per night.

►Longbeech Campsite
Fritham
☎ (0131) 3146100
fax: (0131) 334 0849
Large attractive site bordering The New Forest; pitch price £6-£8.50 per night

►Ocknell Campsite
Fritham
☎ (0131) 314 6100
fax: (0131) 334 0849
An open New Forest site; pitch price from £6 per night.

WHERE TO EAT

RESTAURANTS

❀ Hour Glass
Burgate, Fordingbridge
☎ (01425) 652348
Enjoyable, straightforward modern English dishes in cosy thatched cottage restaurant.
Lunch: 12-1.30
Dinner: 7-9.45
Credit cards 1 3 5

❀❀❀ The Three Lions
Stuckton, Fordingbridge
☎ (01425) 652489
Variety and value from a spontaneous menu and exciting wine list.
Lunch: 12-1.30
Dinner: 7-9
Credit cards 1 3

❀ Langley Wood
Redlynch
☎ (01794) 390348
Straightforward French/English cooking in a relaxed rural setting.
Lunch by arrangement: Sunday lunch £13.75
Dinner: 7-11; £22 à la carte
Credit cards 1 2 3 5

❀ Milford Hall
206 Castle St
☎ (01722) 417411
Interesting and ambitious menus at a Georgian mansion.
Lunch: 12-2
Dinner: 7-9.30

❀ Ashburn
Damerham Rd, Fordingbridge
☎ (01425) 652060
Hillside restaurant with views over the New Forest.
Lunch: 12-1.45
Dinner: 7-9

PUBS

Haunch of Venison
14 Minster St
☎ (01722) 322024
Parts of this tiny pub date from 1320 when it was the church house, and one bar has a 600-year-old fireplace. Beers include Ringwood Best, Courage Best and Directors and there are 100 malt whiskies. Excellent value bar snacks are available, though space is rather limited.
Open: 11am-11pm; Sunday 12-3pm, 7-10.30pm
Bar food: 12-2.30pm, 7-9.30pm, except Sunday evening

Around Salisbury

Horseshoe
Ebbesbourne Wake
☎ (01722) 780474
Delightfully rustic and homely village pub with a pretty garden, beyond which are kept pot-bellied pigs, goats and a donkey. Adnams, Wadworth and Ringwood ales are drawn straight from the cask and hearty portions of reliable bar food are on offer.
Open: 11.30am-2.30pm, 6.30-11pm; Sunday 12-3pm, 7-10.30pm
Bar food: 12-2pm, 7-9.30pm, except Monday evening; Sunday 7-9pm
Restaurant: Tuesday to Saturday 7-9.30pm, Sunday 12-2pm

Cuckoo Inn
Hamptworth, Landford
☎ (01794) 390302
Tucked away down a series of country lanes this isolated thatched inn attracts lovers of real ale, with no less than 12 varieties on offer. Food is limited to rolls, ploughmans and pasties, but is always available. Children are allowed in the family room and garden bar.
Open: 11.30am-2.30pm, 6-11pm; Saturday 11am-11pm; Sunday 12-3pm, 7-10.30pm
Bar food: as opening times

Sandown Park

Sandown is often voted 'Racecourse of the Year', an accolade it richly deserves. It has in fact been awarded this title more than 10 times in the last twenty years which gives a pretty good indication of its justifiable popularity.

Located a mere 15 miles from the centre of London in leafy Esher, this course is the nearest thing to a racing Utopia. The track is set in a spectacular amphitheatre with the grandstand ideally situated to give a superb view of the action. The facilities are exemplary and the atmosphere is second to none.

The quality of racing does justice to the fantastic surroundings and stirring finishes can nearly always be guaranteed on the stiff uphill climb to the winning post. There is a full programme of events under both codes with nearly thirty fixtures staged here annually. The evening meetings are a delight during summer and the jumps fixtures can not be matched for excitement in winter. One of the major attractions of the equine calendar is the Whitbread Gold Cup Day at the end of April. The famous handicap chase of that name is the feature race of an outstanding mixed card which also includes an important Derby trial on the Flat. Crowds are huge at this meeting and it is sensible to purchase tickets in advance as numbers may be restricted for safety reasons. Another highlight is the Coral-Eclipse Stakes in early July, an extremely valuable Group One event that attracts Europe's top middle-distance performers.

FURTHER INFORMATION

Club Secretary
Sandown Park Racecourse, Esher,
Surrey KT10 9AJ
☎ (01372) 463072/464348

LOCATION AND HOW TO GET THERE

Sandown Park is 13 miles from central London via the A3 and four miles southwest of Kingston on the A307. Leave the M3 at junction 1 and take the A308 towards Kingston, passing Kempton Park on the left; turn right onto the A309, then right again onto the A307. From the M25, leave at junction 10, and approach via the A3.

Nearest Railway Station: Esher; the station is within easy walking distance of the course.

ADMISSION

Day Tickets:

Accompanied children under 16 are admitted free to all enclosures.

CLUB feature days £15,(£13 in advance) £10 junior (16-25 years); premium days £16,(£14 in advance) £13 junior; classic days £25,(£20 in advance) £16 junior - access to restaurants, bars, snacks, private rooms, boxes and facilities for disabled racegoers.

GRANDSTAND feature days £10; premium days £11; classic days £15 (reductions for advance booking) - access to self-service restaurant, bars, snacks, facilities for disabled racegoers, creche.

PARK feature days £4; premium £4, classic days £5 - access to bar, snacks and mobile catering; good view of steeplechase fences and flat sprint course

Parking: Members car park £2; Classic days £5; Portsmouth Road car park free

Annual membership: £180, junior £75, includes free members' car park label, exclusive use of Club Bar with balcony, free admission for a guest to one meeting. Season membership: jump season £75; flat season £115

COURSE FACILITIES

Banks:
there are no banks or cashpoint facilities on the course, but cheques can be cashed at the Secretary's office during the hours between gates opening and the last race

For families:
picnic area; children's play area; creche; lost children taken to secretary's office

CALENDAR OF EVENTS

January 10 – jumping
February 7 – jumping; includes Scilly Isles Novices' Steeple Chase
February 19-20 – jumping
March 13-14 – jumping; includes Sunderlands Imperial Cup Handicap Hurdle
March 31 – jumping
April 24-25 – flat; includes Sandown Mile on Friday. Whitbread Gold Cup and Thresher Classic Trial on Saturday
May 25-26 – includes Tripleprint Temple Stakes and Brigadier Gerard Stakes; evening meeting on Tuesday
June 12-13 – flat
July 3-4 – Hong Kong Day on Friday. Coral-Eclipse Day on Saturday
July 15 – flat; evening meeting
July 22-23 – includes Evening Meeting on Wednesday. Milcars Star Stakes on Thursday
August 2 – flat
August 12 – flat; evening meeting
August 21-22 – includes Solario Stakes on Friday. Lyceum Atlanta Stakes on Saturday
September 15-16 – flat
November 7 – National Hunt
December 4-5 – includes Bovis Crowngap Winter Hurdle on Friday. William Hill Handicap Hurdle on Saturday

WHERE TO STAY

HOTELS

Around Sandown Park

★★ 65% Haven
Portsmouth Rd, Esher
☎ 0181-398 0023
fax: 0181-398 9463
20 bedrooms; double B&B from £79
Credit cards 1 2 3 5

Travel Inn
Leatherhead Rd, Chessington
☎ (01372) 744060
fax: (01372) 720889
42 bedrooms; double bedroom £36.50

★★★ 64% Shepperton Moat House
Felix Lane, Shepperton
☎ (01932) 241404
fax: (01932) 245231
156 bedrooms
Credit cards 1 2 3 5

★★★★ ❀ 71% Oatlands Park
146 Oatlands Drive, Weybridge
☎ (01932) 847242
fax: (01932) 842252
128 bedrooms; double B&B £75-£145
Credit cards 1 2 3 5

★★★ ❀ 71% Ship Thistle
Monument Green, Weybridge
☎ (01932) 848364
fax: (01932) 857153
39 bedrooms; double bedroom £86-£125
Credit cards 1 2 3 5

★★★ 65% Forte Posthouse
Bath Rd, Heathrow Airport
☎ 0181-759 2552
fax: 0181-564 9265
186 bedrooms; double room from £69 (room only)
Credit cards 1 2 3 5

★★ 61% Hotel Ibis Heathrow
112/114 Bath Rd, Heathrow Airport
☎ 0181-759 4888
fax: 0181-564 7894
354 bedrooms; double room £53.50-£55
Credit cards 1 2 3 5

★★★★ ❀ 65% Woodlands Park
Woodlands Ln, Stoke D'Abernon
☎ (01372) 843933
fax: (01372) 842704
59 bedrooms; double room from £115
Credit cards 1 2 3 5

Hilton National Cobham
Seven Hills Rd South, Cobham
☎ (01932) 864471
fax: (01932) 868017
149 bedrooms; double bedroom £80-£174

★★★ 69% Kingston Lodge
Kingston Hill, Kingston Upon Thames
☎ 0181-541 4481
fax: 0181-547 1013
62 bedrooms; double bedroom £75-£105
Credit cards 1 2 3 5

BED AND BREAKFAST

Around Sandown Park

QQQ Epsom Downs Hotel
9 Longdown Rd, Epsom
☎ (01372) 740643
fax: (01372) 723259
Charming hotel located in peaceful residential area; modern, well equipped accommodation.
15 bedrooms; double B&B £49-£65
Credit cards 1 2 3 5

QQQQ Ashling Tara Hotel
50 Rosehill, Sutton
☎ 0181-641 6142
fax: 0181-644 7872
Ideal hotel for business and pleasure
14 bedrooms; double B&B from £75
Credit cards 1 2 3

QQQ Shalimar Hotel
215-221 Staines Rd, Hounslow
☎ 0181-577 7070
fax: 0181 569 6789
31 bedrooms; double B&B £45-£49
Credit cards 1 2 3 5

WHERE TO STAY

QQ Warwick
321 Ewell Rd, Surbiton
☎ 0181-296 0516
fax: 0181-296 0517
Small, cheerful guest house.
9 bedrooms; double B&B £40-£46
Credit cards 1 3

QQ Warbeck House Hotel
46 Queens Rd, Weybridge
☎ (01932) 848764
fax: (01932) 847290
Modestly furnished bedrooms in an
attractive Edwardian house.
10 bedrooms; double B&B £45-£55

QQQ Glen Court
St Johns Hill Rd, Woking
☎ (01483) 764154
fax: (01483) 755737
Attractive Edwardian house; spacious
comfortable bedrooms, traditionally
furnished.
12 bedrooms; double B&B £63.45
Credit cards 1 3

WHERE TO EAT

RESTAURANTS

Around Sandown Park

✿✿ Le Raj
211 Firtree Rd, Epsom
☎ (01737) 371371
Excellent Indian cuisine in stylish air-
conditioned restaurant.
Lunch 12-2.15; £20 à la carte
Dinner: 7-10.30; £20 à la carte

✿ Crowthers
481 Upper Richmond Rd West, East Sheen,
London SW14
☎ 0181-876 6372
Popular local restaurant with good modern
cooking and a warm welcome.
Lunch: 12-2
Dinner: 7-10
Credit cards 1 2 3

✿✿✿ Michels
13 High St, Ripley
☎ (01483) 224777 & 222940
Stylish town house where the cooking
shows more than a dash of flair.
Lunch: 12-1.30
Dinner: 7-9
Credit cards 1 2 3

✿ Good Earth
14-18 High St, Esher
☎ (01372) 462489
Popular restaurant serving mainly
Cantonese dishes.
Lunch: 12-2.15; £12 and à la carte
Dinner: 6-11; £17.50 and à la carte

✿✿ Le Petit Pierrot
4 The Parade, Claygate
☎ (01372) 465105
French provincial-style dishes served in
comfortable restaurant.
Lunch: 12.15-2.30
Dinner: 7-10.30

✿✿ Chez Max
168 Ifield Rd, Surbiton
☎ 0171-835 0874
Lunch: 12.30-2.30
Dinner: 7-11

✿✿ Ayudhya
14 Kingston Hill, Kingston upon Thames
☎ 0181-549 5984
A welcoming Thai restaurant.
Lunch: 12-2.30; from £20 à la carte
Dinner: 7-11; from £20 à la carte

✿✿ McClements Bistro
2 Whitton Rd, Twickenham
☎ 0181-744 9610
Interesting variety of mainly rustic French
cooking.
Lunch: 12-2.30
Dinner: 7-11

Sedgefield

With its relaxed, warm and welcoming atmosphere, Sedgefield has rightly gained a reputation for being a friendly racecourse. Recent redevelopment has included a brand new pavilion and the upgrading of the existing facilities, all with the needs of disabled racegoers in mind.

These changes were very necessary as the stands had begun to look antiquated and the amenities were definitely on the limited side. The situation is much improved now and the course has still managed to retain its old-fashioned charm and individual character that makes it such an enticing venue. It is also good to see that admission prices remain amongst the lowest in the land.

The track is in beautiful, rolling countryside and is a peaceful and tranquil setting for around 20 National Hunt meetings staged here every year. The standard of racing is only average and the most valuable event in the calendar is, appropriately enough, a selling hurdle which is run in early May. The oval circuit is undulating and essentially sharp in character, though the run-in rises fairly steeply and long-distance chases provide a thorough test of stamina when the ground is riding soft.

FURTHER INFORMATION

The Racecourse Manager, The Bungalow, Sedgefield Racecourse, Sedgefield, Stockton-on Tees, Cleveland, TS21 2HW
☎ (01740) 621925; Fax:(01740) 620663

LOCATION AND HOW TO GET THERE

The racecourse is situated just outside the southwestern edge of Sedgefield, which is just 10 miles from Teesside and Darlington on the A689 it is three miles east of the A1(M) and seven miles west of the A19, via the A689.
Nearest railway station: Durham and Darlington there is a regular bus service to Sedgefield

ADMISSION

All classes of day ticket give access to full betting facilities, including Tote.

Day Tickets:

Accompanied children under 16 are admitted free. Parking is free, though there is parking in the paddock enclosure for £2 per day.

PADDOCK £8, senior citizens £4 - access to bars, restaurants, private boxes and rooms

COURSE £2 - access to bar and snack bar

COURSE FACILITIES

Banks:
there are no banks or cashpoint facilities on the course.

For families:
lost children's centre in Secretary's office.

CALENDAR OF EVENTS

January 14 – jumping	**September 4**
January 28 – jumping	**September 15**
February 17 – jumping	**September 29**
February 25 – jumping	**October 13**
March 10 – jumping	**October 29**
March 17 – jumping	**November 10**
April 3	**November 19**
April 25 – evening meeting	**December 8**
May 2 – evening meeting	**December 26**
July 11 – evening meeting	
July 29 – evening meeting	

WHERE TO STAY

HOTELS

★★★ 64% Hardwick Hall
☎ (01740) 620253
fax: (01740) 622771
17 bedrooms; double B&B £68-£73
Credit cards 1 2 3 5

★★ 65% Crosshill
1 The Square
☎ (01740) 620153 & 621206
fax: (01740) 621206
8 bedrooms; double B&B £47-£53
Credit cards 1 2 3

Around Sedgefield

★★ 59% The Postchaise
36 Market, Bishop Auckland
☎ (01388) 661296
fax: (01388) 606312
12 bedrooms; double B&B £40-£45
Credit cards 1 3 5

★★★ 69% Hallgarth Country House
Coatham Mundeville, Darlington
☎ (01325) 300400
fax: (01325) 310083
41 bedrooms; double room £60-£75
Credit cards 1 2 3 5

★★★ 68% Headlam Hall
Headlam, Gainford, Darlington
☎ (01325) 730238
fax: (01325) 730790
28 bedrooms; double B&B £78-£98
Credit cards 1 2 3 5

★★★ 69% Swallow King's Head
Priestgate, Darlington
☎ (01325) 380222
fax: (01325) 382006
85 bedrooms; double B&B £90-£110
Credit cards 1 2 3 5

★★★★ 68% Royal Country
Old Elvet, Durham
☎ 0191-386 6821
fax: 0191-386 0704
150 bedrooms; double B&B £125
Credit cards 1 2 3 5

★★★ 72% Ramside Hall
Carrville, Durham
☎ 0191-386 5282
fax: 0191-386 0399
82 bedrooms; double B&B £110-£125
Credit cards 1 2 3 5

★★★ 69% Three Tuns
New Elvet, Durham
☎ 0191-386 4326
fax: 0191-386 1406
47 bedrooms; double B&B £65-£125
Credit cards 1 2 3 5

★★★ 65% Bowburn Hall
Bowburn, Durham
☎ 0191-377 0311
fax: 0191-377 3459
19 bedrooms; double B&B £60
Credit cards 1 2 3 5

★★ 68% Bridge Toby
Croxdale, Durham
☎ 0191-378 0524
fax: 0191-378 9981
46 bedrooms
Credit cards 1 2 3 5

★★ 58% Rainton Lodge
West Rainton, Durham
☎ 0191-5120540 & 5120534,
fax: 0191-584 1221
27 bedrooms; double B&B £40-£45
Credit cards 1 3

★★ 69% Hardwicke Hall Manor
Hesleden
☎ (01429) 836326
fax: (01429) 837676
15 bedrooms; double B&B £57.50-£67.50
Credit cards 1 2 3 5

★★★★ 72% Redworth Hall Hotel & Country Club
Redworth
☎ (01388) 772442
fax: (01388) 775112
100 bedrooms; double room £114-£145
Credit cards 1 2 3 5

★★★ 69% Eden Arms Swallow Hotel
Rushyford
☎ (01388) 720541
fax: (01388) 721871
46 bedrooms; double B&B £95-£110
Credit cards 1 2 3 5

★★★★ 66% Swallow
10 John Walker Square, Stockton-on-Tees
☎ (01642) 679721
fax: (01642) 601714
125 bedrooms; double B&B £60-£125
Credit cards 1 2 3 5

★★★ 71% Parkmore
636 Yarm Rd, Eaglescliffe, Stockton-on-Tees
☎ (01642) 786815
fax: (01642) 790485
55 bedrooms; double B&B £53-£79
Credit cards 1 2 3 5

Forte Posthouse Teeside
Low Ln, Thornaby-on-Tees
☎ (01642) 591213, fax: (01642) 594989
135 bedrooms; double room £43-£69
(room only)
Credit cards 1 2 3 5

★★★ 59% Billingham Arms
The Causeway, Billingham
☎ (01642) 553661 & 360880
fax: (01642) 552104
69 bedrooms; double room £60-£67
Credit cards 1 2 3 5

★★ 66% Claireville
519 Yarm Rd, Eaglescliffe
☎ (01642) 780378
fax: (01642) 784109
18 bedrooms; double B&B £44-£58
Credit cards 1 2 3 5

★★ 63% Crossways
Dunelm Rd, Thornley
☎ (01429) 821248
fax: (01429) 820034
23 bedrooms; double B&B £40-£65
Credit cards 1 2 3 5

WHERE TO STAY

BED AND BREAKFAST

QQQ Dun Cow
High St
☎ (01740) 620894
Charming old inn situated near the
racecourse; unusual bedrooms and
excellent cuisine.
6 bedrooms; double B&B from £45
Credit cards 1 2 3 5

Around Sedgefield

QQQ Woodland
63 Woodland Rd, Darlington
☎ (01325) 461908
fax: (01325) 461908
Victorian terraced house situated on the
A68, with well maintained bedrooms.
9 bedrooms; double B&B £35-42

QQQQ Hillrise
13 Durham Road West, Bowburn, Durham
☎ 0191-377 0302, fax: 0191-377 0302
Lovingly furnished house offering warm
friendly service
5 bedrooms; double B&B £40

QQQ Lothlorien
48/49 Front St, Witton Gilbert, Durham
☎ 0191-371 0067
Quaint roadside cottage; charming
proprietoress.
3 bedrooms; double B&B £34-£36

QQQ Bay Horse
Brandon, Durham
☎ 0191-378 0498
Attractive stone-built inn; comfortable, well
equipped bedrooms. Good value bar meals.
10 bedrooms; double B&B £40
Credit cards 1 3

QQQQ The Edwardian Hotel
72 Yarm Rd, Stockton-on-Tees
☎ (01642) 615655
Bright, very well equipped cosy bedrooms.
6 bedrooms
Credit cards 1 3

WHERE TO EAT

RESTAURANTS

❀ Krimo's
8 The Front, Seaton Carew, Hartlepool
☎ (01429) 266120
Good value Mediterranean cuisine at a
popular sea front restaurant.
Lunch: 12-1.30; £6 and à la carte
Dinner: 7-9; from £13.95 à la carte

PUBS

See **Dun Cow** and **Bay Horse**, under Bed
and Breakfast above.

Southwell

This Midlands course is one of only three in Britain where racing is held both on a turf and an all weather track, the others being Lingfield and Wolverhampton. There are, not surprisingly, many striking similarities between the three venues.

All three stage large numbers of fixtures annually (around 50), the quality of racing is not the highest and attendances on weekdays can be rather low. To be fair to Southwell, though, the atmosphere here is more animated than at Lingfield and spectators are more numerous, particularly at the Saturday meetings which can be quite lively. The best card is over the jumps when all the races carry decent prize money.

This Nottinghamshire course may be somewhat lacking in beauty, but the facilities are substantial. There is a profusion of bars and restaurants from which to choose and particularly recommended is the friendly little eating-house called 'Pam's Pantry', which serves some terrific home-made food at very reasonable prices. The parade ring is attractively laid out while the copious stands provide excellent viewing of the track. An interesting recent initiative here is that some trainers are now actually based at the racecourse stables. This system is prevalent throughout America and has the potential for further development in this country.

New additions include an 18-hole golf course and leisure centre.

FURTHER INFORMATION

R A M Racecourses Ltd
Southwell Racecourse, Rolleston, Near Newark
Notts NG25 0TS
☎ (01636) 814481
Fax: (01636) 812271

LOCATION AND HOW TO GET THERE

The course is seven miles west of Newark, midway between the A1 and the M1. Leave the M1 at junction 28, take the A38 to Mansfield, then the A617 towards Newark on Trent.
Nearest Railway Station: Rolleston, adjacent to racecourse; there is no connecting bus service to the course.

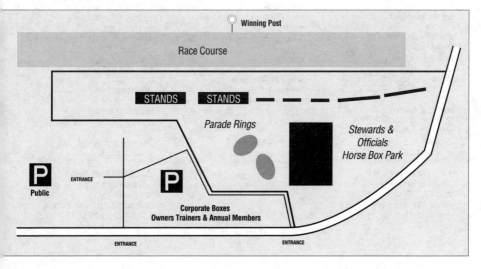

ADMISSION

All classes of day ticket give access to full betting facilities, including Tote.

MEMBERS £12 - access to restaurant, bar and private boxes

TATTERSALLS £6 - access to restaurant, bars and marquee

Diamond Club £4 – over 60s

(£2.50 administration charge)

COURSE FACILITIES

Banks:
there are no banks or cashpoint facilities on the course.

For families:
picnic area; children's play area; baby-changing facilities; lost children centre

CALENDAR OF EVENTS

January 2 – flat	**March 2** – flat	**July 9** – flat
January 5 – flat	**March 9** – flat	**July 11** – flat; evening meeting
January 9 – flat	**March 11** – flat	**July 17** – flat
January 12 – flat	**March 17** – flat	**July 20** – flat
January 16 – flat	**March 20** – flat	**July 25** – flat; evening meeting
January 19 – flat	**March 23** – flat	**August 14** – flat
January 23 – flat	**April 6** – flat	**August 31** – jumping
January 26 – flat	**April 27** – flat	**October 5** – jumping
January 30 – flat	**May 4** – jumping	**October 19** – flat
February 2 – flat	**May 7** – flat	**November 13** – flat
February 6 – flat	**May 11** – flat	**November 20** – flat
February 9 – flat	**May 18** – flat	**November 23** – flat
February 13 – flat	**June 5** – flat	**December 1** – flat
February 16 – flat	**June 12** – flat	**December 18** – flat
February 20 – flat	**June 18** – flat	**December 22** – flat
February 23 – flat	**June 20** – jumping; evening meeting	
February 27 – flat	**June 29** – flat	

WHERE TO STAY

HOTELS

★★★ 64% Saracen's Head
Market Place
☎ (01636) 812701, fax: (01636) 815408
27 bedrooms; double room £60 (room only)
Credit cards 1 2 3 5

Around Southwell

★★ 66% Unicorn
Gunthorpe Bridge, Gunthorpe
☎ (0115) 9663612
fax: (0115) 9664801
16 bedrooms; double £49.50-£59.50
Credit cards 1 2 3

★★ 71% Grange
73 London Rd, Newark-on-Trent
☎ (01636) 703399, fax: (01636) 702328
15 bedrooms; double B&B £52-£72
Credit cards 1 2 3 5

★★ 72% South Parade
117-119 Baldertongate, Newark-on-Trent
☎ (01636) 703008, fax: (01522) 605593
14 bedrooms; double B&B £54-£64
Credit cards 1 2 3

★★★★ 63% Nottingham Royal Moat House
Wollaton Street, Nottingham
☎ (0115) 941 4444, fax:(0115) 947 5888
201 bedrooms; double B&B £129
Credit cards 1 2 3 5

Travelodge
North Muskham, Newark-on-Trent
☎ (01636) 703635
30 bedrooms; double room £35-£50 (room only)
Credit cards 1 2 3

★★ 64% The Haven
Grantham Rd, Whatton
☎ (01949) 850800, fax: (01949) 851454
33 bedrooms; double B&B from £48
Credit cards 1 2 3

★★ 65% Hop Pole
Main St, Ollerton
☎ (01623) 822573
11 bedrooms; double B&B £45
Credit cards 1 2 3

★★ 66% Pine Lodge
281-283 Nottingham Rd, Mansfield
☎ (01623) 22308, fax: (01623) 656819
20 bedrooms; double B&B £40-£60
Credit cards 1 2 3 5

★★★ 65% Westminster
312 Mansfield Rd, Carrington, Nottingham
☎ (0115) 955 5000
fax: (0115) 955 5005
62 bedrooms; double bedroom £60-£98
Credit cards 1 2 3 5

BED AND BREAKFAST

QQ Crown Hotel
11 Market Place
☎ (01636) 812120
Attractive Georgian inn with pretty bedrooms
7 bedrooms; double B&B from £33
Credit cards 1 3

QQQQ Hall Farm House
Gonalston, Nottingham
☎ (0115) 9663112
Attractive 18th-century farmhouse.
3 bedrooms; double B&B £40-£45

WHERE TO EAT

QQQ Grantham Commercial Hotel
24-26 Radcliffe Rd, West Bridgford,
Nottingham
☎ (0115) 9811373
fax: (0115) 9818567
22 bedrooms; double B&B £40-£42
Credit cards 1 2 3

CAMPSITES

►►► Thornton's Holt Camping Park
Stragglethorpe, Radcliffe on Trent
☎ (0115) 9332125 & 933 4204
fax: (0115) 933 3318
Half a mile south of the A52 and 2 miles
north of the A46; pitch price £7-£8 per night

RESTAURANTS

✿✿ Black Swan
Hillside, Beckingham
☎ (01636) 626474
Highly competent modern English cooking
and efficient service in a village inn.
Lunch: 12-2; from £19.50
Dinner: 7-10; from £19.50
Credit cards 1 3

✿✿ Sonny's
3 Carlton St, Hockley, Nottingham
☎ (0115) 9473041
Honest cooking in the café/brasserie style.
Lunch: 12-2.30; from £25
Dinner: 7-10.30; from £25

PUBS

Waggon and Horses
Gypsy La, Bleasby, nr Southwell
☎ (01636) 830283
Good value pub fare, in an attractive and
peacefully located village pub, consists of
substantial, homely dishes. Theakston B,
Old Peculiar, Home Bitter and McEwans
Export are on draught and morning coffee is
available. Children are welcome anywhere
and there is an outdoor play area.
Open: 11am-3pm, 6-11pm; Sunday 12-
3pm, 7-10.30pm
Bar food: Tuesday to Sunday 12-2pm

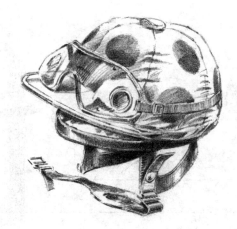

Stratford-upon-Avon

The name of Stratford-upon-Avon is, of course, recognised the world over as the birthplace of William Shakespeare. As a result, this charming town, with its splendid theatrical tradition, is one of the major tourist attractions in Britain.

Indeed, its popularity is second only to London in terms of the number of visitors it receives each year. Anyone planning a trip here should definitely try to fit in a day at the races. National Hunt meetings are held from March to September, with the spring and autumn fixtures particularly recommended.

There is always a lovely atmosphere at this delightful little racecourse. Crowds are really enthusiastic about their sport and horses return to a loud ovation in the winner's enclosure. The facilities are good and this is an ideal place to pack a picnic and drive into the centre of the course where there is also a large indoor bar that serves snacks. A good level of competition is maintained throughout the year with the highlight being the two-day meeting which draws the jumps season to a close at the end of May. There is a terrific end of term feel with a real party mood prevailing. The feature race on the Saturday is the Horse and Hound Cup, a prestigious hunter chase which runners will travel from far and wide to compete in.

FURTHER INFORMATION

Stratford-on-Avon Racecourse Co Ltd
Luddington Road, Stratford-upon-Avon
Warwicks CV37 9SE
☎ (01789) 267949

LOCATION AND HOW TO GET THERE

The course is approximately one mile from the town centre via the A439 Evesham road. From the M5 southbound, leave at junction 6 and take the A4538 southwards before turning left onto the A422 for Stratford; from the M5 northbound, leave at junction 7, and head towards Worcester for a short distance before turning right onto the A422 for Stratford; from the M42 south of Birmingham, leave at junction 4 and take the A44 southwards to Stratford.;Junction 15 off the M40.

Nearest Railway Station: Stratford upon Avon; there is no connecting bus service to the course on racedays.

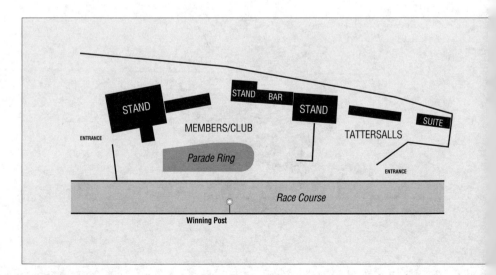

ADMISSION

All classes of day ticket give access to full betting facilities, including Tote.

Day Tickets:

CLUB/MEMBERS ENCLOSURE £13 - access to several bars, champagne bar, Annual Members' tea room, snack bars & new viewing grandstand.

TATTERSALLS £9 - access to Paddock Suite with restaurant and bars, viewing stand, private boxes & new viewing grandstand.

CENTRE COURSE £4 - access to bar, snack bar

Annual membership: £85, Car label £5

COURSE FACILITIES

Banks:
there are no banks or cashpoint facilities on the course.

For families:
picnic area with refreshment kiosk and toilets; children's play area.

CALENDAR OF EVENTS

March 16 – jumping
April 18 – evening meeting
May 8 – evening meeting
May 15 – evening meeting
May 29-30 – Horse and Hound Meeting; evening meetings on Friday; includes Horse and Hound Cup (final Champion Hunters' Steeplechase)
June 26 – evening meeting

July 12
July 25
August 15
September 5
October 17
October 29
December 30

WHERE TO STAY

HOTELS

★★★★ 🏵🏵 76% Welcombe
Warwick Rd
☎ (01789) 295252
fax: (01789) 414666
67 bedrooms; double B&B £150 –£160
Credit cards 1 2 3 5

★★★★ 65% Stratford Moat House
Bridgefoot
☎ (01789) 279988
fax: (01789) 298589
247 bedrooms; double bedroom £125
(room only)
Credit cards 1 2 3 5

★★★★🏵 66% The Shakespeare
Chapel St
☎ (01789) 294771
fax: (01789) 415411
63 bedrooms; double room £115 (room
only)
Credit cards 1 2 3 5

**★★★★ 68% Windmill Park Hotel &
Country Club**
Warwick Rd
☎ (01789) 731173
fax: (01789) 731131
104 bedrooms; double B&B £100–£120
Credit cards 1 2 3 5

★★★ 68% Grosvenor House
Warwick Rd
☎ (01789) 269213
fax: (01789) 266087
67 bedrooms; double B&B from £79.50
Credit cards 1 2 3 5

★★★★ 🏵 65% Alveston Manor
Clopton Bridge
☎ (01789) 204581
fax: (01789) 414095
106 bedrooms; double room £110–£175
(room only)
Credit cards 1 2 3 5

Forte Posthouse
Bridgefoot
☎ (01789) 266761
fax: (01789) 414547
60 bedrooms; double room £56
(room only)
Credit cards 1 2 3 5

★★★ 64% The White Swan
Rother St
☎ (01789) 297022
fax: (01789) 268773
37 bedrooms; double room £70–£90 (room
only)
Credit cards 1 2 3 5

★★★ 63% Falcon
Chapel St
☎ (01789) 279953
fax: (01789) 414260
73 bedrooms; double bedroom £80–£105
Credit cards 1 2 3 4 5

★★ 🏵 70% Stratford House
Sheep St
☎ (01789) 268288
fax: (01789) 295580
11 bedrooms; double B&B £72–£88
Credit cards 1 2 3 5

★★ 65% The Coach House Hotel
16-17 Warwick Rd
☎ (01789) 204109
fax: (01789) 415916
22 bedrooms; double B&B £65–£98
Credit cards 1 2 3 5

Around Stratford-upon-Avon

★★★ 🏵🏵 77% Salford Hall
Abbot's Salford
☎ (01386) 871300
fax: (01386) 871301
33 bedrooms; double B&B £105–£150
Credit cards 1 2 3 5

★★★ 68% Kings Court
Kings Coughton, Alcester
☎ (01789) 763111
fax: (01789) 400242
42 bedrooms; double B&B from £52
Credit cards 1 2 3

★★★★ 🏵🏵 77% Ettington Park,
Alderminster
☎ (01789) 450123
fax: (01789) 450472
48 bedrooms; double room £175
Credit cards 1 2 3

★★★ 67% The Glebe at Barford
Church St, Barford
☎ (01926) 624218
fax: (01926) 624625
41 bedrooms; double B&B £70–£140
Credit cards 1 2 3 5

**★★★★ 🏵🏵🏵 70% Billesley
Manor**
Billesley
☎ (01789) 279955
fax: (01789) 764145
41 bedrooms; double bedroom £160–£172
Credit cards 1 2 3 5

**★★★ 🏵🏵 (Red) Charingworth
Manor**
Charingworth
☎ (01386) 593555,
fax: (01386) 593353
26 bedrooms; double B&B from £132
Credit cards 1 2 3 5

WHERE TO STAY

★★★ 64% Charlecote Pheasant Country
Charlecote
☎ (01789) 279954
fax: (01789) 470222
67 bedrooms; double room £86–£95
Credit cards 1 2 3 5

★★★ (RED) ⚜⚜ Cotswold House
The Square, Chipping Campden
☎ (01386) 840330
fax: (01386) 840310
15 bedrooms; double B&B £120–£150
Credit cards 1 2 3

★★★ ⚜ ⚜ 70% Seymour House
High St, Chipping Campden
☎ (01386) 840429
fax: (01386) 804369
15 bedrooms; double B&B £90–£140
Credit cards 1 2 3

★★ ⚜⚜ 73% Noel Arms
High St, Chipping Campden
☎ (01386) 840317
fax: (01386) 841136
26 bedrooms; double B&B £92–£99
Credit cards 1 2 3 5

★★★ 66% Three Ways
Mickleton
☎ (01386) 438429
fax: (01386) 438118
40 bedrooms; double B&B £83–£110
Credit cards 1 2 3 5

★★ 59% Warwick Arms
High St, Warwick
☎ (01926) 492759
fax: (01926) 410587
35 bedrooms; double B&B £50–£59
Credit cards 1 2 3 5

BED AND BREAKFAST

QQQ Brook Lodge
192 Alcester Rd
☎ (01789) 295988
fax: (01789) 295988
Nicely decorated, well kept guesthouse.
7 bedrooms; double B&B £40–£50
Credit cards 1 2 3

QQQ Craig Cleeve House
67-69 Shipston Rd
☎ (01789) 296573, fax: (01789) 299452
On the A34 south of Clopton Bridge; bright fresh accommodation and friendly hosts.
15 bedrooms; double B&B £39–£50
Credit cards 1 2 3 5

QQQQ Eastnor House Hotel
Shipston Rd
☎ (01789) 268115
fax: (01789) 266516
On the A34, just 300 metres from the theatre; bright, fresh accommodation.
9 bedrooms; double B&B £50–£64
Credit cards 1 2 3

QQQQ Gravelside Barn
Binton
☎ (01789) 750502 & 297000,
fax: (01789) 298056
3 bedrooms; double B&B £50–£60
Credit cards 1 3

QQQ Highcroft
Banbury Rd
☎ (01789) 296293
fax: (01789) 415236
Spacious attractive rooms with antique or pine furniture; well equipped.
1 bedrooms; double B&B £36–£40

QQQ Hollies
'The Hollies', 16 Evesham Place
☎ (01789) 266857
Close to the town centre; a popular guesthouse offering a warm welcome.
6 bedrooms; double B&B £34–£45

QQQQ Melita Private Hotel
37 Shipston Rd
☎ (01789) 292432
fax: (01789) 204867
A friendly family run gueshouse on the A34, close to the river and major attractions.
12 bedrooms; double B&B £45–£72
Credit cards 1 2 3

QQQ Moonraker House
40 Alcester Rd
☎ (01789) 299346 & 267115
fax: (01789) 295504
Unusual guesthouse, spread over four properties, with attractive bedrooms.
22 bedrooms; double B&B £45–£70
Credit cards 1 3

QQQQ Sequoia House Private Hotel
51-53 Shipston Rd
☎ (01789) 268852
fax: (01789) 414559
Opposite the Royal Shakespeare Theatre; several types of room available, from the cosy cottage annexe to the exceptionally well furnished, luxury no-smoking rooms.
24 bedrooms; double B&B £42–£74
Credit cards 1 2 3 5

QQQQ Twelfth Night
Evesham Place
☎ (01789) 414595
Delightfully refurbished Victorian villa; pretty rooms with welcome extra touches.
6 bedrooms; double B&B £44–£56
Credit cards 1 3

QQQQ Victoria Spa Lodge
Bishopton Ln
☎ (01789) 267985
fax: (01789) 204728
Victorian Spa Lodge, enjoying peaceful, leafy setting at the side of the Stratford Canal.
7 bedrooms; double B&B £45–£52
Credit cards 1 3

QQQ Virginia Lodge
12 Evesham Place
☎ (01789) 292157
Well kept, friendly guesthouse close to the centre of Stratford.
8 bedrooms; double B&B £36–£48

WHERE TO STAY

Around Stratford

QQ Woodside Country House
Langley Rd, Claverdon
☎ (01926) 842446
fax: (01926) 842410
4 bedrooms; double B&B £40-£50

QQ Halford Bridge
Fosse Way, Halford
☎ (01789) 740382
fax: (01789) 740382
Spacious Cotswold stone road-house,
situated on the A429, offering pretty, well
equipped bedrooms.
6 bedrooms; double room £35-£42
Credit cards 1 3

QQQQ Northleigh House
Five Ways Rd, Hatton
☎ (01926) 484203
fax: (01926) 484006
Bedrooms have thoughtful extras and high
standards are maintained throughout by the
friendly proprietress.
7 bedrooms; double B&B £40-£58
Credit cards 1 3

QQQ Redlands Farm
Banbury Rd, Lighthorne
☎ (01926) 651241
Open-air swimming pool is available to
guests; Mrs Stanton provides wholesome
dishes.
3 bedrooms; double B&B £36-£40

QQ Newbold Nurseries
Newbold on Stour
☎ (01789) 450285
fax: (01789) 450285
Spacious, simply appointed bed and
breakfast accommodation.
2 bedrooms; double B&B from £30

QQQQ Nolands Farm
Oxhill
☎ (01926) 640309
fax: (01926) 641662
Set in a tranquil valley, with comfortable
bedrooms. Clay pigeon shooting and riding
can be arranged nearby.
9 bedrooms; double B&B from £36-£46
Credit cards 1 3

QQ Austin House
96 Emscote Rd, Warwick
☎ (01926) 493583
Guesthouse offering modest
accommodation.
6 bedrooms; double B&B £31-£37
Credit cards 1 3

QQQ Tudor House
West St, Warwick
☎ (01926) 495447
fax: (01926) 492948
Tudor house retaining much wattle and
daub and timbers; cosy bedrooms.
11 bedrooms; double B&B from £55.90
Credit cards 1 2 3 5

QQ Whitchurch Farm
Whitchurch, Wimpstone
☎ (01789) 450275
Lovely Georgian farmhouse part of a
working farm; bedrooms recently improved
with good en suite facilities.
3 bedrooms; double B&B ££36

CAMPSITES

**►►►► Island Meadow Caravan
Park**
The Mill House, Aston Cantlow
☎ (01789) 488273
fax: (01789) 488273
Quarter of a mile west of Aston Cantlow;
pitch price from £6.50 per night.

►►►► Ranch Caravan Park
Honeybourne
☎ (01386) 830744
fax: (01386) 833503
In the Vale of Evesham 2m from B4035;
pitch price £6-£11 per night.

WHERE TO EAT

RESTAURANTS

❀❀ Dormy House Hotel
Willersley, Broadway
☎ (01386) 852711
A good choice of light classical dishes from a range of menus
Lunch: 12-2
Dinner: 7-9.30

❀❀❀ Lygon Arms
High St, Broadway
☎ (01386) 852255
A good choice of modern English country cooking.
Lunch: 12-2
Dinner: 7-9.15

❀❀ Billesley Manor
Billesley, Alcester
☎ (01789) 279955
Richly classical Anglo/French cooking with a modern twist.
Lunch: 12-2
Dinner: 7-9.30

❀ Alveston Manor
Clopton Bridge
☎ (01789) 204581
Well-prepared dishes using good quality produce.
Lunch: 12-2
Dinner: 6-9.30

❀ Le Filbert Cottage
64 High St, Henley-in-Arden
☎ (01564) 792700
Well-executed French cooking in an English village setting.
Lunch: 12-1.30; £25 and à la carte
Dinner: 7-9.30; from £25 and à la carte

❀❀ Restaurant Bosquet
97a Warwick Rd, Kenilworth
☎ (01926) 852463
Unpretentious, reliably good cooking of French dishes.
Lunch: 12-1.15; from £21 and à la carte
Dinner: 7-9.15; from £21 and à la carte

PUBS

Bell
Alderminster
☎ (01789) 450414
An adventurous menu, a high standard of cooking and a wine list to match are the main attractions of the 17th-century pub. Beers include Marston Pedigree and Flowers Best and Original. Children are welcome.
Open: 12-2.30pm, 7-11pm; Sunday 12-2.30pm, 7-10.30pm
Bar food: 12-2pm, 7-9.30pm; Sunday 12-1.45pm, 7-9pm
Restaurant: times as bar food

Ferry
Alveston
☎ (01789) 269883
Friendly village-centre pub offering well prepared and promptly served food at a range of prices, all good value for money. Theakston Best, Bass, Wadworth 6X and Flowers Original are on sale, along with a selection of wines. Children over 5 years old are welcome.
Open: 11am-2.30pm, 6-11pm; Sunday 12-2.30pm, 7-10.30
Bar food: 11.45am-2pm, 6.30-9pm; Sunday 12-2pm

Kings Head
Aston Cantlow
☎ (01789) 488242
This is an attractive and unspoilt half-timbered pub with a small, well tended garden. Beers include Marston Pedigree, Flowers IPA, Boddingtons Bitter and Mild and Murphy's Stout; there is a reasonable selection of wines and a tasty range of bar meals. No children under 14 in the bar.
Open: 12-2.30pm, 7-11pm; Sunday 12-2.30pm, 7-10.30pm
Bar food: as opening hours, except Sunday and Monday evenings

Broom Tavern
High St, Broom, nr Bidford-on-Avon
☎ (01789) 773656
This busy village pub is popular for its wide choice of well prepared food, served promptly in unstinting portions. Beers include Bass, Flowers Best and Murphy's Stout and there is an extensive wine list. Children are welcome and the small lawned area outside has a bouncy castle.
Open: 11am-3pm, 6.30-11pm (opens at 6pm on Saturday); Sunday 11am-3pm, 7-10.30pm
Bar food: 12-2pm, 7-10pm
Restaurant: as bar food

Taunton

This small West Country course is well patronised by local trainers and attracts an enthusiastic and friendly crowd from all over the South West. The picturesque course is set in unspoilt Somerset countryside against a backdrop of the well-wooded Blackdown Hills.

Taunton is a country course with a country atmosphere, yet boasting modern facilities and newly laid out saddling boxes, Parade Ring and Winners Enclosure which give spectators an excellent view of the horses from the time they arrive on the course until the presentation of trophies after the race. There is a modern high level restaurant with a panoramic view of the track. There are also bars and snack bars and warm stands in which to shelter on cold wet days.

The £5 enclosure is in the centre of the course where racegoers can take their cars for a picnic on a fine day, with close-up views of the starts and all the fences. The course is a one and a quarter mile right-handed oval with two long straights and well-banked bends at both ends. Martin Pipe, the champion trainer, is a near neighbour and regular patron, rarely leaving any of the dozen meetings empty-handed.

FURTHER INFORMATION

Taunton Racecourse
Orchard Portman, Taunton TA3 7BL
☎ (01823) 337172; fax:(01823) 325881

LOCATION AND HOW TO GET THERE

The course is two miles south of Taunton on the B3170 Honiton-Corfe road. Leave the M5 at junction 25, turn towards Taunton and follow the Racecourse signs. From the A303 take the A358 towards Taunton and then proceed as above.

Nearest Railway Station: Taunton; there is no connecting bus service to the course.

ADMISSION

Bookmakers and Tote available to all classes of ticket holders; betting shop situated in paddock area not available to Centre Course.

Day Tickets:

CLUB £11 - access to Members' bars, buffet

PADDOCK £9 - access to bars, restaurant, buffet, hospitality suites

CENTRE COURSE £5 - access to Centre Course bar and buffet

Annual membership: £75 single, £125 double

COURSE FACILITIES

Banks:
there are no banks or cashpoint facilities on the course.

For families:
picnic area with refreshment kiosk and toilet

CALENDAR OF EVENTS

January 22	October 15
February 19	November 12
March 5	November 26
March 16	December 10
April 2	December 29
April 24 – evening meeting	
October 1	

WHERE TO STAY

HOTELS

★★★ (RED) 🏵🏵🏵🏵 Castle
Castle Green
☎ (01823) 272671
fax: (01823) 336066
36 bedrooms; double B&B £120-£195
Credit cards 1 2 3 5

★★★ 71% Rumwell Manor
Rumwell
☎ (01823) 461902
fax: (01823) 254861
20 bedrooms; double B&B £82-£92
Credit cards 1 2 3

Forte Posthouse
Deane Gate Av
☎ (01823) 332222
fax: (01823) 332266
99 bedrooms; double room £49-£59 (room only)
Credit cards 1 2 3 5

Travel Inn
81, Bridgewater Rd
☎ (01823) 321112
fax: (01823) 322054
40 bedrooms; double bedroom £36.50

★★ 61% Falcon
Henlade
☎ (01823) 442502
fax: (01823) 442670
11 bedrooms; double B&B £55-£65
Credit cards 1 2 3 5

★★ 🏵 74% Farthings Hotel & Restaurant
Hatch Beauchamp
☎ (01823) 480664
fax; (01823) 481118
8 bedrooms; double B&B £80-£90
Credit cards 1 2 3 5

Around Taunton

★★★ 72% Walnut Tree Inn
North Petherton, Bridgwater
☎ (01278) 662255
fax: (01278) 663946
32 bedrooms; double B&B £55-£74
Credit cards 1 2 3 5

★★ 67% Friarn Court
37 St Mary, Bridgwater
☎ (01278) 452859
fax: (01278) 452988
16 bedrooms; double B&B £59-£69
Credit cards 1 2 3 5

★★ 65% Shrubbery
Ilminster
☎ (01460) 52108
fax: (01460) 53660
14 bedrooms; double B&B £70-£95
Credit cards 1 2 3 5

Travelodge
Ilminster
☎ (01460) 53748
32 bedrooms; double room £35-£50 (room only)
Credit cards 1 2 3

Roadchef Lodge
Tauton Deane Motorway Service Area, Trull
☎ (01823) 332228
fax: (01823) 338131
39 bedrooms; double room £43.50
Credit cards 1 2 3 5

★★ 64% Beambridge
Sampford Arundel, Wellington
☎ (01823) 672223
fax: (01823) 673100
9 bedrooms; double B&B £47
Credit cards 1 2 3

★★ 🏵 76% The Belfry Country Hotel
Yarcombe
☎ (01404) 861234
fax: (01404) 861579
6 bedrooms; double B&B £68
Credit cards 1 2 3

BED AND BREAKFAST

QQQQ Meryan House Hotel
Bishop's Hull
☎ (01823) 337445
fax: (01823) 322355
Charming period residence; graceful, attractive decoration; early booking strongly recommended.
12 bedrooms; double B&B £50-£65
Credit cards 1 3

QQQQ Higher Dipford Farm
Trull
☎ (01823) 275770 & 257916
Grade II listed farmhouse; friendly proprietors and lots of character.
3 bedrooms; double B&B £46-£54
Credit cards 2

QQQ Brookfield
16 Wellington Rd
☎ (01823) 272786
Comfortable warm relaxed guesthouse.
8 bedrooms; double B&B £32-£40

Around Taunton

QQQQQ Frog Street Farm
Beercrocombe
☎ (01823) 480430
fax: (01823) 480430
Still a working farm; attractive Somerset longhouse, clad in wisteria; friendly, cosy atmosphere.
3 bedrooms; double B&B £46-£60

QQQQQ Whittles Farm
Beercrocombe
☎ (01823) 480301
fax: (01823) 480301
Ivey clad period house with welcoming hosts and attractive en suite bedrooms.
3 bedrooms; double B&B £46-£50

QQQQ Rising Sun
West Bagborough
☎ (01823) 432996
fax: (01823) 433568
A 16th-century inn with attractive colour - co-ordinated bedrooms.
3 bedrooms; double B&B from £45

WHERE TO STAY

QQQQ Higher House
West Bagborough
☎ (01823) 432996
fax: (01823) 433568
Superb views; comfortable bedrooms, a charming place to stay.
3 bedrooms; double B&B from £45

CAMPSITES

►►► Holly Bush Park
Culmhead
☎ (01823) 421515
fax: (01823) 421885
South of Taunton; pitch price from £6 per night.

►►► Gamlins Farm Caravan Park
Gamlins Farm, Greenham, Wellington
☎ (01823) 672596
fax: (01823) 672324
Situated off the A38 on the Greenham road.; pitch price £4-£7 per night

►►► Quantock Orchard Caravan Park
Crowcombe
☎ (01984) 618618
Attractive, quiet site; pitch price £6.90-£9.75 per night.

►►►► Fairways International Touring Caravan & Camp
Woolavington Corner, Bath Rd, Bawdrip
☎ (01278) 685569
A well-planned new site; pitch price £6-£8 per night.

WHERE TO EAT

RESTAURANTS

❀❀ Nightingales
Bath House Farm, Lower West Hatch
☎ (01823) 480806
Imaginative dishes, relaxed unpretentious service, in a simply decorated former cider house.
Dinner only: 7-9.30
Credit cards 1 3

❀❀❀❀ Castle
Castle Green
☎ (01823) 272671
Technically faultless cooking in the modern British style.
Lunch: 12.30-2
Dinner: 7.30-9

❀ Farthings
Hatch Beauchamp
☎ (01823) 480664
Enjoyable modern English food in a popular hotel.
Lunch: 12-1.30
Dinner: 7-8.30

PUBS

Around Taunton

Rising Sun
Knapp, North Curry
☎ (01823) 490436
This whitewashed Somerset longhouse, dating from 1480, is tucked away in a remote village near the Somerset Levels. Exmoor Ale, Boddingtons and Bass are on tap and there is a good wine list to complement the constantly changing menu, which represents good value for money. There is a room where children are allowed and there are gardens at the front and rear of the pub.
Open: 11.30am-2.30pm, 6.30-11pm; Sunday 12-3pm, 7-10.30pm
Bar food: 12-2pm, 7.30-9.30pm. Only ploughmans' are available on Sundays.
Restaurant: 12-2pm, 7-9.30pm. Only a traditional roast on Sunday

Greyhound
Staple Fitzpaine
☎ (01823) 480227
A good choice of beers is available in this former hunting lodge dating from 1640, and a good variety of food is on offer in both the bar and the restaurant. Children are welcome anywhere and there is a play area outside.
Open: 11am-3pm, 5-11pm
Bar food: 12-2pm, 7-10pm
Restaurant: as bar food

Rose & Crown
Wood Hill, Stoke St Gregory
☎ (01823) 490296
This 300-year-old pub (said to be haunted) offers interesting home-cooked bar meals. Beers include Eldridge Pope Royal Oak and Thomas Hardy Country Bitter, Exmoor Ale and Toby Bitter. Children are only allowed in the restaurant, where half-portions are available.
Open: 11am-2.30pm, 7-11pm
Bar food: 12-2pm, 7-10pm
Restaurant: as bar food
Accommodation: double room £34

Thirsk

A North Yorkshire track which is probably unrivalled in the attractiveness of its setting. The picturesque Hambleton Hills form a gorgeous backdrop to this pretty little course which is situated in real James Herriot country.

Given the natural beauty of the surroundings and the wonderfully relaxed atmosphere that pervades the air here, it is a pity that racing is restricted to just 13 fixtures on the Flat. The most popular of these meetings are in May and August when the sun is usually guaranteed to be shining.

The track is a left-handed oval circuit of a mile and a quarter. There is a slightly undulating run in of half a mile with an additional spur to provide a straight six-furlong course (horses drawn high have a big advantage in sprints). The track is deceptively sharp and a good jockey can sometimes steal a race by establishing a big early lead - top northern rider Mark Birch is a past master at this art round here. The standard of competition is fair and there are a couple of significant contests, the Classic Trial in mid-April and the Thirsk Hunt Cup, a competitive handicap that is run at the start of May.

FURTHER INFORMATION

Thirsk Racecourse Ltd
Station Road, Thirsk, North Yorkshire YO7 1QL
☎ (01845) 522276 Fax: (01845) 525353

LOCATION AND HOW TO GET THERE

The course is to the west of Thirsk on the A61, which links directly with the A1 in the west and the A19 in the east.
Nearest Railway Station: Thirsk; there is no connecting bus service, but the course is just ten minutes walk from the station.

ADMISSION

All classes of day ticket give access to full betting facilities, including Tote.

Day tickets:
Accompanied children under 16 are admitted free

MEMBERS £12 – access to restaurants, bars, boxes, private rooms

TATTERSALLS £8, senior citizens £4 – access to bars and self-service restaurant

FAMILY RING £3, £9 for car with up to four adults and all children, senior citizens £1.50 – access to bars and self-service buffet.

Annual membership: £80, Associate (man/woman and one other member of family) £130, junior (17-21) £35 – includes exchange days with other northern racecourses, 9 days free entry to Yorkshire county cricket matches.

COURSE FACILITIES

Banks:
there are no banks or cashpoint facilities on the course.

For families:
picnic area in Number 3 Ring with refreshment kiosk and toilets; supervised creche; baby changing facilities

CALENDAR OF EVENTS

April 17-18
May 2
May 15-16
June 1 – evening meeting
June 16
July 24

July 31-August 1
August 10 – evening meeting
August 28
September 5

WHERE TO STAY

HOTELS

★★ 62% Three Tuns Hotel
Market Place
☎ (01845) 523124
fax: (01845) 526126
11 bedrooms; double B&B £50-£60
Credit cards 1 2 3 5

★ 60% Old Red House
Station Rd
☎ (01845) 524383
10 bedrooms; double B&B £32-£36
Credit cards 1 2 3

Around Thirsk

★★ 63% Motel Leeming
Great North Rd, Bedale
☎ (01677) 422122
fax: (01677) 424507
40 bedrooms; double bedroom £30-£39.50
Credit cards 1 2 3 5

★★ 60% White Rose
Bedale
☎ (01677) 422707 & 424941,
fax: (01677) 425123
18 bedrooms; double B&B from £45
Credit cards 1 2 3 5

★★★ ❀ 69% Solberge Hall
Newby Wiske, Northallerton
☎ (01609) 779191
fax: (01609) 780472
25 bedrooms; double B&B £90-£100
Credit cards 1 2 3 5

★★ 67% The Golden Lion
Market Place, Northallerton
☎ (01609) 777411, fax: (01609) 773250
26 bedrooms; double room £45-£65
Credit cards 1 2 3 5

★★ 65% Nags Head Country Inn
Pickhill
☎ (01845) 567391, fax: (01845) 5672172
15 bedrooms; double room £50
Credit cards 1 3

★★★ 67% Ripon Spa
Park St, Ripon
☎ (01765) 602172, fax: (01765) 690770
40 bedrooms; double room £75-£95
Credit cards 1 2 3 5

★★ 61% Unicorn
Market Place, Ripon
☎ (01765) 602202, fax: (01765) 690734
33 bedrooms; double room £64
Credit cards 1 2 3 5

★★ ❀ 71% Sheppard's
Church Farm, Front St, Sowerby
☎ (01845) 523655, fax: (01845) 524720
8 bedrooms; double B&B £70-£80
Credit cards 1 3

★★ 68% The Angel Inn
Long St, Topcliffe
☎ (01845) 577237, fax: (01845) 578000
15 bedrooms; double B&B £55-£59.50
Credit cards 1 3

BED AND BREAKFAST

QQQQ Elmfield House
Arrathorne, Patrick Brompton
☎ (01677) 450558, fax: (01677) 450557
Large attractive house with all-round
countryside views.
9 bedrooms; double B&B £42-£48
Credit cards 3

QQQ Forresters Arms Hotel
Kilburn
☎ (01347) 868386 & 868550
fax: (01347) 868386
Attractive inn, dating from the 12th-century,
with particularly well furnished bedrooms.
10 bedrooms; double room £49-£58
Credit cards 1 3

QQQQ The Crown
Roecliffe, Boroughbridge
☎ (01423) 322578, fax: (01423) 324060
12 bedrooms
Credit cards 1 3

QQQQ Bank Villa
Masham
☎ (01765) 689605
Charming stone-built Georgian house with
attractive bedrooms.
7 bedrooms; double B&B £39

QQQ Alverton
26 South Pde, Northallerton
☎ (01609) 776207
Attractive and comfortable Victorian terraced
house.
5 bedrooms; double B&B from £37

QQQ Windsor
56 South Pde, Northallerton
☎ (01609) 774100
Thoughtfully furnished and equipped
bedrooms.
6 bedrooms; double B&B £34-£42
Credit cards 1 3

CAMPSITES

►►► Sowerby Caravan Park
Sowerby
☎ (01845) 522753
One mile from Thirsk on the Sowerby Road;
pitch price £6.25-£6.75 per night

►►► Sleningford Water Mill Caravan Site
North Stanley
☎ (01765) 635201
Adajacent to A6108; pitch price £7-£10.50
per night

WHERE TO STAY

►►► Cote Ghyll Caravan Park
Osmotherley
☎ (01609) 883425
Situated off A19; pitch price from £5.25-£6 per night.

►►► Riverside Meadows Country Caravan Park
Ure Bank Top, Ripon
☎ (01765) 602964 & 607764
On high ground overlooking the River Ure. Pitch price from £5-£9.50 per night.

►► Church Farm Caravan Park
Bishop Monkton
☎ (01765) 677405
Tree-lined site; pitch price from £4-£5 per night

WHERE TO EAT

RESTAURANTS

Around Thirsk

❀❀ McCoys (Tontine Inn)
Staddle Bridge
☎ (01609) 882671
Stylish cooking in a relaxed, oriental setting of palms and parasols.
Lunch: 12-2
Dinner: 7-10
Credit cards 1 2 3 5

❀ Sheppard's
Church Farm, Front Street, Sowerby
☎ (01845) 523655
An interesting choice of well-produced dishes.
Lunch: 12-2
Dinner: 7-10

❀ Solberge Hall
Newby Wiske, Northallerton
☎ (01609) 779191
A wide-ranging selection of English/French dishes
Lunch: 12-2
Dinner: 7-9.30

PUBS

Around Thirsk

Crab and Lobster
Asenby
☎ (01845) 577286
This white, thatched cottage with vines and shuttered windows is just outside Asenby on a fairly busy road. The food is of excellent quality and there is an extensive wine list. Draught ales include Youngers and Theakstons and scrumpy is also available. Children are welcome, with the 'snug' area available for families.
Open: 11.30am-3pm, 6.30-11pm; Sunday 12-3
Bar food: 12-2pm, 7-9.30 or 10pm
Restaurant: 11.30am-3pm, 6.30-11pm; Sunday 12-3 (book six weeks in advance for weekends)

Abbey Inn
Coxwold
☎ (013476) 204
An attractive old Yorkshire stone pub near to Byland Abbey, offering very tasty, good value meals. Draught beers include EP Traditional, Theakstons and Guinness and there is a good wine list. Children are welcome in the pub and there is a large garden.
Open: 10am-2.30pm, 6.30-11pm, but closed Sunday evening and all day Monday.
Bar food: as opening times

Towcester

This is, without any shadow of a doubt, the stiffest National Hunt course in Britain. The track is a mile and three quarters in circumference with the last mile providing a punishing test of stamina.

There is a steep climb before the turn into the home straight which then rises steadily all the way to the winning post. On heavy ground, long-distance contests can become a gruelling slog with the runners almost appearing to be moving in slow motion in the closing stages. A jockey even commented once that he was travelling so slowly that he could have finished quicker by jumping off his horse and dragging it to the line.

This is not said to put anyone off making a visit to this charming rural track. Quite the contrary, in fact, as there is no better venue at which to witness the total embodiment of the spirit of National Hunt racing. Winners, both equine and human, have to show real courage and determination in order to triumph here and that is why this course ranks as a firm favourite among jumping enthusiasts. The Grandstands offer fantastic views of the entire course and finishing straight, with excellent facilities available in the new £1million Members Grace Stand

FURTHER INFORMATION

Towcester Race Club
Easton Neston, Towcester, Northants NN12 7HS
☎ (01327) 353414

LOCATION AND HOW TO GET THERE

The course is half a mile south of Towcester on the old Watling Street. Leave the M1 at junction 15A and take the A5.
Nearest Railway Stations: Northampton (9 miles) or Milton Keynes (12 miles); there are no connecting bus services to the course, but there are services from both towns' bus stations to Towcester town centre.

ADMISSION

All classes of day ticket give access to full betting facilities, including Tote.

Day tickets:
MEMBERS £12 – access to bar, restaurant, snack bar, boxes, & new Grace Stand

TATTERSALLS £8 – access to parade ring, grandstand, bar and buffet

COURSE £5– access to bar and snacks

Annual Membership: £95

COURSE FACILITIES

Banks:
there are no banks or cashpoint facilites on the course.

For families:
picnic area with refreshment kiosk and toilets; children's play area.

CALENDAR OF EVENTS

January 9
February 5
March 12
March 25
April 11
April 13
April 22
May 4

May 11 – evening meeting
May 22 – evening meeting
October 7
October 30
November 5
November 15
December 5
December 17

WHERE TO STAY

HOTELS

★★ 65% Saracens Head
219 Watling St
☎ (01327) 350414, fax: (01327) 359879
21 bedrooms; double B&B ££65
Credit cards 1 2 3

Travelodge
☎ (01327) 359105
33 bedrooms; double room £34.95–£49.95
(room only)
Credit cards 1 2 3

Around Towcester

★★★ 66% Buckingham Four Pillars
Ring Rd South, Buckingham
☎ (01280) 822622, fax: (01280) 823074
70 bedrooms; double room £73–£86
Credit cards 1 2 3 5

★★★ 71% Heyford Manor
The High St, Flore
☎ (01327) 349022, fax: (01327) 349017
55 bedrooms; double room £45–£65
Credit cards 1 2 3 5

★★★ 61% Hatton Court
Bullington End, Hanslope
☎ (01908) 510044, fax: (01908) 510945
20 bedrooms; double room £75–£90
Credit cards 1 2 3 5

★★★★ 67% Swallow
Eagle Dr, Northampton
☎ (01604) 768700, fax: (01604) 769011
120 bedrooms; double B&B £70–£115
Credit cards 1 2 3 5

★★★ 65% Northampton Moat House
Silver Street, Town Centre, Northampton
☎ (01604) 739988, fax: (01604) 230614
141 bedrooms; double room £50–£105
Credit cards 1 2 3 5

★★★ 69% Lime Trees
8 Langham Place, Barrack Rd, Northampton
☎ (01604) 32188, fax: (01604) 233012
27 bedrooms; double B&B £57.50–£79.50
Credit cards 1 2 3 5

★★ 67% Thorplands Toby
Talavera Way, Round Spinney, Northampton
☎ (01604) 494241
fax: (01604) 790532
31 bedrooms; double room £49.95–£64.95
Credit cards 1 2 3 5

★★★ 63% Grand
Gold St, Northampton
☎ (01604) 250511
fax: (01604) 234534
56 bedrooms; double B&B £65–£105
Credit cards 1 2 3 5

BED AND BREAKFAST

QQQ Mill Farm
Gayhurst
☎ (01908) 611489
fax: (01908) 611489
Attractive 17th-century farmhouse with
warm, comfortable bedrooms.
4 bedrooms; double B&B £36–£40

QQQ Poplars Hotel
Cross Street, Moulton
☎ (01604) 643983
fax: (01604) 790233
Quiet village location; comfortable
bedrooms and personal service are
provided.
18 bedrooms; double B&B £45–£50
Credit cards 1 2 3

Q Hollington
22 Abington Grove, Northampton
☎ (01604) 32584
Predominantly commercial guesthouse;
modest accommodation, and friendly
owners.
7 bedrooms; double B&B £30–£35
Credit cards 1 3

QQQ Silverthorpe
Abthorpe Rd, Silverstone
☎ (01327) 858020
Modern farm building in five acres of
mushroom farm.
3 bedrooms; double room from £38

QQQQ Quinton Green
Quinton, Northampton
☎ (01604) 863685, fax: (01604) 862230
A mellowed stone longhouse in a totally
secluded rural situation.
3 bedrooms; double B&B £42–£45

CAMPSITES

►►► Barnstones Caravan & Camping Site
Great Bourton, Banbury
☎ (01295) 750289
North of Banbury; about 25 miles west of
Towcester via the A43, A422 and A423.
pitch price £3.50–£5 per night.

WHERE TO EAT

RESTAURANTS

Around Towcester

❀❀ Vine House
100 High St, Paulerspury
☎ (01327) 811267
Skilful, reliable cooking in a small cottage-
style hotel restaurant.
Lunch: 12-2.30
Dinner: 7-10
Credit cards 1 3

❀❀ French Partridge
Horton
☎ (01604) 870033
Superb modern cooking which offers good
value for money in an old-established
village restaurant.
Dinner: 7.30-9

❀ Roadhouse
16 High St, Roade
☎ (01604) 863372
Unassuming enjoyable food in a smart,
cottage-style restaurant.
Lunch: 12-1.45
Dinner: 7-9.30
Credit cards 1 2 3

PUBS

Around Towcester

Bartholomew Arms
30 High St, Blakesley
☎ (01327) 860292
The cosy beamed bars of this welcoming 18th-
century pub are full of interesting collections.
There are three well kept real ales – Websters
Yorkshire Bitter, Ruddles County and Marstons
Pedigree – and an excellent range of 70 malt
whiskies. The homely pub fare represents good
value for money, with half-portions available for
children (welcome in the back room only).
Open: 11am-2.30pm, 5.30-11pm; Sunday 12-
3pm, 7-10.30pm
Bar food: 12-2pm, 6-9.30pm, Sunday 12-2pm,
7-9.30pm

Uttoxeter

This is widely regarded as the most go-ahead track in the British Isles. Under the inspired leadership of its owner, Stan Clarke, the course's management have, in a remarkably short period of time, transformed this Midlands venue from a second-rate site into a major centre of equine excellence.

The numbers of runners and spectators have continued to grow, despite its out of the way location and the recession. This bears testimony to its universal appeal among owners, trainers and punters alike. There has been no resting on any laurels, however, as the recently built Tattersalls stand and the new club restaurant show.

If ever the phrase 'user-friendly' could be legitimately applied to a racecourse, then Uttoxeter fits the bill. Bands frequently play, there are fun-fairs on big days and senior citizens often benefit from generous discount schemes. The staff are genuinely considerate and amongst the most friendly ever encountered on a racecourse. The standard of catering is superb and corporate entertainment is another area that is booming here - there can be few better places to hire a box. Finally, a word about the racing, which is restricted solely to the jumps. Once again, there has been a significant recent improvement in this sphere, with the levels of prize money and the standard of competition rising steadily all the time. The richest race in the calendar is the Marstons Pedigree Midlands Grand National, run in mid-March.

FURTHER INFORMATION

Uttoxeter Leisure & Development Co Ltd
The Racecourse, Wood Lane, Uttoxeter,
Staffordshire ST14 8BD
☎ (01889) 562561; Fax:(01889) 562786

LOCATION AND HOW TO GET THERE

The course is half a mile southeast of Uttoxeter town centre off the B5017. From the M6 southbound leave at junction 15 and take the A50 eastwards; from the northbound direction, leave at junction 13, go into Stafford and take the A518 to Uttoxeter. Alternatively, to avoid the busy M6 around Birmingham, take the M42 to junction 10, then west on the A5. At Tamworth, take the A51 through Lichfield and on to Rugeley. Here turn right onto the B5013 for Uttoxeter. From the M1, leave at junction 22 and take the A50 through Ashby-de-la-Zouch and Burton to Uttoxeter. **Nearest Railway Station:** Uttoxeter; the station adjoins the course. From the inter-city network, it is necessary to change at Derby or Stoke for Uttoxeter; there is also a service from Crewe.

ADMISSION

The SP Betting Shop is in Members and Tattersalls only.

Day tickets:
DAILY CLUB £15, £20 for Midlands National – access to Members' stand, bars, restaurant, champagne and seafood bar, boxes and private rooms

TATTERSALLS £10, £12 for Midlands National – access to bars, restaurant and champagne and seafood bar

CENTRE COURSE £4 – access to bars and snacks

Pensioners: £3 off Club or Tattersalls
Accompanied children under 16 admitted free.

Annual membership: £150, couple £220; senior citizen £120, couple £175; junior (under 21) £70 – includes free racecard at all home fixtures and reciprocal meetings at certain other courses. Members also admitted free to Newcastle Racecourse.

COURSE FACILITIES

Banks:
there are no banks or cashpoint facilities on the course.

For families:
picnic area with refreshment kiosk and toilets; children's play area on Bank Holidays only; lost children centre.
Parking: Free and plentiful.

CALENDAR OF EVENTS

January 3
February 7
March 21 – Midlands Grand National
March 24
April 13-14
May 2 – jumping
May 6 – jumping; evening meeting
May 20 – jumping; evening meeting
May 25 – jumping

May 28
June 10 – jumping; evening meeting
June 28 – jumping
September 1 – jumping
October 3
November 6-7 – jumping
November 26 – jumping
December 18-19 – jumping

WHERE TO STAY

HOTELS

★★ 64% Bank House
Church St
☎ (01889) 566922
fax: (01889) 567565
14 bedrooms; double B&B £69.50-£89.50
Credit cards 1 2 3 5

Travelodge
Ashbourne Rd
☎ (01889) 562043
32 bedrooms; double room £34.95-£49.95
Credit cards 1 2 3

Around Uttoxeter

★★★ 69% Ashbourne Lodge
Derby Rd, Ashbourne
☎ (01335) 346666
fax: (01335) 346549
50 bedrooms; double B&B £78-£86
Credit cards 1 2 3 5

★★★ 66% The Boars Head
Lichfield Rd, Sudbury
☎ (01283) 820344
fax: (01283) 820075
22 bedrooms; double B&B £49.50-£61.50
Credit cards 1 2 3

★★★★ 69% Hoar Cross Hall Health Spa
Hoar Cross, Burton upon Trent
☎ (01283) 575671
fax: (01283) 575652
86 bedrooms; double B&B £148
Credit cards 1 2 3 5

★★★ 64% Ye Old Dog & Partridge
High St, Tutbury
☎ (01283) 813030
fax: (01283) 813178
17 bedrooms; double B&B £49.50-£80
Credit cards 1 2 3

★★★ ❀❀ 75% Callow Hall
Mappleton Rd, Ashbourne
☎ (01335) 343403 & 342412
fax: (01335) 343624
16 bedrooms; double B&B £110-£136.50
Credit cards 1 2 3 5

Travelodge
Western Springs Rd, Rugeley
☎ (01889) 570096
32 bedrooms; double room £34.95-£49.95
Credit cards 1 2 3

BED AND BREAKFAST

QQQQ Hillcrest
3 Leighton Rd, Uttoxeter
☎ (01889) 564627
Family-run guesthouse in elevated position.
7 bedrooms; double B&B £38-£40
Credit cards 1 3

QQ Marsh Farm
Abbots Bromley
☎ (01283) 840323
In pleasant village famed for its ancient annual tradition, the Horn Dance; the farm has been modernised but retains its exposed beams.
2 bedrooms; double B&B £32-£34

QQQQ Dairy House Farm
Alkmonton
☎ (01335) 330359
fax: (01335) 330359
Friendly hosts welcome guests to this comfortably modernised 16th-century house.
7 bedrooms; double B&B £34-£40

WHERE TO STAY

QQQQQ Bank House
Farley Ln, Oakamoor
☎ (01538) 702810
fax :(01538) 702810
High quality accommodation is offered in
this welcoming family home; lovely big old
rooms with antique furniture.
3 bedrooms; double B&B £54-£74
Credit cards 1 3

QQQQ Ribden Farm
Three Lows, Oakamoor
☎ (01538) 702830
fax: (01538) 702830
Stone-built farmhouse with well-maintained
bedrooms
5 bedrooms; double B&B £40-£44
Credit cards 1 3

QQQQ Lichfield
Bridge View, Mayfield, Ashbourne
☎ (01335) 344422
fax: (01335) 344422
Pleasant cottage-style accommodation .
4 bedrooms; double B&B £40-£42

QQ Ye Olde Crown
Waterhouses
☎ (01538) 308204
Old stone-built inn.
7 bedrooms; double B&B £37

QQQ Delter Hotel
5 Derby Rd, Burton upon Trent
☎ (01283) 535115
fax: (01283) 535115
Bright, clean bedrooms in a modernised
house.
5 bedrooms; double B&B £42.50
Credit Cards 1 3

CAMPSITES

►►► Caravan Club Site
Uttoxeter Racecourse
☎ (01889) 564172 & 562561
Off the B5017; pitch price from £7.50 per
night.

►► Sandybrook Hall Holiday Park
Buxton Rd, Ashbourne
☎ (01335) 342679
One mile north of Ashbourne on A515; pitch
price from £7 per night.

►► Star Caravan & Camping Park
Cotton, Oakamoor
☎ (01538) 702256 & 702219
One and a quarter miles northeast off
B5417; pitch price £6 per night.

WHERE TO EAT

RESTAURANT

Around Uttoxeter

❀❀ Callow Hall
Mappleton Rd, Ashbourne
☎ (01335) 343403
A wide range of English and French dishes.
Lunch: 12-1.30
Dinner: 7-9.15

PUBS

Around Uttoxeter

Horseshoe Inn
Main St, Tatenhill, nr Burton upon Trent
☎ (01283) 64913
This charming old building in the village
centre has an attractive garden for summer
days and a wood-burning stove for wintry
nights. It specialises in wines from the
Beaujolais and Macon regions of France
and there is a good selection of malt
whiskies; draught beers on offer are
Marston's and Guinness. The bar food is
well presented and reasonably priced. There
is a family room and an outdoor play area
for children.
Open: 11 or 11.30am-3pm, 5.30-11pm;
Sunday 12-3pm, 7-10.30pm
Bar food: Monday 12-2pm; Tuesday to
Saturday 12-2pm, 6-9.15pm; Sunday 12-
1.30pm
Restaurant: times as bar food

Warwick

Races were first held at Warwick during the 18th century, when crowds of 50,000 watched the renowned 'King's Plates'. Steeplechases were staged here from the beginning of the 19th century and, in the 1900s, this course was several times host to the National Hunt Chase, a contest now permanently based at Cheltenham.

Another interesting historical fact about this venue is that the longest ever recorded leap by a racehorse took place here in 1836 when The Chandler cleared a distance of 36 feet.

It would probably be fair to say that Warwick's past is more illustrious than its present. It is now very much a bread and butter type track, offering a fair standard of racing in a pleasant laid-back atmosphere. Some two dozen meetings are split almost evenly between the Flat and National Hunt, with the jumps fixtures holding a slight edge in quality. The most prestigious contest of the year is the Tote Trio Warwick National in January, while there is also an excellent card in February which features several important trials for the Cheltenham Festival. Facilities have been generally upgraded, with the addition of new bars and private boxes, but the viewing areas are rather cramped and the big hill in the middle of the course obscures some of the action in the back straight.

FURTHER INFORMATION

Warwick Racecourse Company Ltd
Hampton Street, Warwick CV34 6HN
☎ (01926) 491553 Fax:(01926) 403223

LOCATION AND HOW TO GET THERE

The racecourse is within half a mile of the centre of Warwick, 20 miles southeast of Birmingham and two miles from Royal Leamington Spa. Leave the M40 at junction 15 and take the A429 into the centre of Warwick, from where the course is signposted.

Nearest Railway Station: Warwick; there are no connecting bus services to the course

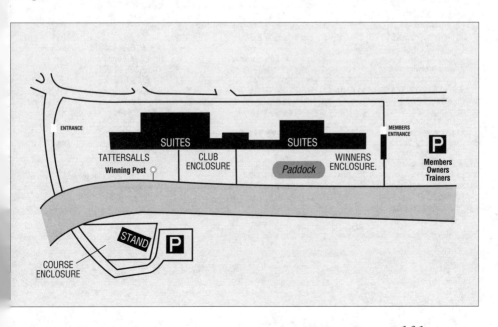

ADMISSION

All classes of day ticket give access to full betting facilities, including Tote.

Day tickets:
Accompanied children under 16 are admitted free to all enclosures.

CLUB £12 – access to members bar, all grandstands, hospitality suites

TATTERSALLS (GRANDSTAND & PADDOCK) £8 – access to paddock, winners enclosure, betting shop, bar and restaurant

COURSE £5 – access to bar, snack bar, betting shop (Saturdays and Bank Holidays), picnic area, parking

Annual Membership: £120 full, £65 National Hunt, £50 junior – includes vouchers for new members, redeemable against racecards and refreshments; reciprocal arrangements at certain other courses on certain days; two days of polo at the local club. Members may bring a guest racing on two occasions during the year. National Hunt members enjoy these benefits on National Hunt Racedays only.

COURSE FACILITIES

Banks:
there are no banks or cashpoint facilities on the course.

For families:
picnic area with refreshment kiosk and toilets, children's play area

---

CALENDAR OF EVENTS

January 10 – jumping
January 17 – jumping
February 10 – jumping
February 21 – jumping
March 7 – jumping
March 28 – flat
April 13 – flat
April 24 –National Hunt; evening meeting
May 4 – flat

May 23 –National Hunt; evening meeting
June 3 – flat
June 8 – flat; evening meeting
June 24 – flat
July 3 – flat;
July 11 – flat; evening meeting
July 18 – flat; evening meeting
August 14 – flat; eveing meeting
August 31 – flat

September 22 – flat
October 4 – flat
November 3 – National Hunt
November 19 – National Hunt
November 28 – National Hunt
December 19 – National Hunt
December 31 – National Hunt

WHERE TO STAY

HOTELS

★★ 56% Warwick Arms
High St
☎ (01926) 492759
fax: (01926) 410587
35 bedrooms; double B&B £50–£59
Credit cards 1 2 3 5

Around Warwick

★★★ ✿ 67% The Glebe at Barford
Church St, Barford
☎ (01926) 624218
fax: (01926) 624625
41 bedrooms; double B&B £70–£140
Credit cards 1 2 3 5

★★★★ ✿✿ 72% Nailcote Hall
Nailcote Ln, Berkswell, Balsall Common
☎ (01203) 466174
fax: (01203) 470720
38 bedrooms; double B&B from £135
Credit cards 1 2 3

★★★ 64% Charlecote Pheasant Country Hotel
Charlecote
☎ (01789) 279954
fax: (01789) 470222
67 bedrooms; double room £86–£95
Credit cards 1 2 3 5

★★★★ 59% De Vere
Cathedral Square, Coventry
☎ (01203) 633733
fax: (01203) 225299
190 bedrooms; double room £75–£120
Credit cards 1 2 3 5

★★★ ✿✿ 74% Brooklands Grange Hotel & Restaurant
Holyhead Rd, Coventry
☎ (01203) 601601
fax: (01203) 601277
30 bedrooms; double B&B £95–£100
Credit cards 1 2 3 5

★★★ 68% Coventry Knight
Ryton on Dunsmore, Coventry
☎ (01203) 301585
fax: (01203) 301610
49 bedrooms; double room £60–£75
Credit cards 1 2 3 5

★★★ 61% Leofric
Broadgate, Coventry
☎ (01203) 221371
fax: (01203) 551352
94 bedrooms; double room £65–£115
(room only)
Credit cards 1 2 3 5

Forte Crest
Hinckley Rd, Walsgrave, Coventry
☎ (01203) 613261
fax: (01203) 621736
147 bedrooms; double room £59
(room only)
Credit cards 1 2 3 5

WHERE TO STAY

★★★ 60% The Chace
London Rd, Willenhall, Coventry
☎ (01203) 303398
fax: (01203) 301816
66 bedrooms; double bedroom £70-£120
(room only)
Credit cards 1 2 3 5

★★★ 66% Hylands
Warwick Rd, Coventry
☎ (01203) 501600
fax: (01203) 501027
54 bedrooms; double B&B £89-£95
Credit cards 1 2 3 5

★★★ 61% Novotel Coventry
Wilsons Ln, Coventry
☎ (01203) 365000
fax: (01203) 362422
98 bedrooms; double room £55
Credit cards 1 2 3 5

★★★ 58% Coventry Hill
Rye Hill, Allesley, Coventry
☎ (01203) 402151
fax: (01203) 402235
180 bedrooms; double bedroom from £60
(room only)
Credit cards 1 2 3 5

Campanile
4 Wigston Rd, Walsgrave, Coventry
☎ (01203) 622311
fax: (01203) 602362
50 bedrooms; double room £29.95-£36.50
Credit cards 1 2 3

★★★ 66% Honiley Court
Honiley
☎ (01926) 484234, fax: (01926) 484474
62 bedrooms; double room £76-£110
Credit cards 1 2 3 5

★★★ 64% De Montfort
The Square, Kenilworth
☎ (01926) 855944, fax: (01926) 857830
103 bedrooms; double room £75-£180
Credit cards 1 2 3 5

★★ 64% Clarendon House
Old High St, Kenilworth
☎ (01926) 857668 & (0800) 16883,
fax: (01926) 850669
30 bedrooms; double B&B £75-£85
Credit cards 1 3

★★★ (RED) ❀❀❀ Mallory Court
Harbury Ln, Bishop's Tachbrook,
Leamington Spa tel: (01926) 330214,
fax: (01926) 451714
10 bedrooms; double B&B £185-£250
Credit cards 1 2 3 5

★★★ ❀ 76% Regent
77 The Parade, Leamington Spa
☎ (01926) 427231
fax: (01926) 450728
80 bedrooms
Credit cards 1 2 3 5

★★★ 61% Falstaff
16-20 Warwick New Rd, Leamington Spa
☎ (01926) 312044, fax: (01926) 450574
63 bedrooms; double B&B £40-£75
Credit cards 1 2 3 5

★★★ 60% Manor House
Avenue Rd, Leamington Spa
☎ (01926) 423251, fax: (01926) 425933
53 bedrooms; double room from £84
Credit cards 1 2 3 5

★★ 71% Adams
22 Avenue Rd, Leamington Spa
☎ (01926) 450742 & 422758,
fax: (01926) 313110
14 bedrooms; double B&B £58-£70
Credit cards 1 2 3 5

★★ 65% Beech Lodge
Warwick New Rd, Leamington Spa
☎ (01926) 422227
fax: (01926) 435288
14 bedrooms; double B&B £45-£60
Credit cards 1 2 3 5

★★★ 63% Angel
143 Regent St, Leamington Spa
☎ (01926) 881296
fax: (01926) 881296
50 bedrooms; double B&B £50-£65
Credit cards 1 2 3

★ (RED) ❀ Lansdowne
87 Clarendon St, Leamington Spa
☎ (01926) 450505
fax: (01926) 421313
14 bedrooms; double B&B £61.90-£69.90
Credit cards 1 3

★★★★ ❀❀ 76% Welcombe
Warwick Rd, Stratford-upon-Avon
☎ (01789) 295252
fax: (01789) 414666
67 bedrooms; double B&B from £150-£160
Credit cards 1 2 3 5

★★★★ 65% Stratford Moat House
Bridgefoot, Stratford-upon-Avon
☎ (01789) 279988,
fax: (01789) 298589
247 bedrooms; double room £96-£125
Credit cards 1 2 3 5

WHERE TO STAY

★★★★✿ 66% The Shakespeare
Chapel St, Stratford-upon-Avon
☎ (01789) 294771, fax: (01789) 415411
63 bedrooms; double room £115 (room only)
Credit cards 1 2 3 5

★★★★ 68% Stratford Manor
Warwick Rd, Stratford-upon-Avon
☎ (01789) 731173, fax: (01789) 731131
104 bedrooms; double room £100-£120
Credit cards 1 2 3 5

★★★ 68% Grosvenor House
Warwick Rd, Stratford-upon-Avon
☎ (01789) 269213
fax: (01789) 266087
67 bedrooms; double room from £79.50
Credit cards 1 2 3 5

★★★★ ✿ 65% Alveston Manor
Clopton Bridge, Stratford-upon-Avon
☎ (01789) 204581
fax: (01789) 414095
106 bedrooms; double room £110-£175
(room only)
Credit cards 1 2 3 5

★★★✿✿ 77% Salford Hall
Abbot's Salford
☎ (01386) 871300, fax: (01386) 871301
33 bedrooms; double B&B £105-£150
Credit cards 1 2 3 5

Forte Posthouse
Bridgefoot, Stratford-upon-Avon
☎ (01789) 266761, fax: (01789) 414547
60 bedrooms; double room £56
(room only)
Credit cards 1 2 3 5

★★★ 64% The White Swan
Rother St, Stratford-upon-Avon
☎ (01789) 297022, fax: (01789) 268773
37 bedrooms; double room £90-£115
(room only)
Credit cards 1 2 3 5

★★★ 63% Falcon
Chapel St, Stratford-upon-Avon
☎ (01789) 279953,
fax: (01789) 414260
73 bedrooms; double B&B £99-£120
Credit cards 1 2 3 5

★★ ✿ 70% Stratford House
Sheep St, Stratford-upon-Avon
☎ (01789) 268288
fax: (01789) 295580
11 bedrooms; double B&B £72-£88
Credit cards 1 2 3 5

★★ 65% The Coach House Hotel
16-17 Warwick Rd, Stratford-upon-Avon
☎ (01789) 204109 & 299468,
fax: (01789) 415916
22 bedrooms; double B&B £65-£98
Credit cards 1 2 3 5

BED AND BREAKFAST

QQQQ The Old Rectory
Vicarage Ln, Sherbourne,
☎ (01926) 624562
fax: (01926) 624995
Tastefully restored house offering very comfortable accommodation and home-cooked food.
14 bedrooms; double B&B £40-£70
Credit cards 1 3

QQ Austin House
96 Emscote Rd,
☎ (01926) 493583
Guesthouse offering modest accommodation.
6 bedrooms; double B&B £32-£40
Credit cards 1 3

QQQ Tudor House
West St
☎ (01926) 495447, fax: (01926) 492948
Tudor house retaining much wattle and daub and timbers; cosy bedrooms.
11 bedrooms; double room £56-£65
Credit cards 1 2 3 5

WHERE TO STAY

Around Warwick

QQ Woodside Country House
Langley Rd, Claverdon
☎ (01926) 842446
fax: (01926) 842410
4 bedrooms; double B&B £40–£50

QQ Hearsall Lodge Hotel
1 Broad Ln, Coventry
☎ (01203) 674543 & 678749
Professionally run guesthouse situated
close to the A45
12 bedrooms; double B&B £34
Credit cards 1 2 3

QQ Ashleigh House
17 Park Rd, Coventry
☎ (01203) 223804
Compact rooms with modest furnishings.
10 bedrooms; double B&B £30–£36

QQ Croft Hotel
23 Stoke Green, Off Binley Rd, Coventry
☎ (01203) 457846
fax: (01203) 457846
Pleasant guesthouse with friendly owners.
11 bedrooms; double B&B £42–£58
Credit cards 1 3

QQQQ Croft
Haseley Knob
☎ (01926) 484447
fax: (01926) 484447
Five miles northwest of Warwick.
5 bedrooms; double B&B from £44

QQQQ Northleigh House
Five Ways Rd, Hatton
☎ (01926) 484203
fax: (01926) 484006
Bedrooms have many thoughtful extras in
this charming guesthouse, with high
standards throughout ensured by friendly
hostess.
7 bedrooms; double B&B £40–£58
Credit cards 1 3

QQQ Abbey
41 Station Rd, Kenilworth
☎ (01926) 512707
fax: (01926) 859148
A warm welcome is assured at this
guesthouse, set in a residential area.
7 bedrooms; double B&B £36–£42

QQQ Castle Laurels Hotel
22 Castle Rd, Kenilworth
☎ (01926) 856179
fax: (01926) 854954
Attractive, spacious Victorian house
opposite the castle and Abbey Fields.
12 bedrooms; double B&B £53–£60
Credit cards 1 3

QQQ Ferndale
45 Priory Rd, Kenilworth
☎ (01926) 853214
fax: (01926) 858336
Attractive, comfortable accommodation.
7 bedrooms; double B&B £36–£42

QQQ Hollyhurst
47 Priory Rd, Kenilworth
☎ (01926) 853882
Friendly and welcoming guesthouse, with
bright fresh bedrooms providing a good
range of facilities.
7 bedrooms; double B&B £38–£46

QQQQ Victoria Lodge Hotel
180 Warwick Rd, Kenilworth
☎ (01926) 512020
fax: (01926) 58703
Charming hosts and excellent standards of
cleanliness and maintenance throughout.
7 bedrooms; double B&B £45–£49
Credit cards 1 2 3

QQQ Coverdale Private Hotel
8 Portland St, Leamington Spa
☎ (01926) 330400
fax: (01926) 833388
Attractive well situated Georgian house,
offering a high level of comfort.
7 bedrooms; double room £46–£48
Credit cards 1 3

QQQ Flowerdale House
58 Warwick New Rd, Leamington Spa
☎ (01926) 426002
fax: (01926) 883699
Delightful Victorian property offering
attractive accommodation.
6 bedrooms; double B&B £36–£46
Credit cards 1 3

QQQ Hill Farm
Lewis Rd, Radford, Leamington Spa
☎ (01926) 337571
This popular farmhouse is just off the A45.
5 bedrooms; double B&B £32–£40

QQ Charnwood
47 Avenue Rd, Leamington Spa
☎ (01926)831074
Close to town centre, providing attractive,
well equipped accommodation.
6 bedrooms; double B&B £32–£37
Credit cards 1 3

QQ The Dell
8 Warwick Place, Leamington Spa
☎ (01926) 422784
fax: (01926) 422784
Situated on the main road into Leamington
Spa; offering generally spacious
accommodation.
9 bedrooms; double room £34–£50

QQQ Redlands Farm
Banbury Rd, Lighthorne
☎ (01926) 651241
Open-air swimming pool is available to
guests; Mrs Stanton provides wholesome
dishes.
3 bedrooms; double B&B £36–£40

WHERE TO STAY

QQQ Brook Lodge
192 Alcester Rd, Stratford-upon-Avon
☎ (01789) 295988
fax: (01789) 295988
Nicely decorated, well kept guesthouse.
7 bedrooms; double B&B £40-£50
Credit cards 1 2 3

QQQ Craig Cleeve House
67-69 Shipston Rd, Stratford-upon-Avon
☎ (01789) 296573
fax: (01789) 299452
On the A34 south of Clopton Bridge; bright
fresh accommodation; friendly hosts.
15 bedrooms; double room £39-£50
Credit cards 1 2 3 5

QQQQ Eastnor House Hotel
Shipston Rd, Stratford-upon-Avon
☎ (01789) 268115
fax: (01789) 266516
On the A34, just 300m from the theatre;
bright, fresh accommodation.
9 bedrooms; double B&B £50-£64
Credit cards 1 2 3

QQQQ Gravelside Barn
Binton, Stratford-upon-Avon
☎ (01789) 750502 & 297000,
fax: (01789) 298056
3 bedrooms; double room £50-£60
Credit cards 1 3

QQQ Highcroft
Banbury Rd, Stratford-upon-Avon
☎ (01789) 296293
fax: (01789) 415236
Spacious attractive rooms which are well
equipped and have antique or pine furniture.
1 bedrooms; double B&B £36-£40

QQQ Hollies
16 Evesham Place, Stratford-upon-Avon
☎ (01789) 266857
Close to the town centre; popular hostess
who gives a warm welcome.
6 bedrooms; double room £34-£45

QQQQ Melita Private Hotel
37 Shipston Rd, Stratford-upon-Avon
☎ (01789) 292432
fax: (01789) 204867
A friendly family run guesthouse on the A34
close to the river and major attractions.
12 bedrooms; double B&B £45-£72
Credit cards 1 2 3

QQQ Moonraker House
40 Alcester Rd, Stratford-upon-Avon
☎ (01789) 299346
fax: (01789) 295504
Unusual guesthouse, spread over four
properties, with attractive bedrooms.
22 bedrooms; double B&B £45-£70
Credit cards 1 3

QQQQ Sequoia House Private Hotel
51-53 Shipston Rd, Stratford-upon-Avon
☎ (01789) 268852
fax: (01789) 414559
Opposite the Royal Shakespeare Theatre;
several types of room are available, from the
cosy cottage annexe to the exceptionally
well furnished, luxury no-smoking rooms.
24 bedrooms; double B&B £42-£74
Credit cards 1 2 3 5

QQQQ Twelfth Night
Evesham Place, Stratford-upon-Avon
☎ (01789) 414595
Delightfully refurbished Victorian villa;
pretty rooms with welcome extra touches.
6 bedrooms; double B&B £44-£56
Credit cards 1 3

QQQQ Victoria Spa Lodge
Bishopton Ln, Stratford-upon-Avon
☎ (01789) 267985
fax: (01789) 204728
Victorian Lodge in a peaceful, leafy setting
at the side of the Stratford Canal.
7 bedrooms; double B&B £45-£52
Credit cards 1 3

QQQ Virginia Lodge
12 Evesham Place, Stratford-upon-Avon
☎ (01789) 292157
Well kept, friendly guesthouse close to the
centre of Stratford.
8 bedrooms; double B&B £36-£48

CAMPSITES

►►►► Island Meadow Caravan Park
The Mill House, Aston Cantlow
☎ (01789) 488273
Quarter of a mile west of Aston Cantlow;
pitch price from £6.50 per night.

WHERE TO EAT

RESTAURANTS

Around Warwick

✸✸ Restaurant Bosquet
97A Warwick Rd, Kenilworth
☎ (01926) 852463
Generous portions of honest-to-goodness provincial French cooking and friendly, helpful service.
Credit cards 1 2 3

✸ Le Filbert Cottage
64 High St, Henley- In-Arden
☎ (01564) 792700
Well-executed french cooking and charming Gallic service.
Lunch: 12-1.30, from £25
Dinner: 7-9.30; from £25 à la carte.

✸ Lansdowne
87 Clarendon St, Royal Leamington Spa
☎ (01926) 450505
Simple but effective cooking full of natural flavours.

✸✸✸ Mallory Court
Harbury Lane, Bishop's Tachbrook
☎ (01926) 330214
Creatively presented and expensive modern french cuisine.
Lunch: 12-2
Dinner: 7-9.45

✸ Regent
77 The Parade, Royal Leamington Spa
☎ (01926) 427231
A choice of two dining places and a range of menus.
Lunch: 12-2, from £24 and à la carte
Dinner: 7-10; from £24 and à la carte

PUBS

Around Warwick

Bell
Alderminster
☎ (01789) 450414
An adventurous menu, a high standard of cooking and a wine list to match are the main attractions of the 17th-century pub. Beers include Marston Pedigree and Flowers Best and Original. Children are welcome.
Open: 12-2.30pm, 7-11pm; Sunday 12-2.30pm, 7-10.30pm
Bar food: 12-2pm, 7-9.30pm; Sunday 12-1.45pm, 7-9pm
Restaurant: times as bar food

Ferry
Alveston
☎ (01789) 269883
Friendly village-centre pub offering well prepared and promptly served food at a range of prices, all good value for money. Theakston Best, Bass, Wadworth 6X and Flowers Original are on sale, along with a selection of wines. Children over 5 years old are welcome.
Open: 11am-2.30pm, 6-11pm; Sunday 12-2.30pm, 7-10.30
Bar food: 11.45am-2pm, 6.30-9pm; Sunday 12-2pm

Kings Head
Aston Cantlow
☎ (01789) 488242
This is an attractive and unspoilt half-timbered pub with a small, well tended garden. Beers include Marston Pedigree, Flowers IPA, Boddingtons Bitter and Mild and Murphy's Stout; there is a reasonable selection of wines and a tasty range of bar meals. No children under 14 in the bar.
Open: 12-2.30pm, 7-11pm; Sunday 12-2.30pm, 7-10.30pm
Bar food: as opening hours, except Sunday and Monday evenings

Malt Shovel
Lower End, Bubbenhall, nr Coventry
☎ (01203) 301141
Beer on tap include Ansells Bitter and Mild, Bass and Tetley Bitter. Dating from the 16th century, the brick and timber pub has a small patio at the front and a garden adjoining a bowling green. Children welcome anywhere at lunchtime and early evening.
Open: 11.30am-2.30pm, 6-11pm; Sunday 12-2.30pm, 7-10.30pm
Bar food: 12-2pm, 6.30-9.30pm. No food Sunday evening.

Wetherby

Yorkshire is blessed with an abundance of racecourses, of which Wetherby is undoubtedly the premier jumping venue. This popular National Hunt track offers first class facilities to racegoers and provides superb all-round visibility of the course from the stands.

It is conveniently located just off the A1, making access exceptionally easy, and has a large catchment area, the major cities of Harrogate, Leeds and York all being within a close radius. As a consequence, crowds are always large, creating a cracking atmosphere.

There are 15 or so meetings held here annually and the quality of the runners is usually high. Part of the reason for this is that the track is regarded as one of the fairest in Britain. The mile and a half oval circuit has wide straights and easy bends, suiting the long-striding horse, and the stiff fences are a good test of an animal's jumping ability. Trainers, therefore, find it more difficult than usual to come up with excuses for beaten horses here. The best fixtures are on Boxing Day, at the end of October, when an outstanding Saturday televised card includes three top events, the Charlie Hall

Chase, the Tote West Yorkshire Hurdle and the Wensleydale Novices' Hurdle.

This National Hunt course offers first class facilities to racegoers and provides superb all-round visibility of the course from the stands.

FURTHER INFORMATION

Wetherby Racecourse
York Rd, Wetherby LS22 5EJ
☎ (01937) 582035

LOCATION AND HOW TO GET THERE

The course is on the B1224 Wetherby-York road, adjacent to, and visible from, the A1.
Nearest Railway Stations: Leeds or York; there are no connecting bus services to the course.

ADMISSION

All classes of day ticket give access to full betting facilities, including Tote

Day tickets:
Accompanied children under 16 are admitted free.

MEMBERS/CLUB £12 – access to bar, restaurant (limited availability)

GRANDSTAND/TATTERSALLS £8 – access to bar, self-service restaurant

COURSE £2, or £8 for car and up to four adults – access to bar, self-service restaurant

COURSE FACILITIES

Banks:
there are no banks or cashpoint facilities on the course.

For families:
picnic area with refreshment kiosk and toilets; children's play area

CALENDAR OF EVENTS

January 15	October 14
February 7	October 25
February 26	October 30-31
March 4	November 17
April 13-14	December 5
May 6 – evening meeting	December 26
May 25	December 28

WHERE TO STAY

HOTELS

★★★ (RED) ⊛ Wood Hall
Trip Ln, Linton
☎ (01937) 587271, fax: (01937) 584353
43 bedrooms; double room £109
Credit cards 1 2 3 5

Around Wetherby

★★★ 70% Aldwark Manor
Aldwark
☎ (01347) 838146, fax: (01347) 838867
20 bedrooms
Credit cards 1 2 3 5

Travelodge
Bilbrough
☎ (01973) 531823
36 bedrooms; double room £34.95-£49.95
(room only)
Credit cards 1 2 3

★★★ 63% Harewood Arms
Harrogate Rd, Harewood
☎ (0113) 288 6566
fax: (0113) 288 6064
24 bedrooms; double B&B £60-£80
Credit cards 1 2 3 5

★★★★ 65% Harrogate Moat House
Kings Rd, Harrogate
☎ (01423) 849988,
fax: (01423) 524435
214 bedrooms; double room £134
Credit cards 1 2 3 5

★★★★ 61% The Majestic
Ripon Rd, Harrogate
☎ (01423) 568972,
fax: (01423) 502283
156 bedrooms; double room £79-£100
(room only)
Credit cards 1 2 3 5

★★★ 70% Grants
3-13 Swan Rd, Harrogate
☎ (01423) 560666
fax: (01423) 502550
42 bedrooms; double B&B £104
Credit cards 1 2 3 5

★★★ ⊛⊛ 68% White House
10 Park Pde, Harrogate
☎ (01423) 501388
fax: (01423) 527973
11 bedrooms; double B&B £90-£135
Credit cards 1 2 3 5

★★★ 65% St George Swallow
1 Ripon Rd, Harrogate
☎ (01423) 561431
fax: (01423) 530037
90 bedrooms; double B&B £110-£125
Credit cards 1 2 3 5

★★★ 61% The Crown
Crown Place, Harrogate
☎ (01423) 567755
fax: (01423) 502284
121 bedrooms; double room £94-£140
Credit cards 1 2 3 5

★★★⊛ 65% Studley
Swan Rd, Harrogate
☎ (01423) 560425,
fax: (01423) 530967
36 bedrooms; double B&B £88-£98
Credit cards 1 2 3 5

★★★ 61% Hospitality Inn
Prospect Place, West Park
☎ (01423) 564601,
fax: (01423) 507508
71 bedrooms; double room £80-£95 (room
only)
Credit cards 1 2 3 5

**★★ ⊛ 68% Harrogate Brasserie
Hotel & Bar**
28-30 Cheltenham Pde, Harrogate
☎ (01423) 505041
fax: (01423) 530920
13 bedrooms; double B&B £55-£65
Credit cards 1 3 5

★★ 70% The Manor
3 Clarence Dr, Harrogate
☎ (01423) 503916
fax: (01423) 568709
17 bedrooms; double B&B £62-£89
Credit cards 1 3

★★ 70% Ascot House
53 Kings Rd, Harrogate
☎ (01423) 531005
fax: (01423) 503523
18 bedrooms; double B&B £69-£100
Credit cards 1 2 3 5

★★ 67% Abbey Lodge
29-31 Ripon Rd, Harrogate
☎ (01423) 569712
fax: (01423) 530570
19 bedrooms; double B&B £55-£59
Credit cards 1 2 3

★★ 69% Green Park
Valley Dr, Harrogate
☎ (01423) 504681
fax: (01423) 530811
43 bedrooms; double B&B £65-£83
Credit cards 1 2 3 5

★★ 64% Valley
93-95 Valley Dr, Harrogate
☎ (01423) 504868
fax: (01423) 531940
16 bedrooms; double B&B £52-£65
Credit cards 1 2 3 5

WHERE TO STAY

★ **72% Britannia Lodge**
16 Swan Rd, Harrogate
☎ (01423) 508482
fax: (01423) 526840
12 bedrooms; double B&B £54-£75
Credit cards 1 2 3

★ **70% Gables**
2 West Grove Rd, Harrogate
☎ (01423) 505625
fax: (01423) 561312
9 bedrooms; double B&B £55-£70
Credit cards 1 3

★★ **67% Grafton**
1-3 Franklin Mount, Harrogate
☎ (01423) 508491
fax: (01423) 523168
17 bedrooms; double B&B £54-£68
Credit cards 1 2 3 5

★ **69% Alvera Court**
76 Kings Rd, Harrogate
☎ (01423) 505735
fax: (01423) 507996
12 bedrooms; double B&B £58-£84
Credit cards 1 3

★ **67% The Croft**
42-46 Franklin Rd, Harrogate
☎ (01423) 563326
fax: (01423) 530733
13 bedrooms; double B&B £52
Credit cards 1 2 3 5

★★★ ❀ **70% Dower House**
Bond End, Knaresborough
☎ (01423) 863302
fax: (01423) 867665
32 bedrooms; double B&B £75-£100
Credit cards 1 2 3 5

BED AND BREAKFAST

QQ Prospect House
8 Caxton St
☎ (01937) 582428
Close to town centre, offering clean, simple
bedrooms.
6 bedrooms; double B&B £45-£50

Around Wetherby

QQQQ Alexa House & Stable Cottages
26 Ripon Rd, Harrogate
☎ (01423) 501988
fax: (01423) 504086
Yorkshire hospitality in very congenial
surroundings, with high standards
throughout.
13 bedrooms; double B&B £55-£65
Credit cards 1 3

QQQQ Acacia Lodge
21 Ripon Rd, Harrogate
☎ (01423) 560752
fax: (01423) 503725
A few minutes walk from the town centre;
very attractively furnished and decorated
throughout.
6 bedrooms; double B&B £48-£68

QQQQ Ashley House Hotel
36-40 Franklin Rd, Harrogate
☎ (01423) 507474
fax: (01423) 560858
Attractive, friendly hotel with very well
equipped bedrooms.
18 bedrooms; double B&B £50-£70
Credit cards 1 2 3 5

QQQ Ashwood House
7 Spring Grove, Harrogate
☎ (01423) 560081
fax: (01423) 527928
Bedrooms are mostly spacious and
comfortable.
8 bedrooms; double B&B £46-£50

QQQQ Delaine Hotel
17 Ripon Rd, Harrogate
☎ (01423) 567974 & 529034
fax: (01423) 561723
Family-run Victorian house with attractive
flower gardens and tastefully decorated
bedrooms.
10 bedrooms; double B&B £52-£56
Credit cards 1 2 3

QQQ Newton House Hotel
5/7 York Place, Knaresborough
☎ (01423) 863539, fax: (01423) 869748
Lovely Grade II listed house with
individually decorated, spacious bedrooms.
12 bedrooms; double B&B £50-£60
Credit cards 1 3

QQQ The Villa
47 Kirkgate, Knaresborough
☎ (01423) 865370
fax: (01423) 867740
Situated high above the River Nidd;
bedrooms furnished in period style.
6 bedrooms

QQQ Wellgarth House
Wetherby Rd, Rufforth
☎ (01904) 738592 & 738595
fax (01904) 738595
A large well appointed modern house on the
edge of the village.
7 bedrooms; double B&B £34-£44
Credit cards 1 3

WHERE TO STAY

CAMPSITES

►►►► Allerton Park Caravan Site
Allerton Mauleverer, Allerton Park
☎ (01423) 330569
Quarter of a mile east of the A1, off the A59:
Pitch price £7.75-£9.75 per night

►► Moor Lodge Park
Blackmoor Ln, Bardsey
☎ (01937) 572424
West of Wetherby; pitch price from
£6.50 per night.

►►► Shaws Trailer Park
Knaresborough Rd, Harrogate
☎ (01423) 884432 & 883622
On the A59 Harrogate-Knaresborough road;
pitch price from £6.50 per night.

►►►► High Moor Farm Park
Skipton Rd, Harrogate
☎ (01423) 563637 & 564955
fax: (01423) 529449
On the A59 Harrogate-Skipton road; pitch
price £9 per night.

►►►► Rudding Holiday Park
Follifoot, Harrogate
☎ (01423) 870439
fax: (01423) 870859
Situated 3m SE of Harrogate;
pitch price from £6 per night.

WHERE TO EAT

RESTAURANTS

Around Wetherby

🏵 Grundy's
21 Cheltenham Crescent, Harrogate
☎ (01423) 502610
Bright flavours, unusual combinations and
an admirable wine list.
Dinner: 6.30-10
Credit cards 1 2 3 5

🏵🏵 The Bistro
1 Montpellier Mews, Harrogate
☎ (01423) 530708
Ambitious and accomplished cooking in a
small mews restaurant.
Lunch: 12-2
Dinner: 7-10
Credit cards 1 3

🏵🏵 Henry's
Franklin Mount, Harrogate
☎ (01423) 508208
A town centre hotel with good menus.
Dinner: 7-9.30

🏵🏵 Melton's
7 Scarcroft Rd, York
☎ (01904) 634341
A wide variety of dishes from around the
world.
Lunch: 12-2
Dinner: 7-10

PUBS

Around Wetherby

Bingley Arms
37 Church Lane, Bardsley
☎ (01937) 572462
This ancient ivy-clad pub is in the centre of
a pretty village, its two bars quiet and roomy
with old beams and panelling. Tetley Bitter
and Mild are on draught and bar meals are
good value. Children are welcome and there
is a lovely terraced garden, full of flowers.
Open: Monday to Thursday 11am-3pm, 6-
11pm; Friday and Saturday 11am-11pm;
Sunday 12-3pm, 7-10.30pm
Bar food: 12-2pm, 6-8pm; Sunday 12-2pm.
Restaurant: Wednesday to Saturday 6-9pm;
Sunday 12-2pm

White Swan
Wighill
☎ (01937) 832217
This is a very pretty and unspoilt old pub,
and was used as a location for the TV
series,'The Darling Buds of May'. Lots of
pictures of horses adorn the interior where a
fairly standard selection of good bar meals
is on offer. Beers include Tetley's, Stones
and Theakstons and there is an above
average wine list. Children are welcome in
the pub and there are two grassed gardens.
Open: 12-3pm, 6-11pm; Sunday 12-3pm,
7-10.30pm
Bar food: 12-2pm, 6-9.30pm; Sunday 12-
2pm.
Restaurant: 6-9.30pm.

Wincanton

This small and very charming West Country course is the ideal place to visit for anyone wanting to get a real feel for the jumping game. The crowds here are made up of professionals and genuine enthusiasts who know and love their sport.

Officials will be only too pleased to answer questions and make newcomers feel part of the occasion. Facilities are good and the catering deserves a special mention.

Top-class National Hunt horses can be seen in action on most race days throughout the winter months at this popular venue. One of the highlights of the early part of the jumps season is the Desert Orchid South Western Pattern Chase in late October. This famous grey, in whose honour the race is named, was a tremendous course specialist in his day, thrilling the public with his spectacular front running displays. Now in happy retirement, he still usually attends this meeting, leading the pre-race parade in front of the stands. Other notable contests are the Jim Ford Challenge Cup and K.J. Pike & Sons Kingwell Hurdle, both run on the same Thursday at the end of Feburary. These are well established trials for the Gold Cup and Triumph Hurdle at Cheltenham in March and a big turnout is always in evidence, as is the case at the Boxing Day fixture.

FURTHER INFORMATION

Racecourse Secretary, Wincanton Racecours Wincanton, Somerset BA9 8BJ
Telephone: (01963) 32344; Fax:(01963) 34668

LOCATION AND HOW TO GET THERE

The course is north of Wincanton, off the B308 From the M3, leave at junction 8 and take the A303 to Wincanton; from the M4, leave junction 17 and take the A429 south throug Chippenham, then the A350. Keep on the A35 until it joins the A303, then turn right for Wincanton. From the M5, leave at junction 2 and take the A358 eastwards towards Ilminste Join the A303 and continue eastwards Wincanton.

Nearest Railway Stations: Gillingham (Dorse Castle Cary, or Temple Combe. A courtes coach is available all race days. Ring for detail

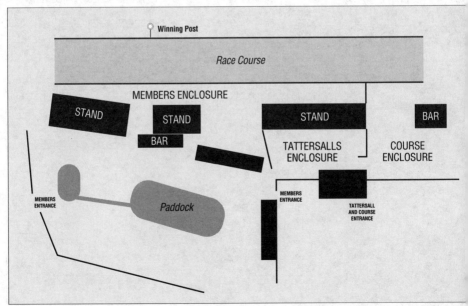

ADMISSION

All classes of day ticket give access to full betting facilities.

Day tickets:
MEMBERS/CLUB £13, premier days £14; junior 17-22, £7
– access to members' stand, and Hatherleigh stand, paddock and parade ring, bars, restaurant, boxes and private rooms

TATTERSALLS £8, premier days £9 – access to grandstand, paddock and winners enclosure, bars, hot and cold snacks

COURSE £4, car £4 plus £4 for each occupant – access to stand, bar with hot and cold snacks, free parking

Annual Membership: £100 – includes reciprocal racing days at other courses

COURSE FACILITIES

Banks:
there are no banks or cashpoint facilities on the course.

For families:
picnic area with refreshment kiosk and toilets, lost children centre at raceday office and police hut.

CALENDAR OF EVENTS

January 15
January 29
February 12
February 26
March 13
March 26
May 8 – evening meeting
October 8

October 25 – includes The Desert Orchid S W Pattern Steeplechase
November 7 – includes The Tanglefoot Elite Hurdle
November 19
December 3
December 26

WHERE TO STAY

HOTELS

Around Wincanton

★★ 63% Pecking Mill Inn & Hotel
Evercreech
☎ (01749) 830336
fax: (01749) 831316
6 bedrooms; double B&B from £40
Credit cards 1 2 3 5

★★★ (RED) ❀❀❀ Stock Hill House
Stock Hill, Gillingham
☎ (01747) 823626
fax: (01747) 825628
10 bedrooms; double B&B £190-£280 including dinner
Credit cards 1 3 5

★★ 62% Holbrook House
Holbrook, Wincanton
☎ (01963) 32377
fax: (01963) 32681
30 bedrooms; double room £75-£110
Credit cards 1 2 3 5

★★★ ❀❀ 72% Royal Chase
Royal Chase Roundabout, Shaftesbury
☎ (01747) 853355
fax: (01747) 851969
35 bedrooms; double room £87-£97
Credit cards 1 2 3 5

★★★ 59% The Grosvenor
The Commons, Shaftesbury
☎ (01747) 852282
fax: (01747) 854755
35 bedrooms; double room £70-£80 (room only)
Credit cards 1 2 3 5

★★★❀ 69% Eastbury
Long St, Sherborne
☎ (01935) 813131
fax: (01935) 817296
15 bedrooms; double B&B £66-£89
Credit cards 1 2 3 5

★★★ 65% Antelope
Greenhill, Sherborne
☎ (01935) 812077
fax: (01935) 816473
19 bedrooms; double B&B £50-£70
Credit cards 1 2 3 5

★★★ 61% Sherborne Hotel
Horsecastle Ln, Sherborne
☎ (01935) 813191, fax: (01935) 816493
59 bedrooms; double room £59.50
Credit cards 1 2 3 5

★ 63% The Talbot
The Square, Mere
☎ (01747) 860427
7 bedrooms; double B&B £40-£63
Credit cards 1 2 3 5

BED AND BREAKFAST

Around Wincanton

QQQQ Lower Church Farm
Rectory Ln, Charlton Musgrove, Wincanton
☎ (01963) 32307
Small, very welcoming farmhouse with old beams, exposed brickwork and fireplaces.
3 bedrooms; double B&B £32

QQQ Toomer Farm
Henstridge
☎ (01963) 250237
fax: (01963) 250237
Old farmhouse providing pleasant accommodation.
3 bedrooms

WHERE TO STAY

QQQQ Chetacombe House Hotel
Chetcombe Rd, Mere
☎ (01747) 860219
fax: (01747) 860111
Elegant and comfortable detached property
on the edge of the village.
5 bedrooms; double B&B from £50
Credit cards 1 2 3

QQQQ The Alders
Sandford Orcas, Sherborne
☎ (01963) 220666
2 bedrooms; double B&B £40-£45

QQQ The Half Moon
Main Street, Mudford, Yeovil
☎ (01935) 850289, fax; (01935) 850842
17th century inn with well-equipped
bedrooms.
11 bedrooms
Credit cards 1 2 3 5

QQQQQ Holywell House
Holywell, East Coker, Yeovil
☎ (01935) 862612
fax: (01935) 863035
Charming 18th-century house in 3
acres of delightful gardens.
3 bedrooms; double B&B £60-£65

QQ Venn Farm
Sherborne
☎ (01963) 250598
Located on the A30, this farm offers a warm
and friendly atmosphere.
3 bedrooms; double B&B from £28

QQQ The Ship
West Stour
☎ (01747) 838640
Fine views of Blackmore Vale; cosy bars.
7 bedroom; double B&B £40-£45
Credit cards 1 3

CAMPSITE

►► Wincanton Racecourse Caravan Club Site
☎ (01963) 34276
One mile from the town centre off the
A3081; pitch price from £5 per night

►► Batcombe Vale Caravan Park
Batcombe, Bruton
☎ (01749) 830246
North of Wincanton
Pitch price £7-£8 per night

WHERE TO EAT

RESTAURANTS

Around Wincanton

🏵🏵 Truffles
95 High St, Bruton
☎ (01749) 812255
Skilful modern interpretation of classic
French traditions in a pleasant cottagey
setting.
Lunch: 12-2
Dinner: 7-9.30

🏵🏵 La Fleur de Lys
25 Salisbury St, Shaftesbury
☎ (01747) 853717
Enjoyable modern French/English cooking
in pretty and comfortable surroundings.
Lunch: 12-2.30
Dinner: 7-10
Credit cards 1 3

🏵🏵 Pheasants
24 Greenhill, Sherborne
☎ (01935) 815252
An attractive stone house offering modern
English cooking with the emphasis on
game.
Lunch: 12-2
Dinner: 7-10
Credit cards 1 3

🏵🏵 Royal Chase
Royal Chase Roundabout, Shaftesbury
☎ (01747) 853355
Formal hotel restaurant
Lunch: 12-2
Dinner: 7-9.30

🏵🏵 Plumber Manor
Hazelbury Bryan Rd, Sturminster Newton
☎ (01258) 472507
Highly recommended cooking in a friendly
Jacobean manor house

Wolverhampton

This Midlands venue has recently undergone a major facelift. It was granted a £2 million loan from the Levy Board to become the third course to lay down an all weather track, with the intention of introducing both floodlit and trotting races into this country.

Such ventures have proved incredibly successful elsewhere in the world, most notably Australia and Hong Kong, and it will be fascinating to see how they fare in Britain.

This ambitious redevelopment plan, which includes both a Holiday Inn and a conference centre and cost a staggering total of £15 million, was officially opened by Her Majesty The Queen in June 1994.

Clearly, then, the future looks very exciting for Wolverhampton. Meetings are run under both codes, many of them on Wednesdays with the Boxing Day and evening fixtures attracting healthy attendances. Visitors are afforded a genuinely warm welcome and the massive programme of improvements has provided many new facilities. A new tiered restaurant offers excellent views of the track which is triangular in shape and extremely sharp in nature, greatly favouring front-runners.

FURTHER INFORMATION

Wolverhampton Racecourse
Gorsebrook Road, Wolverhampton BV6 0PE
☎ (01902) 424481; Fax:(01902) 716626

LOCATION AND HOW TO GET THERE

The course is in Gorsebrook Road, Wolverhampton. From M6 junction 10a, turn onto the M54, leaving at junction 2 to drive south on the A449. At the fifth roundabout turn right and the racecourse is on the right-hand side.

Nearest Railway Station: Wolverhampton; there is a connecting bus service to the course on racedays.

ADMISSION

All classes of day ticket give access to full betting facilities, including Tote.

Day tickets:
MEMBERS/CLUB £15 – access to bars, boxes, banqueting suite.
COURSE £6 – access to bars

Viewing restaurant £25.90 dinner and admittance

Annual Membership: £150

(Please note: The above are 1997 prices and are subject to review in 1998)

COURSE FACILITIES

Banks:
there are no banks or cashpoint facilities on the course.

For families:
picnic area with refreshment kiosk and toilets.

CALENDAR OF EVENTS

January 7 – flat	March 28 – flat; evening meeting	August 22 – flat; evening meeting
January 10 – flat; evening meeting	April 4 – flat; evening meeting	September 5 – flat; evening meeting
January 14 – flat	April 7 – flat	September 19 – flat; evening meeting
January 21 – flat	April 11 – flat; evening meeting	September 29 – flat
January 24 – flat; evening meeting	April 18 – flat; evening meeting	October 3 – flat; evening meeting
January 28 – flat	April 25 – flat; evening meeting	October 17 – flat; evening meeting
February 4 – flat	April 30 – flat	October 31 – flat; evening meeting
February 7 – flat; evening meeting	May 29 – flat	November 14 – flat; evening meeting
February 11 – flat	June 6 – flat; evening meeting	November 16 – flat
February 18 – flat	June 17 – flat	November 28 – flat; evening meeting
February 21 – flat; evening meeting	June 20 – flat; evening meeting	December 2 – flat
February 25 – flat	June 26 – flat	December 5 – flat
March 4 – flat	July 10 – flat	December 12 – flat; evening meeting
March 7 – flat; evening meeting	July 13 – jumping; evening meeting	December 16 – flat
March 14 – flat	July 24 – flat	December 26 – flat
March 21 – flat; evening meeting	August 7 – flat	

195

WHERE TO STAY

HOTELS

★★★ 65% Goldthorn
Penn Rd
☎ (01902) 429216
fax: (01902) 710419
93 bedrooms; double room £60-£100
(room only)

★★ 68% Ely House
53 Tettenhall Rd
☎ (01902) 311311
fax: (01902) 21098
18 bedrooms; double B&B £48-£78
Credit cards 1 2 3 5

★★ 58% York
138-140 Tettenhall Rd
☎ (01902) 758211
fax: (01902) 758212
15 bedrooms; double B&B £43-£48
Credit cards 1 2 3 5

Around Wolverhampton

★★★ 66% Roman Way
Watling St, Hatherton, Cannock
☎ (01543) 572121
fax: (01543) 502749
56 bedrooms; double room £80-£175
Credit cards 1 2 3

Travel Inn
Watling St, Longford, Cannock
☎ (01543) 572721
fax: (01543) 466130
38 bedrooms; double room £36.50

★★★ 58% Ward Arms
Birmingham Rd, Dudley
☎ (01384) 458070
fax: (01384) 457502
72 bedrooms; double room £70-£108
Credit cards 1 2 3

Travelodge
Dudley Rd, Dudley
☎ (01384) 481579, Central Reservations:
(01800) 850950
32 bedrooms; double room £34.95-£49.95
(room only)
Credit cards 1 2 3

Forte Posthouse Birmingham
Chapel Ln, Great Barr
☎ 0121-357 7444
fax: 0121-357 7503
192 bedrooms; double room £56-£69
(room only)
Credit cards 1 2 3 5

**★★★ 61% Great Barr Hotel &
Conference Centre**
Pear Tree Dr, off Newton Rd, Great Barr
☎ 0121-357 1141
fax: 0121-357 7557
105 bedrooms; double room £69-£73
(room only)
Credit cards 1 2 3 5

★★ 60% Talbot
High St, Stourbridge
☎ (01384) 394350
fax: (01384) 371318
25 bedrooms; double room £70-£104
Credit cards 1 2 3

**★★★ ✿ 70% The Fairlawns at
Aldridge**
178 Little Aston Road, Aldridge, Walsall
☎ (01922) 55122
fax: (01922) 743210
35 bedrooms; double B&B £89.50-£105
Credit cards 1 2 3 5

★★★ 66% Quality Friendly Hotel
20 Wolverhampton Rd West, Bentley
☎ (01922) 724444
fax: (01922) 723148
155 bedrooms; double room £92 (room
only)
Credit cards 1 2 3 5

★★★ 65% Boundary
Birmingham Rd, Walsall
☎ (01922) 33555
fax: (01922) 612034
94 bedrooms; double room £39-50-£55.50
(room only)
Credit cards 1 2 3 5

★★★ 63% Beverley
58 Lichfield Rd, Walsall
☎ (01922) 614967 & 22999,
fax: (01922) 724187
30 bedrooms; double room £45-£85
Credit cards 1 2 3

★★★ 62% Barons Court
Walsall Rd, Walsall Wood, Walsall
☎ (01543) 452020
fax: (01543) 361276
94 bedrooms; double room from £65
Credit cards 1 2 3

★★ 65% Abberley
Bescot Rd, Wallsall
☎ (01922) 27413
fax: (01922) 720933
28 bedrooms; double B&B £40-£59
Credit cards 1 2 3 5

★★★ ✿✿✿ 78% Old Vicarage
Worfield
☎ (01746) 716497
fax: (01746) 716552
14 bedrooms; double B&B £107-£152
Credit cards 1 2 3 5

★★ 63% Fountain Court Hotel
339-343 Hagley Rd, Edgbaston,
Birmingham
☎ 0121-429 1754
fax: 0121-429 1209
Bright, warm and clean bedrooms.
25 bedrooms; double B&B £45-£55
Credit cards 1 2 3 5

WHERE TO STAY

BED AND BREAKFAST

Around Wolverhampton

QQ Highfield House Hotel
Holly Rd, Rowley Regis, Blackheath
☎ 0121-559 1066
Commercial guesthouse with friendly proprietors.
14 bedrooms; double B&B £38–£47
Credit cards 1 3

QQQ Moors Farm & Country Restaurant
Chillington Ln, Codsall
☎ (01902) 842330
fax: (01902) 847878
A busy working farm, well known in the area for both its accommodation and restaurant.
6 bedrooms; double B&B £40–£50

QQQ Kinfayre Restaurant
41 High St, Kinver
☎ (01384) 872565
fax: (01384) 877724
A modernised inn with well-equipped bedrooms.
11 bedrooms; double B&B from £50
Credit cards 1 3

QQ Coppers End
Walsall Rd, Muckley Corner, Lichfield
☎ (01543) 372910
fax: (01543) 372910
Former police station with modern bedrooms.
6 bedrooms; double B&B £36–£42
Credit cards 1 2 3 5

WHERE TO EAT

RESTAURANTS

❀ Chung Ying Garden
17 Thorp St, Birmingham
☎ 0121-666 6622
Many specialities and an excellent selection of dim sum.

❀ Shimla Pinks
214 Broad St, Birmingham
☎ 0121-633 0366
Modern versions of popular Indian dishes.
Lunch: 12-2.30
Dinner: 6-11

PUBS

Around Wolverhampton

The Crooked House
Coppice Mill, nr Himley
☎ (01384) 238583
This is a local curiosity – a 19th-century building affected by subsidence to the point where its floors, walls and doors all slope noticeably! Three bars in Victorian style serve draught Banks's Bitter and Mild, Harp, Kronenberg 1664 and Grolsch lager and Woodpecker cider. Bar menus offer snacks and salads alongside a range of traditional hot dishes. Only children having meals are permitted in the bars.
Open: 11am-11pm; Sunday 12-3pm, 7-10.30pm
Bar food: 12-2pm, Sunday lunch.

The Little Dry Dock
Windmill End, Netherton, nr Dudley
☎ (01384) 235369
The front door wings of this canalide Victorian pub are narrowboat rudders and the bar itself is an authentic narrowboat. With its floor covered with lino and sawdust, this is an effective reminder of another era. The value-for-money menu of good, home-cooked food may be accompanied by a pint of 'Mad' O'Rourke's Little Lumphammer or Holts Mild or Entire. Children are welcome.
Open: 11am-3pm, 7-11pm; Sunday 12-3pm, 7-10.30pm
Bar food: 11am-2.30pm, 6-10pm; Sunday 12-3pm, 7-9.30pm

Church Tavern
High St, Quarry Bank, nr Brierley Hill
☎ (01384) 68757
The ample portions of tasty bar food served in this early Victorian 'local' in the town's High Street represents excellent value for money. Holts Entire, Bitter and Mild are available on draught and the atmosphere is quiet and pleasant. No children under 14 in the bar, but there is outside seating.
Open: 11am-3pm, 5-11pm; Friday and Saturday 11am-11pm; Sunday 12-3pm, 7-10.30pm
Bar food: 12-2pm for main meals; snacks at other times.

Worcester

Worcester is the favourite racetrack of many National Hunt trainers. The long oval circuit of 13 furlongs has easy bends and very fair fences. There is always plenty of room for jockeys to manoeuvre, making this a perfect venue to introduce novices, both over hurdles and fences. As a result, fields are large, creating an open betting market that proves a boon to punters.

The emphasis is usually on quantity rather than quality, although there are a couple of valuable Grade Two events, including the Worcester Novice's Chase in mid-November.

Meetings are held during nine months of the jumps season. The vast majority of fixtures are run on Wednesdays and Saturdays, with the evening cards a particular delight in summer. There are some fine facilities available to racegoers and these are being improved all the time. One slight disadvantage of this beautiful course is that it is situated right on the banks of the River Severn, which makes it prone to flooding during the depths of winter. On rare occasions, the whole track has even become submerged, with only the grandstand remaining above water, causing the site to look more like a marina than a racecourse.

FURTHER INFORMATION

Mr Stephen Brice
Pitchcroft,
Worcester WR1 3EJ
☎ (01905) 23936

LOCATION AND HOW TO GET THERE

The course is on the eastern bank of the River Severn, five minutes' walk from the city centre. From the north, leave the M5 at junction 6, from the south leave the M5 at junction 7.
Nearest Railway Station: Worcester (Foregate Street); there is no connecting bus service, but the course is within easy walking distance.

ADMISSION

All classes of day ticket give access to full betting facilities, including Tote.

Day tickets:
MEMBERS/CLUB £12.50 – access to bar, restaurant, boxes and private rooms.

TATTERSALLS £9.50 – access to bar and boxes.

CENTRE COURSE £5, senior citizens £2.50 – access to bar, picnic parking and children's play area.
There are group discounts on all classes of ticket.

(Please note: The above are 1997 prices and will be subject to review in 1998)

COURSE FACILITIES

Banks:
there are no banks or cashpoint facilities on the course.

For families:
picnic area with refreshment kiosk and toilets, children's play area, lost children centre.

CALENDAR OF EVENTS

April 25 – jumping; evening meeting
May 9 – jumping
May 20 – jumping
June 6 – jumping
June 17 – jumping; evening meeting
June 27 – jumping
July 8 – jumping; evening meeting
July 15 – jumping; evening meeting
July 22 – jumping
August 1 – jumping

August 7 – jumping; evening meeting
August 10 – jumping
August 26 – jumping
September 11-12 – jumping
September 26 – jumping
October 10 – jumping
October 24 – jumping
November 11 – jumping; includes Worcester Novices' Steeple Chase
November 30 – jumping

WHERE TO STAY

HOTELS

★★★ ❀ 68% Fownes Resort
City Walls Rd
☎ (01905) 613151
fax: (01905) 23742
61 bedrooms; double room £78-£95 (room only)
Credit cards 1 2 3 5

★★★ 63% Star
Foregate St
☎ (01905) 24308
fax: (01905) 23440
46 bedrooms; double room £70-£114
Credit cards 1 2 3

★★★ 62% The Giffard
High St
☎ (01905) 726262
fax: (01905) 723458
95 bedrooms; double room £62.50-£70 (room only)
Credit cards 1 2 3 5

★★ 65% Loch Ryan Hotel
119 Sidbury Rd
☎ (01905) 351143
fax: (01905) 351143
10 bedrooms; double B&B from £55
Credit cards 1 2 3 5

★★ 66% Ye Olde Talbot
Friar St
☎ (01905) 23573
fax: (01905) 612760
29 bedrooms; double B&B £49.50-£59.50
Credit cards 1 2 3 5

★ 64% Park House
12 Droitwich Rd
☎ (01905) 21816
fax: (01905) 612178
7 bedrooms; double B&B £38-£44

Around Worcester

★★★★ 66% Chateau Impney
Droitwich
☎ (01905) 774411
fax: (01905) 772371
67 bedrooms; double room £59.95-£129.95 (room only)
Credit cards 1 2 3 5

★★★★ 64% Raven
Droitwich
☎ (01905) 772224, fax: (01905) 797100
72 bedrooms
Credit cards 1 2 3 5

Travelodge
Rashwood Hill, Droitwich
☎ (01527) 866545
32 bedrooms; double £34.95-£49.95 (room only)
Credit cards 1 2 3

★★ 65% The Chequers Inn
Chequers Lane, Fladbury
☎ (01386) 860276 & 860527
fax:(01386) 861286
8 bedrooms; double B&B £55-£65
Credit cards 1 2 3

★★★ 64% Abbey
Abbey Rd, Malvern
☎ (01684) 892332
fax: (01684) 892662
107 bedrooms; double B&B from £95
Credit cards 1 2 3 5

★★★ 64% Foley Arms
Worcester Rd, Malvern
☎ (01684) 573397
fax: (01684) 569665
28 bedrooms; double B&B £88-£110 (room only)
Credit cards 1 2 3 5

★★ 66% Great Malvern
Graham Rd, Malvern
☎ (01684) 563411
fax: (01684) 560514
14 bedrooms; double B&B £60-£75
Credit cards 1 2 3 5

★★ 66% Mount Pleasant
Belle Vue Terrace, Malvern
☎ (01684) 561837
fax: (01684) 569968
15 bedrooms; double B&B £64-£79
Credit cards 1 2 3 5

★★ 64% Cotford
51 Graham Rd, Malvern
☎ (01684) 574680
fax: (01684) 572952
17 bedrooms; double B&B from £60
Credit cards 1 3

★★★ ❀❀ 72% Cottage in the Wood
Holywell Rd, Malvern Wells
☎ (01684) 575859
fax: (01684) 560662
20 bedrooms; double B&B £89-£140
Credit cards 1 2 3

WHERE TO STAY

★★ 64% Star
High St, Upton upon Severn
☎ (01684) 592300
fax: (01684) 592929
16 bedrooms; double B&B £45-£75
Credit cards 1 2 3 5

★★ ❀❀ 75% Holdfast Cottage
Welland, Little Malvern
☎ (01684) 310288
fax: (01684) 311117
8 bedrooms; double room £78-£85
Credit cards 1 3

BED AND BREAKFAST

QQ Wyatt
40 Barbourne Rd
☎ (01905) 26311
fax: (01905) 26311
Well maintained guesthouse with spacious
lounge and pretty dining room.
8 bedrooms; double B&B £34-£38
Credit cards 1 3

Around Worcester

QQQQQ Nightingale Hotel
Bishampton
☎ (01386) 462521
fax (01386) 462522
Mock-Tudor farmhouse in 200 acres of land
offering warm hospitality, a high standard of
accommodation and excellent food.
3 bedrooms; double B&B £50
Credit cards 1 3

QQQQ Old Parsonage Farm
Hanley Castle
☎ (01684) 310124
A fine old house with views of the castle and
Malvern Hills, offering a high standard of
accommodation in spacious, well furnished
rooms, good food and over 100 wines
available.
3 bedrooms; double B&B £41-£47

QQQQ Phepson Farm
Himbleton
☎ (01905) 391205
Rambling 17th-century farmhouse with
cosy bedrooms and comfortable lounge,
just 5 miles from the M5.
4 bedrooms; double B&B £40

QQ Croft
Bransford
☎ (01886) 832227
5 bedrooms; double B&B £37-£44
Credit cards 1 3

QQQ Sidney House Hotel
40 Worcester Rd, Malvern
☎ (01684) 574994
fax: (01684) 574994
Grade II listed house with views over the
Severn Valley. Bedrooms are particularly
well equipped and hosts are hospitable.
8 bedrooms; double B&B £39-£59
Credit cards 1 2 3

QQQQ Wyche Keep
22 Wyche Road, Malvern
☎ (01684) 567018, fax: (01684) 892304
An impeccably maintained, castellated
country house.
3 bedrooms; double B&B £50-£60

CAMPSITES

Around Worcester

►►► Riverside Caravan Park
Little Clevelode, Malvern
☎ (01684) 310475
fax: (01684) 310475
An open field site; pitch price from £6 per
night

WHERE TO EAT

RESTAURANTS

🌸🌸 Brown's
The Old Cornmill, South Quay
☎ (01905) 26263
Spacious and attractive restaurant serving interesting English and French food.
Last lunch 1.45pm
Last dinner 9.45pm
Credit cards 1 2 3 5

Around Worcester

🌸🌸 Elms
Abberley
☎ (01299) 896666
French and British food of a high standard
Lunch 12-2, from £11.95
Dinner 7-9.30; from £24

🌸🌸 Cottage in the Wood
Holywell Rd, Malvern Wells
☎ (01684) 575859
A good range of modern English food
Lunch 12-2
Dinner 7-9

🌸🌸 Holdfast Cottage
Little Malvern, Malvern
☎ (01684) 310288
Imaginative traditional and continental cooking
Dinner 7-9

🌸 Fownes
City Walls Rd, Worcester
☎ (01905) 613151
International cuisine in a converted glove factory
Lunch 12-2.30
Dinner 7-9.45

PUBS

Around Worcester

Bluebell
4 Charlford Rd, Barnard's Green, Great Malvern
☎ (01684) 575031
The combination of sensibly priced, well cooked food and an appealing setting guarantees this pub's popularity. Marston Pedigree and Banks's Mild are among the beers on draught, along with half a dozen lagers. Children are only permitted in the eating areas, but there is an outdoor play area and seating in the patio garden.
Open: 11.30am-3pm, 6-11pm; Sunday 12-3pm, 7-10.30pm
Bar food: 12-2pm, 6.30-10pm; Sunday 12-2.3opm, 7-9.30pm

Three Kings
Hanley Castle
☎ (01684) 592686
This brick and timber village centre pub has remained largely unspoilt since it was built around 500 years ago. Butcombe and Thwaites Bitters are served, along with guest beers from the likes of Bunces, Shepherd Neame and Smiles. A range of reasonably priced bar meals and snacks are available. Children are welcome in the room without a bar.
Open: 11am-2.30pm, 7-11pm, but flexible, depending on trade; Sunday 12-3pm, 7-10.30pm
Bar food: As opening hours within reason, but not Sunday evening

Kings Arms
Ombersley
☎ (01905) 620315
The kitchen here works to provide provide interesting and varied menu of value-for-money dishes. Bass and Boddingtons Mild are on sale, along with a wide selection of malt whiskies. Some 600 years old, the pub is an impressive black and white building with a courtyard in front and garden at the back. Children over 8 years are welcome if eating.
Open: 11am-2.45pm, 5.30-11pm; Sunday 12-3pm, 7-10.30pm (possibly extending opening hours for the dining area in the afternoon)
Bar food: 12-2.15pm, 6-10pm; Sunday as opening times, until 10pm

Anchor
Wyre Piddle
☎ (01386) 552799
There is an excellent, well-balanced wine list, and beer drinkers are not overlooked, with Flowers, Boddingtons and Banks's on tap. The low, white-painted building dates back to the 17th century and at the back a terraced garden drops steeply down to the River Avon.
Open: 11am-2.30pm, 6-11pm; Sunday 12-3pm, 7-10.30pm
Bar food: 12-2.30pm, 7-9.30pm; Sunday 12-2pm, 7-9pm
Restaurant: times as bar food, but closed Sunday evening

Yarmouth

This popular Norfolk coastal resort, 20 miles east of Norwich, offers the perfect opportunity to combine a break at the seaside with some exciting Flat racing.

The course caters for families and provides a bouncy castle and a train for families to keep the children happy. There are plenty of outlets selling fast food and snacks.

This is one of the nearest venues to the major equine centre of Newmarket and many of the top trainers there like to frequent this course. The quality of racing is therefore usually well above average, particularly in the contests for two-year-olds. The track is a narrow oval circuit with a long run-in of five furlongs which also forms part of the straight mile course. It is very level and galloping in nature, suiting big, long-striding horses. Fixtures are held throughout the summer, with the three-day meeting in mid-September and the evening cards in July the main highlights of the year.

FURTHER INFORMATION

The Racecourse
Jellicoe Road, Great Yarmouth, Norfolk NR30 4AU
☎ (01493) 842527

LOCATION AND HOW TO GET THERE

The racecourse is on the A1064 Caister road, one and a half miles north of Great Yarmouth and is signposted from the roundabout at the end of the A47.
Nearest Railway Station: Great Yarmouth

ADMISSION

All classes of day ticket give access to full betting facilities, including Tote.

Day tickets:
Accompanied children under 16 are admitted free.

MEMBERS £12 – access to bar, lawn, restaurant.

TATTERSALLS £8.50 – access to seafood restaurant, carvery & à la carte restaurant, bars, seafood counters and fast food

SILVER RING/FAMILY £4.50 – access to bars, snacks and ice cream

Annual Membership: £100, first guest £75

COURSE FACILITIES

Banks:
there are no banks or cashpoint facilities on the course.

For families:
picnic area with refreshment kiosk and toilets; children's play area with train, pony rides, bouncy castle and fair in Silver Ring/Family enclosure; baby changing facilities; lost children centre.

CALENDAR OF EVENTS

May 27 – flat
June 4 – flat
June 11 – flat
June 22 – flat; evening meeting
July 1-2 – flat; evening meeting
July 15 – flat
July 21 – flat

July 27 – flat; evening meeting
August 5 – flat; evening meeting
August 9 – flat
August 20 – flat
September 15-17 – flat; includes John Musker Stakes
October 20 – flat
October 28 – flat

WHERE TO STAY

HOTELS

★★★ 73% Cliff
Gorleston
☎ (01493) 662179
fax: (01493) 653617
39 bedrooms
Credit cards 1 2 3 5

★★★ ⊛ 66% Imperial
North Dr
☎ (01493) 851113
fax: (01493) 852229
39 bedrooms; double B&B from £80
Credit cards 1 2 3 5

★★★ 68% Regency Dolphin
Albert Square
☎ (01493) 855070
fax: (01493) 853798
50 bedrooms; double room £80
Credit cards 1 2 3 5

★★ 64% Burlington
11 North Dr
☎ (01493) 844568 & 842095,
fax: (01493) 331848
28 bedrooms; double B&B £68-£85
Credit cards 1 2 3 5

★★ 68% Regency
5 North Dr
☎ (01493) 843759
fax: (01493) 330411
14 bedrooms; double B&B £40-£54
Credit cards 1 2 3 5

Around Great Yarmouth

Travelodge
Acle
☎ (01493) 751970, Central Reservations:
(01800) 850950
40 bedrooms; double room £34.95-£49.95
(room only)
Credit cards 1 2 3

★★★ 64% Hotel Hatfield
The Esplanade, Lowesloft
☎ (01502) 565337
fax: (01502) 511885
33 bedrooms; double B&B £63-£75
Credit cards 1 2 3 5

★★★ 64% South Walsham Hall
The Street, South Walsham
☎ (01603) 270378
fax: (01603) 270519
16 bedrooms; double B&B £80-£180
Credit cards 1 2 3 5

BED AND BREAKFAST

QQ Avalon Private Hotel
54 Clarence Road, Gorleston-on-Sea,
Great Yarmouth
☎ (01493) 662114, fax: (01493) 661521
Close to the cliff tops and the sandy beach.
9 bedrooms; double B&B £30-£38

QQQ Georgian House
☎ (01493) 842623
Popular, good value establishment.
19 bedrooms; double B&B £32-£46

QQ Spindrift
36 Wellesley Rd
☎ (01493) 858674
fax: (01493) 858674
Victorian building on a tree-lined avenue
parallel with the seafront.
7 bedrooms; double B&B £30-£45
Credit cards 1 2 3

QQQ Squirrels Nest
71 Avondale Rd
☎ (01493)) 662746
fax: (01493) 662746
A few steps from the beach in a quiet area of
Gorlestone; friendly proprietor.
9 bedrooms; double B&B £40-£60
Credit cards 1 2 3

QQ Frandor
120 Lowestoft Rd
☎ (01493) 662112
Situated close to town centre; simply
furnished guesthouse with relaxed
atmosphere.
6 bedrooms; double room £33-£40
Credit cards 3

QQ Jennis Lodge
63 Avondale Rd
☎ (01493) 662840
A well located guesthouse a few steps from
the seafront.
11 bedrooms; double B&B £28-£36

Around Yarmouth

QQQ Sonnerton House
7 Kirkley Cliff, Lowestoft
☎ (01502) 565665
fax: (01502) 501176
A distinctive blue and white house on the
seafront.
8 bedrooms; double B&B £37-£45
Credit cards 1 2 3 5

QQ Fairways
398 London Rd South, Lowestoft
☎ (01502) 572659
Friendly, carefully maintained guesthouse.
7 bedrooms; double B&B £32-£36
Credit cards 1 2 3

QQ Kingsleigh
44 Marine Pde, Lowestoft
☎ (01502) 572513
Nicely kept guesthouse with some sea
views.
5 bedrooms; double B&B£32-£38

QQQ Rockville House
6 Pakefield Rd, Lowestoft
☎ (01502) 581011 & 574891
A professional approach and genuine
consideration for guests is evident at this
popular guesthouse.
4 bedrooms; double B&B from £45
Credit cards 1 3

WHERE TO STAY

CAMPSITES

►►► Rose Farm Touring & Camping Park
Stepshort, Belton
☎ (01493) 780896
fax: (01493) 780896
Off A143 south of Great Yarmouth; pitch price £5-£6.50 per night.

►►► Wild Duck Caravan & Chalet Park
Belton
☎ (01493) 780268
fax: (01493) 782308
South of Great Yarmouth; pitch price from £6 per night.

►►► Grasmere Caravan Park
9 Bultitude's Loke, Yarmouth Rd, Caister-on-Sea
☎ (01493) 720382
Off A149; pitch price £5.30-£7.50 per night.

►►► Old Hall Leisure Park
High St, Caiser-on-Sea
☎ (01493) 720400
fax: (01493) 720261
Close to the A149; pitch price from £6 per night.

►►► Clippesby Holidays
Clippesby
☎ (01493) 369367
fax: (01493) 368181
Southwest of Great Yarmouth; pitch price £8.50-£15 per night.

►►► Scratby Hall Caravan Park
Scratby
☎ (01493) 730283
North of Great Yarmouth, close to the beach and Norfolk Broads; pitch price £4.50 - £9.90 per night.

Vauxhall Holiday Park
4 Acle New Rd, Gt Yarmouth
☎ (01493) 857231
fax: (01493) 331122
A very large holiday complex; pitch price £14-£20 per night.

WHERE TO EAT

RESTAURANTS

❀ Imperial
North Drive, Gt Yarmouth
☎ (01493) 851113
Restaurant with the feel of a French brasserie
Lunch: 12-2.30
Dinner: 7-10

PUBS

Around Yarmouth

Fisherman's Return
The Lane, Winterton-on-Sea
☎ (01493) 393305
The fact that it is just ten minutes' walk from the beach and has a garden filled with play equipment in summer makes this pub very popular with families. Very good, sensibly priced meals include seasonal daily specials and Adnams Best Bitter and Courage Directors are available on draught. There is also a choice of 20 to 25 malt whiskies and a guest wine. Children under are 14 not permitted in the bar, but there is a family room and a garden room in summer.
Open: summer every day 11am-2.30pm, 6-11pm; winter Monday to Saturday 11-2.30pm, 7-11pm; Sunday 11-3pm, 7-10.30pm
Bar food: summer 11am-2pm, 6-9.30pm; winter 11am-2pm, 7-9.30pm

Sutton Staithe Hotel
Sutton Staithe
☎ (01692) 580244
This 18th-century red brick inn, halfway between a pub and an hotel, enjoys a rural setting right beside Sutton Broad. A good range of draught beers includes Adnams, Ruddles and Websters Bitters, with Adnams on cask, while a decent wine list accompanies a menu of fairly priced bar food. Children are welcome in the eating area.
Open: summer all day; winter 11am-2.30pm, 6-11pm; Sunday 12-3pm, 7-10.30pm
Bar food: 12-2pm, 7-9pm daily
Restaurant: 7-9.30pm (booking necessary)

The Lodge
Vicarage Rd, Salhouse
☎ (01603) 782828
Originally a Georgian rectory, this large and comfortable red brick pub is set in its own extensive grounds on the edge of the village. The range of beverages on offer includes over 80 malt whiskies as well as a good choice of draught beers (Woodfordes, Stones, Greene King IPA and Murphy's Stout). It is advisable to book a table in the carvery at popular times. Children are welcome if eating and there is an outdoor play area.
Open: 10.30am-3pm, 5.30-11pm; Sunday 12-3pm, 7-10.30pm
Bar food: 12-2pm, 7.30-9.30pm (except Sunday evenings in winter)

The Reedham Ferry Inn
Reedham
☎ (01493) 700429
A marvellous place to moor – or, if you are land based, to sit and watch passing boats or the ferry plying back and forth across the Yare, this white-painted, grey-roofed inn dating from the late 17th century stands right on the waterfront with tables on its jetty. The modern sun room running across the front of the bar and restaurant provides a suitable area for children (welcome anywhere except in the bar and until 9pm in the restaurant). Beverages range from Scrumpy Jack to continental lagers and local wines, with Adnams and Woodfordes beer on draught. Good-value bar food is available.
Open: 11am-3pm, 6.30-11pm (7-11pm in winter); Sunday 12-3pm, 7-10.30pm
Bar food: 12-2pm, 7-10pm
Restaurant: as bar food; booking preferred

The Swan
Ingham, nr Stalham
☎ (01692) 581099
A good choice of bottled beers supplements those on draught (Woodfordes Wherry, Adnams Bitter and Mild, Murphy's, Double Dragon and guest beers) at this lovely 14th-century thatched inn, and a decent wine list is also available. Set next to the church in the centre of the village, the Swan offers reasonably priced excellent home-cooked food. Children are welcome and there is a family room as well as an outdoor play area.
Open: 11am-3pm, 6-11pm; Sunday 12-3pm, 7-10.30pm
Bar food: Tuesday to Saturday 12-2pm, 6.30-9pm; Sunday 12-2.30pm

York

This beautiful cathedral city is steeped in history, as indeed is the racecourse. Top-class Flat racing has been held since 1731 on the turf of The Knavesmire, renowned as the place where Dick Turpin was hanged.

Fifteen fixtures are now scheduled here each year, with more than two million pounds in prize money attracting some of the finest bloodstock to compete. The highlights are the three-day mid-week meetings in May and August.

The former includes two significant Classic trials, the Grosvenor Casinos Dante and Tattersalls Musidora Stakes while the latter is regarded as one of the most influential meetings in the racing calendar. It is known as the Ebor Festival, named after the famous handicap of that title, and features a plethora of important races. Best of these are the Juddmonte International, Aston Upthorpe Yorkshire Oaks and Nunthorpe Stakes, all prestigious Group One contests.

These meetings have also become important social events and York is often described as the Royal Ascot of the north, although locals prefer to think of Royal Ascot as the York of the south. Entrance fees are suitably steep for the Members Enclosure on the big occasions, but the champagne is considerably cheaper than at most southern tracks and the atmosphere is unsurpassed anywhere. The new Knavesmire Stand (opened 1996) has added a new dimension to race-going at York and set new standards. As well as increasing facilities for Tattersalls and County Stand customers, the Knavesmire Stand has created an impressive 500-seater "dine and view" restaurant on the third floor.

York Racing Museum

Permanently on display on the fourth floor of the grandstand is a fine collection of old prints and racing memorabilia. The museum has a close affiliation with the National Racing Museum at Newmarket, who participate in an exchange of exhibits throughout the year.

Open: from 11.30am on each raceday; by appointment at other times.

FURTHER INFORMATION

York Race Committee
The Racecourse, York YO2 1EX
☎ (01904) 620911; Fax:(01904) 611071
24-hr Credit card hotline for bookings of £30+
(0345) 585642 (no junior badge orders in advance)

LOCATION AND HOW TO GET THERE

The racecourse is to the south of the city centre on Knavesmire Road. From the south or west take the A64; from the northeast take the northern bypass linking the A19 to the A64; from the north on the A1, take the A59 turning to York, just south of Boroughbridge, and join the northern bypass.

Nearest Railway Station: York, one mile from the course; there are connecting bus services on racedays. The journey from London Kings Cross to York station is around two hours.

There are landing facilities for light aircraft close to the course – contact the racecourse office for details.

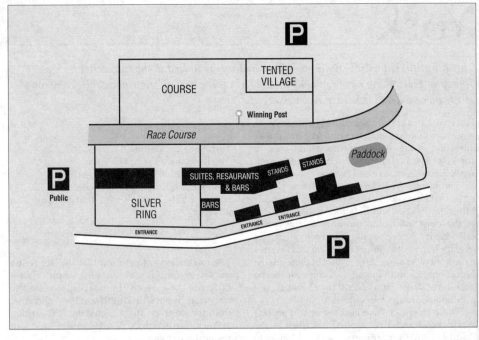

ADMISSION

All classes of day ticket give access to full betting facilities, including Tote.

Day tickets:
Tickets may be purchased in advance for all enclosures. Three-day passes may be purchased for all enclosures at the May and August Meetings at a reduced price. Accompanied children under 16 are admitted free to all enclosures, but children under 12 are not admitted to the County Stand during the May and August meetings.

COUNTY STAND £18-£35, (junior 16-23 £12-£18), (3-day badge £45-£80) – access to Members dining room, champagne bar, seafood bar, bars and snacks
TATTERSALLS £10-£17 (3-day badge £28-£35) – access to bar and self-service restaurant
SILVER RING £5 (3-day £10) – access to self-service restaurant & fish 'n' chip shop
COURSE £3 (3-day £6)

Annual Membership: £150, family £255; junior £60

COURSE FACILITIES

Banks:
There are no banks or cashpoint facilities on the course.

For families:
picnic area with refreshment kiosk and toilets; children's play area at some meetings; baby changing facilities; free creche on Saturdays; lost children centre.

CALENDAR OF EVENTS

May 12-14 – includes Tattersalls Musidora Stakes, The Grosvenor Casinos Dante Stakes, The Yorkshire Cup and Duke of York International Factors Stakes
June 12-13 – includes William Hill Trophy and Daniel Prenn Royal Yorkshire Rated Stakes
July 10-11 – includes John Smith's Magnet Cup
August 18-20 – includes The Juddmonte International Stakes, Great Voltigeur, Tote Ebor, Scottish Equitable Gimcrack, Aston Upthorpe Yorkshire Oaks, Nunthorpe Stakes, Bradford and Bingley and

Weatherbys/Hiscox Household Insurance Lonsdale Stakes
September 2-3 – includes Strensall Stakes on Thursday
October 7-8
October 10

WHERE TO STAY

HOTELS

★★★★ 64% Swallow
Tadcaster Rd
☎ (01904) 701000
fax: (01904) 702308
113 bedrooms; double B&B £125–£140
Credit cards 1 2 3 5

★★★★ 65% Royal York
Station Rd
☎ (01904) 653681
fax: (01904) 653271
158 bedrooms; double room £125–£160
Credit cards 1 2 3 5

★★★★ 60% York Viking Moat House
North St
☎ (01904) 459988
fax: (01904) 641793
200 bedrooms; double room £125–£140
Credit cards 1 2 3 5

★★★ (RED) ❀ The Grange
Clifton
☎ (01904) 644744
fax: (01904) 612453
30 bedrooms; double B&B £110–£190
Credit cards 1 2 3 5

★★★ (RED) ❀❀❀ Middlethorpe Hall
Bishopthorpe Rd
☎ (01904) 641241
fax: (01904) 620176
30 bedrooms; double room £131–£215
(room only)
Credit cards 1 2 3 5

★★★❀ 72% Dean Court
Duncombe Place
☎ (01904) 625082
fax: (01904) 620305
41 bedrooms; double B&B £95–£145
Credit cards 1 2 3 5

★★★ ❀ 67% Ambassador
125 The Mount
☎ (01904) 641316
fax: (01904) 640259
24 bedrooms
Credit cards 1 2 3

★★★ ❀ 73% Mount Royal
The Mount
☎ (01904) 628856
fax: (01904) 611171
23 bedrooms
Credit cards 1 2 3 5

★★★ ❀ 70% York Pavilion
45 Main St, Fulford
☎ (01904) 622099
fax: (01904) 626939
35 bedrooms; double B&B £110–£120
Credit cards 1 2 3 5

Forte Posthouse
Tadcaster Rd
☎ (01904) 707921
fax: (01904) 702804
143 bedrooms; double room £59
(room only)
Credit cards 1 2 3 5

★★★ 64% Novotel
Fishergate
☎ (01904) 611660
fax: (01904) 610925
124 bedrooms
Credit cards 1 2 3 5

★★★ 64% Monkbar
Monkbar
☎ (01904) 638086; fax: (01904) 629195
48 bedrooms; double B&B £105–£125
Credit cards 1 2 3 5

★★★❀ 69% Kilima
129 Holgate Rd
☎ (01904) 658844 & 625787,
fax: (01904) 612083
15 bedrooms; double B&B from £78
Credit cards 1 2 3 5

★★ 67% Heworth Court
76-78 Heworth Green
☎ (01904) 425156
fax: (01904) 415290
25 bedrooms; double B&B £44–£78
Credit cards 1 2 3 5

★★ 69% Beechwood Close
19 Shipton Rd, Clifton
☎ (01904) 658378, fax: (01904) 647124
14 bedrooms; double B&B £65–£75
Credit cards 1 2 3 5

★★ 68% Hudsons
60 Bootham
☎ (01904) 621267, fax: (01904) 654719
30 bedrooms
Credit cards 1 2 3 5

★★ 64% Cottage
3 Clifton Green
☎ (01904) 643711, fax: (01904) 611230
19 bedrooms
Credit cards 1 2 3 5

★★ 64% Holgate Bridge
106-108 Holgate Rd
☎ (01904) 635971, fax: (01904) 670049
14 bedrooms; double B&B from £38
Credit cards 1 2 3

★★ 65% Clifton Bridge
Water End, Clifton
☎ (01904) 610510, fax: (01904) 640208
14 bedrooms; double B&B £50–£68
Credit cards 1 2 3 5

★★ 63% Elliotts
Sycamore Place, Bootham
☎ (01904) 623333
fax: (01904) 654908
18 bedrooms
Credit cards 1 3

★★ 63% Savages
15 St Peters Grove
☎ (01904) 610818
fax: (01904) 627729
20 bedrooms; double B&B £50–£68
Credit cards 1 2 3 5

★★ 64% Alhambra Court
31 St Mary's, Bootham
☎ (01904) 628474
fax: (01904) 610690
24 bedrooms
Credit cards 1 3

★★ 69% Ashcroft
294 Bishopthorpe Rd
☎ (01904) 659286
fax: (01904) 640107
15 bedrooms; double B&B £60–£85
Credit cards 1 2 3 5

★★ ❀ 68% Knavesmire Manor
302 Tadcaster Rd
☎ (01904) 702941
fax: (01904) 709274
21 bedrooms; double B&B £49–£79
Credit cards 1 2 3 5

WHERE TO STAY

★★ 62% Abbot's Mews
6 Marygate Ln, Bootham
☎ (01904) 634866
fax: (01904) 612848
53 bedrooms; double B&B £39-£51
Credit cards 1 2 3 5

★★ 64% Lady Anne Middletons Hotel
Skeldergate
☎ (01904) 632257 & 630456,
fax: (01904) 613043
55 bedrooms; double B&B £100
Credit cards 1 2 3

★★ 63% Newington
147 Mount Vale
☎ (01904) 625173
fax: (01904) 679917
40 bedrooms; double B&B £50-£66
Credit cards 1 2 3

Travelodge
Bilbrough
☎ (01973) 531823
Central Reservations: (01800) 850950
36 bedrooms; double room £34.95-£49.95
(room only)
Credit cards 1 2 3

★★★ ❀ 71% Parsonage Country House
Main St, Escrick
☎ (01904) 728111
fax: (01904) 728151
17 bedrooms; double B&B £105-£125
Credit cards 1 2 3 5

★★ 64% Old Rectory
Sutton upon Derwent
☎ (01904) 608548
6 bedrooms; double B&B £50-£54
Credit cards 1

BED AND BREAKFAST

QQQQQ Arndale Hotel
290 Tadcaster Rd
☎ (01904) 702424
Beautifully furnished Victorian residence
with delightful character.
10 bedrooms; double B&B £49-£70

QQQQ Grasmead House Hotel
1 Scarcroft Hill, The Mount
☎ (01904) 629996
fax: (01904) 629996
Charming small, family-run hotel furnished
with antiques and run by friendly owners.
6 bedrooms; double B&B £58-£60
Credit cards 1 3

QQQ Alfreda
61 Heslington Ln, Fulford
☎ (01904) 631698
Surrounded by spacious gardens in quiet
location.
10 bedrooms; double B&B £35-£50
Credit cards 1 2 3

QQQQ Ashbourne House
139 Fulford Rd
☎ (01904) 639912
fax: (01904) 631332
In quiet area on the fringe of the city;
friendly service.
6 bedrooms; double B&B £40-£50
Credit cards 1 2 3 5

QQQ Bedford
108/110 Bootham
☎ (01904) 624412
Nicely decorated, neatly maintained
Victorian property.
17 bedrooms; double B&B £46-£56
Credit cards 1 3

QQQ Beech House
6-7 Longfield Terrace, Bootham
☎ (01904) 634581 & 630951
Family-run guesthouse situated in a quiet
street near the town centre.
10 bedrooms; double B&B £42-£50

QQQ Bootham Bar Hotel
4 High Petergate
☎ (01904) 658516
Delightful 18th-century house just inside
one of the fortified gateways to the city.
14 bedrooms; double B&B £40-£58
Credit cards 1 3

QQQ Cavalier Private Hotel
39 Monkgate
☎ (01904) 636615
fax: (01904) 636615
Early Georgian listed building close to the
town centre.
10 bedrooms; double B&B £44-£52
Credit cards 1 2 3

QQQQ Curzon Lodge and Stable Cottages
23 Tadcaster Rd, Dringhouses
☎ (01904) 703157
Attractive whitewashed listed building close
to the racecourse.
10 bedrooms; double B&B £45-£65
Credit cards 1 3

WHERE TO STAY

QQQ Field House Hotel
2 St George's Place
☎ (01904) 639572
Conveniently situated for both the racecourse and town centre.
17 bedrooms; double B&B £40-£59
Credit cards 1 2 3

QQQ Four Poster Lodge
68-70 Heslington Rd, off Barbican Rd
☎ (01904) 651170
Victorian villa, near city-centre, with attractive bedrooms.
12 bedrooms; double B&B £40-£54
Credit cards 1 2 3

QQQQ Midway House Hotel
145 Fulford Rd
☎ (01904) 659272
fax: (01904) 659272
Tastefully modernised detached Victorian house, with well appointed, comfortable accommodation.
12 bedrooms; double B&B £36-£55
Credit cards 1 2 3 5

QQQ Orchard Court Hotel
4 St Peters Grove
☎ (01904) 653964
fax: (01904) 653964
Close to city centre; bedrooms are well appointed.
14 bedrooms; double B&B £50-£65
Credit cards 1 3

QQQQ St Denys Hotel
St Denys Rd
☎ (01904) 622207
fax: (01904) 624800
Former vicarage offering comfortable spacious accommodation.
10 bedrooms; double B&B £40-£50
Credit cards 1 3

Around York

QQQ Ship
Acaster Malbis
☎ (01904) 705609 & 703888
fax: (01904) 705971
Once frequented by Cromwell's soldiers, this is an attractive building and most rooms have views of the river.
8 bedrooms; double B&B £34.50
Credit cards 1 3

QQQ High Catton Grange
High Catton
☎ (01759) 371374
Attractive farmhouse with its own working farm; tastefully decorated bedrooms.
3 bedrooms; double B&B £34

QQQ Ivy House
Kexby
☎ (01904) 489368
Situated on the A1079 York-Hull road, this farmhouse offers neat bedrooms and cosy public rooms, all run by a friendly owner.
3 bedrooms; double B&B £30

QQQQ Derwent Lodge
Low Catton
☎ (01759) 371468
Eight miles south of York; owned and run by a charming family and offering high level of comfort.
5 bedrooms; double B&B £47

QQQ Wellgarth House
Wetherby Rd, Rufforth
☎ (01904) 738592 & 738595
fax: (01904) 738595
A large well appointed modern house on the edge of the village.
7 bedrooms; double B&B £34-£44
Credit cards 1 3

QQ Cuckoo Nest Farm
Wilberfoss
☎ (01759) 380365
Small traditional farmhouse on the A1079; simple, well maintained accommodation.
3 bedrooms; double B&B £36-£44

CAMPSITES

►►►► Rawcliffe Caravan Site
Manor Lane, Shipton Rd
☎ (01904) 624422
Situated on an ex-RAF bomber airfield; pitch price £4.20-£11 per night.

Around York

►►► Chestnut Farm Caravan Park
Acaster Malbis
☎ (01904) 704676
fax: (01904) 704676
South of York; pitch price from £7.50 per night.

►► Moor End Farm
Acaster Malbis
☎ (01904) 706727
fax: (01904) 706727
South of York; pitch price from £7 per night.

►►►► Cawood Holiday Park
Ryther Rd, Cawood
☎ (01757) 268450
fax: (01757) 268537
Half a mile northwest of Cawood on B1233; pitch price from £8.50 per night.

►► Swallow Hall Caravan Park
Crockey Hill
☎ (01904) 448219
fax: (01904) 448219
Near the A19 south of York; pitch price from £7.50 per night.

WHERE TO STAY

►►► Weir Caravan Park
Stamford Bridge
☎ (01759) 371377
Off A166; pitch price £7.75-£9.75 per night.

►►►► Goosewood Caravan Park
Sutton-on-the-Forest
☎ (01347) 810829
North of York; pitch price £7.50-£9 per night.

►►► Camping & Caravanning Club Site
Bracken Hill, Sheriff Hutton
☎ (01347) 878660 & (01203) 694995
fax :(01203) 694886
Within easy reach of York; pitch price £8.70-£11.30 per night.

WHERE TO EAT

RESTAURANTS

✸✸ 19 Grape Lane
19 Grape Ln
☎ (01904) 636366
Atmospheric little restaurant with sound modern English cooking.
Lunch: 12-1.45
Dinner: 7-10
Credit cards 1 3

✸✸ Melton's
7 Scarcroft Rd
☎ (01904) 634341, fax: (01904) 629233
Careful, accurate cooking at reasonable prices in a simple, stylish restaurant.
Lunch: 12-2
Dinner: 7-10
Credit cards 1 3

✸✸✸ Middlethorpe Hall
Bishopthorpe Rd
☎ (01904) 641241
Delightful, well-presented dishes from a talented chef.
Lunch: 12.30-1.45
Dinner: 7.30-9.45

✸ Ambassador
125 The Mount
☎ (01904) 641316
An interesting menu in a former merchant's residence.
Dinner: 7.30-10

✸ Grange
Clifton
☎ (01904) 644744
A formal restaurant serving modern British cooking.
Lunch: 12-2
Dinner: 7-10
Credit cards 1 3

✸ Mount Royale
The Mount
☎ (01904) 628856
A fixed price dinner menu augmented by daily specialities.
Dinner: 7-9.30

✸ York Pavilion
45 Main St, Fulford
☎ (01904) 622099
Modern English cuisine with some French influence.
Lunch: 12-2
Dinner: 6.30-9.30

PUBS

Around York

Abbey Inn
Coxwold
☎ (013476) 204
An attractive old Yorkshire stone pub near to Byland Abbey, offering very tasty, good value meals. Draught beers include EP Traditional, Theakstons and Guinness and there is a good wine list. Children are welcome in the pub and there is a large garden.
Open: 10am-2.30pm, 6.30-11pm, but closed Sunday evening and all day Monday.
Bar food: as opening times

Fauconberg Arms
Coxwold
☎ (013476) 214
Pretty Yorkshire stone pub in the centre of the village, with a relaxed and friendly atmosphere. The fresh, home-made food is above average and includes some interesting choices. Draught beers include John Smiths, Theakstons, Tetley and Guinness and there is a large wine list. Children are welcome.
Open:11am-3pm, 6.30-11pm; Sunday 12-3pm, 7-10.30pm
Bar food: 12-2pm, 7-9.45pm

The Curragh

The Curragh is the premier Flat course in Ireland. It is situated in the beautiful rolling countryside of County Kildare and the facilities are some of the best to be found anywhere in the country.

This venue is regarded as the home of Irish Flat racing and it plays host to all five Irish Classics.

The 2000 and 1000 Guineas are held on the last Saturday and Sunday in May and then the highlight of the Turf calendar comes on the last Sunday in June, in the shape of the Budweiser Irish Derby. This is an immensely valuable contest, both in terms of prestige and prize money, and it often attracts both the Epsom and French Derby winners. A huge attendance is guaranteed, as is the case two weeks later at the Kildangan Stud Irish Oaks. Mid-September sees the final Classic, the Jefferson Smurfit Irish St Leger, the feature event of an outstanding weekend card which also includes the National Stakes, an important Group One contest for two-year-olds.

FURTHER INFORMATION

The Curragh Racecourse
Co Kildare, Republic of Ireland
☎ (045) 441205; fax:(045) 441442

LOCATION AND HOW TO GET THERE

The course is about 27 miles southwest of Dublin on the N7, one mile past Newbridge (Droichead Nua).
Nearest Railway Station: Curragh; special train services run to most meetings from the principal stations in the south and west as well as from Dublin. For full details contact Iarnrod Eireann (01) 8 366222.

Bus Eireann run a special Race Bus from Dublin's Central Bus Station (Busarus) on racedays. For full details contact Bus Eireann (01) 8 366111.

ADMISSION

There is no reserved enclosure at the Curragh, except during the Budweiser Irish Derby Meeting in June, and apart from this meeting, all facilities – bars, restaurant, self-service restaurant etc – are available to all racegoers. Boxes, reserved seats on the upper levels of the Stands and private suites are let on a yearly basis – contact The Manager for details.

Day tickets:
Regular Meetings: Saturdays IR£7,
Sundays IR£8
Classic and Group 1 Meetings: IR£10
Irish Derby Meeting: West End Enclosure
IR£12, children under 14 IR£4; Reserved
enclosure IR£30, children under 14 IR£8
Accompanied children under 14 are admitted
free to all meetings except the Irish Derby ;
there is a 50% reduction for senior citizens
and students showing evidence of age

transfers: available from West End to Reserved Enclosure on Derby Day on payment of the appropriate difference in admission charges, as long as it is not sold out in advance.

Annual Membership: IR£110, senior citizens and students IR£55; combined membership for Punchestown, Naas and the Curragh, £IR195 – includes free parking, access to the Members, Owners and Trainers Bar and a reserved portion of the Stand at the West End.

COURSE FACILITIES

Banks:
The Bank of Ireland is available at some, but not all meetings. As dates and times vary, it is advisable to check with the racecourse in advance. There are no cashpoint facilities on the course.

For families:
A creche is provided at the west end of the Stand and there is an outdoor children's playground in the same area, both under qualified supervision. Neither facility is available on Irish Derby Day. There are also baby-changing facilities and a lost children centre.

CALENDAR OF EVENTS

1998 Calendar not known at time of press. Please contact racecourse or the Irish Horseracing Authority for details of fixtures.

WHERE TO STAY

HOTELS

Around The Curragh

★★★ **56% Downshire House**
Blessington
☎ (045) 865199
fax: (045) 865335
25 bedrooms; double B&B IR£75
Credit cards 1 3

The following hotels are within about 20 miles or so:

★★ **61% Doyle Green Isle**
Naas Road, Clondalkin (northeast of The Curragh on the outskirts of Dublin)
☎ (01) 4593406,
fax: (01) 4592178
90 bedrooms
Credit cards 1 2 3 5

★★★ **66% Finnstown Country House Hotel & Golf Course**
Newcastle Rd, Lucan (northeast of The Curragh)
☎ (01) 6280644
fax: (01) 6281088
45 bedrooms; double B&B IR£80-IR£140
Credit cards 1 2 3 5

★★★ **56% Lucan Spa**
Lucan (northeast of The Curragh)
☎ (01) 6280494
fax: (01) 6280841
59 bedrooms; double B&B £70-£75
Credit cards 1 2 3 5

Dublin Hotels
Dublin is about 27 miles from The Curragh. The following hotels are in the central or southern part of the city with easy access to the N7.

★★★★ ✿✿ **72% Conrad**
Earlsfort Terrace
☎ (01) 6765555
fax: (01) 6765424
191 bedrooms; double room IR£200-IR£210 (room only)
Credit cards 1 2 3 5

★★★★ ✿ **70% Jurys**
Ballsbridge
☎ (01) 6 605000, telex: 93723,
fax: (01) 6 605540
294 bedrooms; double room IR£202.50 (room only)
Credit cards 1 2 3 5

★★★★ **68% Burlington**
Leeson St
☎ (01) 6 605222
fax: (01) 6 608496
526 bedrooms; double room IR£149
Credit cards 1 2 3 5

★★★✿✿ **63% Stephen's Hall**
14-17 Lower Leeson St
☎ (01) 6 610585
fax: (01) 6 610606
37 bedrooms; double room IR£150 (room only)
Credit cards 1 2 3 5

★★★ **68% Doyle Montrose**
Stillorgan Rd
☎ (01) 2693311
fax: (01) 2691164
179 bedrooms; double room IR£95-IR£103
Credit cards 1 2 3 5

★★★ **64% Doyle Tara Tower**
Merrion Rd
☎ (01) 2694666
fax: (01) 2691027
113 bedrooms; double room IR£79-IR£95
Credit cards 1 2 3 5

★★★ ✿✿ **65% Longfield's**
Fitzwilliam St
☎ (01) 6 761367
fax: (01) 6 761542
26 bedrooms
Credit cards 1 2 3 5

WHERE TO STAY

BED AND BREAKFAST

Around The Curragh

QQ Setanta Farm
Castlekeely, Carragh, nr Naas
☎ (045) 876481
Modern farm bungalow in peaceful area,
about six miles north of The Curragh.
5 bedrooms; double B&B IR£34

QQQQ Kingswood Country House,
Old Kingswood, Naas Rd, Clondalkin
☎ (01) 4 592428 & 4 592207
fax: (01) 4 592428
On the southwestern outskirts of the city on
the N7.
7 bedrooms; double B&B IR£55–IR£70
Credit cards 1 3

Dublin Bed and Breakfast
(See note under Dublin Hotels)

QQQQQ Aberdeen Lodge
53-55 Park Av
☎ (01) 2838155, fax: (01) 2837877
Edwardian house, tastefully refurbished to
the highest standards with excellent
bedrooms.
16 bedrooms
Credit cards 1 2 3 5

QQQQQ Ariel House
52 Lansdowne Rd
☎ (01) 6 685512, fax: (01) 6 685845
Luxurious Victorian mansion with antique-
furnished rooms and charming proprietors.
28 bedrooms; double room IR£78–IR£168
Credit cards 1 2 3

QQQ Beddington
181 Rathgar Rd
☎ (01) 4 978047, fax: (01) 4 78275
14 bedrooms; double B&B IR£55–IR£60
Credit cards 1 2 3

QQQ The Fitzwilliam
41 Upper Fitzwilliam St
☎ (01) 6 600199
fax: (01) 6 767488
Newly renovated to a very high standard,
this house is in the heart of Georgian
Dublin.
12 bedrooms; double B&B IR£50–IR£75
Credit cards 1 2 3 5

QQQQQ The Grey Door
22-23 Upper Pembroke St
☎ (01) 6 763286
fax: (01) 6 76387
Elegant, tastefully restored Georgian house
in the heart of the City – the AA's Best
Newcomer for the Republic of Ireland for
1992-3 – with a choice of two restaurants.
7 bedrooms; double room IR£95
Credit cards 1 2 3 5

QQQ Marelle
92 Rathfarnham Rd, Terenure
☎ (01) 4 904590
Attractive house, recently refurbished, set
back from the N81 road, south of the city.
6 bedrooms; double B&B from IR£52–IR£60
Credit cards 1 3

QQQQ Morehampton Lodge
113 Morehampton Rd, Donnybrook
☎ (01) 2837499, fax: (01) 2837595
Beautifully restored to a high standard, this
Victorian house to the south of the city
centre, has excellent bedrooms and
particularly charming proprietors. Breakfasts
are highly recommended.
12 bedrooms; double B&B IR£55–IR£70
Credit cards 1 3

QQQ St Aiden's
32 Brighton Rd, Rathgar
☎ (01) 4 902011 & 4 906178,
fax: (01) 4 92034
10 bedrooms; double B&B IR£40–IR£77
Credit cards 1 3

CAMPSITES

Around The Curragh

►►► Shankill Caravan Park
Sherrington Park, Shankill
☎ (01) 2820011
On the east coast, just south of Dublin;
about 30 miles drive from The Curragh.

Down Royal

This is one of only two racecourses in Northern Ireland, the other being Downpatrick, and visitors from the mainland can be assured of a tremendously warm welcome from the knowledgeable locals - all of whom will be only too willing to pass on a few hot tips.

In past years, the facilities could best be described as rudimentary, but the course has been greatly modernised, with the construction of a new covered grandstand with boxes, a restaurant and several fast-food outlets.

The Down Royal Corporation was originally launched by James II in 1685 and racing has been held at this venue for over 200 years. Eleven meetings now take place here annually under both codes, the cards often including a mixture of both Flat and National Hunt contests. The standard of competition is high and the bookmakers are fair and offer a wide variety of interesting bets. The highlight of the year is the Ulster Harp Derby meeting. This attracts runners from all over Ireland and the UK, and there is a real carnival atmosphere.

FURTHER INFORMATION

Down Royal Corporation of Horse Breeders
Maze, Lisburn, Co Antrim BT7 5BW
Northern Ireland
☎ (01846) 621256; fax:(01846) 621433

LOCATION AND HOW TO GET THERE

The course is at Maze, near Lisburn, about 12 miles southwest of the centre of Belfast on the A1 then the A3. It is signposted from the Sprucefield Roundabout in Lisburn.
Nearest Railway Station: Lisburn; there is no connecting bus service to the course.

ADMISSION

There are no separate enclosures at Down Royal; all racegoers have access to all the facilities.

Day tickets: £6, and £10 on Derby Day.
– access to bar, restaurant, boxes, private rooms

Annual Membership: £60

COURSE FACILITIES

Banks:
there are no banks or cashpoint facilities on the course.

For families:
picnic area

CALENDAR OF EVENTS

1998 Calendar not available at time of press. Please contact racecourse or Irish Horseracing Authority for details of fixtures.

WHERE TO STAY

HOTELS

Around Down Royal

★★★★ 64% Stormont
587 Upper Newtonards Rd, Belfast
☎ (01232) 658621
fax: (01232) 480240
109 bedrooms; double room £125
Credit cards 1 2 3 5

★★★ 62% Plaza
15 Brunswick St, Belfast
☎ (01232) 333555
fax: (01232) 232999
76 bedrooms; double room £89
Credit cards 1 2 3 5

★★ 61% Renshaws
75 University St, Belfast
☎ (01232) 333366
fax: (01232) 333399
20 bedrooms; double B&B £39–£69.50
Credit cards 1 2 3 5

BED AND BREAKFAST

Around Down Royal

QQQQ Brook Lodge
Old Ballynahinch Rd, Cargacroy, Lisburn
☎ (01846) 638454
A high standard of accommodation and
good home-cooked food are offered at this
modern farmhouse just off the A49.
6 bedrooms; double room £36

QQQ Malone
79 Malone Rd, Belfast
☎ (01232) 669565
Spacious, comfortable accommodation in
detached Victorian villa to the south of the
city centre, close to the University.
8 bedrooms; double B&B £40–£48

QQ Camera
44 Wellington Park, Belfast
☎ (01232) 660026 & 667856
In a quiet residential road between the
Lisburn and Malone roads, close to the
University. Simple accommodation with a
relaxed, friendly atmosphere.
9 bedrooms; double B&B £25–£30
Credit cards 1 2 3

WHERE TO EAT

RESTAURANT

Around Down Royal

⊛⊛⊛ Roscoff
2 Lesley House, Shaftesbury Sq, Belfast
☎ (01232) 331532
Vibrant, friendly and relaxing restaurant
providing high standards of French food in
smart surroundings. Good quality local
produce, including fresh fish, meat, game
and organic vegetables, are used and an
excellent value lunch menu is available.
Last lunch: 2.15pm
Last dinner: 10.30pm

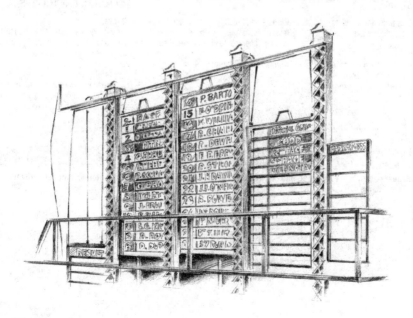

Fairyhouse

This glorious country venue became the first official steeplechase course in Ireland when it was inaugurated in 1851. In keeping with its proud tradition, the quality of the jumping events is still high, although racing here is mixed now, with fixtures being staged throughout the year.

One of the major high spots of the Irish equestrian calendar is the three-day Easter Festival meeting. This begins on Easter Monday with the Jameson Irish Grand National, a handicap chase which carries nearly IR£100,000 in prize money and attracts plenty of British competitors - Desert Orchid was a past winner of this race.

There are many other valuable contests spread over the three days and this is a marvellous place to take a break over the Easter period. The hospitality of the Irish is legendary and newcomers to the sport will be welcomed with open arms - after all, racing is part of the national heritage. The facilities at the course are excellent and the almost square-shaped track has stiff fences, which certainly catch out any dodgy jumpers.

FURTHER INFORMATION

Fairyhouse Racecourse
Ratoath, Co Meath, Republic of Ireland
☎ (01) 8 256167; fax:(01) 8256051

LOCATION AND HOW TO GET THERE

The course is about 12 miles northwest of the centre of Dublin, between the N2 and the N3. It is clearly signposted on each side of Ashbourne on the N2, and between Clonee and Dunshaughlin on the N3.

Nearest Railway Station: Dublin; there is a direct bus service from Dublin to the racecourse. For full details contact Bus Eireann (01) 8 366111.

ADMISSION

All classes of day ticket give access to full betting facilities, including Tote.

Day tickets:
RESERVED IR£7-IR£10 – access to bars, restaurants, members' room, boxes, private rooms, indoor Tote facilities, bookmakers.

GENERAL IR£5-IR£7 – access to bars, restaurants, parade ring, Owners & Trainers' bar and stand, Tote facilities, bookmakers.

Annual membership: IR£90

COURSE FACILITIES

Banks:
there is a mobile office of the Allied Irish Bank on the course, open throughout racing, as well as cashpoint facilities.

For families:
picnicking is allowed outside the enclosures; there is a children's play area, baby changing facilities and a lost children centre.

CALENDAR OF EVENTS

1998 Calendar of events not known at time of press. Please contact racecourse or the Irish Horseracing Authority for details of fixtures.

WHERE TO STAY

HOTELS

Around Fairyhouse

★★★★ 🏵🏵 72% Conrad
Earlsfort Terrace, Dublin
☎ (01) 6 765555,
fax: (01) 6 765424
191 bedrooms; double room from IR£200
(room only)
Credit cards 1 2 3 5

★★★★ 🏵 70% Jurys
Ballsbridge, Dublin
☎ (01) 6 605000
fax: (01) 6 605540
294 bedrooms; double room IR£202.50
 (room only)
Credit cards 1 2 3 5

★★★★ 68% Burlington
Leeson St, Dublin
☎ (01) 6 605222,
fax: (01) 6 608496
526 bedrooms; double room IR£149
Credit cards 1 2 3 5

★★★ 🏵🏵 63% Stephen's Hall
14-17 Lower Leeson St, Dublin
☎ (01) 6 610585
fax: (01) 6 610606
37 bedrooms; double room IR£150
(room only)
Credit cards 1 2 3 5

★★★ 🏵🏵 69% Marine
Sutton, Dublin
☎ (01) 8 390000
fax: (01) 8 390442
26 bedrooms; double B&B IR£80-IR£120
Credit cards 1 2 3 5

★★★ 67% Doyle Skylon
Drumcondra Rd, Dublin
☎ (01) 8 379121
fax: (01) 8 372778
92 bedrooms
Credit cards 1 2 3 4 5

★★★ 68% Doyle Montrose
Stillorgan Rd, Dublin
☎ (01) 2693311
fax: (01) 2691164
179 bedrooms; double room IR£95-IR£103
Credit cards 1 2 3 5

★★★ 64% Doyle Tara Tower
Merrion Rd, Dublin
☎ (01) 2694666
fax: (01) 2691027
113 bedrooms; double room IR£79-IR£95
Credit cards 1 2 3 4 5

★★★ 🏵🏵 65% Longfield's
Fitzwilliam St, Dublin
☎ (01) 6 761367
fax: (01) 6 761542
26 bedrooms

**★★★ 66% Finnstown Country House
Hotel & Golf Course**
Newcastle Rd, Lucan
☎ (01) 6280644
fax: (01) 6281088
45 bedrooms; double B&B IR£80-IR£140
Credit cards 1 2 3 5

★★★ 56% Lucan Spa
Lucan
☎ (01) 6280494
fax: (01) 6280841
59 bedrooms; double B&B IR£70-IR£75
Credit cards 1 2 3 5

BED AND BREAKFAST

Around Fairyhouse

QQQQQ Aberdeen Lodge
53-55 Park Av, Dublin
☎ (01) 2838155
fax: (01) 2837877
Edwardian house, tastefully refurbished to
the highest standards with excellent
bedrooms.
16 bedrooms
Credit cards 1 2 3 5

QQQQQ Ariel House
52 Lansdowne Rd, Dublin
☎ (01) 6 685512
ax: (01) 6 685845
Luxurious Victorian mansion with antique-
furnished rooms and charming proprietors.
28 bedrooms; double room IR£78-IR£168
Credit cards 1 2 3

QQQQ Charleville Guest Inn
268-272 North Circular Rd, Dublin
☎ (01) 8 386633
fax: (01) 8 385854
In an elegant terrace of renovated Victorian
houses close to the city centre.
20 bedrooms; double B&B IR£55-IR£90
Credit cards 1 2 3

QQQ Egan's
7-9 Iona Park, Glasnevin, Dublin
☎ (01) 8 303611 & 303818,
fax: (01) 8 303312
Comfortable Victorian house in a quiet
suburb in the northern part of the city;
renowned for its friendly and cheerful
atmosphere.
25 bedrooms; double room IR£42-IR£50
Credit cards 1 3

WHERE TO STAY

QQQ The Fitzwilliam
41 Upper Fitzwilliam St, Dublin
☎ (01) 6 600199, fax: (01) 6 767488
Newly renovated to a very high standard,
this house is in the heart of Georgian
Dublin.
12 bedrooms;
Credit cards 1 2 3 5

QQQQQ The Grey Door
22-23 Upper Pembroke St, Dublin
☎ (01) 6 763286, fax: (01) 6 76387
Elegant, tastefully restored Georgian house
in the heart of the City – the AA's Best
Newcomer for the Republic of Ireland for
1992-3 – with a choice of two restaurants.
7 bedrooms; double room IR£95
Credit cards 1 2 3 5

QQQ Iona House
5 Iona Park, Dublin
☎ (01) 8 306217 & 306855,
fax: (01) 8 306732
Family-run Victorian house in quiet
residential area to the north of the city; large
modern bedrooms, comfortable lounge and
small garden.
12 bedrooms; double B&B IR£62
Credit cards 1 3

QQQ Marelle
92 Rathfarnham Rd, Terenure
☎ (01) 4 904590
Attractive house, recently refurbished, set
back from the N81 road, south of the city.
6 bedrooms; double B&B from IR£52-IR£60
Credit cards 1 3

QQQQ Morehampton Lodge
113 Morehampton Rd, Donnybrook
☎ (01) 2837499
fax: (01) 2837595
Beautifully restored to a high standard, this
Victorian house to the south of the city
centre, has excellent bedrooms and
particularly charming proprietors.
Breakfasts are highly recommended.
12 bedrooms: double B&B IR£70-IR£120
Credit cards 1 3

Leopardstown

There are a total of 26 racecourses in Ireland, of which Leopardstown is the most likely to top any popularity poll. This picturesque track has many virtues, including its superb location just five miles from the centre of Dublin.

Admission charges are low and the facilities outstanding. There are three main restaurants all offering a good standard of catering and an even wider choice of bars. The stands provide excellent viewing of the action.

Another great advantage of this galloping, left-handed track is that the turf drains very well, so that meetings rarely have to be abandoned because of waterlogging (a common problem in Ireland). This is particularly beneficial during the early months of the year, when some high class National Hunt contests are staged here. The second Saturday in January sees the Ladbroke, a fiercely contested handicap hurdle which always produces a close finish. Towards the end of the month comes the AIG Europe Champion Hurdle and then early February witnesses the valuable and prestigious Hennessy Cognac Gold Cup Chase. These last two events take place on Sundays and are acknowledged as extremely important trials for the Cheltenham Festival. A consistently high level of competition is also maintained on the

Flat. The highlights are the Heinz 57 Phoenix Stakes in early August and the Guinness Champion Stakes in early September, both Group One events that draw runners from all over Europe.

FURTHER INFORMATION

Leopardstown Racecourse
Stillorgan, Dublin, Republic of Ireland
☎ (01) 2893607

LOCATION AND HOW TO GET THERE

The course is six miles south of Dublin City centre at Stillorgan. Take the N11 Wexford road and follow signs.
Nearest Railway Station: Blackrock (DART services); there is a connecting bus service to the course on racedays, except Sundays. There is also a direct bus service from Dublin's Central Bus Station (Busarus). For full details contact Bus Eireann (01) 8 302222.

ADMISSION

All classes of day ticket give access to full betting facilities, including Tote.

Day tickets:
BOX LEVEL IR£20-£25 – access to bars, boxes, private rooms

RESERVED IR£8-IR£13 – access to bars, restaurant and snack bar

GRANDSTAND IR£6-IR£10 – access to bars and snack bar

Annual Membership: IR£110

COURSE FACILITIES

For families:
Children's play area; creche.

CALENDAR OF EVENTS

1998 Calendar not known at time of press. Please contact racecourse or Irish Horseracing Authority for details of fixtures.

WHERE TO STAY

HOTELS

★★★ 60% Royal
Main St, Bray
☎ (01) 2862935
fax: (01) 2867373
91 bedrooms; double B&B IR£90-IR£150
Credit cards 1 2 3 5

★★★ 64% Fitzpatrick Castle
Killiney
☎ (01) 2840700
fax: (01) 2850207
112 bedrooms; double room IR£96-IR£130
Credit cards 1 2 3 5

★★★ 63% Court
Killiney
☎ (01) 2851622
fax: (01) 2852085
86 bedrooms; double room IR£96-IR£107
Credit cards 1 2 3 5

Around Leopardstown

★★★★ ❀❀ 72% Conrad
Earlsfort Terrace, Dublin
☎ (01) 6 765555
fax: (01) 6 765424
191 bedrooms; double room from IR£200-
IR£210 (room only)
Credit cards 1 2 3 5

★★★★ ❀ 70% Jurys
Ballsbridge, Dublin
☎ (01) 6 605000,
fax: (01) 6 605540
294 bedrooms; double room IR£202.50
(room only)
Credit cards 1 2 3 5

★★★★ 68% Burlington
Leeson St, Dublin
☎ (01) 6 605222
fax: (01) 6 608496
526 bedrooms; double room IR£149
Credit cards 1 2 3 5

★★★❀❀ 63% Stephen's Hall
14-17 Lower Leeson St, Dublin
☎ (01) 6 610585
fax: (01) 6 610606
37 bedrooms; double room IR£150 (room
only)
Credit cards 1 2 3 5

★★★ 68% Doyle Montrose
Stillorgan Rd, Dublin
☎ (01) 2693311
fax: (01) 2691164
179 bedrooms; double room IR£95-IR£103
Credit cards 1 2 3 5

★★★ 64% Doyle Tara Tower
Merrion Rd, Dublin
☎ (01) 2694666
fax: (01) 2691027
113 bedrooms; double room IR£79-IR£95
Credit cards 1 2 3 4 5

★★★ 61% Doyle Green Isle
Clondalkin, Dublin
☎ (01) 4 593406,
fax: (01) 4 592178
83 bedrooms
Credit cards 1 2 3 5

★★★ ❀❀ 65% Longfield's
Fitzwilliam St, Dublin
☎ (01) 6 761367
fax: (01) 6 761542
26 bedrooms

★★ 71% Pierre
Victoria Terrace, Seafront, Dun Laoghaire
☎ (01) 2800291
ax: (01) 2843332
32 bedrooms; double B&B IR£58-IR£65
Credit cards 1 2 3

BED AND BREAKFAST

Around Leopardstown

QQQQQ Aberdeen Lodge
53-55 Park Av Dublin
☎ (01) 2838155
fax: (01) 2837877
Edwardian house, tastefully refurbished to
the highest standards with excellent
bedrooms.
16 bedrooms
Credit cards 1 2 3 5

QQQQQ Ariel House
52 Lansdowne Rd, Dublin
☎ (01) 6 685512
fax: (01) 6 685845
Luxurious Victorian mansion with antique-
furnished rooms and charming proprietors.
28 bedrooms; double room IR£78-IR£168
Credit cards 1 2 3

QQQ Beddington
181 Rathgar Rd, Dublin
☎ (01) 4 978047
fax: (01) 4 978275
14 bedrooms; double B&B IR£55-IR£60
Credit cards 1 2 3

QQQ The Fitzwilliam
41 Upper Fitzwilliam St, Dublin
☎ (01) 6 600199
fax: (01) 6 767488
Newly renovated to a very high standard,
this house is in the heart of Georgian
Dublin.
12 bedrooms; double B &B £50-£75
Credit cards 1 2 3 5

WHERE TO STAY

QQQQQ The Grey Door
22-23 Upper Pembroke St, Dublin
☎ (01) 6 763286
fax: (01) 6 76387
Elegant, tastefully restored Georgian house in the heart of the City – the AA's Best Newcomer for the Republic of Ireland for 1992-3 – with a choice of two restaurants.
7 bedrooms; double room IR£95
Credit cards 1 2 3 5

QQQQ Kingswood Country House,
Old Kingswood, Naas Rd, Clondalkin, Dublin
☎ (01) 4 592428 & 4 592207
fax: (01) 4 592428
On the southwestern outskirts of the city on the N7.
7 bedrooms; double B&B IR£55-IR£70
Credit cards 1 2 3 5

QQQ Marelle
92 Rathfarnham Rd, Terenure, Dublin
☎ (01) 4 904590
Attractive house, recently refurbished, set back from the N81 road, south of the city.
6 bedrooms; double B&B from IR£52
Credit cards 1 3

QQQQ Morehampton Lodge
113 Morehampton Rd, Donnybrook, Dublin
☎ (01) 2837499, fax: (01) 2837595
Beautifully restored to a high standard, this Victorian house to the south of the city centre, has excellent bedrooms and particularly charming proprietors.
Breakfasts are highly recommended.
12 bedrooms: double B&B IR£70-IR£120
Credit cards 1 3

QQQ St Aiden's
32 Brighton Rd, Rathgar, Dublin
☎ (01) 4 902011 & 4 906178,
fax: (01) 4 92034
10 bedrooms; double B&B IR£40-IR£77
Credit cards 1 3

QQ Ferry
15 Clarinda Park North, Dun Laoghaire
☎ (01) 2808301
fax: (01) 2846530
Large Victorian house overlooking People's Park.
6 bedrooms; double B&B IR£37-IR£42
Credit cards 1 3

CAMPSITES

Around Leopardstown

►►► Shankill Caravan Park
Sherrington Park, Shankill
☎ (01) 2820011
On the east coast, just south of Dublin

►►►► Roundwood Caravan Park
Roundwood
☎ (01) 2818163
fax: (01) 2818163
About 17 miles south, on the R755 between Enniskerry and Laragh, in the Wicklow Mountains; pitch price IR£7-IR£9 per night.

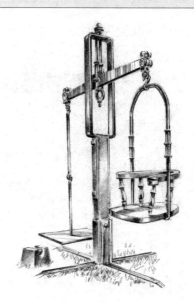

Punchestown

The Emerald Isle is renowned for its lush verdancy and there is certainly plenty in evidence at this jewel of a racecourse. With the scenic Wicklow Mountains in the background and the sweeping countryside of County Kildare in the foreground, this is an idyllic site at which to enjoy the spectacle of some of Ireland's finest thoroughbreds in action.

One of the biggest meetings of the entire year is held at this course towards the end of April. This three-day mid-week National Hunt Festival is growing in importance every season, with the levels of sponsorship and prize money increasing all the time. A great number of British horses travel across to participate and the standard of competition now rivals that at the Cheltenham and Aintree Festivals. A wide variety of contests are run over the undulating track, which provides a stiff test of stamina. Among the most interesting is a novel four-mile 'bank race', where runners have to negotiate a series of natural obstacles, including walls, ditches and Irish banks.

FURTHER INFORMATION

Punchestown Racecourse
Naas, Co Kildare, Republic of Ireland
☎ (045) 897704; Fax:(045) 897319

LOCATION AND HOW TO GET THERE

The course is twenty miles south of Dublin on the N7, two miles outside Naas.
Nearest Railway Station: Sallins, 5 miles.

ADMISSION

All classes of day ticket give access to full betting facilities, including Tote.

3 Day tickets
Admission & Reserved Enclosure £48,
(Admission only £30)

Daily tickets
Admission & Reserved Enclosure £18,
(Admission only £12)
Reserved Car Park: £5 daily,
Reserved Enclosure £8 daily

COURSE FACILITIES

Banks:
A mobile facility and cashpoint is available during the Festival Meeting and at weekends open throughout racing

For families:
Picnicking is possible, though there is no formal area; there is a childrens play area and a lost children centre.

CALENDAR OF EVENTS

January 8
January 24
February 22
April 28-30 – Festival Meeting
October 1
October 22
November 1
November 14
December 6
December 31

WHERE TO STAY

HOTELS

Around Punchestown

★★★ 56% Downshire House
Blessington
☎ (045) 865199, fax: (045) 865335
25 bedrooms; double B&B IR£75
Credit cards 1 3

The following hotels are within about 20 miles:

★★★ 61% Doyle Green Isle
Clondalkin (about 18 miles northeast on the outskirts of Dublin)
☎ (01) 4 593406
fax: (01) 4 592178
90 bedrooms
Credit cards 1 2 3 5

★★★ 66% Finnstown Country House Hotel & Golf Course
Newcastle Rd, Lucan (about 15 miles northeast)
☎ (01) 6280644, fax: (01) 6281088
25 bedrooms; double B&B IR£80–IR£140
Credit cards 1 2 3 5

★★★ 56% Lucan Spa
Lucan (about 15 miles northeast)
☎ (01) 6280494, fax: (01) 6280841
59 bedrooms; double B&B IR£70–IR£75
Credit cards 1 2 3 5

Dublin Hotels
Dublin is about 20 miles from Punchestown. The following hotels are in the central or southern part of the city with easy access to the N7.

★★★★ 🌸🌸 72% Conrad
Earlsfort Terrace
☎ (01) 6 765555
fax: (01) 6 765424
191 bedrooms; double room from IR£200 (room only)
Credit cards 1 2 3 5

★★★★ 🌸 70% Jurys
Ballsbridge
☎ (01) 6 605000
fax: (01) 6 605540
294 bedrooms; double room IR£202.50 (room only)
Credit cards 1 2 3 5

★★★★ 68% Burlington
Leeson St
☎ (01) 6 605222
fax: (01) 6 608496
526 bedrooms; double room IR£149
Credit cards 1 2 3 5

★★★🌸🌸 63% Stephen's Hall
14-17 Lower Leeson St
☎ (01) 6 610585, fax: (01) 6 610606
37 bedrooms; double room IR£150 (room only)
Credit cards 1 2 3 5

★★★ 68% Doyle Montrose
Stillorgan Rd
☎ (01) 2693311
fax: (01) 2691164
179 bedrooms; double room IR£95–IR£103
Credit cards 1 2 3 5

★★★ 64% Doyle Tara Tower
Merrion Rd
☎ (01) 2694666
fax: (01) 2691027
113 bedrooms; double room IR£79–IR£95
Credit cards 1 2 3 5

★★★ 🌸🌸 65% Longfield's
Fitzwilliam St
☎ (01) 6 761367, fax: (01) 6 761542
26 bedrooms
Credit cards 1 2 3 5

BED AND BREAKFAST

Around Punchestown

QQ Setanta Farm
Castlekeely, Carragh, nr Naas
☎ (045) 876481
Modern farm bungalow in peaceful area close to the racecourse.
5 bedrooms; double B&B IR£34

QQ Westown Farm
Johnstown
☎ (045) 97006
Modern house half a mile off the N7 north of Naas.
5 bedrooms; double B&B IR£30–IR£32

Dublin Bed and Breakfast
(See note under Dublin Hotels)

QQQQQ Aberdeen Lodge
53-55 Park Av
☎ (01) 2838155, fax: (01) 2837877
Edwardian house, tastefully refurbished to the highest standards with excellent bedrooms.
16 bedrooms
Credit cards 1 2 3 5

QQQQQ Ariel House
52 Lansdowne Rd
☎ (01) 6 685512, fax: (01) 6 685845
Luxurious Victorian mansion with antique-furnished rooms and charming proprietors.
28 bedrooms; double B&B IR£78–IR£168
Credit cards 1 2 3

WHERE TO STAY

QQQ Beddington
181 Rathgar Rd
☎ (01) 4 978047, fax: (01) 4 978275
14 bedrooms; double B&B IR£55–IR£60
Credit cards 1 2 3

QQQ The Fitzwilliam
41 Upper Fitzwilliam St
☎ (01) 6 600199, fax: (01) 6 767488
Newly renovated to a very high standard, this house is in the heart of Georgian Dublin.
12 bedrooms;
Credit cards 1 2 3 5

QQQQQ The Grey Door
22-23 Upper Pembroke St
☎ (01) 6 763286, fax: (01) 6 76387
Elegant, tastefully restored Georgian house in the heart of the City, with a choice of two restaurants.
7 bedrooms; double room IR£95
Credit cards 1 2 3 5

QQQQ Kingswood Country House,
Old Kingswood, Naas Rd, Clondalkin
☎ (01) 4 592428 & 4 592207
On the southwestern outskirts of the city on the N7.
7 bedrooms; double B&B IR£55–IR£70
Credit cards 1 2 3 5

QQQ Marelle
92 Rathfarnham Rd, Terenure
☎ (01) 4 904590
Attractive house, recently refurbished, set back from the N81 road, south of the city.
6 bedrooms; double B&B from IR£52
Credit cards 1 3

QQQQ Morehampton Lodge
113 Morehampton Rd, Donnybrook
☎ (01) 2837499, fax: (01) 2837595
Beautifully restored to a high standard, this Victorian house to the south of the city centre, has excellent bedrooms and particularly charming proprietors. Breakfasts are highly recommended.
12 bedrooms: double B&B IR£70–IR£120
Credit cards 1 3

QQQ St Aiden's
32 Brighton Rd, Rathgar
☎ (01) 4 902011 & 4 906178,
fax: (01) 4 92034
10 bedrooms; double B&B IR£40–IR£77
Credit cards 1 3

CAMPSITES

Around Punchestown

►►► Shankill Caravan Park
Sherrington Park, Shankill
☎ (01) 2820011
On the east coast, just south of Dublin.

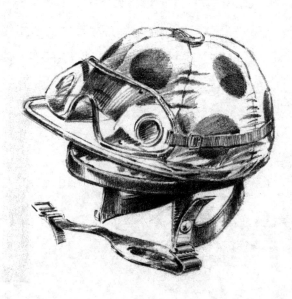

Other Irish Racecourses

Ballinrobe Racecourse
Ballinrobe
Co Mayo
Republic of Ireland
☎ (092) 41083

Bellewstown Racecourse
Bellewstown
Drogheda
Co Louth
Republic of Ireland
☎ (01) 2892888; fax (01) 2892019

Clonmel Racecourse
Powerstown Park
Clonmel
Co Tipperary
Republic of Ireland
☎ (052) 22611; fax: (052) 26446

Cork Racecourse
Mallow
Co Cork
Republic of Ireland
☎ (022) 21592, fax:(022) 42750

Downpatrick Racecourse
Downpatrick
Co Down, BT30 7EY
Northern Ireland
☎ (01396) 612054

Dundalk Racecourse
Dowdaliehill
Dundalk
Co Louth
Republic of Ireland
☎ (042) 34800

Galway Racecourse
Ballybrit
Galway
Co Galway
Republic of Ireland
☎ (091) 753870; fax:(091) 752592

Gowran Park Racecourse
Gowran
Co Kilkenny
Republic of Ireland
☎ (056) 26120 or 26225
fax: (056) 26173

Kilbeggan Racecourse
Kilbeggan
Co Westmeath
Republic of Ireland
☎ (0506) 32176; fax: (0506) 32125

Killarney Racecourse
Killarney
Co Kerry
Republic of Ireland
☎ (064) 31125

Laytown Racecourse
Laytown
Co Meath
Republic of Ireland
☎ (041) 23425

Limerick Racecourse
Limerick
Co Limerick
Republic of Ireland
☎ & fax: (061) 229377

Listowel Racecourse
Listowel
Co Kerry
Republic of Ireland
☎ & fax: (068) 21144

Naas Racecourse
Kingsfurze
Tipper Road
Naas
Co Kildare
Republic of Ireland
☎ (045) 897391; fax:(045) 879486

Navan Racecourse
Proudstown
Navan
Co Meath
Republic of Ireland
☎ (01) 2893607, fax:(01) 2892634

Roscommon Racecourse
Lenabane
Roscommon
Co Roscommon
Republic of Ireland
☎ (0903) 26231, fax:(0903) 25065

Sligo Racecourse
Cleveragh
Sligo
Co Sligo
Republic of Ireland
☎ (071) 62484; fax:(071) 83342

Thurles Racecourse
Tipperary
Co Tipperary
Republic of Ireland
☎ & fax (0504) 22253

Tipperary Racecourse
Limerick Junction
Co Tipperary
Republic of Ireland
☎ (062) 51357; fax:(062) 51303

Tralee Racecourse
Ballybeggan Park
Tralee
Co Kerry
Republic of Ireland
☎ (066) 26188 or 36148; fax:(066)28007

Waterford & Tramore Racecourse
Tramore
Co Waterford
Republic of Ireland
☎ (051) 381574; mobile (088) 599478

Wexford Racecourse
Bettyville
Newtown Road
Wexford
Co Wexford
Republic of Ireland
☎ (051) 21681; fax:(051) 21830

Principal Races

Races are listed in date order throughout the month. Please check days and times with the courses themselves. Due to a reworking of the 1998 Fixtures List, these dates are provisional and are subject to alteration.

JANUARY

3 Newbury	Challow Novices' Hurdle
10 Sandown Park	Anthony Mildmay, Peter Cazelet Memorial Handicap Steeple Chase
10 Sandown Park	Pertemps Cream Tolworth Novices' Hurdle
10 Haydock Park	Newton Steeple Chase
15 Wetherby	Towton Novices' Steeple Chase
17 Ascot	Victor Chandler Chase (Handicap)
17 Newcastle	Adversport Dipper Novices' Steeple Chase
17 Warwick	Tote Trio Warwick National Handicap Chase
23 Ascot	PML Lightning Novices' Steeple Chase
24 Haydock Park	Peter Marsh Steeple Chase (Handicap)
24 Haydock Park	Tote Premier Long Distance Hurdle
24 Haydock Park	Bellcharm Mitsubishi Champion Hurdle Trial
24 Kempton Park	The Sun King of the Punters Lanzarote Handicap Hurdle
30 Doncaster	Rossington Main Novices' Hurdle
31 Cheltenham	The Cleeve Hurdle
31 Cheltenham	Finesse Four Years Old Novices' Hurdle
31 Doncaster	Pertemps Great Yorkshire Chase (Handicap)
31 Doncaster	Napoleons Racing River Don Novices' Hurdle

FEBRUARY

7 Sandown Park	Tote Bookmakers Sandown Hurdle (Handicap)
7 Sandown Park	Scilly Isles Novices' Steeple Chase
7 Sandown Park	Agfa Diamond Steeple Chase (Limited Handicap)
7 Uttoxeter	Singer & Friedlander National Trial (Handicap Steeple Chase)
11 Ascot	Comet Steeple Chase
11 Ascot	HSBC James Capel Reynoldstown Novices' Chase
14 Newbury	Tote Gold Trophy (Handicap Hurdle)
14 Newbury	Mitsubishi Shogun Game Spirit Steeple Chase
21 Chepstow	Colin Davies Persian War Premier Novices' Hurdle
21 Chepstow	John Hughes Grand National Trial (Handicap Chase)
21 Chepstow	Prestige Novices' Hurdle
21 Newcastle	Tote Eider Handicap Steeple Chase
21 Warwick	Michael Page Group Kingmaker Novices' Chase
26 Wincanton	K.J.Pike & Sons Kingwell Hurdle
28 Haydock Park	Greenalls Grand National Trial (Handicap Chase)
28 Kempton Park	Racing Post Steeple Chase (Handicap)
28 Kempton Park	Pendil Novices' Steeple Chase
28 Kempton Park	Rendlesham Hurdle (Limited Handicap)
28 Kempton Park	Dovecote Novices' Hurdle
28 Kempton Park	The Voice Newspaper Adonis Juvenile Novices' Hurdle

MARCH

14 Sandown Park	Sunderlands Imperial Cup (Handicap Hurdle)
17 Cheltenham	Smurfit Champion Hurdle Challenge Trophy
17 Cheltenham	Guinness Arkle Challenge Trophy Novices' Chase
17 Cheltenham	Citroen Supreme Novices' Hurdle
18 Cheltenham	Queen Mother Champion Steeple Chase
18 Cheltenham	Royal SunAlliance Novices' Steeple Chase
18 Cheltenham	Royal SunAlliance Novices' Hurdle
18 Cheltenham	Weatherbys Champion Bumper

19 Cheltenham	Tote Cheltenham Gold Cup Steeple Chase
19 Cheltenham	Bonusprint Stayers Hurdle
19 Cheltenham	Elite racing Club Triumph Hurdle (Novices')
19 Cheltenham	Vincent O'Brien County Handicap Hurdle
21 Uttoxeter	Marstons Pedigree Midlands Grand National (Handicap Steeple Chase)
26 Doncaster	Sporting Life Doncaster Mile
27 Doncaster	Worthington Spring Mile (Handicap)
28 Doncaster	Worthington Lincoln Handicap
28 Doncaster	The Cammidge Trophy
28 Newbury	Hoechst Roussel Vet Panacur EBF Mares' NH Final (Novices' Hurdle)

APRIL

2 Aintree	Glenlivet Anniversary Novices' Hurdle
2 Aintree	Martell Cup Steeple Chase
2 Aintree	Sandeman Maghull Novices' Steeple Chase
2 Aintree	Seagram Top Novices' Hurdle
3 Aintree	Mumm Melling Steeple Chase
3 Aintree	Mumm Mildmay Novices' Steeple Chase
3 Aintree	Belle Epoque Sefton Novices' Hurdle
3 Aintree	Martell Mersey Novices' Hurdle
4 Aintree	Martell Grand National Steeple Chase (Handicap)
4 Aintree	Martell Aintree Hurdle
4 Aintree	Martell Red Rum Steeple Chase (Limited Handicap)
4 Aintree	Martell Champion Standard Bumper
8 Ascot	Letheby & Christopher Long Distance Hurdle
11 Haydock Park	Daihatsu Field Marshal Stakes
11 Kempton Park	Milcars Easter Stakes (colts & geldings)
11 Kempton Park	Milcars Masaka Stakes (fillies)
13 Kempton Park	Magnolia Stakes
14 Newmarket	Shadwell Stud Nell Gwyn Stakes (fillies)
14 Newmarket	Scottish Equitable/Jockeys Association Abernant Stakes
15 Cheltenham	Faucets for Mira Rada Showers Silver Trophy Steeple Chase
15 Cheltenham	EBF 'NH' Novices' Hurdle Series Final
15 Newmarket	Earl of Sefton Stakes
15 Newmarket	NGK Spark Plugs European Free Handicap
16 Newmarket	City Index Craven Stakes (colts & geldings)
16 Newmarket	Greene King Feilden Stakes
17 Newbury	Dubai Duty Free Fred Darling Stakes (fillies)
18 Ayr	Stakis Casinos Scottish Grand National (Handicap Steeple Chase)
18 Ayr	Samsung Electronics Scottish Champion Hurdle (Handicap)
18 Ayr	Edinburgh Woollen Mill's Future Champion Novices' Steeple Chase
18 Newbury	Lanes End John Porter Stakes
18 Newbury	Tripleprint Greenham Stakes (colts & geldings)
24 Sandown Park	The Sandown Mile
25 Sandown Park	Thresher Classic Trial
25 Sandown Park	David Lloyd Leisure Gordon Richards Stakes
25 Sandown Park	42nd Whitbread Gold Cup (Handicap Steeple Chase)
25 Leicester	Tote Leicestershire Stakes
29 Ascot	Insulpak Sagaro Stakes
29 Ascot	Insulpak Victoria Cup (Handicap)

MAY

1 Newmarket	Grangewood Jockey Club Stakes
1 Newmarket	Kuwait Green Ridge Stables Newmarket Stakes (colts)
1 Newmarket	Dahlia Stakes (fillies)
2 Haydock Park	Crowther Homes Swinton Handicap Hurdle
2 Haydock Park	Haydock Park Spring Trophy Rated Stakes
2 Newmarket	Pertemps 2000 Guineas Stakes
2 Newmarket	Dubai Racing Club Palace House Stakes
3 Newmarket	Pertemps 1000 Guineas Stakes (fillies)
3 Newmarket	R.L. Davison Pretty Polly Stakes (fillies)
4 Kempton Park	Jubilee Handicap Stakes
5 Chester	The Chester Vase

6 Chester	Tote Chester Cup (Handicap)
6 Chester	Shadwell Stud Cheshire Oaks (fillies)
7 Chester	The Ormonde Stakes
7 Chester	The 186th Year of the Dee Stakes
9 Lingfield Park	Tripleprint Derby Trial Stakes
9 Lingfield Park	Lingfield Oaks Trial Stakes (fillies)
9 Lingfield Park	Milcars Chartwell Stakes (fillies)
12 York	Tattersalls Musidora Stakes (fillies)
13 York	Grosvenor Casinos Dante Stakes
13 York	Grosvenor Casinos Hambleton Rated Stakes
13 York	Grosvenor Casinos Middleton Stakes (fillies)
14 York	The Yorkshire Cup
14 York	Duke of York International Factors Stakes
15 Newbury	Vodafone Group Fillies' Trial Stakes
15 Newbury	Juddmonte Lockinge Stakes
15 Newmarket	King Charles II Stakes
16 Newbury	Quantel Aston Park Stakes
19 Goodwood	Westminster Taxi Insurance Predominate Stakes (colts & geldings)
20 Goodwood	Tripleprint Lupe Stakes (fillies)
21 Goodwood	Royal Sussex Regiment Festival Stakes
21 Goodwood	Ruinart Champagne Conqueror Stakes (fillies)
23 Haydock Park	Tote Credit Silver Bowl (Handicap)
23 Haydock Park	Leahurst Sandy Lane Rated Stakes
23 Kempton Park	Crawley Warren Heron Stakes
25 Redcar	Tote Zetland Gold Cup (Handicap)
25 Sandown Park	Tripleprint Temple Stakes
25 Sandown Park	Bonusprint Henry II Stakes
26 Sandown Park	Brigadier Gerard Stakes
26 Sandown Park	The National Stakes
30 Kempton Park	Holsten Pils Achilles Stakes
30 Lingfield Park	Tote Credit Leisure Stakes
30 Newmarket	Coral Sprint Handicap Stakes
30 Newmarket	Bairstow Eves Charlotte Fillies' Stakes
30 Stratford-on-Avon	Horse and Hound Cup (Hunters' Steeple Chase)

JUNE

5 Epsom Downs	Vodafone Oaks (fillies)
5 Epsom Downs	Vodafone Coronation Cup
5 Epsom Downs	Vodacall Victress Stakes (fillies)
5 Epsom Downs	Vodata Woodcote Stakes
6 Epsom Downs	Vodafone Derby (colts & fillies)
6 Epsom Downs	Vodafone Diomed Stakes
6 Epsom Downs	Vodac 'Dash' Rated Stakes
6 Haydock Park	The John of Gaunt Stakes
11 Newbury	Ballymacoll Stud Stakes (fillies)
12 York	Anthony Fawcett Memorial Sprint Handicap
13 Leicester	Leicester Mercury Stakes
13 York	William Hill Trophy (Handicap)
13 York	Daniel Prenn Royal Yorkshire Rated Stakes
16 Royal Ascot	St James's Palace Stakes (colts & fillies)
16 Royal Ascot	The Prince of Wales's Stakes
16 Royal Ascot	The Queen Anne Stakes
16 Royal Ascot	The Coventry Stakes
17 Royal Ascot	The Coronation Stakes (fillies)
17 Royal Ascot	The Queen's Vase Stakes
17 Royal Ascot	The Jersey Stakes
17 Royal Ascot	The Queen Mary Stakes (fillies)
18 Royal Ascot	The Gold Cup
18 Royal Ascot	Ribblesdale Stakes (fillies)
18 Royal Ascot	Cork and Orrery Stakes
18 Royal Ascot	The Norfolk Stakes
18 Royal Ascot	The Chesham Stakes
19 Royal Ascot	The Hardwicke Stakes
19 Royal Ascot	King's Stand Stakes
19 Royal Ascot	King Edward VII Stakes (colts & geldings)

20 Ascot	London Clubs Fern Hill Rated Stakes (fillies)
24 Epsom Downs	The Gala Stakes
27 Newcastle	'Newcastle Brown Ale' Northumberland Plate (Handicap)
27 Newcastle	Colonel Porter Brown Chipchase Stakes
27 Newmarket	Van Greest Critierion Stakes
27 Newmarket	NGK Spark Plugs Fred Archer Stakes
27 Newmarket	Ladbroke Empress Stakes (fillies)

JULY

3 Sandown Park	Hong Kong Jockey Club Trophy (Handicap)
3 Sandown Park	Wates Centenary Dragon Stakes
4 Haydock Park	Haydock Park July Trophy (colts & geldings)
4 Haydock Park	Letheby & Christopher Lancashire Oaks Stakes (fillies)
4 Haydock Park	Letheby & Christopher Old Newton Cup (Handicap)
4 Sandown Park	The Coral-Eclipse Stakes
4 Sandown Park	Sandown Park Sprint Stakes
7 Newmarket	Princess of Wales's Stakes
7 Newmarket	Charles Heidsieck Champagne Cherry Hinton Stakes
8 Newmarket	Amcor Falmouth Stakes (fillies)
8 Newmarket	TNT International Aviation July Stakes (colts & geldings)
9 Newmarket	The Darley July Cup
9 Newmarket	Ladbroke Bunbury Cup (Handicap)
9 Newmarket	The Bahrain Trophy
9 Newmarket	Weatherbys Superlative Stakes
10 York	Singapore Summer Stakes (fillies)
11 Lingfield Park	Daily Mail Classified Silver Trophy Rated Stakes
11 York	John Smith's Magnet Cup (Handicap)
11 York	Foster's Silver Cup Rated Stakes
18 Newbury	Weatherbys Super Sprint (auction race)
18 Newbury	The Steventon Stakes
18 Newbury	Ruinart Champagne Hackwood Stakes
18 Newbury	The Rose Bowl Stakes
18 Newmarket	Food Brokers Animal Health Trust Trophy (Handicap)
18 Newmarket	Food Brokers Aphrodite Stakes (fillies)
20 Ayr	Tennent Caledonian Breweries Scottish Classic
23 Sandown Park	Milcars Star Stakes (fillies)
24 Chepstow	Golden Daffodil Stakes (fillies)
25 Ascot	King George VI and The Queen Elizabeth Diamond Stakes
25 Ascot	Princess Margaret Stakes (fillies)
25 Newcastle	Thomas Lonsdale Gallagher Beeswing Stakes
28 Goodwood	The William Hill Cup (Handicap)
28 Goodwood	The King George Stakes
28 Goodwood	Westminster Taxi Insurance Gordon Stakes
29 Goodwood	The Sussex Stakes
29 Goodwood	Lanson Champagne Vintage Stakes
29 Goodwood	Tote Gold Trophy (Handicap)
30 Goodwood	Salomon Brothers Richmond Stakes (colts & geldings)
30 Goodwood	Schweppes Golden Mile (Handicap)
30 Goodwood	Crowson Goodwood Cup
30 Goodwood	Oak Tree Stakes (fillies)
31 Goodwood	Schroders Glorious Rated Stakes
31 Goodwood	Volvo Contracts Globetrotter Stakes (Handicap)
31 Goodwood	Jockey Club of Kenya Molecomb Stakes

AUGUST

1 Goodwood	Vodafone Stewards' Cup (Handicap)
1 Goodwood	Vodafone Nassau Stakes (fillies)
8 Haydock Park	Petros Rose of Lancaster Stakes
8 Newmarket	Enza New Zealand Sweet Solera Stakes (fillies)
12 Salisbury	Upavon Stakes (fillies)
14 Newbury	Grosvenor Casinos Hungerford Stakes
14 Newbury	Grosvenor Casinos Washington Singer Stakes
15 Newbury	Triprint Geoffrey Freer Stakes

15 Newbury	Swettenham Stud St Hugh's Stakes (fillies)
15 Ripon	William Hill Great St Wilfrid Handicap Stakes
18 York	Juddmonte International Stakes
18 York	Great Voltigeur Stakes (colts & geldings)
18 York	Weatherbys/Hiscox Household Insurance Lonsdale Stakes
19 York	Aston Upthorpe Yorkshire Oaks (fillies)
19 York	Scottish Equitable Gimcrack Stakes (colts & geldings)
19 York	Tote Ebor (Handicap)
19 York	Roses Stakes (colts & geldings)
20 York	Stakis Casinos Lowther Stakes (fillies)
20 York	Nunthorpe Stakes
20 York	Bradford & Bingley Rated Stakes
20 York	The Galtres Stakes (fillies)
20 York	The City of York Stakes
21 Sandown Park	The Solario Stakes
22 Chester	The Chester Stakes (Handicap)
22 Sandown Park	Lyceum Atalanta Stakes (fillies)
26 Goodwood	Prestige Stakes (fillies)
27 Goodwood	Tripleprint Celebration Mile
27 Goodwood	Sport on 5 March Stakes
28 Newmarket	The Hopeful Stakes
29 Windsor	The Winter Hill Stakes
31 Newcastle	Northern Virginia Rated Stakes
31 Ripon	Ripon Champion Two Years Old Trophy

SEPTEMBER

3 York	The Strensall Stakes
4 Epsom Downs	H & V News Fortune Stakes
5 Epsom Downs	Grosvenor Casinos September Stakes
5 Haydock Park	Haydock Park Sprint Cup
9 Doncaster	The Park Hill Stakes
9 Doncaster	Tote-Portland Handicap
9 Doncaster	Doncaster Bloodstock Sales Scarborough Stakes
9 Kempton Park	The Sirenia Stakes
10 Doncaster	Great North Eastern Railway Doncaster Cup
10 Doncaster	Britain's Fastest Railway Park Stakes
10 Doncaster	May Hill Stakes (fillies)
10 Doncaster	Kyoto Sceptre Stakes (fillies)
11 Doncaster	Laurent-Perrier Rose Champagne Stakes (colts & geldings)
11 Doncaster	The O&K Troy Stakes
11 Goodwood	Bellway Homes Stardom Stakes
12 Doncaster	Pertemps St Leger Stakes (colts & fillies)
12 Doncaster	Polypipe Plc Flying Childers Stakes
12 Goodwood	Westminster Taxi Insurance Select Stakes
15 Great Yarmouth	The John Musker Stakes (fillies)
17 Ayr	Timeform Harry Rosebery Trophy
17 Newbury	The Dubai Duty Free Cup
17 Newbury	Doubleprint Arc Trial
17 Newbury	Dubai Airport World Trophy
18 Ayr	Shadwell Stud Firth of Clyde Stakes (fillies)
19 Ayr	Ladbroke (Ayr) Gold Cup (Handicap)
19 Ayr	Stakis Casinos Doonside Cup
19 Newbury	Bonusprint Mill Reef Stakes
23 Goodwood	R.O.A. Foundation Stakes
24 Goodwood	Charlton Hunt Supreme Stakes
26 Ascot	Queen Elizabeth II Stakes
26 Ascot	Racal Diadem Stakes
26 Ascot	Tote Festival Handicap
26 Ascot	Cumberland Lodge Stakes
26 Ascot	Rosemary Rated Stakes (fillies)
27 Ascot	The Fillies' Mile
27 Ascot	Gtech Royal Lodge Stakes (colts & geldings)
27 Ascot	Tote Sunday Special Handicap

27 Ascot	Mail on Sunday Final (Handicap)
27 Ascot	The Harvest Stakes (fillies)
29 Newmarket	Shadwell Stud Cheveley Park Stakes (fillies)

OCTOBER

1 Newmarket	Middle Park Stakes (colts)
1 Newmarket	Hearth Court Hotel Joel Stakes
1 Newmarket	JRA Nakayama Rous Stakes
2 Newmarket	Racing Post Godolphin Stakes
2 Newmarket	Somerville Tattersall Stakes (colts & geldings)
3 Newmarket	Tote Cambridgeshire Handicap Stakes
3 Newmarket	Sun Chariot Stakes (fillies)
3 Newmarket	Portland Place Properties Jockey Club Cup
3 Newmarket	Oh So Sharp Stakes (fillies)
9 Ascot	Bonusprint October Stakes (fillies)
10 Ascot	Princess Royal Stakes (fillies)
10 Ascot	Willmott Dixon Cornwallis Stakes
10 Ascot	McGee Autumn Stakes
16 Newmarket	Bedford Lodge Hotel Bentinck Stakes
16 Newmarket	Baring International Darley Stakes
17 Newmarket	Dubai Champion Stakes
17 Newmarket	Tote Cesarewitch (Handicap)
17 Newmarket	The Challenge Stakes
17 Newmarket	Dewhurst Stakes (colts & fillies)
17 Newmarket	Owen Brown Rockfel Stakes (fillies)
17 Redcar	Comcast Teesside Two-Year-Old Trophy
19 Pontefract	Tote Silver Tankard
23 Newbury	Vodafone Horris Hill Stakes (colts & geldings)
24 Doncaster	Racing Post Trophy (colts & fillies)
24 Doncaster	Charles Sidney Mercedes Benz Doncaster Stakes
24 Newbury	Perpetual St Simon Stakes
24 Newbury	The Radley Stakes (fillies)
25 Wincanton	Desert Orchid South Western Pattern Steeple Chase (Ltd Handicap)
30 Newmarket	George Stubbs Rated Stakes
30 Newmarket	James Seymour Stakes
31 Newmarket	Ladbroke Autumn Handicap
31 Newmarket	Ben Marshall Stakes
31 Newmarket	NGK Spark Plugs Zetland Stakes
31 Wetherby	Charlie Hall Steeple Chase
31 Wetherby	Tote West Yorkshire Hurdle
31 Wetherby	Wensleydale Novices' Hurdle

NOVEMBER

3 Exeter	William Hill Haldon Gold Cup Chase (Ltd Handicap)
7 Chepstow	Tote Silver Trophy Hurdle (Handicap)
7 Chepstow	Rising Stars Novices' Steeple Chase
7 Doncaster	Tote Credit November Handicap
7 Doncaster	Co-Operative Bank Serlby Stakes
7 Doncaster	The Wentworth Stakes
7 Uttoxeter	Classic Nov Hurdle
7 Wincanton	Tanglefoot Elite Hurdle
11 Worcester	Worcester Novices' Steeple Chase
13 Cheltenham	Sporting Index Cross Country Steeple Chase
14 Cheltenham	Murphy's Gold Cup Handicap Steeple Chase
14 Cheltenham	Mackeson Novices' Hurdle
15 Cheltenham	Stakis Casinos November Novices' Steeple Chase
20 Ascot	Coopers & Lybrand Ascot Hurdle
21 Aintree	Crowther Homes Becher Chase (Handicap)
21 Ascot	First National Bank Gold Cup Chase (Handicap)
21 Huntingdon	Peterborough Steeple Chase
28 Newcastle	Newcastle Building Society "Fighting Fifth" Hurdle (Ltd Handicap)
28 Newbury	Hennessy Cognac Gold Cup Handicap Steeple Chase
28 Newbury	Gerry Feilden Hurdle
28 Newbury	Long Distance Hurdle

DECEMBER

4 Sandown Park	Bovis Crowngap Winter Novices' Hurdle
5 Chepstow	Coral Rehearsal Steeple Chase (Handicap)
5 Sandown Park	Mitsubishi Shogun Tingle Creek Trophy Chase
5 Sandown Park	William Hill Handicap Hurdle
5 Sandown Park	Henry VIII Novices' Steeple Chase
5 Wolverhampton	The Bass Wulfrun Stakes
12 Cheltenham	Tripleprint Gold Cup (Handicap Steeple Chase)
12 Cheltenham	Bonusprint Bula Hurdle
12 Cheltenham	Bristol Novices' Hurdle
12 Lingfield Park	Lambert Fenchurch December Novices' Chase
12 Lingfield Park	Summit Novices' Hurdle
19 Ascot	Jefferson Smurfit Group Long Walk Hurdle
19 Ascot	Betterware Cup (Handicap Steeple Chase)
19 Ascot	'Book of Music' Novices' Steeple Chase
19 Ascot	Mitie Group Kennel Gate Novices' Hurdle
26 Kempton Park	Pertemps King George VI Steeple Chase
26 Kempton Park	Pertemps Recruitment Partnership Feltham Novices' Steeple Chase
26 Wetherby	Rowland Meyrick Handicap Steeple Chase
28 Chepstow	Coral Welsh National (Handicap Steeple Chase)
28 Chepstow	Finale Junior Novices' Hurdle
28 Kempton Park	Pertemps Christmas Hurdle
28 Wetherby	Castleford Steeple Chase

Racing Fixtures

The fixtures are reproduced by kind permission of the British Horseracing Board. They have been divided into three areas as defined by the Racecourse Association, namely North, Midlands and South

Capital letters are used to represent the Flat Race Meetings and the symbol † denotes evening racing. (AWT) following the name of a meeting indicates an All Weather Track fixture. Each month's fixtures are divided into weeks. Please check the precise day and time with the racecourses themselves.

	JANUARY		
	NORTH	MIDLANDS	SOUTH
1	Catterick Bridge	Cheltenham	Exeter
		Leicester	LINGFIELD PARK (AWT)
			Windsor
2	Ayr	SOUTHWELL (AWT)	Newbury
3	Musselburgh	Uttoxeter	LINGFIELD PARK (AWT)
			Newbury
5		SOUTHWELL (AWT)	Folkestone
6		Ludlow	LINGFIELD PARK (AWT)
7	Musselburgh	WOLVERHAMPTON (AWT)	Lingfield Park
8	Catterick Bridge	Market Rasen	LINGFIELD PARK (AWT)
9		SOUTHWELL (AWT)	Exeter
		Towcester	
10	Haydock Park	Warwick	LINGFIELD PARK (AWT)
		†WOLVERHAMPTON (AWT)	Sandown Park
12		SOUTHWELL (AWT)	Plumpton
13		Leicester	LINGFIELD PARK (AWT)
14	Sedgefield	WOLVERHAMPTON (AWT)	Folkestone
15	Wetherby		LINGFIELD PARK (AWT)
			Wincanton
16	Musselburgh	SOUTHWELL (AWT)	Kempton Park
17	Newcastle	Warwick	Ascot
			LINGFIELD PARK (AWT)
19		SOUTHWELL (AWT)	Fontwell Park
20	Carlisle		LINGFIELD PARK (AWT)
21		Huntingdon	Windsor
		WOLVERHAMPTON (AWT)	
22		Ludlow	LINGFIELD PARK (AWT)
			Taunton
23	Kelso	SOUTHWELL (AWT)	Ascot
24	Catterick Bridge	†WOLVERHAMPTON (AWT)	Kempton Park
	Haydock Park		LINGFIELD PARK (AWT)
26		SOUTHWELL (AWT)	Windsor
27		Leicester	LINGFIELD PARK (AWT)
28	Sedgefield	WOLVERHAMPTON (AWT)	Lingfield Park
29		Huntingdon	LINGFIELD PARK (AWT)
			Wincanton
30	Doncaster	SOUTHWELL (AWT)	Folkestone
31	Ayr	Cheltenham	LINGFIELD PARK (AWT)
	Doncaster		

	FEBRUARY	
NORTH	**MIDLANDS**	**SOUTH**
2	SOUTHWELL (AWT)	Plumpton
3 Musselburgh		LINGFIELD PARK (AWT)
4	Leicester	Windsor
	WOLVERHAMPTON (AWT)	
5 Kelso	Towcester	LINGFIELD PARK (AWT)
6 Catterick Bridge	SOUTHWELL (AWT)	Lingfield Park
7 Wetherby	Uttoxeter	LINGFIELD PARK (AWT)
	†WOLVERHAMPTON (AWT)	Sandown Park
9 Newcastle	SOUTHWELL (AWT)	Fontwell Park
10 Carlisle	Warwick	LINGFIELD PARK (AWT)
11	Ludlow	Ascot
	WOLVERHAMPTON (AWT)	
12	Huntingdon	LINGFIELD PARK (AWT)
		Wincanton
13	Bangor-On-Dee	Newbury
	SOUTHWELL (AWT)	
14 Ayr	Market Rasen	LINGFIELD PARK (AWT)
Catterick Bridge		Newbury
16	Hereford	Plumpton
	SOUTHWELL (AWT)	
17 Sedgefield	Leicester	LINGFIELD PARK (AWT)
18 Musselburgh	WOLVERHAMPTON (AWT)	Lingfield Park
19		LINGFIELD PARK (AWT)
		Sandown Park
		Taunton
20	Fakenham	Sandown Park
	SOUTHWELL (AWT)	
21 Newcastle	Warwick	Chepstow
	†WOLVERHAMPTON (AWT)	LINGFIELD PARK (AWT)
		Windsor
23	SOUTHWELL (AWT)	Fontwell Park
24 Doncaster		LINGFIELD PARK (AWT)
25 Sedgefield	WOLVERHAMPTON (AWT)	Folkestone
26	Huntingdon	LINGFIELD PARK (AWT)
		Wincanton
27 Haydock Park	SOUTHWELL (AWT)	Kempton Park
28 Haydock Park		Kempton Park
		LINGFIELD PARK (AWT)
Musselburgh		

MARCH

	NORTH	MIDLANDS	SOUTH
2	Newcastle	SOUTHWELL (AWT)	Plumpton
3	Catterick Bridge	Leicester	LINGFIELD PARK (AWT)
4	Wetherby	WOLVERHAMPTON (AWT)	Chepstow
5		Ludlow	Lingfield Park
			Taunton
6	Doncaster		Newbury
	Kelso		
7	Doncaster	Huntingdon	Newbury
		Warwick	
		†WOLVERHAMPTON (AWT)	
9		SOUTHWELL (AWT)	Newton Abbot
10	Sedgefield	Leicester	Exeter
11	Catterick Bridge	Bangor-On-Dee	
		SOUTHWELL (AWT)	
12	Carlisle	Towcester	Wincaton
13	Ayr	Market Rasen	Sandown Park
14	Ayr	WOLVERHAMPTON (AWT)	Chepstow
			Sandown Park
16		Stratford-On-Avon	Plumpton
			Taunton
17	Sedgefield	Cheltenham	
		SOUTHWELL (AWT)	
18		Cheltenham	Newton Abbot
		Huntingdon	
19	Hexham	Cheltenham	LINGFIELD PARK (AWT)
20		Fakenham	Folkestone
		SOUTHWELL (AWT)	
21	Newcastle	Hereford	Lingfield Park
		Uttoxeter	
		†WOLVERHAMPTON (AWT)	
23	Newcastle	SOUTHWELL (AWT)	
24		Uttoxeter	Chepstow
			Fontwell Park
25		Ludlow	Exeter
		Towcester	
26	DONCASTER		Plumpton
			Wincanton
27	DONCASTER		Newbury
	Kelso		
28	DONCASTER	Bangor-On-Dee	Newbury
		WARWICK (MIXED)	
		†WOLVERHAMPTON (AWT)	
30	HAMILTON PARK		LINGFIELD PARK (AWT)
	Hexham		
31	NEWCASTLE (MIXED)	NOTTINGHAM	Sandown Park

| | APRIL | |
NORTH	MIDLANDS	SOUTH
1 CATTERICK BRIDGE		Ascot
		FOLKESTONE
2 Aintree	LEICESTER	Taunton
3 Aintree		LINGFIELD PARK (AWT)
Sedgefield		
4 Aintree	Hereford	
HAMILTON PARK	†WOLVERHAMPTON (AWT)	
6 Kelso	SOUTHWELL (AWT)	Fontwell Park
7	NOTTINGHAM	FOLKESTONE
	WOLVERHAMPTON (AWT)	
8 RIPON	Ludlow	Ascot
9 MUSSELBURGH	LEICESTER	LINGFIELD PARK (AWT)
11 Carlisle	Towcester	KEMPTON PARK
HAYDOCK PARK	†WOLVERHAMPTON (AWT)	Newton Abbot
		Plumpton
13 Carlisle	Fakenham	Chepstow
NEWCASTLE (MIXED)	Hereford	KEMPTON PARK
Wetherby	Huntingdon	Plumpton
	Market Rasen	Wincanton
	NOTTINGHAM	
	Towcester	
	Uttoxeter	
	WARWICK	
14 Wetherby	NEWMARKET	Exeter
	Uttoxeter	
15 PONTEFRACT	Cheltenham	
	NEWMARKET	
16 RIPON	NEWMARKET	
	Cheltenham	
17 Ayr		NEWBURY
THIRSK		
18 Ayr	Bangor-On-Dee	NEWBURY
THIRSK	Stratford-On-Avon	
	†WOLVERHAMPTON (AWT)	
20 Hexham	NOTTINGHAM	BRIGHTON
21 PONTEFRACT		Chepstow
		FOLKESTONE
22 CATTERICK BRIDGE	Towcester	EPSOM DOWNS
Perth		
23 BEVERLEY		Fontwell Park
Perth		
24 CARLISLE	†Ludlow	SANDOWN PARK
Perth	†Warwick	†Taunton
25 RIPON	LEICESTER	SANDOWN PARK (MIXED)
†Sedgefield	Market Rasen	
	†Worcester	
	†WOLVERHAMPTON (AWT)	
27 PONTEFRACT	SOUTHWELL(AWT)	
28	†Huntingdon	†Ascot
	NOTTINGHAM	BATH
29 †Kelso	†Cheltenham	ASCOT
		Exeter
		Plumpton
30 REDCAR	WOLVERHAMPTON (AWT)	BRIGHTON

MAY

	NORTH	MIDLANDS	SOUTH
1	MUSSELBURGH †Sedgefield	†Bangor-On-Dee NEWMARKET	Newton Abbot
2	HAYDOCK PARK (MIXED) Hexham THIRSK	Hereford NEWMARKET Uttoxeter	
3	HAMILTON PARK	NEWMARKET	SALISBURY
4	DONCASTER NEWCASTLE	Ludlow Southwell Towcester WARWICK	Fontwell Park KEMPTON PARK
5		CHESTER	BRIGHTON Exeter
6	MUSSELBURGH †Wetherby	CHESTER †Uttoxeter	Chepstow
7	HAMILTON PARK	CHESTER SOUTHWELL (AWT)	
8	CARLISLE	NOTTINGHAM †Stratford-On-Avon	LINGFIELD PARK †Wincanton
9	BEVERLEY Hexham	Worcester	ASCOT LINGFIELD PARK
10	BEVERLEY HAYDOCK PARK		BATH
11	REDCAR	SOUTHWELL(AWT) †Towcester	†WINDSOR
12	YORK	Hereford	
13	†Perth YORK	†Huntingdon	Chepstow †Folkestone LINGFIELD PARK (AWT)
14	Perth YORK		SALISBURY
15	†Aintree †HAMILTON PARK THIRSK	NEWMARKET †Stratford-On-Avon	NEWBURY
16	THIRSK	Bangor-On-Dee NOTTINGHAM	NEWBURY
17	RIPON	Fakenham	KEMPTON PARK
18	†MUSSELBURGH	SOUTHWELL (AWT)	BATH †WINDSOR
19	BEVERLEY		GOODWOOD
20	Kelso	†Uttoxeter Worcester	GOODWOOD †Newton Abbot
21	NEWCASTLE		Exeter GOODWOOD
22	HAYDOCK PARK †PONTEFRACT	NOTTINGHAM †Towcester	BRIGHTON
23	Cartmel DONCASTER HAYDOCK PARK Hexham	†WARWICK	KEMPTON PARK †LINGFIELD PARK
25	Cartmel REDCAR Wetherby	Hereford Huntingdon LEICESTER Uttoxeter	CHEPSTOW Fontwell Park SANDOWN PARK
26	†Hexham REDCAR	LEICESTER	†SANDOWN PARK
27	Cartmel †RIPON	YARMOUTH	FOLKESTONE †NEWBURY
28	AYR	Uttoxeter	BRIGHTON
29	AYR CATTERICK BRIDGE	†Stratford-On-Avon WOLVERHAMPTON (AWT)	†BATH
30	CATTERICK BRIDGE †MUSSELBURGH	†Market Rasen NEWMARKET Stratford-On-Avon	†KEMPTON PARK LINGFIELD PARK

	JUNE	
NORTH	**MIDLANDS**	**SOUTH**
1 HAMILTON PARK	†Hereford	†WINDSOR
†THIRSK	LEICESTER	
2 PONTEFRACT		BRIGHTON
3 †BEVERLEY	†CHESTER	†FOLKESTONE
NEWCASTLE	WARWICK	GOODWOOD
4 HAYDOCK PARK	YARMOUTH	
Perth		
5 CATTERICK BRIDGE	SOUTHWELL (AWT)	EPSOM DOWNS
†HAYDOCK PARK		†GOODWOOD
†Perth		
6 DONCASTER	†NEWMARKET	EPSOM DOWNS
HAYDOCK PARK	†WOLVERHAMPTON (AWT)	†Newton Abbot
	Worcester	
8 PONTEFRACT	NOTTINGHAM	†WINDSOR
	†WARWICK	
9 REDCAR		SALISBURY
10 BEVERLEY	†Uttoxeter	†KEMPTON PARK
†HAMILTON PARK		SALISBURY
11 CARLISLE	YARMOUTH	NEWBURY
12 YORK	†Market Rasen	†CHEPSTOW
	SOUTHWELL (AWT)	†GOODWOOD
		SANDOWN PARK
13 †Hexham	†LEICESTER	BATH
YORK	Market Rasen	†LINGFIELD PARK
		SANDOWN PARK
15 MUSSELBURGH		BRIGHTON
†PONTEFRACT		†WINDSOR
16 THIRSK		ASCOT
17 HAMILTON PARK	†NOTTINGHAM	ASCOT
†RIPON	WOLVERHAMPTON (AWT)	
	†Worcester	
18 RIPON	SOUTHWELL (AWT)	ASCOT
19 AYR	†NEWMARKET	ASCOT
†Hexham		†GOODWOOD
REDCAR		
20 AYR	†Southwell	ASCOT
REDCAR	†WOLVERHAMPTON	†LINGFIELD PARK
		Newton Abbot
22 MUSSELBURGH	NOTTINGHAM	†WINDSOR
	†YARMOUTH	
23 BEVERLEY		LINGFIELD PARK
24 CARLISLE	†CHESTER	†EPSOM DOWNS
†HAMILTON PARK	WARWICK	SALISBURY
25 CARLISLE		SALISBURY
NEWCASTLE		
26 †NEWCASTLE	NEWMARKET	FOLKESTONE
	†Stratford-On-Avon	†GOODWOOD
	WOLVERHAMPTON (AWT)	
27 †DONCASTER	NEWMARKET	BATH
NEWCASTLE	Worcester	†LINGFIELD PARK
		†Newton Abbot
28 DONCASTER	Uttoxeter	GOODWOOD
29 †MUSSELBURGH	SOUTHWELL (AWT)	†WINDSOR
PONTEFRACT		
30 HAMILTON PARK		CHEPSTOW

	NORTH	MIDLANDS	SOUTH
		JULY	
1	REDCAR	†YARMOUTH	BRIGHTON
			†KEMPTON PARK
2	CATTERICK BRIDGE	YARMOUTH	
	HAYDOCK PARK		
3	†BEVERLEY	Market Rasen	SANDOWN PARK
	†HAMILTON PARK	WARWICK	
	†HAYDOCK PARK		
4	BEVERLEY	†NOTTINGHAM	CHEPSTOW
	†CARLISLE	†Wolverhampton	SANDOWN PARK
	HAYDOCK PARK		
6	MUSSELBURGH		BATH
	†RIPON		†Newton Abbot
			†WINDSOR
7	PONTEFRACT	NEWMARKET	
8		NEWMARKET	FOLKESTONE
		†Worcester	†KEMPTON PARK
9		NEWMARKET	LINGFIELD PARK
		SOUTHWELL (AWT)	
10	†HAMILTON PARK	†CHESTER	†CHEPSTOW
	YORK	WOLVERHAMPTON (AWT)	LINGFIELD PARK
11	†Sedgefield	CHESTER	LINGFIELD PARK
	YORK	†SOUTHWELL (AWT)	SALISBURY
		†WARWICK	
12	HAYDOCK PARK	Stratford-On-Avon	NEWBURY
13	AYR	†Wolverhampton	BRIGHTON
			†WINDSOR
14	BEVERLEY		BRIGHTON
15	CATTERICK BRIDGE	†Worcester	FOLKESTONE
	†DONCASTER	YARMOUTH	†SANDOWN PARK
16	DONCASTER	LEICESTER	BATH
17	CARLISLE	†NEWMARKET	NEWBURY
	†PONTEFRACT	SOUTHWELL (AWT)	†SALISBURY
18	†AYR	NEWMARKET	NEWBURY
	†REDCAR	NOTTINGHAM	
	RIPON	†WARWICK	
20	AYR	SOUTHWELL (AWT)	†WINDSOR
	†BEVERLEY		
21		YARMOUTH	BATH
22	CATTERICK BRIDGE	†LEICESTER	†SANDOWN PARK
		Worcester	
23	Sedgefield		BRIGHTON
			SANDOWN PARK
24	THIRSK	†NEWMARKET	ASCOT
		†NOTTINGHAM	†CHEPSTOW
		WOLVERHAMPTON (AWT)	
25	NEWCASTLE	Market Rasen	ASCOT
	†REDCAR	†SOUTHWELL (AWT)	†LINGFIELD PARK
		Stratford-On-Avon	
27	NEWCASTLE	†YARMOUTH	FOLKESTONE
			†WINDSOR
28	BEVERLEY		GOODWOOD
29	†DONCASTER		GOODWOOD
	Sedgefield		†EPSOM DOWNS
30	DONCASTER		GOODWOOD
			Newton Abbot
31	THIRSK	Bangor-On-Dee	GOODWOOD
		†NEWMARKET	†SALISBURY

AUGUST

	NORTH	MIDLANDS	SOUTH
1	†HAMILTON PARK THIRSK	†Market Rasen NEWMARKET Worcester	GOODWOOD †LINGFIELD PARK
2	NEWCASTLE	CHESTER	SANDOWN PARK
3	†CARLISLE RIPON		Newton Abbot †WINDSOR
4	CATTERICK BRIDGE		BATH
5	NEWCASTLE PONTEFRACT	†LEICESTER †YARMOUTH	BRIGHTON †KEMPTON PARK
6	HAYDOCK PARK		FOLKESTONE
7	†HAYDOCK PARK	†NEWMARKET WOLVERHAMPTON (AWT) †Worcester	SALISBURY
8	HAYDOCK PARK REDCAR	NEWMARKET	ASCOT
9	REDCAR	YARMOUTH	EPSOM DOWNS
10	†THIRSK	†LEICESTER Worcester	WINDSOR
11	AYR		BATH
12	BEVERLEY †HAMILTON PARK	†NOTTINGHAM	BRIGHTON SALISBURY †SANDOWN PARK
13	BEVERLEY		CHEPSTOW
14	†CATTERICK BRIDGE	SOUTHWELL (AWT) †WARWICK	FOLKESTONE NEWBURY
15	RIPON	Bangor-On-Dee Stratford-On-Avon	NEWBURY
16	PONTEFRACT		LINGFIELD PARK Newton Abbot
17	HAMILTON PARK		WINDSOR
18	YORK		BRIGHTON
19	MUSSELBURGH YORK	†LEICESTER	†KEMPTON PARK
20	YORK	YARMOUTH	SALISBURY
21	Perth	CHESTER	SANDOWN PARK
22	Perth RIPON	CHESTER †Market Rasen †WOLVERHAMPTON (AWT)	†LINGFIELD PARK SANDOWN PARK
24	BEVERLEY		BRIGHTON
25	PONTEFRACT		LINGFIELD PARK
26	CARLISLE	Worcester	GOODWOOD
27	†Cartmel MUSSELBURGH		GOODWOOD
28	THIRSK	NEWMARKET	FOLKESTONE
29	BEVERLEY †Cartmel †REDCAR	NEWMARKET †NOTTINGHAM	LINGFIELD PARK †WINDSOR
31	Cartmel NEWCASTLE RIPON	Huntingdon Southwell WARWICK	CHEPSTOW EPSOM DOWNS Fontwell Park Newton Abbot

SEPTEMBER

	NORTH	MIDLANDS	SOUTH
1	RIPON	Uttoxeter	
2	YORK		BRIGHTON
			Newton Abbot
3	YORK		Fontwell Park
			SALISBURY
4	HAYDOCK PARK		EPSOM DOWNS
	Sedgefield		
5	HAYDOCK PARK	Stratford-On-Avon	EPSOM DOWNS
	THIRSK	†WOLVERHAMPTON (AWT)	
7	HAMILTON PARK		BATH
8	NEWCASTLE	LEICESTER	LINGFIELD PARK
9	DONCASTER		KEMPTON PARK
10	DONCASTER		CHEPSTOW
			Newton Abbot
11	DONCASTER	Worcester	GOODWOOD
12	DONCASTER	Bangor-On-Dee	GOODWOOD
		Worcester	
14	MUSSELBURGH	NOTTINGHAM	Plumpton
15	Sedgefield	YARMOUTH	SANDOWN PARK
16	BEVERLEY	YARMOUTH	SANDOWN PARK
17	AYR	YARMOUTH	NEWBURY
18	AYR	Huntingdon	NEWBURY
19	AYR	Market Rasen	NEWBURY
	Carlisle	†WOLVERHAMPTON (AWT)	
	CATTERICK BRIDGE		
21		Hereford	KEMPTON PARK
		LEICESTER	
22	BEVERLEY	WARWICK	Fontwell Park
23	Perth	CHESTER	GOODWOOD
24	Perth		GOODWOOD
	PONTEFRACT		
25	HAYDOCK PARK		FOLKESTONE
	REDCAR		
26	HAYDOCK PARK	NOTTINGHAM	ASCOT
		Worcester	
27	MUSSELBURGH	Huntingdon	ASCOT
28	HAMILTON PARK		BATH
			Exeter
29	Sedgefield	NEWMARKET	
		WOLVERHAMPTON (AWT)	
30	NEWCASTLE		BRIGHTON
			SALISBURY

OCTOBER

	NORTH	MIDLANDS	SOUTH
1		Hereford	Taunton
		NEWMARKET	
2	Hexham	NEWMARKET	LINGFIELD PARK
3	CATTERICK BRIDGE	NEWMARKET	Chepstow
		Uttoxeter	
		†WOLVERHAMPTON (AWT)	
4	Kelso	Market Rasen	
		WARWICK	
5	PONTEFRACT	Southwell	BRIGHTON
6	REDCAR	NOTTINGHAM	Fontwell Park
7	YORK	Towcester	Exeter
8	YORK	Ludlow	Plumpton
			Wincanton
9	Carlisle	Huntingdon	ASCOT
10	Hexham	Bangor-On-Dee	ASCOT
	YORK	Worcester	
12	AYR	LEICESTER	Newton Abbot
13	AYR	LEICESTER	
	Sedgefield		
14	HAYDOCK PARK	NOTTINGHAM	
	Wetherby		
15	CATTERICK BRIDGE	NEWMARKET	Taunton
16	CATTERICK BRIDGE	Hereford	
		NEWMARKET	
17	Kelso	NEWMARKET	Kempton Park
	REDCAR	Stratford-On-Avon	
		†WOLVERHAMPTON (AWT)	
19	PONTEFRACT	SOUTHWELL (AWT)	Plumpton
20		YARMOUTH	Exeter
			FOLKESTONE
21	NEWCASTLE	NOTTINGHAM	Chepstow
22		Ludlow	BRIGHTON
		NOTTINGHAM	
23	DONCASTER	Fakenham	NEWBURY
24	Carlisle	Market Rasen	NEWBURY
	DONCASTER	Worcester	
25	Wetherby	LEICESTER	Wincanton
26		LEICESTER	LINGFIELD PARK
		Bangor-On-Dee	
27	REDCAR	Cheltenham	BATH
28		Cheltenham	Fontwell Park
		YARMOUTH	
29	Sedgefield	NOTTINGHAM	
		Stratford-On-Avon	
30	NEWCASTLE	Towcester	
	Wetherby	NEWMARKET	
31	Kelso	NEWMARKET	Ascot
	Wetherby	†WOLVERHAMPTON (AWT)	

NOVEMBER

	NORTH	MIDLANDS	SOUTH
2	REDCAR	NOTTINGHAM	Plumpton
3	CATTERICK BRIDGE	Warwick	Exeter
4	MUSSELBURGH		Kempton Park
			Newton Abbot
5	Haydock Park	Towcester	BRIGHTON
6	DONCASTER	Uttoxeter	
	Hexham		
7	DONCASTER	Uttoxeter	Chepstow
			Sandown Park
			Wincanton
9	Carlisle		Fontwell Park
			LINGFIELD PARK (AWT)
10	Sedgefield	Huntingdon	Newbury
11	Kelso	Worcester	Newbury
12		Ludlow	LINGFIELD PARK (AWT)
			Taunton
13	Newcastle	Cheltenham	
		SOUTHWELL (AWT)	
14	Ayr	Cheltenham	Windsor
		Market Rasen	
		†WOLVERHAMPTON (AWT)	
15	Ayr	Cheltenham	
		Towcester	
16		Leicester	Plumpton
		WOLVERHAMPTON (AWT)	
17	Wetherby		LINGFIELD PARK (AWT)
			Newton Abbot
18	Haydock Park	Hereford	Kempton Park
19	Sedgefield	Warwick	Wincanton
20		SOUTHWELL (AWT)	Ascot
			Exeter
21	Aintree	Huntingdon	Ascot
	Catterick Bridge		
23		Ludlow	Windsor
		SOUTHWELL (AWT)	
24		Cheltenham	LINGFIELD PARK (AWT)
		Market Rasen	
25	Hexham		Chepstow
			LINGFIELD PARK (AWT)
26	Carlisle	Uttoxeter	Taunton
27		Bangor-On-Dee	LINGFIELD PARK (AWT)
			Newbury
28	Haydock Park	Warwick	Newbury
	Newcastle	†WOLVERHAMPTON (AWT)	
30	Kelso	Worcester	Folkestone

DECEMBER

	NORTH	MIDLANDS	SOUTH
1	Newcastle	SOUTHWELL (AWT)	Newton Abbot
2	Catterick Bridge	WOLVERHAMPTON (AWT)	Fontwell Park
3		Leicester	Wincanton
			Windsor
4		Hereford	Exeter
			Sandown Park
5	Wetherby	Towcester	Chepstow
		WOLVERHAMPTON (AWT)	Sandown Park
7	Ayr	Fakenham	LINGFIELD PARK (AWT)
8	Sedgefield	Huntingdon	Plumpton
9	Hexham	Leicester	LINGFIELD PARK (AWT)
10		Ludlow	Taunton
		Market Rasen	
11	Doncaster	Cheltenham	LINGFIELD PARK (AWT)
12	Doncaster	Cheltenham	Lingfield Park
	Haydock Park	†WOLVERHAMPTON (AWT)	
14	Newcastle		Newton Abbot
15	Musselburgh	Hereford	Folkestone
16	Catterick Bridge	Bangor-On-Dee	
		WOLVERHAMPTON (AWT)	
17	Catterick Bridge	Towcester	Exeter
18		SOUTHWELL PARK (AWT)	Lingfield Park
		Uttoxeter	
19		Uttoxeter	Ascot
		Warwick	LINGFIELD PARK (AWT)
21	Kelso		LINGFIELD PARK (AWT)
22		Ludlow	
		SOUTHWELL (AWT)	
26	Ayr	Hereford	Kempton Park
	Sedgefield	Huntingdon	Newton Abbot
	Wetherby	Market Rasen	Wincanton
		WOLVERHAMPTON (AWT)	
28	Wetherby	Leicester	Chepstow
			Kempton Park
29	Haydock Park		LINGFIELD PARK (AWT)
	Musselburgh		Taunton
30	Carlisle	Stratford-On-Avon	Plumpton
31	Catterick Bridge	Warwick	Fontwell Park

○ *RACING RECORD KEEPER*

COURSE

Date

FIRST RACE

Winner	Second	Third	Fourth
SP			

SECOND RACE

Winner	Second	Third	Fourth
SP			

THIRD RACE

Winner	Second	Third	Fourth
SP			

FOURTH RACE

Winner	Second	Third	Fourth
SP			

FIFTH RACE

Winner	Second	Third	Fourth
SP			

SIXTH RACE

Winner	Second	Third	Fourth
SP			

SEVENTH RACE

Winner	Second	Third	Fourth
SP			

EIGHTH RACE

Winner	Second	Third	Fourth
SP			

COURSE

Date	

FIRST RACE

Winner	Second	Third	Fourth
SP			

SECOND RACE

Winner	Second	Third	Fourth
SP			

THIRD RACE

Winner	Second	Third	Fourth
SP			

FOURTH RACE

Winner	Second	Third	Fourth
SP			

FIFTH RACE

Winner	Second	Third	Fourth
SP			

SIXTH RACE

Winner	Second	Third	Fourth
SP			

SEVENTH RACE

Winner	Second	Third	Fourth
SP			

EIGHTH RACE

Winner	Second	Third	Fourth
SP			

COURSE

Date			

FIRST RACE

Winner	Second	Third	Fourth
SP			

SECOND RACE

Winner	Second	Third	Fourth
SP			

THIRD RACE

Winner	Second	Third	Fourth
SP			

FOURTH RACE

Winner	Second	Third	Fourth
SP			

FIFTH RACE

Winner	Second	Third	Fourth
SP			

SIXTH RACE

Winner	Second	Third	Fourth
SP			

SEVENTH RACE

Winner	Second	Third	Fourth
SP			

EIGHTH RACE

Winner	Second	Third	Fourth
SP			

COURSE			
Date			

FIRST RACE			
Winner	Second	Third	Fourth
SP			

SECOND RACE			
Winner	Second	Third	Fourth
SP			

THIRD RACE			
Winner	Second	Third	Fourth
SP			

FOURTH RACE			
Winner	Second	Third	Fourth
SP			

FIFTH RACE			
Winner	Second	Third	Fourth
SP			

SIXTH RACE			
Winner	Second	Third	Fourth
SP			

SEVENTH RACE			
Winner	Second	Third	Fourth
SP			

EIGHTH RACE			
Winner	Second	Third	Fourth
SP			

COURSE

Date

FIRST RACE

Winner	Second	Third	Fourth
SP			

SECOND RACE

Winner	Second	Third	Fourth
SP			

THIRD RACE

Winner	Second	Third	Fourth
SP			

FOURTH RACE

Winner	Second	Third	Fourth
SP			

FIFTH RACE

Winner	Second	Third	Fourth
SP			

SIXTH RACE

Winner	Second	Third	Fourth
SP			

SEVENTH RACE

Winner	Second	Third	Fourth
SP			

EIGHTH RACE

Winner	Second	Third	Fourth
SP			

COURSE

Date

FIRST RACE

Winner	Second	Third	Fourth
SP			

SECOND RACE

Winner	Second	Third	Fourth
SP			

THIRD RACE

Winner	Second	Third	Fourth
SP			

FOURTH RACE

Winner	Second	Third	Fourth
SP			

FIFTH RACE

Winner	Second	Third	Fourth
SP			

SIXTH RACE

Winner	Second	Third	Fourth
SP			

SEVENTH RACE

Winner	Second	Third	Fourth
SP			

EIGHTH RACE

Winner	Second	Third	Fourth
SP			

COURSE

Date			

FIRST RACE

Winner	Second	Third	Fourth
SP			

SECOND RACE

Winner	Second	Third	Fourth
SP			

THIRD RACE

Winner	Second	Third	Fourth
SP			

FOURTH RACE

Winner	Second	Third	Fourth
SP			

FIFTH RACE

Winner	Second	Third	Fourth
SP			

SIXTH RACE

Winner	Second	Third	Fourth
SP			

SEVENTH RACE

Winner	Second	Third	Fourth
SP			

EIGHTH RACE

Winner	Second	Third	Fourth
SP			

COURSE

Date	

FIRST RACE

Winner	Second	Third	Fourth
SP			

SECOND RACE

Winner	Second	Third	Fourth
SP			

THIRD RACE

Winner	Second	Third	Fourth
SP			

FOURTH RACE

Winner	Second	Third	Fourth
SP			

FIFTH RACE

Winner	Second	Third	Fourth
SP			

SIXTH RACE

Winner	Second	Third	Fourth
SP			

SEVENTH RACE

Winner	Second	Third	Fourth
SP			

EIGHTH RACE

Winner	Second	Third	Fourth
SP			

COURSE

Date	

FIRST RACE

Winner	Second	Third	Fourth
SP			

SECOND RACE

Winner	Second	Third	Fourth
SP			

THIRD RACE

Winner	Second	Third	Fourth
SP			

FOURTH RACE

Winner	Second	Third	Fourth
SP			

FIFTH RACE

Winner	Second	Third	Fourth
SP			

SIXTH RACE

Winner	Second	Third	Fourth
SP			

SEVENTH RACE

Winner	Second	Third	Fourth
SP			

EIGHTH RACE

Winner	Second	Third	Fourth
SP			

COURSE

Date	

FIRST RACE

Winner	Second	Third	Fourth
SP			

SECOND RACE

Winner	Second	Third	Fourth
SP			

THIRD RACE

Winner	Second	Third	Fourth
SP			

FOURTH RACE

Winner	Second	Third	Fourth
SP			

FIFTH RACE

Winner	Second	Third	Fourth
SP			

SIXTH RACE

Winner	Second	Third	Fourth
SP			

SEVENTH RACE

Winner	Second	Third	Fourth
SP			

EIGHTH RACE

Winner	Second	Third	Fourth
SP			

COURSE

Date	

FIRST RACE

Winner	Second	Third	Fourth
SP			

SECOND RACE

Winner	Second	Third	Fourth
SP			

THIRD RACE

Winner	Second	Third	Fourth
SP			

FOURTH RACE

Winner	Second	Third	Fourth
SP			

FIFTH RACE

Winner	Second	Third	Fourth
SP			

SIXTH RACE

Winner	Second	Third	Fourth
SP			

SEVENTH RACE

Winner	Second	Third	Fourth
SP			

EIGHTH RACE

Winner	Second	Third	Fourth
SP			

COURSE

Date

FIRST RACE

Winner	Second	Third	Fourth
SP			

SECOND RACE

Winner	Second	Third	Fourth
SP			

THIRD RACE

Winner	Second	Third	Fourth
SP			

FOURTH RACE

Winner	Second	Third	Fourth
SP			

FIFTH RACE

Winner	Second	Third	Fourth
SP			

SIXTH RACE

Winner	Second	Third	Fourth
SP			

SEVENTH RACE

Winner	Second	Third	Fourth
SP			

EIGHTH RACE

Winner	Second	Third	Fourth
SP			